Welcome back to C&L. We look forward to a long relationship of providing service to you and your company.

W. Gary Farmer

Bob Bird

Thomas J. Fehrman

Toby Shelly

Mary Davis

John P. Lawrence

EVALUATING
INTERNAL
CONTROL

EVALUATING INTERNAL CONTROL

CONCEPTS, GUIDELINES, PROCEDURES, DOCUMENTATION

KENNETH P. JOHNSON, C.P.A.
Coopers & Lybrand

HENRY R. JAENICKE, C.P.A., Ph.D.
Franklin and Marshall College

A RONALD PRESS PUBLICATION

JOHN WILEY & SONS, New York • Chichester • Brisbane • Toronto

Published by John Wiley & Sons, Inc.
Copyright © 1980 by Coopers & Lybrand

This publication is designed to provide accurate and
authoritative information in regard to the subject matter
covered. It is sold with the understanding that
the publisher is not engaged in rendering legal, accounting,
or other professional service. If legal advice or other
expert assistance is required, the services of a competent
professional person should be sought. *From a Declaration
of Principles jointly adopted by a Committee of the
American Bar Association and a Committee of Publishers.*

Library of Congress Cataloging in Publication Data:

Johnson, Kenneth Paul, 1928-
    Evaluating internal control.

    Includes index.
    1. Auditing.   I. Jaenicke, Henry R.,
joint author.   II. Title.

HF 5668.25.J63   657'.45   79-23172
ISBN 0-471-05620-0

Printed in the United States of America

10 9 8 7 6 5 4 3 2 1

Preface

Seldom has a single element of enterprise activity received the degree or span of attention that has been devoted to internal control in the past two years. The post-Watergate revelations of acts of questionable legality by businesses initially raised the question, "But where were the auditors?" As the public and its elected and appointed representatives came to understand the issues better, the focus properly shifted and the concern became, "But where were the controls?"

First the report of tentative conclusions in the Spring of 1977 and then the *Report, Conclusions, and Recommendations* of the Commission on Auditors' Responsibilities at the beginning of 1978 called for a formal report by enterprise management on the "condition of the controls over the accounting system." The independent auditor, under the Commission's proposal, would "report on whether he agrees with management's description of the company's accounting controls" and would be required to "describe material uncorrected weaknesses not described in the report."

Congressional concern culminated, at least for the time being, in the Foreign Corrupt Practices Act of 1977. The accounting provisions of the Act include a requirement that companies registered with the Securities and Exchange Commission "devise and maintain a system of internal accounting controls sufficient to provide reasonable assurances" that certain specified objectives are met.

In 1978, the Financial Executives Institute recommended that a "Statement of Management Responsibility for Financial Statements" be presented in annual reports. The "Statement" would include a "discussion of management's responsibility for maintaining internal control systems" and "management's assessment of the effectiveness of the internal accounting control system." Many companies had already made such statements, in greater or lesser degree, in their 1977 annual reports.

The time is ripe, then, for a book that covers both the conceptual aspects of internal control systems and a practical approach to conducting a formal review and evaluation of existing systems. This book is intended to enable a company to design its own review and evaluation program. While specific forms, questionnaires, and procedures are suggested and illustrated, they are included only as guidance, not as gospel. We have included (in the Appendices) detailed procedures for only one activity cycle. This was intentional, for the objective of the book is to encourage management to design evaluation procedures tailored to the specific needs of an individual enterprise. If, because of staff limitations or other reasons, management cannot design a tailored evaluation program, the company should retain outside evaluators or purchase a manual containing detailed procedures for the evaluation. Coopers & Lybrand offers both of those services. The authors believe, however, that organizations should undertake their own reviews and create their own detailed evaluation procedures, preferably using their CPAs in a review and consulting capacity.

The Special Advisory Committee on Internal Accounting Control of the American Institute of Certified Public Accountants, organized to develop criteria for evaluating internal accounting control, published its report in 1979. The "cycle approach" discussed and illustrated by the Committee is essentially the approach followed in this book. (The only divergence between the two approaches is discussed in Chapter 2.) While the Committee report provides broad guidance for performing an evaluation, it does not consider the issues and problems that must be resolved before a review can be implemented. It is the purpose of this book to provide practical help for resolving those issues and for implementing the review.

Much of the thinking behind this book is based on concepts and procedures developed by Coopers & Lybrand, initially as a basis for meeting their responsibility for reviewing internal control under professional auditing standards, and later as a basis for extending that review beyond the requirements of the ordinary audit engagement. The evaluation technique in this book is now being used effectively by many organizations as a basis for self-evaluations.

This book is intended primarily for those levels of management responsible for evaluating internal control and for overseeing the maintenance of the proper degree of control. It will also be helpful to internal auditors, who will often have the primary responsibility for designing and conducting the evaluation. External, independent auditors who will review the evaluation process will find the book useful as a standard for determining the overall effectiveness of the evaluation.

The approach used in this book evolved over several decades and went through many stages of development. In preparing the manuscript we have drawn upon a number of Coopers & Lybrand publications. These include several of the Firm's technical policy statements and *Montgomery's Auditing,* 9th Edition.* The authors acknowledge with thanks the permission granted by Coopers & Lybrand (International) to use their materials.

Special thanks are due for permitting us to make extensive use of selected portions of *An Audit Approach to Computers* by Brian Jenkins and Anthony Pinkney.† The authors of that book are partners in the United Kingdom firm of Coopers & Lybrand; accordingly, their approach to evaluating computer controls closely parallels the approach in this book. The following sections of this book benefitted greatly from the analysis and presentation in *An Audit Approach to Computers:* Internal Control in a Computer Environment (Chapter 2), Integrity Control Weaknesses in Computer Systems (Chapter 3), Flowcharting Computer Systems (Chapter 4), Computer Questions (Chapter 5), Functional Tests in a Computer System (Chapter 5), Levels of Tests in Computer Systems (Chapter 5), and Internal Control in Computer Systems (Chapter 6). *An Audit Approach to Computers* is a useful reference source for the reader whose interests in computer controls extend beyond the coverage in this book.

In a broader sense, this book represents the efforts and ideas of many people. While we would like to, it is impossible to honor each contributor individually. Within the Coopers & Lybrand organization, two people in particular, however—Philip L. Defliese (retired chairman) and Jean W. Horton—contributed significantly to the development of the materials that underlie the approach to evaluating internal control described in this book; also, Stanley D. Halper and Raymond W. Elliott provided valuable assistance with the materials on computer systems. We owe a special acknowledgment to Ronald J. Murray, also of Coopers & Lybrand, for the thoughtful and incisive comments that resulted from his penetrating "audit" of the manuscript. In addition, Warren W. Brown and Thomas D. Smith of the American Telephone and Telegraph Company, Albert S. Martin, Jr. of the Sun Company, and John J. Begley of Johnson & Johnson provided the authors with helpful advice in the early stages of the book's development. Particular thanks are due to Myra Cleary for her skillful editing of the text for style, grammar, and consistency. To all those

---

*Philip L. Defliese, Kenneth P. Johnson, and Roderick K. Macleod, *Montgomery's Auditing,* 9th Ed. (New York: Ronald Press Division, John Wiley & Sons, 1975.)

†Brian Jenkins and Anthony Pinkney, *An Audit Approach to Computers.* (London: The Institute of Chartered Accountants in England and Wales, 1978.)

individuals go not only our thanks, but also the usual absolution from blame for errors and omissions.

KENNETH P. JOHNSON
HENRY R. JAENICKE

New York, New York
January 1980

Contents

EVALUATING INTERNAL CONTROL

1

Internal Control in a Risk Environment

Risk is the potential for realization of unwanted, negative consequences of an event.

* * *

When risks, especially new ones, arise, man experiences anxiety and is motivated to worry and to invoke a risk analysis process, either qualitatively or quantitatively, either cursorily or in depth, resulting in a risk evaluation. This risk evaluation leads either to risk acceptance or risk aversion.

* * *

As technology develops, new methods to control risk are being found: risks hitherto considered uncontrollable can now be controlled to various degrees, and more effective controls are found for risks that are already controllable.

—WILLIAM D. ROWE

All enterprises assume risks in achieving their goals. Profits are the result, at least in part, of the assumption of those risks. Risk results from the chance that enterprise activities—financial, production, marketing—will not turn out as planned. Sound management entails assessing risks, limiting them to those the enterprise's management has consciously decided to assume, and then instituting accounting and operating controls to reduce those risks as much as possible.

William D. Rowe, *An Anatomy of Risk.* (New York: John Wiley & Sons, 1977; pp. 22, 46, 49.)

The system of controlling and reporting on enterprise activity includes policies, procedures, and the means of monitoring compliance with them. Collectively, these policies and procedures are designated as *internal controls* because they operate within an enterprise as a means of reducing its unintentional exposure to business, financial, and accounting risks. Before a system of internal control can be designed, or an existing system evaluated, management must know something about the kinds of risks that exist in its particular organization, assess their significance, and determine which ones cannot be avoided. Only then can controls be designed to reduce the remaining risks to those that are consciously acceptable to management and are at a level that management has consciously determined. This book presents a framework for evaluating an internal control system based on identification of the risks to which the enterprise is exposed as a result of internal control deficiencies. Suggestions for correcting specific control deficiencies are also provided.

KINDS OF RISKS

Financial management requires assessing risks in several related areas. Among them are financial risks—the loss of assets by fraudulent conversion and inappropriate financial management policies—and accounting risks—errors in the records and reports by which accountability for assets is maintained. Failure to safeguard assets from theft, and mismanagement of assets through inefficient operations create the risk of loss to owners and creditors. Failure to safeguard accounting records and reports creates the risk of error, intentional and unintentional, in financial information that is used for decision-making purposes both inside and outside the enterprise.

REDUCING RISKS THROUGH CONTROLS

Risks can be controlled by establishing policies to avoid or reduce the level of risk, and then instituting procedures to ensure that the policies are complied with. For example, in the financial area, the risk of loss from bad debts can be avoided completely by establishing a policy of not engaging in credit sales and creating procedures to enforce and monitor that policy. Alternatively, policies and procedures can be established to reduce the risk of loss to an acceptable level without prohibiting all credit sales. In the accounting area, risk of errors can be reduced by policies and procedures for controlling information and transaction flows.

The size and nature of the business, the type of assets employed, and the degree of involvement of the owner are among the factors that influence the risk of fraudulent or unauthorized use of assets, the risk of error in the accounting records and reports, and the controls that should be instituted to reduce those risks. Of those factors, the involvement of the owner is the most significant. As an example, consider a newsstand that is operated by the owner. The owner, who bears the cost if a risk materializes, has no concerns about fraudulent conversion of assets because he alone operates the business. His concerns about asset loss through operating inefficiencies are overcome by his knowledge of the business. Books and records are necessary for tax purposes, but the accounting system can be extremely simple. He doesn't even need a cash register.

The owner's risks change significantly if he hires an employee to operate the newsstand. While the amount and nature of the fixed assets (the newsstand) suggest low risks and therefore little need for controls, the high convertibility of cash indicates a high risk worthy of significant controls. The practical inability to segregate duties, particularly the physical custodianship of cash from the related recordkeeping, increases the risk that cash will be misappropriated. The risk can be avoided by not being an absentee owner or it can be reduced by the imposition of a (very expensive) control, a second employee. The owner will in all likelihood accept some risk of fraudulent conversion of cash by installing only minimal controls—for example, overall reconciliations of daily deposits with deliveries and returns of newspapers and magazines. As the size of the business grows and ownership becomes even more remote from operations, the potential consequences of control weaknesses and the likelihood of improper conversion of cash increase. That may lead to a different assessment of risk, and more expensive controls may be installed.

The newsstand owner is now dependent on the work of other people to safeguard his assets from misappropriation or unauthorized use. He is also dependent on accounting records and reports as the means by which his employees are held accountable for their stewardship and use of those assets, including potentially improper use of the assets, such as for conducting one's own business "off the books." As the enterprise expands and the number of employees increases, professional managers will be hired and the owner's span of control will be reduced. Employees will be held accountable to the professional managers, who, in turn, will be accountable to the owner. The particular means by which accountability is achieved—the internal accounting control system—will then depend, as suggested earlier, primarily on the size of the business and the degree to which the owner is removed from its operations, and to a lesser extent on the nature of the business and the type of assets it employs.

The newsstand example illustrates several additional factors. First, there is a point at which it makes good business sense to accept a risk, such as small cash defalcations or the use of enterprise assets for an employee's own business on the side, rather than avoid the risk or seek to reduce it. Second, that point can generally be determined by identifying the potential risks and weighing the costs and benefits of reducing them. Third, such cost/benefit analyses are, at least at present, very imprecise. (The entire area of risk evaluation is currently under study on several fronts.) Fourth, ultimately, subjective judgment must be applied in determining and evaluating particular risks; this includes a decision on whether it is good business to incur the cost of reducing them.

EVALUATING RISKS AND CONTROLS

While we do not presently have the methodology to make a complete analysis of accounting and financial risk, some guidelines exist, as suggested in the newsstand example, which are at least a starting point. Coupling those guidelines with the judgment derived from broad experience with internal control systems generally and a knowledge, again from experience, of the level of risk that business management generally is willing to accept, we have developed a framework for evaluating a system of internal control that gives appropriate, though not precise, recognition to risks and the costs of controlling them.

Our framework does not require determining and evaluating each accounting and financial risk faced by a business. The approach described in this book, in effect, represents a "shortcut" to evaluating risks. It is based on an analysis of the potential risks inherent in accounting and financial activity and the development of internal control objectives that, if attained, reduce those risks. The control objectives, and the apparatus for obtaining evidence that they are met, provide the means for informing management about *particular* risks; management can then decide whether to accept a risk or incur the cost to avoid or reduce it.

Experience with systems of internal control shows that only a relatively small number of control tasks exist, and that, with minor changes in language, they are applicable to virtually all businesses, regardless of industry, size, or whether the system is operated by people or computerized. The approach to designing and evaluating systems of internal control explained in this book does not view business activities by function or department. For example, it does not focus on controls in the receiving department. Instead, it focuses on *transactions,* which cross many departmental lines; a purchase transaction, for example, touches the purchasing, receiving, and accounting departments. Using the transaction as the focal point has the distinct advantage of removing much of the uniqueness from specialized industries. Thus, the objective of assuring control over imprest cash funds is equally applicable to a manufacturing company's petty cash fund, a bank teller's cash drawer, and a supermarket's check-out register.

Internal controls should not be confused with, or limited to, the accounting system. While an accounting system is a necessary element of a system of internal control, the control system is much larger in scope. A good system of internal control contains elements that have little or no relationship to accounting activities. For example, personnel policies that are aimed at hiring honest and competent employees, requirements for approval before transactions can be entered into, and restrictions on physical access to assets are all examples of internal controls that reduce the risk of errors; they also operate outside of the accounting system. Internal controls are introduced into the accounting system and into other aspects of enterprise operations to prevent errors from occurring in the first place, and to detect them on a timely basis if they do occur.

THE CHANGING ENVIRONMENT

Changes in the business and legal environment over the past few years have magnified the importance of internal control to management. These changes have also created the need for a formal process of studying and evaluating the adequacy of a system of internal control for meeting stated objectives at minimum cost. This book is intended to fill that need.

The traditional view of management's responsibility for internal control was recently restated by the Securities and Exchange Commission (SEC):

> The establishment and maintenance of a system of internal control is an important management obligation. A fundamental aspect of management's stewardship responsibility is to provide shareholders with reasonable assurance that the business is adequately controlled. Additionally, management has a responsibility to furnish shareholders and potential investors with reliable information on a timely basis. An adequate system of internal accounting control is necessary to management's discharge of these obligations.*

---

*Exchange Act Release No. 13185, January 19, 1977, "Promotion of the Reliability of Financial Information, Prevention of the Concealment of Questionable or Illegal Corporate Payments and Practices, and Disclosure of the Involvement of Management in Specified Types of Transactions; Proposed Amendments to Rules and Schedules."

That position was codified into law by the Foreign Corrupt Practices Act of 1977. The Act has two parts: one deals with specific acts and penalties associated with certain corrupt practices; the second, with "accounting standards" (actually, internal accounting controls). Companies may have to demonstrate compliance with the Act in the area of "accounting standards." Since the Act amends the Securities Exchange Act of 1934, responsibility for its enforcement falls to the SEC. Beyond that, a number of Commissioners have spoken out on the need for public reporting on the adequacy of internal accounting controls, and the SEC is presently considering whether to require registrants to report on their system of internal accounting control.*

Much in the same vein, the report of the Commission on Auditors' Responsibilities (the Cohen Commission), an independent study group created by the American Institute of Certified Public Accountants (AICPA), suggested that management should make some form of representation about its internal accounting control as part of its annual financial disclosure. Some companies presently include statements on internal control and related management responsibilities in their annual reports, further underscoring the trend toward public disclosure by management about its internal control system. This topic is discussed at length in Chapter 7.

Recent years have seen a growing interest in corporate governance in general and one aspect in particular—the role and responsibilities of boards of directors and audit committees of boards. Both the Foreign Corrupt Practices Act and public reporting on systems of internal accounting control, should it become either more widespread or required, will force audit committee and board members to seek comfort that the company's system of internal accounting control is sufficient to support an opinion that the objectives of internal accounting control have been met, that is, that financial and accounting risks have been reduced to a level acceptable to management. That comfort comes primarily from ongoing supervision that should be an integral part of a system of internal control. It may also come from the work of the company's internal auditors and external auditors (that is, CPAs). Both groups of auditors need means of assessing the quality of internal controls and recommending appropriate improvements. Boards of directors and their audit committees will then seek assurances that control deficiencies have been corrected to reduce those risks to an appropriate level.

In August 1977, the AICPA created a Special Advisory Committee on Internal Accounting Control "to develop criteria, in reasonable detail and

*Exchange Act Release No. 15772, April 30, 1979.

susceptible to objective application by companies and their auditors, for evaluating internal accounting controls." The Committee issued its report in April 1979.* The Committee's approach and the criteria it developed are intended to serve as broad management tools for the evaluation and monitoring of control systems rather than as detailed rules. The Committee's approach is similar to the approach of this book, which is the approach to evaluating internal control that Coopers & Lybrand has used for many years in the course of performing audits. The evaluation framework discussed here, though compatible with the Committee's approach, is more detailed and has had the benefit of almost a decade of experimentation and use.

DEFINITIONS AND OBJECTIVES OF INTERNAL CONTROL

The formal definition of *internal control,* originally published by the accounting profession in 1949 and repeated in subsequent publications, including Statement on Auditing Standards (SAS) No. 1 (paragraph 320.09), states:

> Internal control comprises the plan of organization and all of the coordinate methods and measures adopted within a business to safeguard its assets, check the accuracy and reliability of its accounting data, promote operational efficiency, and encourage adherence to prescribed managerial policies . . . . [A] "system" of internal control extends beyond those matters which relate directly to the functions of the accounting and financial departments.

Thus, two kinds of internal controls are included in this broad definition: internal accounting and administrative (or operational) controls. Both are directed at reducing exposure to possible losses of an accounting or financial nature.

Internal accounting control is defined in SAS No. 1 (paragraph 320.28) as:

> . . . the plan of organization and the procedures and records that are concerned with the safeguarding of assets and the reliability of financial records and consequently are designed to provide reasonable assurance that:
> a. Transactions are executed in accordance with management's general or specific authorization.
> b. Transactions are recorded as necessary (1) to permit preparation of financial statements in conformity with generally accepted accounting principles or any other criteria applicable to such statements and (2) to maintain accountability for assets.

Report of the Special Advisory Committee on Internal Accounting Control. (New York: American Institute of Certified Public Accountants, 1979.)

    c. Access to assets is permitted only in accordance with management's authority.

    d. The recorded accountability for assets is compared with the existing assets at reasonable intervals and appropriate action is taken with respect to any differences.

Internal accounting controls "check the accuracy and reliability of . . . accounting data" or, more precisely, are designed to bring about accurate and suitable recording and summarization of authorized financial transactions. Failure to achieve the objectives implicit in the definition means that the risk of loss or error may be present. The responsibility for the installation and maintenance of internal accounting controls is clearly that of an entity's management; ordinarily the task is delegated in turn to the accounting (or financial) department.

Internal accounting controls also include those accounting procedures or physical, statistical, or other controls designed to safeguard assets against fraudulent conversion or against avoidable loss from other causes. Some forms of internal accounting control of a physical nature, such as fences, gates, security guards, and inspection of outgoing material or personnel, are ordinarily the responsibility of operating departments. The accounting department is usually responsible for the installation and maintenance of those internal accounting controls that may be achieved through accounting procedures or by proper segregation of accounting duties. Coordination among departments is, of course, necessary for an efficient system.

Administrative or *operational control* (the words are sometimes used interchangeably) is described in SAS No. 1 (paragraph 320.27) as including, but not limited to:

> . . . the plan of organization and the procedures and records that are concerned with the decision processes leading to management's authorization of transactions. Such authorization is a management function directly associated with the responsibility for achieving the objectives of the organization and is the starting point for establishing accounting control of transactions.

Broadly, the prime responsibility of management is to operate an enterprise at a profit, or within the available resources if it is a not-for-profit organization. In both types of enterprise, management must produce goods or services at acceptable cost; it must develop markets in which the goods or services can be sold at proper prices; and, because of pressure of competition, changes in customer demand, and other factors that cause obsolescence, it must develop new or improved goods or services.

To accomplish those goals, management must develop policies and procedures to promote efficiency in every area of activity; implement them through proper personnel selection, training, and compensation; communicate the means of effecting them; and monitor performance through adequate supervision. In this book, the "plan of organization and all of the coordinate methods and measures adopted within a business to . . . promote operational efficiency and encourage adherence to prescribed managerial policies" (SAS No. 1, paragraph 320.09) are referred to as *administrative* or *operational* controls.

Operational controls are distinguished from internal accounting controls by their primary purpose. The definitions of administrative control and internal accounting control are, however, not mutually exclusive. Some of the methods and procedures comprehended in administrative control may also be involved in internal accounting control. For example, sales and cost records classified by products may be used both for accounting control purposes and for making management decisions about unit prices. Other operational controls may be based on or integrated with accounting data, or more than one purpose may be served by the same controls. For example, certain administrative controls may be based on data or information furnished by accounting or financial departments, such as investigating and acting on the underlying causes of variances found in variance reports. On the other hand, some administrative controls may also satisfy internal accounting control objectives.

In practice, the various objectives of accounting control and administrative control can be achieved in many ways. In some instances they may be embodied in the same procedure; in other cases each may require a separate procedure. For example, a separate receiving department can "promote operational efficiency" by providing for efficient acceptance, inspection, and forwarding of all items received; it can "check the . . . reliability of . . . accounting data" by checking and documenting the quantity and condition of goods received; it can "safeguard . . . assets" (discourage defalcations) because its place in the organization is separate from the ordering of goods, disbursing of funds, and keeping of records. As the definition states, internal control usually involves "coordinate methods."

The problem of drawing the line between administrative or operational control and accounting control has more than only conceptual or semantic significance. The distinction is important to independent auditors because of their relatively narrowly defined responsibilities for the study and evaluation of internal accounting control under generally accepted auditing standards. The distinction is also important to management because of the specific requirements of the Foreign Corrupt Practices Act. Management, however, and particularly internal auditors, will often want to evaluate administrative or operational controls as well as accounting controls. The framework of the approach to evaluating internal control described in this book, while initially oriented toward accounting controls, will easily expand to include administrative or operational controls. Moreover, many operational controls, particularly those of a financial nature, can be evaluated with little additional effort and a high potential for improving the system.

MANAGEMENT'S RESPONSIBILITY FOR INTERNAL ACCOUNTING CONTROL UNDER THE FOREIGN CORRUPT PRACTICES ACT

Management's responsibility for designing, implementing, and maintaining a system of internal control has already been noted, particularly the unambiguous statement by the SEC. Statement on Auditing Standards No. 1 (paragraph 320.31) states that ''the system of internal control should be under continuing supervision by management to determine that it is functioning as prescribed and is modified as appropriate for changes in conditions.'' The Foreign Corrupt Practices Act has, in effect, increased those management responsibilities for companies registered with the SEC, and it is only slightly speculative to suggest that the day is not far off when the requirements of the Act will apply to many enterprises beyond present SEC registrants.

"Accounting Standards" Provisions of the Act

The Act's wording dealing with ''accounting standards'' is deceptively short and simple. Although the section on internal accounting control is taken largely from the current auditing standards of the American Institute of Certified Public Accountants, its new stature as law imposes many new legal obligations on companies that have a continuous reporting requirement with the SEC. Specifically, the legislation requires every registrant to devise and maintain a system of internal accounting control sufficient to provide reasonable assurances that transactions are executed in accordance with management's authorization. The system must also provide for the recording of transactions to permit preparation of financial statements in conformity with generally accepted accounting principles and to maintain accountability for assets. The system is further required to provide reasonable assurances that access to assets is permitted only with management's authorization and that recorded accountability for assets is compared with existing assets at reasonable intervals so that appropriate action can be taken with respect to any differences.*

---

*The actual wording of the Act with respect to ''accounting standards'' is as follows:

The four objectives of internal accounting control as specified in the Foreign Corrupt Practices Act are quite broad—too broad to serve as a basis for evaluating a system of accounting controls for compliance with the Act. Management must identify control objectives in more specific terms before the controls designed to accomplish those objectives can be evaluated. This book is intended to help management meet that need.

Many believe that not only will companies be required to meet the criteria established for a system of internal accounting control, but they will also have to set up a means of monitoring the system and evaluating its effectiveness. Although organizations have long had systems of internal accounting control and have assigned to management the responsibility for maintaining them, and although the systems were subject to review by CPAs, decisions about the extent of control were, until now, based on management's usually subjective identification of risks and of the costs and benefits of controlling them. A subjective appraisal of the internal accounting control system will no longer be acceptable; management will want to demonstrate compliance with the Act and a desire to minimize business risks in a positive, objective manner. The approach in this book provides both a framework for evaluating a system of controls to meet those objectives and a means of documenting the evaluation.

Early in 1978, soon after the Act was signed into law, the SEC brought its first court action under the ''accounting standards'' provisions. The Commission alleged that the defendants failed to ''make and keep books, records, and accounts which, in reasonable detail, accurately and fairly reflect the transactions and dispositions of the assets . . .; and devise and maintain a system of internal accounting controls sufficient to provide

---

Every issuer which has a class of securities registered pursuant to section 12 of this title and every issuer which is required to file reports pursuant to section 15(d) of this title shall—

(A) make and keep books, records and accounts, which in reasonable detail, accurately and fairly reflect the transactions and dispositions of the assets of the issuer; and

(B) devise and maintain a system of internal accounting controls sufficient to provide reasonable assurances that—

    (i) transactions are executed in accordance with management's general or specific authorization;

    (ii) transactions are recorded as necessary (I) to permit preparation of financial statements in conformity with generally accepted accounting principles or any other criteria applicable to such statements, and (II) to maintain accountability for assets;

    (iii) access to assets is permitted only in accordance with management's general or specific authorization; and

    (iv) the recorded accountability for assets is compared with the existing assets at reasonable intervals and appropriate action is taken with respect to any differences.

reasonable assurances that [the objectives of a system of internal accounting control as specified in the Act were met]."*

The SEC further alleged that the violations of the "accounting standards" provisions of the Act were intended to conceal fraudulent activities involving the diversion of corporate funds to certain officers of the company and other entities they controlled. This action thus suggests that the SEC intends to use the "accounting standards" provisions in enforcement actions even if foreign bribery (the ostensible reason for the Act and its accounting provisions) is not involved. The SEC is clearly attaching great significance to the "accounting standards" provisions of the Act. This particular codification of management responsibilities may well encourage other federal and state regulatory agencies, legislatures, and courts to seek a comparable level of responsibility from non-SEC registrants as well.

Guidelines for Defining the "Accounting Standards"

In addition to being too broad to be useful, the objectives are not adequately defined. What, for example, is meant by a "general or specific authorization"? Management, accountants, and attorneys will have to grapple with defining the objectives; they cannot afford to wait for professional, regulatory, or judicial interpretations that may not be forthcoming soon enough to be useful. For that reason, we have formulated the following guidelines for defining the "accounting standards" of the Act:

"Accounting standard" (B)(i) states ". . . transactions are executed in accordance with management's general or specific authorization." A definition of this "standard" should include the following points:

1. Management is not considered to have authorized a transaction unless that authorization is recorded on a form that the company subjects to accounting control. If management authorizes transactions orally or puts them in writing on a form that is not subject to accounting control, e.g., an unnumbered internal memorandum, this does not constitute an authorization for the purpose of determining compliance with the "accounting standards" section of the Foreign Corrupt Practices Act.

2. The phrase "general or specific authorization" means an authorization that is sufficiently specific to permit an employee to carry it out without seeking further clarification. For example, an authorization to purchase "the appropriate number of spare parts for the company's milling machines" would not be an authorization for this purpose because it does not indicate the specific parts or quantity to be purchased, or the unit price. In other words, the terms of the authorization should be sufficiently specific so that

---

*SEC v. Aminex Resources Corp. *et al.*, 78 Civ. 0410 (D.C. 1978).

another person could determine whether the authorization was complied with.

"Accounting standard" (B)(iii) states ". . . access to assets is permitted only in accordance with management's general or specific authorization." A definition of this "standard" should include the following points:

1. In broad terms, there are two aspects to the access question. The first involves processing fraudulent transactions through the accounting system by making them appear to be valid. Examples of this would include (a) processing fraudulent suppliers' invoices with dummy receiving reports and (b) shipping goods to a non-company location and not preparing a sales invoice. The second aspect is the direct theft of the company's assets. This might include stealing incoming cash receipts or inventory. It might also include stealing blank checks and forging the signatures of authorized check signers. The distinction between these two aspects is not clearcut and reasonable people could differ as to whether a particular "unauthorized access" fell into one or the other category.
2. The accounting controls that should be applied to apparently routine transactions usually result in documented evidence of some kind. The existence of such documents would normally constitute prima facie evidence that the controls have operated.
3. The kinds of theft described in 1 above as direct theft would be facilitated by weaknesses in custodial controls or segregation of duties.* Those controls tend to be applied on a general basis rather than transaction-by-transaction. Accordingly, proof that they are operating might be found by analyzing organization charts or accounting manuals and by interview and observation, rather than by examining evidence. For example, the company's procedures may require that storekeepers keep their storage areas locked when not in use and not permit access to unauthorized persons. However, the storekeeper is unlikely to sign a document indicating that the storage area was kept locked all day. Further, unless another, independent person is present at all times, it would be difficult to demonstrate that an unauthorized person was not admitted to the storage area.

"Accounting standard" (B)(iv) states ". . . the recorded accountability for assets is compared with the existing assets at reasonable intervals and appropriate action is taken with respect to any differences." In some respects, this is the most difficult "standard" to deal with, since many companies do not inventory fixed assets or apply other procedures that give them reasonable assurance that the fixed assets actually on hand are reasonably equivalent to the fixed assets recorded on the books. A definition of this "standard" should include the following points:

---

*See the discussion of disciplinary controls in Chapter 2.

1. Companies need not physically count fixed assets if there are other records upon which reliance can be placed, e.g., equipment maintenance records, standard store layouts, and the like.

2. In appropriate circumstances, companies can control their fixed assets even with a system that groups them by operating units or locations rather than by individual assets. For example, an oil company may have accounting records for individual refineries rather than for the component pieces of equipment at each refinery.

3. The intervals between counts of fixed assets can be longer than in the case of current assets because there is less likelihood of misappropriations or unauthorized disposals. This presumption is rebuttable depending on the circumstances.

4. The reasonable interval between counts may depend, in part, on a company's depreciation policies. If assets are fully depreciated now, or will be in the next few years, the fact that they are missing may not have a material effect on the financial statements, i.e., the "recorded accountability" for those assets.

THE CONCEPT OF "REASONABLE ASSURANCE"

Professional auditing literature (SAS No. 1, paragraph 320.32), the Foreign Corrupt Practices Act, and sound financial management all recognize that a system of internal accounting control comprehends reasonable, but not absolute, assurance that its objectives will be accomplished. While internal accounting control aims at preventing and detecting errors, absolute prevention or 100 percent detection is costly and probably impossible. Since controls have a cost in both time and money, management must always make economic judgments as to whether a further degree of risk reduction is worth the cost of providing it.

The judgments that must be made are similar to most other judgments by management. How they are made reflects the ability to identify and measure risks; it also reflects management's broad philosophy or style of managing, for example, a policy of maintaining a "lean" organization. Fortunately, management needs only reasonable, not absolute, assurance that errors will be prevented or will be detected if and when they occur. SAS No. 1 (paragraph 320.32) expresses this idea in words that have been in the auditing literature for many years but are equally relevant today in discussing management's decisions on internal control:

> The concept of reasonable assurance recognizes that the cost of internal control should not exceed the benefits expected to be derived. The benefits consist of reductions in the risk of failing to achieve the objectives implicit in the definition of accounting control. Although the cost–benefit relationship is the primary criterion

that should be considered in designing a system of accounting control, precise measurement of costs and benefits usually is not possible; accordingly, any evaluation of the cost–benefit relationship requires estimates and judgments by management.

Determining the level of risk that should "reasonably" be accepted is a subjective process. The costs of particular controls are not always measurable, and the benefits are even less so. As a result, applying the concept of reasonable assurance requires reliance on subjective determinants. Cost/benefit analysis, while important to the decision process, is presently not developed to the point where it alone should be used. As the AICPA Special Advisory Committee on Internal Accounting Control noted, "Subjective knowledge, experience, specific industry and business conditions, management style, cost–benefit judgments, among other factors, affect the selection of appropriate control procedures and techniques. . . . There is a necessary element of subjectivity inherent in an evaluation by management of internal accounting control."*

Subjectivity, however, does not imply that guidelines cannot be developed for determining the appropriate level of risk that management should accept, that is, for determining how "significant" a control weakness must be before action is taken to correct it. Research is taking place in the area of risk analysis in general, and, spurred by the current interest in internal control, in techniques to improve the measurement process specifically in that area. While more study is needed, the progress to date has made the waters less murky and uncharted than they were several years ago. The results of our research and thinking on how to determine the significance of control weaknesses are presented in Chapter 3.

MEETING MANAGEMENT'S RESPONSIBILITY

Until recently, management devoted relatively little attention to formal evaluation of the entity's internal controls. In most instances, only auditors were concerned with assessing the quality of internal control; as a result, their concepts and procedures for evaluating controls were the only ones that existed. Most of the evaluation methodology was developed by CPAs in the course of formulating auditing strategy. While some internal audit departments have been involved with systems review and evaluation, management's emphasis on profitability rather than accountability often resulted inappropriately in support of the internal audit function below the level necessary for an adequate, ongoing evaluation program.

*Report of the Special Advisory Committee on Internal Accounting Control, p. 27.

The current environment requires that management be more directly involved. Evaluating and revising an existing control system require judgments that only management is in a position to make. It would be inappropriate for the independent auditor, an "outsider" who faces pressures quite different from those faced by management, to make those decisions. While a CPA firm can provide management with some information on the quality of internal control, that information is based on an evaluation intended to meet a single specific and limited objective—an external audit of financial statements.

Consequently, management should not be lulled into false complacency because the company's system of internal accounting control is reviewed as part of the normal annual independent audit. That review alone probably does not have the breadth or depth necessary to provide comfort to the company that it is in reasonable compliance with the Act. There are two reasons for this:

1. The objectives of CPA firms in testing controls are different from the objectives of management. Independent audits relate to the fair presentation of financial statements rather than to a determination of system adequacy in reducing exposure to risk. Accordingly, while the review procedures may be similar, their application may be significantly different because of differing objectives. Controls are only selectively tested for external audit purposes; management needs a more comprehensive review. In particular, the levels of materiality may be different for management's purposes than for audit purposes.
2. In addition to evaluating internal accounting control, CPAs use other procedures and techniques to a significant extent in reaching their conclusions about the fairness of financial statements. Thus, the audit testing program may be substantially different from the evaluation procedures used by management for testing the internal accounting control system.

This book's approach to evaluating internal control will be useful to any enterprise that has not had an evaluation program and now wishes to install one; it can also serve as a standard against which to compare an evaluation program that is already in place. Under this approach, management will be led to focus on specific objectives of internal control, to determine whether specific controls are in place and working to accomplish those objectives, and to identify gaps or weaknesses in the control system.

Our approach enables both the auditor and manager to determine the risk from gaps or weaknesses in the system. The system evaluator will be able to determine whether there are significant weaknesses in the system that could lead to failure to meet one or more control objectives, that is, whether a risk of loss or error is present. A decision to correct a control weakness and reduce the risk must, in the final analysis, be made by management, based on its evaluation of potential costs and, particularly, potential benefits. Similarly, a decision not to correct a control weakness requires an explicit determination by management to accept the risk caused by that weakness.

Those decisions will reflect, in part, management's operating style and philosophy of control. Since internal controls provide information that management needs for making operating decisions, the sophistication of the control system appropriate for a particular organization will also reflect the extent to which management uses existing information and seeks more information. The decisions that have to be made regarding internal controls are not very different from the decisions that management is accustomed to making in other areas, and the skills and techniques management brings to bear in other aspects of an enterprise's operations will also be appropriate in the evaluation of internal controls.

2

Control Concepts and Definitions

The approach followed in this book for evaluating a system of internal control is an adaptation of the approach to auditing that has been used by Coopers & Lybrand in their practice for a decade. The approach uses standardized techniques and documents for developing an understanding and appraisal of the internal control system, thereby encouraging uniformity in application and consistency in judgments among system designers and evaluators. The approach identifies the common characteristics of all internal control systems as a foundation for analyzing individual systems. Among the key aspects of the approach are identification of:

Conditions of control;

Activity *cycles* based on either transaction flows or events related to the passage of time;

Control *objectives* in each cycle; and

Tasks necessary to meet each objective.

CONDITIONS OF CONTROL

Certain conditions must exist before control is possible: there must be some degree of systemization, competent people to operate the system, and documents that record transactions and what is done with them. Under the approach adopted in this book, those control conditions are not directly tested or evaluated, because there is no way in which this can be done. Rather, they are assumed to be present unless evidence to the contrary is found, primarily in the accounting output. An evaluator can thus focus attention on the controls themselves, while retaining an awareness of the underlying influence of the conditions of control. For example, "competence" cannot ordinarily be measured directly in the work environment, but an employee's competence will be questioned if the documents prepared or the work performed by that employee consistently contains errors.

It is often impossible—and always inefficient—to test the degree to which a given condition of control is present. No one has designed an adequate means of testing for the presence of honesty, so no testing at all is possible in this area. Employee competence is a function of training and experience. While it is possible to directly test the quality of the company's training function, system evaluators and auditors do not have the education or background to do so. The system evaluator can more efficiently measure competence by testing employees' skill in performing their tasks, which is done by determining whether the employees make errors. And this is done by functionally testing for compliance with the control system, which an evaluator already does as part of the evaluation process. Testing for competence by reviewing training programs is beyond the expertise of most evaluators, an inefficient means of determining competence, and redundant, since the work of employees will be tested in any event.

Moreover, even if factors such as competence and integrity could be measured with any degree of precision or reliability, there is little assurance that their presence is not ephemeral. The most honest and trusted employee may suddenly seek a change in lifestyle that causes him to steal. A person previously judged to be competent may, on a particular day, not feel well or have personal problems. Under those and similar conditions, the presence of supervisory controls and the checks and balances provided by separation of duties—controls that can be evaluated (as explained below)—prevent dishonesty and incompetence from affecting the output of the accounting system.

We have argued that an attempt to evaluate control conditions directly is sometimes impossible and always inefficient. In some cases, it may also be useless. Suppose, for example, that Diogenes had been successful in his quest for an honest person and that he also had devised a test guaranteed to confirm his success. We have asked scores of our colleagues, "If you could hire that person, what controls would you eliminate?" and we have yet to receive an answer. Systems of internal accounting control are designed to prevent and detect errors, and errors can be made by people of the highest integrity. Honest personnel are a means to an end —a work product that is error-free—not the end itself. Controls are necessary to ensure that the objective is met, not to ensure that personnel are and will remain honest.

That is not to say, however, that the conditions of control, such as competence and integrity, are not relevant to the evaluation. On the contrary, the system evaluator should maintain a high degree of awareness of those factors. In all phases of the work, the evaluator should be especially alert to evidence suggesting their absence, which would be indicated by accounting output of unacceptable quality. Notions such as competence and integrity are useful in diagnosing the causes of unacceptable error rates and may be relevant to management's consideration of the appropriate response to control weaknesses and decisions about corrective action.

If the evaluator finds that errors are caused by the absence of a condition of control, management will have to decide whether the risk of error should be reduced and, if so, the least costly way of doing it. Specifying the level (i.e., the complement of the error rate) at which a control must operate to be considered adequate is management's responsibility. That level may be high or low. For example, management may make a conscious decision to employ workers of relatively low competence and accept the existence of a high error rate, with the understanding either that a supervisory control will detect the errors or that reducing the error rate is not cost-effective. The level at which the conditions of control are present within an enterprise is thus an aspect of administrative, not internal accounting, control.

The job of the system evaluator is not to specify the level at which a control should operate (i.e., the allowable error rate) or the means of achieving that level. Rather, it is to determine whether the actual error rate exceeds the allowable error rate, as determined by management. If it does, the cause must be determined. The cause, e.g., changed circumstances in the form of more complex transactions, employee dishonesty, or incompetent workers, dictates the response to the weakness. Thus, it is not the absence of a control condition or even the resultant errors that are significant; it is the existence of an *unacceptable* error rate, known to have resulted from the absence of a control condition, that requires management action.

Three conditions of control are described below.

Systemization

A systematic plan is fundamental to the control of any operation. Most accountants accept the idea that a double-entry accounting system is a basic necessity for all but the simplest enterprises. The more explicitly an operation is defined, the easier it is to carry it out reliably and to keep it under control. Ideally, everyone involved in an operation should know exactly what should and should not be done under every possible condition, including how to handle unauthorized, incomplete, or erroneous transactions. Without a system, control is impossible, or at best substantially more difficult and time-consuming, and the risk of out-of-control events is significantly greater. The more effective the system, the more effective the other controls are likely to be. The "Conditions of Control Questionnaire" (pages 25–28) includes many questions designed to enhance the system evaluator's understanding of the degree of systemization.

Wide ranges of the degree of systemization are found in practice. The degree in computerized information systems generally exceeds that in systems operated by people, primarily because the computer requires extremely precise instructions that are rigidly followed. An equivalent degree of systemization is not found in systems operated by people, mainly because the human "computer" can handle complex tasks with far less detailed instructions. The degree of systemization, in turn, affects the types of control employed and the way in which controls are evaluated. For example, the high degree of systemization in a computer system enables the evaluator to study controls over the design, implementation, security, and use of computer programs (integrity controls) rather than controls over the mechanical processes by which the computer operates.

Documentation

Data must be recorded for many organizational purposes: communication between people, analysis, accountability, and control. Many financial data serve several purposes simultaneously. Adequate documentation of those data permits correct accounting and helps prevent errors in processing and recording. Some documentation is required solely for internal accounting control purposes: the performance of an activity may be documented (usually by requiring the initials or other means of identification of the performer) to fix responsibility for and permit supervision of it. Documentation required primarily for accounting control purposes may contribute secondarily to operational control purposes: numbering of documents is primarily a means of providing accountability to ensure that all authorized transactions are processed, but it also serves to identify documents for various purposes.

Documentation is inherent and implicit in systemization. It is enumerated as a separate condition of control because it is an essential prerequisite to adequate control. Obviously, without a complete and accurate description of a transaction, its authorization, and each operation through which it passes, exercise of control over it is not possible. In short, for a control to be most effective, its operation should result in the creation or revision of a document.

Competence and Integrity

Systems and all other control procedures are useless unless the people assigned to carry them out do so conscientiously, consistently, and honestly. The competence and integrity of individuals in an organization are influenced by many factors: the organization's reputation and physical location, its personnel selection and training policies, the difficulty of the work, the degree of systemization, and, most importantly, the amount and quality of supervision. Supervision serves as a constant check on the competence and integrity of personnel. On the other hand, competence and integrity influence the appropriate level of supervision and other aspects of the system. Sometimes the people must be selected in the light of the work to be done; sometimes the system, the supervision, and the work itself have to be modified to be appropriate to the level of competence available. The appropriate mix of the level of supervisory and non-supervisory personnel is an administrative decision that should be based on an analysis of costs and benefits over a range of alternatives.

THE CONTROL ENVIRONMENT

Some accountants believe that the internal accounting control environment established by management has "a significant impact on the selection and effectiveness of a company's accounting control procedures and techniques."* The definition of the control environment often overlaps what we have called the conditions of control; it also contains elements of both basic and disciplinary controls, which are discussed below. For example, the AICPA Special Advisory Committee on Internal Accounting Control included the following elements in its discussion of the internal accounting control environment:

---

*Report of the Special Advisory Committee on Internal Accounting Control. (New York: AICPA, p. 12.)

The company's organizational structure,

The competence and integrity of personnel,

The manner and extent of the delegation of authority,

The use of budgets and financial reports as a means of formulating and communicating company goals and objectives,

The presence of organizational checks and balances that separate incompatible activities and provide for supervision by higher levels of management,

The method of data processing used by a company, and in particular the degree of control exercised by management over the development and maintenance of a computer system.

A review of this listing suggests that grouping such diverse elements is not useful. For example, "organizational structure" is too broad a concept to be useful in analyzing the effectiveness of a control system. Similarly, the concept of delegating authority must be broken down into the separate components of granting permission to someone to enter into transactions and requiring that person's approval of specific transactions. The reader will note that competence and integrity have already been discussed as conditions of control; segregation of duties and supervision are included among the disciplinary controls described below; the authorization of transactions is a basic control task common to all transaction cycles in all internal accounting control systems; computer systems are processing techniques that are part of specific internal control systems and should be evaluated as part of each transaction cycle, along with other related controls; and so on with the remaining items on the Committee's list. This book discusses each of those environmental factors as a condition of control, a disciplinary control task, a basic control task, or a specific technique for carrying out a task, as appropriate.

Reassigning the so-called environmental factors in the manner suggested above is more than simply an alternative classification scheme; we believe it is necessary to create groupings that are meaningful for evaluating a system of internal accounting control. Most notably, the basic and disciplinary controls must be tested and evaluated in specific control applications, while the conditions of control, such as personnel competence and integrity, need not be directly evaluated at all. Their existence and operation are demonstrated by the presence and effectiveness of the basic and disciplinary controls.

The AICPA Special Advisory Committee on Internal Accounting Control believes that it is possible to make an overall evaluation of a company's internal accounting control environment, and that such an evaluation is "a necessary prelude to the evaluation of control procedures and techniques." Our experience in evaluating internal accounting control systems indicates that the usefulness of the suggested preliminary assessment is limited to improving the evaluator's awareness of the control environment. Moreover, the preliminary assessment must be carefully structured so as not to include elements that some would call environmental factors but that are in reality basic or disciplinary control tasks. Those controls should be evaluated as part of specific transaction cycles; their assessment is the *purpose* of the evaluation process, not a "necessary prelude."

THE CONDITIONS OF CONTROL QUESTIONNAIRE

The system evaluator should have a general understanding of the operations being evaluated and the control environment in the organization. The Conditions of Control Questionnaire (pages 25–28) is designed to improve the evaluator's awareness of that environment. Although it does not cover all environmental conditions that might be found in a business organization, it does include many that are likely to be of greatest interest to the system evaluator.

The aspects of the environment dealt with in the questionnaire are those organizational arrangements and control procedures that:

1. Provide conditions under which the system of internal accounting and operational controls can operate efficiently (e.g., use of organization charts and procedures manuals); and
2. In part, monitor performance of the accounting system through reporting and analyzing the results that it produces (e.g., budget preparation and variance analysis).

Because of the importance of understanding the control environment when planning a system evaluation, the questionnaire should be completed and reviewed at the start of the evaluation. The significance of "No" answers to questions is restricted to making the evaluator aware of some aspect of the control environment. The evaluation of internal accounting controls is not affected by the presence or absence of an item referred to in the questionnaire, any more than the evaluation is affected by the presence or absence of operational controls. In fact, the items in the questionnaire *are* operational controls.

The questionnaire should normally be completed by the evaluator in charge of a particular location, after discussions with and inquiries of senior management (especially financial management) at the location. The evaluator should report to senior management any "No" answers to questions.

For many of the questions, the end product (e.g., an internal financial statement) is in itself evidence of the control environment. Because the evaluator will not be relying directly on the environmental conditions, it will not always be necessary to examine evidence of their existence before recording a "Yes" answer. Nevertheless, reviewing the related documentation at the time the questionnaire is completed will frequently facilitate the evaluation.

Conditions of Control Questionnaire

A. Overall Organization of Business

    1. Is the overall management and departmental structure of the company, including the duties, lines of responsibility, and accountability of its key employees, defined in:

        a. organization charts;

        b. written job descriptions?

    2. Are the organization charts and written job descriptions:

        a. reviewed periodically to determine whether they are appropriate and up-to-date;

        b. approved by appropriate levels of management?

    3. With regard to financial interests of officers and key employees in vendors, customers, and the like:

        a. does the company have a well-defined policy as to the extent (if any) to which such investments are permitted;

        b. do officers and key employees report periodically on their compliance with that policy?

    4. With regard to possibly questionable payments, political contributions, and the like:

        a. is there a well-defined corporate conduct policy;

        b. has the policy been distributed to all corporate persons;

        c. are there adequate procedures for monitoring compliance with the policy?

B. Organization of the Accounting Department

    5. Are the duties, lines of responsibility, and accountability of the accounting department staff adequately defined in:

        a. organization charts;

        b. written job descriptions?

    6. Are the organization charts and written job descriptions:

        a. reviewed periodically to determine whether they are appropriate and up-to-date;

        b. approved by appropriate levels of management?

    7. Are there written policies regarding accounting department staff that relate to:

        a. delegation of duties when staff are absent;

        b. annual vacations for all staff;

        c. obtaining references for new staff?

C. Accounting Policies and Procedures

    8. Has the company written policies relating to:

        a. distinguishing capital expenditures from charges to expense;

        b. depreciation rates to be used for each type of property, plant, and equipment;

        c. depreciation calculations in the year of acquisition or disposal of capital assets;

        d. accounting treatment of gains and losses on the disposal of capital assets;

        e. accounting for and amortization of deferred expenditures and intangible assets;

    f. basis of calculation of provisions for doubtful accounts, obsolete and slow-moving inventory, warranties and guarantees, and similar provisions;

    g. where required, the timing of profit recognition on sales;

    h. the disposition in the accounts of variances from standard costs and/or under- and over-absorptions of overhead costs;

    i. basis of establishing costs for inventories;

    j. other accounting matters of particular significance to the business (specify)?

9. Are the policies in 8 above:
   a. reviewed periodically to determine whether they are appropriate;
   b. approved by appropriate levels of management;
   c. distributed to appropriate accounting personnel?

10. Has the company prepared:
    a. manuals of accounting procedures;
    b. a list of account codes (chart of accounts);
    c. accounting instructions for the preparation of financial statements?

11. Does the company review accounting documents and forms on a pre-issuance basis to ensure that they are:
    a. understandable;
    b. easy to use?

12. Are there written policies relating to:
    a. physical safeguarding of critical accounting forms, records, transaction processing areas, and procedural manuals;
    b. record retention criteria that meet corporate needs and legal requirements?

13. Is the documentation in 10 to 12 above:
    a. reviewed periodically to determine whether it is appropriate;
    b. approved by appropriate levels of management;
    c. distributed to appropriate accounting personnel?

14. Are the following prohibited as a matter of written policy:
    a. checks issued in blank;
    b. checks issued to "cash" or "bearer";
    c. alteration of checks or bank transfers?

15. Are the following used in the preparation of checks:
    a. check protection machines (where appropriate);
    b. protective paper?

D. Computer Department

16. Are the duties, lines of responsibility, and accountability of the computer department staff adequately defined in:
    a. organization charts;
    b. written job descriptions?

17. Are the organization charts and written job descriptions:
    a. reviewed periodically to determine whether they are appropriate and up-to-date;
    b. approved by appropriate levels of management?

18. Are there written policies regarding computer department staff that relate to:
    a. delegation of duties when staff are absent;
    b. annual vacations for all staff;
    c. obtaining references for new staff?

19. Are there written policies with respect to:
    a. development and maintenance of systems;

    b. selection of purchased hardware, software, and other computer services;

    c. security of important software and data stored on computer media;

    d. privacy and confidentiality of information stored in computer files, output, and documentation;

    e. physical safeguarding of equipment, documentation, and computer files?

20. Does the company review input forms, output formats, and CRT terminal screen formats on a pre-implementation basis to ensure that they are understandable and easy to use?

21. Does the company have adequate back-up arrangements or plans covering:

    a. processing and transmission equipment;

    b. data files, program files, and systems files stored on computer media;

    c. documentation and instructions?

E. Preparation of Budgets

[Note: These questions need not be answered where it is apparent that there are no effective budgeting (short-term planning) procedures.]

22. Are budgets prepared for the current or impending fiscal period for each significant function or activity within the company following the organizational structure of the company as a basis for responsibility reporting?

23. With respect to the budgeting system:

    a. Is there a written statement of assumptions supporting the budget?

    b. Are the programs of the various functional areas (e.g., research, marketing, production) integrated and related to long-term plans?

    c. Is a senior officer responsible for the preparation of operating budgets?

    d. Are budgets approved by the board of directors or an appropriate committee thereof?

    e. If budgets are revised during the year, are the revisions subject to the controls in (a) to (d) above?

24. Are sales and cost of sales budgets:

    a. based on both budgeted quantities and prices;

    b. detailed by product line, sales manager, or other appropriate category;

    c. approved at departmental levels by department heads?

25. Are operating expense budgets:

    a. based on individual expense captions (as opposed to broad, general categories);

    b. approved at departmental levels by department heads?

26. Do budgets include:

    a. "other income";

    b. provisions for known contingencies;

    c. forecast balance sheets at the end of the periods covered;

    d. cash flow?

27. Are actual sales, cost of sales, and operating expenses analyzed by the same categories used in preparation of budgets, and compared with the original and/or revised budgets?

F. Authority for Transactions

28. Does an appropriate level of management establish policy for the authorization of transactions?

29. Is there a policy concerning the maintenance of records of the names and/or specimen signatures/initials of all persons who are authorized to approve specific transactions?

Conditions of Control Questionnaire (Continued)

30. Are there clearly defined authority limits as to approval and execution of significant contracts and other agreements, not in the ordinary course of business (e.g., approval by board of directors or designated officials)?
31. Are minutes kept of decisions made at meetings of the board of directors, committees thereof, and senior management committees?

G. Insurance Coverage and Employee Fidelity Bonds

32. Does the company take appropriate steps to confirm the adequacy of its insurance coverage (e.g., by ensuring that the coverage is regularly reviewed by a knowledgeable person who strives to make a professional-type evaluation)?
33. Does the company carry fidelity bond coverage of the appropriate type and amount?

ACTIVITY CYCLES

The approach described in this book requires that transaction flows be viewed in terms of ''cycles'' into which they can be conveniently grouped and for which specific internal control objectives and tasks can be identified. The system evaluator identifies types of activities (transactions and time-related events) common to most businesses, such as purchasing, selling, and producing. Groupings of similar transaction types are referred to as ''transaction cycles.'' The importance of the cycle concept is its focus on whether appropriate control exists over each type of transaction as the transaction flows through the processing system. The entire ''life span'' of each transaction, from initiation to ultimate disposition, is studied to determine whether it is under control.

Perceived in this manner, control is a continuous element, typically crossing departmental lines of authority and inextricably linked to transaction flows. This approach permits management to oversee and evaluate the controls over transaction cycles as a whole, rather than requiring discrete judgments about specific control processes within a particular department or function. The purpose of internal accounting controls is to provide reasonable assurances about the authorization, execution, and recording of transactions and the safeguarding of assets, not about the operation of the departments or functions through which transactions pass. The purpose of an accounting system is to process transactions; controls are added to the system and operated by specific departments or functions to encourage the accuracy of that processing. Focusing on the transaction, rather than on the departments through which the transaction passes, provides a convenient and direct means of evaluating whether specific controls meet the purposes for which they were created.

Four cycles corresponding to most major business activities have been identified:

Payments Cycle. Transaction flows relating to expenditures and payments and related controls over (among other activities) ordering and receipt of purchases, accounts payable, and cash disbursements.

Production Cycle. Transaction flows relating to production of goods or services and related controls over such activities as inventory transfers and charges to production for labor and overhead.

Revenue Cycle. Transaction flows relating to revenue generating and collection functions and related controls over such activities as sales orders, shipping, and cash collection.

Time Cycle. Not strictly related to transaction flows, this cycle includes events caused by the passage of time, controls that are applied only periodically, certain custodial activities, and the financial reporting process.

Taken together, these four cycles form the internal accounting control system for most enterprises. In a computer environment, a fifth set of controls, also called a "cycle" for convenience, should be added:

Integrity Cycle. Controls over the creation, implementation, security, and use of computer programs, and controls over the security of data files. These controls, technically referred to as integrity controls, constitute a cycle because they operate continuously from the time programs are instituted and data are introduced into the computer records.

CONTROL OBJECTIVES

The control objectives to be achieved by the system of internal control are broken down by cycle. Those objectives must be attained to provide reasonable assurance of control over the authorization, recording, summarization, and reporting of transactions flowing through each cycle. An example of a control objective from the payments cycle is that all valid accounts payable transactions, and only those transactions, should be accurately recorded as accounts payable. If a control objective is not attained, risk has increased because the possibility of accidental errors or irregularities exists. Risk analysis will then determine the appropriate response on the part of management to the possibility of both kinds of errors.

The control objectives fit every enterprise; they remain essentially the same regardless of how the processing is performed. For example, it does not matter whether procedures are performed by people on visible data or by computer. The focus on control objectives on a cycle-by-cycle basis allows the evaluator of the system logically and realistically to identify the control objectives and assess the tasks necessary to accomplish the purposes of internal control.

Objectives that apply to transaction processing activities common to most industrial and commercial enterprises, as in the earlier example of a control objective, are referred to as standard control objectives. Objectives that relate to activities that are important to a particular industry or enterprise are referred to as supplementary control objectives. For example, supplementary control objectives might logically be identified for organizations in which vacation pay is processed differently from regular payrolls or in which inventory is held on consignment.

One of the key differences between the objectives of the Foreign Corrupt Practices Act (which are the same as in SAS No. 1) and our concept of control objectives for each cycle is that the latter are tailored to the flow of transactions and related control tasks in a system, whereas those in the Act are not. Nevertheless, the four general objectives in SAS No. 1 and the Act can be traced directly to the cycle control objectives.* Accordingly, the control objectives are crucial to any practical approach to demonstrating compliance with the Act; they are the means of correlating the objectives in the Act with the usual transaction processing.

As an example, one control objective in the payments cycle is that controls should be established over goods and services received as a basis for (1) determining and recording the liability for goods and services received but not entered as accounts payable, and (2) posting the items to detailed inventory records, if appropriate. This objective relates to Section B(ii) and B(iii) of the Foreign Corrupt Practices Act. (See footnote on page 10.)

CONTROL TASKS

For each control objective, we have identified control tasks † that must be accomplished to provide reasonable assurance that the control objective is being met. We have identified the few fundamental elements that must be present in one form or another in every business activity and then described the limited number of actions that can be taken to achieve control objectives, no matter what the pattern of transaction flow or the sophistication of the data processing technology. Every transaction has to go through certain steps: it has to be authorized, initiated, executed, and recorded. For purposes of internal accounting control, the system should make reasonably sure:

1. That *only* appropriate transactions are authorized, executed, and recorded.
2. That *all* authorized transactions are initiated, executed, and recorded as intended.
3. That errors in execution or recording are detected as soon as possible.

---

*This linkage is further demonstrated and discussed in Chapter 5.

†As will be seen in Chapter 5, a control task is simply a question from an internal control questionnaire expressed as an assertion.

An important feature of our approach is the emphasis on control tasks in the context of transaction flows through the system, rather than on specific control procedures, which may vary greatly among different transaction types within a cycle. For example, the completeness and accuracy of processing and recording cash receipts are confirmed by agreeing the amount deposited in the bank with a record of remittances received. This requires that a detailed record of cash and checks received be made when the mail is opened. That detailed record could consist of a listing of the payer and amount of each check received; it could also consist of photocopies of each check received. This focus on tasks rather than on procedures allows the system evaluator to adapt the analytical approach to fit the specific system. The relationship among cycles, control objectives, control tasks, and control procedures is shown in Exhibit 1.

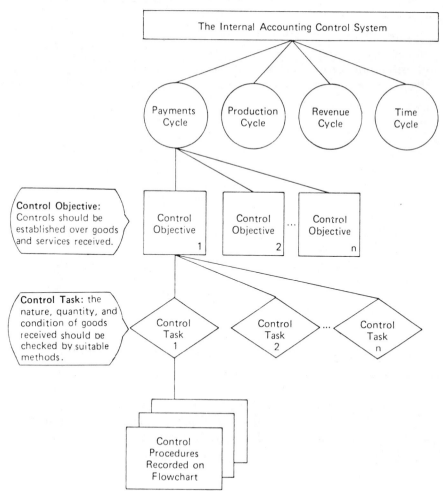

Exhibit 1. The Cycle Concept.

We have identified two groupings of control tasks. *Basic* control tasks are those necessary to meet the system's objectives. *Disciplinary* control tasks are necessary to ensure the continued functioning of the basic control tasks, and include supervision, segregation of duties, and custodial arrangements. In practice, this distinction between basic and disciplinary controls facilitates and adds flexibility to the evaluation of control weaknesses and any action required to correct a weakness. For example, lack of supervision over preparation of purchase orders would constitute a different kind of weakness, and evoke a different level of concern, than if there were no control procedures over purchase orders at all.

Basic Control Tasks

Basic control tasks are those tasks designed to ensure that transactions are recorded completely and accurately and that errors in execution or recording are detected as soon as possible, regardless of whether the error is the processing of an unauthorized transaction, the failure to process an authorized one, or the failure to process it accurately.

If control over accounting data is analyzed into its most basic elements, it becomes apparent that there are only a few control tasks and that they are common to all activity cycles in all internal accounting control systems. The control tasks are:

1. *Authorizing transactions*—assuring that proposed transactions are compared with plans, conditions, constraints, or general knowledge of what constitutes propriety, and deciding that they are proper.
2. *Validating transactions*—assuring that the processing system excludes all transactions that are invalid, that is, fictitious or nonexistent.
3. *Checking for completeness*—assuring that all transactions and data relevant for accounting purposes that should be present are present at each step in the information processing flow.
4. *Checking for accuracy*—assuring that all transactions are recorded at correct amounts, in the proper accounts (both general and subsidiary ledger), and on a timely basis.

These basic tasks appear in many forms and encompass virtually all the specific transaction control procedures a system evaluator is likely to encounter. There are many ways of accomplishing a given task, even within an enterprise. In the following discussion, the exact names of the control tasks are not important; it is the wide variety of means by which the tasks are accomplished that is worth noting.

Authorization.* The primary control over individual transactions is the

*Chapter 1 discussed several definitional aspects of "authorization" and suggested guidelines for a definition of that term as used in the Foreign Corrupt Practices Act.

act of authorizing them. This is the principal means for making sure that only valid transactions are processed and that all other transactions are rejected.

Authorization can be general or specific. A general authorization may take the form of giving a department or function permission to enter into transactions against some budgeted amount. The approval of the budget for a capital expenditure, for example, in effect serves as an authorization to commit the enterprise for expenditures up to the budgeted amount. Another example, from the retail industry, is the "open to buy" concept in which a buyer is authorized to buy merchandise up to a specified amount. A specific authorization, on the other hand, would grant permission to a person to enter into a specific transaction, for example, to buy a specific amount of a raw material needed for the production of a made-to-order item.

Controls over authorization of transactions are increasingly being automated by specifying in advance the conditions under which a transaction will be automatically authorized and executed. For example, a production order can be automatically authorized when the on-hand amount of an inventory item falls to a predetermined point requiring replenishment. Even in nonautomated systems, general authorizations can be used to accomplish the same objective. It should be noted that, for control to exist, some form of authorization must be carried out before, after, or during the initiation and execution of a transaction.

There is potential confusion in another common use of the term "authorization." The control operation of authorizing individual transactions must be distinguished from that aspect of systemization that spells out which member of an organization is authorized to do what. The control operation of authorizing individual transactions is frequently referred to as "approval." For example, a designated person approves a transaction or the validity of a document. For a transaction to be properly authorized, not only must it be approved; it must be approved by a person having the right and competence to do so or under conditions specified by the system.

Validation. Recorded transactions can be checked in various ways for compliance with the requirements of the system, to assure that they are valid. In its most elementary form, validation consists of the examination of documentation, by someone who understands the accounting system, for evidence that a recorded transaction actually took place and that it took place in accordance with prescribed procedures. In more sophisticated systems, validation is built into the system itself so that transactions are tested against predetermined expectations.

Validation of transactions requires establishing controls to:

Ensure that only valid transactions are recorded, i.e., entered on a document or into a computer file that can later be compared with accounting records, reports, or other documents. For example, only goods received are recorded on a receiving report; only goods shipped are recorded on a shipping report. The vendor's invoice can then be compared to the receiving report and the sales invoice can be compared to the shipping report. As another example, cancelling the voucher and related documents at the time of payment prevents their reuse to support a second payment for a nonexistent purchase.

Ensure that all relevant details about a transaction are appropriately recorded. For example, the nature, quantity, and condition of goods received are checked by suitable methods (e.g., by counting or weighing and inspecting) and recorded at the time of receipt.

Completeness. Control operations for ensuring that all transactions that occur are entered on a control document (e.g., receiving report or shipping advice) and included in the accounting records are an important part of internal accounting control. Once again, completeness operations are performed in a variety of ways. Examples are:

Numbering all transactions as soon as (or preferably before) they originate and then accounting for all the transactions after they have been processed. Numbering documents is part of the documentation condition; the control operation is the act of checking to see that all numbered documents complete the expected processing. The possibility of purposeful or accidental errors in the numbering process is reduced if the numerical sequence is printed in advance on the forms to be used for documenting transactions. If the risk of error or misuse is not considered significant, the numbering is often originated simultaneously with the document. For example, a computer preparing checks in the course of an accounts payable processing run can be programmed to number the checks sequentially.

Making sure that all data are processed by using "control totals." This can be done by totalling the critical numbers before and after processing; the assumption is that the processing is correct if the two totals agree. There is, of course, a possibility of one error exactly offsetting another error or omission, but the possibility is slight. Control totals do not provide control in themselves; they provide information by means of which control is exercised. The actual control operation is the comparison of two totals and the searching out and correction of errors giving rise to differences. Control totals appear in many forms. The double-entry system provides control totals in the sense that the totals of the debits always have to equal the total of the credits, both in individual entries and in the accounts as a whole. Batches of transactions may be totalled before recording or other processing. Control totals over some kinds of computations can be established by making the same computations in the aggregate. Another way to make sure that all transactions are processed is to match data from different sources. For example, unmatched documents (e.g., receiving records or vendors' invoices) can be reviewed periodically and long outstanding items investigated to be sure that a document has not been lost in the processing.

Making sure that all transactions are entered in a register. For example, all chargeable service hours may be recorded in a service register that is reconciled to the hours for which payment is made.

Completeness controls are also needed to ensure proper summarization of information and proper preparation of financial reports for both internal and external purposes. Controls over posting of control and other accounting documents serve this purpose.

Since individual transactions are the source of the balances used in financial statements and other financial data, subsidiary records and control accounts must be maintained to provide for proper summarization of recorded transactions and to serve as a check thereon. Typical control steps include establishing control totals before posting subsidiary records, reconciling subsidiary records with control accounts, and investigating differences disclosed by reconciliations.

Accuracy. Control operations are necessary to check that each transaction is recorded at the correct amount, in the right account, and on a timely basis. The accuracy of amount and account is most frequently achieved by establishing controls to check calculations, extensions, additions, and account classifications. For example, those checks might be performed and evidenced on sales invoices, credit memoranda, or payroll summaries. Occasionally an additional "double-check" is made by another individual who repeats the calculations, extensions, and additions, and reviews the account classifications.

Control operations to ensure that transactions are recorded on a timely basis are also essential since processing of most transactions occurs in sequence so that the results of one phase determine the detail of the next. Such control operations also serve to establish the dates on which transactions took place so that controls used for cut-off procedures can operate effectively, thus assuring that transactions are recorded and reported in the proper accounting period. As an example, goods received are checked and recorded at the time of their receipt. Usually the receiving records are matched with related vendors' invoices as part of a further check on the timely recording of transactions.

Disciplinary Control Tasks

We have categorized four kinds of control tasks as "disciplines" because in different ways they share the characteristic of monitoring, enforcing, or "disciplining" accounting activity, including the basic control tasks, and its results. A system without disciplinary controls is conceivable, but it would be error-prone, even if it were actually error-free. Disciplines are important because their presence affords reasonable assurance that the basic accounting and control operations are functioning as designed, at times other than those selected for formal review. They also help assure that errors that do occur are detected on a timely basis.

The value of disciplinary controls has been implicitly recognized for many years, but we believe they deserve much more explicit consideration than they have received in the past. Three disciplines are necessary features of an adequate system of control, and one is an optional feature whose value is becoming increasingly recognized. As with the basic controls, the disciplinary controls are tasks that must be accomplished if control objectives are to be met. Those tasks can be accomplished by many different procedures.

The necessary features are segregation of duties, custodial arrangements, and supervision. Segregation of duties causes the work of one person to act as a check on the work of another. Custodial controls are necessary to prevent unauthorized activity of all sorts, from loss or misuse of assets to loss or misuse of the general ledger. Supervising the system and those who operate it has an obvious effect on accuracy and reliability. Supervisory controls are probably the most important group of controls because they are the means of detecting and correcting errors caused by weaknesses in the basic controls.

The optional feature, but one that is achieving increasingly widespread acceptance, is internal audit. An internal audit function reviews and ''disciplines'' the adequacy of accounting and control activities; as such it serves as a ''super-control.''

Segregation of Duties. The separation of one activity from another serves several purposes. Quite aside from the objectives of accounting control, it is usually more efficient to specialize tasks and people, provided that the volume of activity is sufficient. For example, it is usually better to select and train one person to handle cash or the spare parts inventory exclusively and another person to keep the records than to try to find, train, and supervise someone versatile enough to handle the assets and also keep the records. Thus, in evaluating the costs and benefits of further segregating duties, management must realize that the benefits often include operating efficiencies.

However, the control features of segregation of duties may be so important that this disciplinary control should be adopted, regardless of whether it leads to operating efficiencies and even if it results in inefficiencies. An analysis of the potential risk of errors and fraudulent asset conversion may justify the segregation of duties even if it is inefficient. For example, the volume of transactions and the dollar amounts passing through cash registers in a department store may justify having one person obtain the totals from a register for accounting purposes and another clear the machine for the next salesclerk.

If two parts of a single transaction are handled by different people, each serves as a check on the other. For example, one bookkeeper can process a day's cash receipts received through the mail and another post the receipts to the accounts receivable records. Checking the total of the postings to the total receipts provides some assurance that each operation was accurately performed.

Segregation of duties also serves as a deterrent to fraud or concealment of error because of the need to recruit another individual's cooperation (collusion) to conceal it. As noted below, the separation of responsibility for the physical security of assets and the related recordkeeping is a significant custodial control; the treasurer who signs checks should not be able to hide an unauthorized disbursement through the ability to make a false entry in the disbursements records. That custodial control is even further enhanced if neither the treasurer nor the bookkeeper is responsible for periodically comparing the cash on hand and in the bank with the cash records and taking appropriate action if there are any differences.

Custodial Arrangements. If unauthorized transactions are to be prevented, whether they constitute theft or simply well-intentioned activity not consistent with the system, it is necessary to restrict access to all items that could be used to initiate or process a transaction. Custodial arrangements are most commonly thought of in connection with the physical security of negotiable assets—cash, securities, and sometimes inventory and other items that are easily convertible to cash or personal use. These arrangements apply equally to access to the books and records and the means of altering them—unused forms, unissued checks, check signature plates, files, computer tapes, ledgers, and everything important to the accounting process. In this regard, an internal accounting control system should deal with two kinds of situations:

1. The separation of responsibilities for the physical security of assets and the related recordkeeping.
2. Physical arrangements that prevent unauthorized access to assets and accounting records.

Not all physical safeguards are accounting controls. If the absence of a custodial control cannot cause accounting errors, the control is operational rather than accounting in nature. For example, management may consciously accept a degree of risk of pilferage of small tools in preference to installing toolroom procedures. As long as any losses are properly accounted for, the books and financial statements will reflect accurately what has taken place. As noted on several occasions, we recommend that management include operational controls in its review of internal controls, even though not required to do so by law.

In its simplest form, physical security is evidenced by such things as a safe, a vault, a locked door, a storeroom having a custodian, or a guarded fence. Physical safeguards are useless, however, without a discipline that prevents unauthorized persons from entering. The discipline can be automated to some degree. Issuing a key to only one person is an elementary form of "automated" authorization to enter a locked area; or, computers can be programmed to reject commands or transaction data unless specific tests for authorization and propriety are met. Physical security measures should also protect assets and records from physical harm such as accidental destruction, deterioration, or simply being mislaid.

Supervision. While the procedures used to perform the basic control tasks are important, the amalgam that holds the system together is one of the disciplinary controls, supervision. Effective supervision of personnel performing the work will lead to necessary modifications of the system when new types of transactions occur, corrective action when the system reveals errors, and follow-up when weaknesses in the system become evident. A control cannot be regarded as effective in the absence of adequate supervision.

Together with systemization, supervision is essential to control operations. If supervision exists, it provides the means for correcting other weaknesses. Without adequate supervision, the best of accounting systems and control operations run the risk of becoming erratic or undependable on short notice. Under pressure, systems and disciplines may be cut short or bypassed, reconciliations omitted, errors and exceptions left unattended, and documents lost, mislaid, or simply not journalized or posted to ledgers. Supervisory and administrative personnel may be drawn into the day-to-day work of processing data and correcting errors, and so find themselves less able to perform their supervisory control duties.

Even in a well-designed system, lack of supervisory controls may be signalled by problems in the accounts: an inordinate number of errors and exceptions, backlogs and bottlenecks, and instances of prescribed procedures that are not followed. If problems proliferate and it appears that supervisors are bogged down with detail or have inadequate knowledge of the matters for which they are responsible, management is on notice that it should not rely on the continuity of other control procedures, no matter how well designed.

Many of these controls consist of specific, observable routines for regularly assuring supervisors that the specified conditions of control and the required basic control operations are maintained. The performance of these administrative routines must be documented by: checklists; exception reports; initials evidencing review of batch controls, bank reconciliations, vouchers, and the like; log books for review routines; and written reports. The documentation can then be tested to obtain evidence of the quality of the supervisory controls.

Internal Audit. An internal audit function provides an additional level of discipline. With more and more companies establishing internal audit departments, the function has grown in size and stature.

The term "internal audit" covers a wide variety of activities. In mid-1978, the Institute of Internal Auditors adopted *Standards for the Professional Practice of Internal Auditing*. According to the *Standards,* "the scope of the internal audit should encompass the examination and evaluation of the adequacy and effectiveness of the organization's system of internal control and the quality of performance in carrying out assigned responsibilities."[*] In addition, the *Standards* address:

The organizational status and objectivity of the internal auditing department;

The professional care that internal auditors should exercise;

The performance of internal auditing assignments; and

The management of the internal auditing department.

Management should evaluate the internal audit function, both as part of its overall evaluation of internal control and because it relies on internal audit reports in reaching conclusions about the degree to which the system meets its internal control objectives. At the time of this writing, however, there is no formal mechanism for evaluating the internal audit function, although several accounting firms and government audit agencies have taken some first steps toward that end. Early in 1978, the Institute of Internal Auditors commissioned a research study, to be completed by the end of 1979, to develop a methodology for evaluating internal audit.[†] That methodology will presumably be useful for a self-evaluation, an evaluation by senior levels of management, and an evaluation by independent auditors, according to the purposes of each group.

---

[*]*Standards for the Professional Practice of Internal Auditing,* Section 300: "Scope of Work." (Altamonte Springs, Fla.: Institute of Internal Auditors, 1978.)

[†]Alan S. Glazer and Henry R. Jaenicke, *A Framework for Evaluating an Internal Control Function.* (Altamonte Springs, Fla.: Institute of Internal Auditors, 1980.)

OPERATIONAL CONTROLS

The relationship between administrative or operational controls and accounting controls is described in Chapter 1. Although operational controls aim primarily at efficiency of operations and adherence to policy, they have a feedback type of disciplinary effect on the efficiency of the accounting control system. For example:

Sales, production, and inventory data are used in a modern inventory system to forecast production needs and trigger production orders. That information, which is also essential to the financial accounting system, controls production planning to such a degree that the production planning department serves as an effective control over the accuracy of the financial data. The operational users of the system are constantly checking the accuracy of inventory balances; this may substitute in part for formal inventory cycle count procedures.

The comparison of actual income statements and balance sheets with budgeted figures is widely used as a tool of managerial control over departmental operations. If the budgets are actively used by management, the operations may serve to a degree as a control over the accuracy of the financial statements, because an error in the data processed would cause a variance that would have to be explained by an operating manager. However, one should guard against the tendency of managers to accept without question favorable variances which may shelter errors and make discovery more difficult.

Standard costs are a managerial accounting tool used to identify variations from plan. An investigation of variances may identify accounting errors, thus serving as an internal accounting control.

Other operational controls have an important bearing on enterprise profitability, but they have no accounting control implications. Thus:

Effective sales forecasts and inventory and production management help to prevent inventory overstocking and obsolescence.

Effective credit management helps to minimize bad debt losses.

Effective maintenance programs help to minimize maintenance costs and, by prolonging the life of equipment, depreciation charges.

These examples illustrate the effect of operational controls on earnings. In each case, however, internal accounting controls are necessary to assure the appropriate accounting for and reporting of inventory obsolescence, bad debts, and depreciation, respectively.

Since operational controls can have a profound effect on financial position and results of operations and can, on occasion, serve as accounting controls, they are an appropriate subject of interest to a system evaluator. An evaluator who does not understand them or ignores them can no doubt still do an evaluation. Some unneccessary tests may be made or some accounting problems may be investigated that are adequately taken care of by operational controls. The evaluator can nevertheless finish the evaluation effectively, though perhaps not efficiently, and gain reasonable assurance that internal accounting control objectives are being met.

An evaluator who *does* understand operational controls, however, will usually be able to plan a more efficient and effective evaluation by relying on the controls, where appropriate, and by recognizing the potential for problems if the controls are weak. Moreover, the evaluator may be able to provide comments on operational controls that can lead to improvements in the system.

INTERNAL CONTROL IN A COMPUTER ENVIRONMENT

The objectives of internal control are not affected by the means used to process data. A thorough knowledge of operating techniques of computers is necessary to design computer software, but that level of expertise is not necessary for understanding and evaluating controls in computerized systems. In fact, the evaluator may be better off with the openness of mind that frequently accompanies a degree of knowledge below that required of a computer system designer but nevertheless sufficient to enable the evaluator to seek support for and evaluate an existing system.

The form of the controls or the manner in which they are applied in processing transactions, of course, will be different in a computerized system. Some controls that are carried out by people are unchanged, such as the custodial controls over cash received. Other controls are accomplished by a combination of computer and human operations, for example, the action taken by individuals on a computer report of suppliers' invoices for which no goods have been recorded as received. In a computer environment, some controls that are not usually recognized in a non-computer environment are necessary to ensure the accuracy of processing within the computer itself, for example, the testing of program changes before implementation.*

Computer systems involve the use of computer programs that require specific definitions of tasks and precise instructions for accomplishing

---

*As noted below, testing program changes prior to implementation is an example of an integrity control.

them. Those programs and their use can be controlled so that the instructions are consistently followed. This combination of precise instructions plus consistent operation affects the way in which controls are applied and hence the way in which the system evaluator appraises them. Usually, the effective and consistent application of instructions can be assured by controlling the design, security, and use of computer programs and data files. *
The same assurance might be achieved by checking the results of the processing, although this is usually less efficient if there is a large volume of data that would have to be reported and checked. In some situations, however, the activities performed by the computer may be uncomplicated and may generate complete printouts of information, so that a user department can check the completeness and accuracy of computer processing. Reliance on ''user controls'' in those situations may enable the evaluator to avoid becoming deeply involved in the controls over computer processing. Since we believe the opportunities for this approach are limited, however, we do not refer to them further in this book.

As in non-computer systems, the objective of controls in computer systems is to ensure that authorized data are completely and accurately processed. Control tasks that are performed on visible data by individuals—tasks found mainly in user departments—are somewhat similar to those in non-computer systems and are termed *user controls*. However, the nature of computer processing imposes, and provides the opportunities for, significant changes in the methods of controlling and processing data. The extent of change will depend on the scope of computer processing in each system. The principal changes are:

1. Many accounting and control procedures that were previously carried out on visible data by individuals are replaced by steps in the computer programs. The steps of concern to the system evaluator are referred to as *programmed procedures*. Controls in computer systems are a combination of programmed procedures and tasks performed by people.
2. The continued and proper operation of programmed procedures can be controlled by effective *integrity controls*. This term describes the controls, which are found mainly in the computer department, over the creation, implementation, security, and use of computer programs. In most computer systems, effective control over design, security, and use of computer programs and data on file is achieved through a combination of user controls and integrity controls. Integrity controls assure the consistent operation of programmed

---

* ''Data files'' are transactions and records that can be accessed through the computer. Data files include tapes or discs that are loaded on the computer for a specific processing run or that are permanently loaded and available for inquiry or updating. Files in the latter category may be part of a data base, which is a form of data organization that stores data for use in more than one application.

procedures; user controls are usually limited to investigating computer-generated data on incomplete processing, such as a list of missing invoice numbers.

3. The reduced checking of the output from processing means that extra care is necessary to ensure that the data used in processing are valid.* This is particularly true of *standing data*, such as rates of pay or inventory prices, which are held permanently in master files. As in a non-computer system, specific controls are needed to ensure that the data remain properly held. Controls normally comprise a combination of checking the data on files and preventing unauthorized access to the files. These controls are termed *data file security controls* and form part of the integrity controls referred to above.

Thus, in evaluating a computer system, the reviewer will be concerned with the user controls and the procedures and controls that are unique to computer systems, that is, the programmed procedures and integrity controls mentioned above. These three types of procedures and controls are considered further in the following paragraphs.

User Controls

User controls are controls performed by people on visible data generated by the computer, primarily for the purpose of checking the completeness, validity, and accuracy of computer processing. The term ''user controls'' also describes controls that are unrelated to computer processing, for example, checking the quality and condition of goods received or ensuring that all transactions are initially recorded.

The computer highlights the need for controls over the completeness of information processing; it also enhances the accomplishment of that control task. For example, the computer generates printouts of missing receiving reports that can be investigated to determine whether some receiving reports sent to the computer department for processing were in fact not processed. The investigation, not the printout, is an example of a user control.

Those user controls that are related to computer processing will be effective only if the related programmed procedure operates properly. For example, the investigation of items reported by the computer as missing or exceptional, such as the list of missing receiving reports referred to

---

*Entering data into the computer is costly. As a result, most systems are designed to eliminate, insofar as possible, entering the same information more than once. Once data are entered, they can be used in many different ways. For example, the computer can match information with other information held in a file, as a means of checking the validity of the information. Care must be taken to assure that what is being matched is not information that has been accumulated in two different files from the same source.

previously, can be effective only if the list is complete. As a result, programmed procedures and integrity controls are also needed to assure the completeness of computer-generated data. Certain user controls serve as a check on programmed procedures, for example, the detailed checking to source data of a printout of standing data amendments.

User control techniques are broadly similar to those in non-computer systems. The main difference is that many of the controls are carried out on computer output rather than on reports produced by people. Also, certain procedures are more formalized, for example, the correction of errors. User controls include such techniques as checking computer output to source data or predetermined totals, checking computer reconciliations, and investigating computer-produced rejections and exception reports.

Programmed Procedures

Programmed procedures can be divided into two types:

1. Programmed procedures that replace control functions previously carried out by people, which test the completeness, accuracy, and validity of the data being processed. An example is a sequence check and preparation of a list of missing numbers. (The investigation of the list of missing numbers is a user control, as noted above. Strictly speaking, the sequence check and list preparation are not controls; they enable a control to operate, namely, the investigation.)
2. Programmed procedures that replace operations of an accounting rather than a control nature that are performed by individuals, for example, the calculation and production of sales invoices, the updating of master files, and the generation of data within the computer.

Integrity Controls

In a computer environment, procedures are needed to establish control over the creation, implementation, security, and use of computer programs and the security of data files. Those controls are collectively known as integrity controls. In a non-computer system, separate controls exist over each activity in each cycle, and those controls can be evaluated. In a computer system, this would be impracticable, and even unnecessary, because the integrity controls over programs and files apply to all cycles in which there are computerized procedures. Most controls operate on data; integrity controls operate on procedures. They control "system transactions" rather than "data transactions." Since separate integrity controls do not exist for each data transaction cycle, all integrity controls can be evaluated at one time.

We have already referred to the preciseness of instructions necessary in a computer environment. That same degree of preciseness is not necessary in a non-computer environment. If a clerk finds an unusual transaction, he or she can seek help. The computer cannot. Consequently, the procedures and instructions for creating or revising computer programs and the arrangement of information on computer files must also exhibit a high degree of precision, order, and discipline. Those procedures and instructions are themselves subject to control.

The control objectives and tasks for integrity controls are the same for all activity cycles and for all industries. The methods and procedures for achieving the objectives differ depending on the type of computer. Because our approach is objective- and task-oriented rather than procedure-oriented, this book will not consider the effect of differences in types of computers on integrity controls.

It is convenient to divide the integrity controls according to their purpose, as follows:

Implementation controls are designed to ensure that appropriate programmed procedures are effectively included in the program, both when the system originally becomes operational and when changes are subsequently made. They include controls over the design, testing, and initial operational use of new systems and program changes, and the related documentation.

Program security controls are designed to ensure that unauthorized changes cannot be made in programmed procedures. They include the controls over the security of programs both while in use (i.e., in the computer) and when not in use (in a physical library).

Computer operations controls are designed to ensure that programmed procedures are consistently applied. They include the controls that ensure that programs and data files are properly set up and run in accordance with authorized instructions.

Data file security controls are designed to ensure that unauthorized changes cannot be made in data files. They include controls over the security of data files both while in use, particularly from unauthorized access through remote terminals, and when not in use (in a physical library).

Integrity controls are a combination of controls over operations performed by people and controls over system software. The former are similar to those in a non-computer environment; for example, programs or changes in programs require authorization, development, implementation, and the achievement of user satisfaction. Controls over system software comprise controls over the creation or amendment of computer programs. The controls are not specific to any particular application but may be used in the creation, processing, and control of all applications. System software includes operating systems, compilers, and utility programs. For example, programs may be protected against unauthorized change by program library software; use of the correct files may be assured by software label checks; and the proper processing of jobs may depend on procedures included in the operating system and related software. Integrity controls over system software are as important as the integrity controls over application programs and data files that are discussed in the next paragraph.

Programs and data files may be protected against unauthorized access or change by incorporating requirements for a password into the instructions for accessing and amending the program or file. In some applications, the system will make a record of access to the program or file. This list can then be reviewed for unauthorized access and its consequences, e.g., a change made in a program. The computer's ability to create records of attempts to access programs and data files creates opportunities for enhanced control. Even here, however, the control is a human one because the control is the investigation of the attempt, not the computer record. The machine makes the record; a person does the investigating.

Disciplines

The disciplines over basic controls in computer systems are similar to those in non-computer systems—supervisory controls, segregation of duties, and custodial arrangements. Those disciplines, which use the same techniques as in non-computer systems, operate in both user and computer departments; they are discussed further in the following paragraphs. Note that the concepts and the techniques are the same as in a non-computer system.

Supervisory Controls. Supervisory controls consist of supervising the operation of a basic control to ensure that it continues to operate. For example, in a user department, a responsible official should periodically check that the investigation of data rejected by the computer is being carried out regularly. Likewise, in the computer department, the adequacy of the testing procedures for program changes should be reviewed and approved by a suitable computer department manager.

Segregation of Duties. Segregation of duties involves the work of one person providing a check over the work of another. In relation to user controls, an obvious example is that the person investigating a list of missing documents should be independent of computer operations. In relation to integrity controls, it is important, for example, that personnel responsible for testing and implementing new programs should not also be responsible for operating those programs.

Custodial Arrangements. Custodial arrangements concern the custody of assets and records and involve:

1. Separation of responsibility for the custody of assets from responsibility for the related records; for example, the user controls relating to a computer inventory file should be performed or checked by persons other than those who maintain physical custody of the inventory.
2. Physical arrangements that prevent unauthorized access to assets and the related records; for example, the security arrangements applied to the cashier's department or terminals.

3

A Framework for Evaluating Internal Control

Management's responsibility to create, maintain, and evaluate a system of internal control is discussed in Chapter 1. Until now, management's decisions about the extent of control were based on usually subjective appraisals of risks and the costs of reducing them. The need to demonstrate compliance with the Foreign Corrupt Practices Act and the likelihood in the near future of public reporting on systems of internal control suggest that the evaluation process must become less subjective and more formal. This requires a framework for evaluating internal control, including rules for carrying out the review process.

CPAs have been evaluating systems of internal accounting control for decades, usually for the purpose of defining the nature, timing, and extent of subsequent audit procedures required for the expression of an opinion on the financial statements. The techniques developed by CPAs can, in many cases, be used by corporate management to provide a framework for performing a "self-review" of control systems. While the approach described in this book was originally devised for use on audit engagements, it has also been used, and tested, as a means for management to meet its internal accounting control responsibilities—responsibilities that include reviewing the system of internal accounting controls and reporting to the board, the audit committee, and the public on its effectiveness.

OVERVIEW OF THE FRAMEWORK

The approach to evaluating internal accounting control contains six steps or tasks, with specific procedures to accomplish each task. As explained in greater detail below and summarized in Exhibit 2, the steps, very briefly, are: obtaining and recording an understanding of the internal accounting control system; confirming the understanding; evaluating the system, as planned, to determine whether there are any inherent control weaknesses; assessing control weaknesses to determine whether they are potentially significant; assessing established controls to determine whether they are, in fact, operating effectively; and reporting on control deficiencies. Each step and corresponding procedures are discussed in detail in Chapters 4 and 5. Several appendices provide instructions and forms for the various procedures.

The first step is to obtain and record an understanding of the internal accounting control procedures established for each transaction type.* If responsibility for the evaluation of internal control has been assigned to individuals not familiar with the system, such as internal auditors from another division, they should first "consider the environment in which the accounting control procedures operate, including the nature of the company's business and the industry in which it operates, management's philosophy of operations, and related policies, . . . [and] consider the transactions in which the company engages and classify them by, for example, functions, operating units, or cycles."† This book assumes that the evaluators are familiar with the segment of the enterprise whose controls they are evaluating and the activity cycles entered into by those segments.

---

*"Transaction" and "transaction type" are defined and discussed on page 72.

†*Report of the Special Advisory Committee on Internal Accounting Control,* p. 23. As noted in Chapter 2 of this book, the authors strongly favor classifying transactions by activity cycles, as did the *Report* of the AICPA Special Advisory Committee.

The understanding is the basis for evaluating the system; it is normally obtained through structured interview procedures with accounting personnel and recorded on flowcharts.

Next, the understanding of the system recorded in the flowcharts is confirmed by means of a transaction review. A transaction review is the process of following the documentation for one transaction of each type through the accounting system.

Step	Procedure
☐ Obtain and record an understanding of the internal accounting control system	☐ Conduct site interviews, identify transaction types, and prepare flowcharts
☐ Confirm understanding of the system	☐ Review documentation flow for one transaction of each type and modify flowchart if necessary
☐ Evaluate the system to determine whether there are any inherent control weaknesses	☐ Complete Internal Control Questionnaire using Internal Control Reference Manual
☐ Assess control weaknesses to determine whether they are potentially significant	☐ Complete Record of Control Weaknesses
☐ Assess controls that are in place, to determine whether they are operating effectively	☐ Perform functional tests by testing controls over several transactions of each type, to gain reasonable assurance that procedures are being applied as prescribed. Complete Record of Control-Operation Exceptions
☐ Report to senior management on internal control weaknesses	☐ Draft report on system review

Exhibit 2. A Six-Step Approach to Control Evaluation.

The third step is to evaluate the system to determine whether there are control weaknesses resulting from the absence of controls. The presence or absence of specific controls is determined by completing an Internal Control Questionnaire (ICQ), aided by an Internal Control Reference Manual. The ICQ is organized by cycles, control objectives, and control tasks (as described in Chapter 2). Under each control objective there are questions concerning the control tasks that ordinarily must be performed if the objective is to be met. The ICQ also contains supplementary control objectives that the system evaluator may use, on an optional basis, to tailor the format of the questionnaire to a particular enterprise's circumstances. An excerpt from the ICQ is shown in Exhibit 3. Only questions relating to those tasks considered relevant to realizing the objectives of internal *accounting* control need be answered if the purpose of the evaluation is limited to determining whether the objectives of internal accounting control were achieved. The ICQ also includes optional questions about *operational* control tasks (for example, Question 2.2 in Exhibit 3); Chapter 2 noted the advantages of reviewing operational controls at the same time accounting controls are evaluated.

Control Objective

2. **Control should be established over goods and services received as a basis for:**

    (a) Determining and recording the liability for goods and services received but not entered as accounts payable;

    (b) Where required, posting the items to detailed inventory records.

Questionnaire	Flowchart Ref.	"Yes"	"No"
Initial Recording of Receipt of Goods and Services			
2.1 Are the following checked by suitable methods (e.g., by counting or weighing and inspecting goods received) and the results recorded at the time of their receipt for subsequent checking with the related invoices:			
(a) nature, quantity and condition of goods received (including property, plant and equipment and major supplies, e.g., fuel, stationery);			
(b) major services received (to the extent practicable)?			
2.2 Are procedures in effect to foster: (a) accurate weights (e.g., by periodically testing scales); (b) weighing routines that are not unduly expensive (e.g., by using statistical sampling)?			

Exhibit 3. Excerpt From Payments Cycle Internal Control Questionnaire.

The ICQ is designed so that a "Yes" answer means that a control exists; procedures accomplishing control tasks are identified by cross-references to the flowchart. A "No" answer means a specific control task is not accomplished—a weakness exists. If computer-based systems are used to process accounting data, a combination of the standard ICQ and a separate computer ICQ should be completed in most cases, as explained in Chapter 5.

The Internal Control Reference Manual is used to help in understanding and responding to the accounting control questions. Designed to be used as a reference source that would bridge theory and practice, it explains the purpose of each control task listed under each control objective. It also details various procedures that might be effective for performing the task and cites examples of how these procedures might operate in practice. By providing for a more uniform appraisal, the Reference Manual helps bring consistency to subjective judgments about accounting control systems. It also includes a discussion and chart relating the ICQ control objectives to the general objectives of the Foreign Corrupt Practices Act. The introduction to the manual contains detailed instructions for its use. Some portions of the manual have been incorporated into the text of this book; other portions are reproduced in Appendix D.

Any control weaknesses found, that is, any "No" answers in the ICQ, are then assessed to determine whether the weaknesses are potentially significant. This is accomplished by completing a Record of Control Weaknesses, which summarizes all control weaknesses identified in the ICQ and requires a decision about whether the possible effect of a particular weakness is significant. General guidelines for making this decision are discussed below. The purpose of the form is to bring together in one document all control weaknesses identified during the evaluation and the results of discussing those weaknesses with site personnel. It also provides a ready means of reviewing the possible effects of weaknesses on internal accounting control objectives.

The next step is to assess the controls that are in place to determine whether they are operating effectively. This is done by performing "functional tests," often also referred to as "compliance tests." The system evaluator tests "Yes" answers to the ICQ to gain reasonable assurance that controls are operating as planned. Testing consists of examining evidence and reperforming operations to determine whether control procedures are, in fact, being performed. A breakdown in prescribed procedures places the system evaluator in the same position as if a "No" answer had been identified at the time of the completion of the internal control questionnaire. As noted below, however, management's response will differ in the two cases.

It will normally be possible to rely on the continuing operation of the basic controls only in those areas where there are disciplines over the basic controls. If the functional tests indicate that the disciplines have been in force during the period, testing of the basic controls can usually be restricted to one period, namely, the time of the test.* It is not necessary to test the operation of any control if its failure to function is not significant, as defined below. Further instructions on the performance and documentation of functional tests are set out in Chapter 5 and Appendix E. Chapter 5 also contains guidance concerning reviews of operational controls.

A Record of Control-Operation Exceptions should be completed after the functional tests have been performed. This form summarizes areas of control ineffectiveness (in this case, only those discovered by the functional tests) and requires a decision about whether an inoperative control is significant. The Record of Control Weaknesses summarizes control weaknesses in the design of the system; the Record of Control-Operation Exceptions summarizes breakdowns in prescribed procedures. We have separated the two kinds of control deficiencies because management's response to each should be different, even though the effect of both is the same, namely, the absence of control. For example, a common procedure that facilitates control over the validity of cash disbursements is the cancellation of vouchers and supporting documents after a disbursement so that the same voucher and documents could not support another disbursement. If that procedure is not being followed in a particular enterprise, it may be either because the system design omitted it or because the procedure was included in the system but the employee responsible for carrying out the cancellation failed to do so. The control deficiency in the first case is remedied by redesigning the system to include the cancellation procedure, assuming that alternative procedures do not accomplish the same control task. The control deficiency in the second case may be remedied by strengthening supervision.

The final step is to report to the appropriate level of management on internal control weaknesses noted during the evaluation of the system and the functional tests. The form and content of the report and the level of management to which it should be addressed will be dictated by the needs of the individual company and the significance of the control weakness.

RANKING CONTROL WEAKNESSES

The summaries of control weaknesses and exceptions, described earlier, are used as the basis for reporting to management at various levels whether the internal accounting control system is sufficient to provide reasonable

---

* Chapter 5 discusses the possibility that management may decide not to functionally test, but instead to rely on supervision and segregation of duties as ongoing monitoring devices.

assurance that management is meeting its responsibilities under the Foreign Corrupt Practices Act. Both forms are designed to force the system evaluator to make a judgment as to the level of management to which an internal control weakness or an inoperative or ineffective control* is to be reported for possible corrective action. Ordinarily, every control weakness should be documented and reported to someone. Then, a decision must be made, based on the significance† of the control weakness, regarding the appropriate level of management to which it should be further reported. Senior management will also have to judge whether a control weakness is of sufficient significance to require inclusion in its report to the board of directors or audit committee or in a public report on internal accounting control.

Some kind of scheme for ranking control weaknesses is necessary as a basis for those determinations. In addition, the ranking process will be helpful in making a preliminary evaluation of the significance of potential control weaknesses to determine where the initial review effort should be concentrated (described below), and in determining the level of functional testing that should take place (discussed in Chapter 5).

We suggest that a practical approach to thinking about "levels of significance" is to group control weaknesses into several broad categories. Based on its knowledge of the business and its philosophy and style of managing (see the discussion in Chapter 1), management should formulate a strategy for determining an "exposure threshold," that is, a cut-off level of exposure (considering both the quantitative and qualitative aspects of exposure discussed below) to determine those control weaknesses that would be accumulated and documented, but otherwise ignored. Control weaknesses in this lowest category would not be subjected to cost/benefit analyses because, as a practical matter, the potential exposure to adverse consequences is clearly insignificant.

The strategy for determining the exposure threshold must be periodically reviewed in the light of changing conditions and management philosophy. The number of errors resulting from control weaknesses in the lowest category might increase to the point where the enterprise's exposure exceeded the threshold. For this reason, a knowledge of the number of errors that occur is important and should be accumulated, even though it would be known at the time that the errors were discovered that the control weakness would not be corrected.

A strategy should also be formulated for determining whether a control weakness is so significant as to put it in the highest category. That category

---

*For convenience, the term "control weakness" will be used to refer to a control weakness or an inoperative or ineffective control, that is, a control breakdown or deficiency of any kind.

†As explained later in this section, the concepts of "significance" and "materiality" are different, though they are related.

would be reserved for those weaknesses deemed "most significant." They would be reported to the audit committee, would have high priority for being corrected, and might be publicly reported if uncorrected. Potential control weaknesses in this category would suggest specific areas to receive attention during the preliminary evaluation and would signal the need for relatively high levels of functional testing. Weaknesses in this category would also not be subjected to further cost/benefit analyses, since that would be academic given the decision in a particular case that the risk should not be run. Weaknesses in this category would generally be endemic to the system in that they would affect a substantial part of the financial information reporting system, such as a weakness involving integrity controls in the computer department. Similarly, the exposure could be great because of qualitative factors, as in the case of a system that permitted payments proscribed by law.

Between the highest and the lowest categories would be weaknesses to be reported to intermediate levels of management and to be subjected to cost/benefit analysis to determine whether corrective action is required under the "reasonable assurance" test. There are no precise measurements for determining where the two thresholds are, but precision usually is not needed. As in other management problems, decisions are possible without precise measurements and must be formulated using judgment.

We believe, moreover, that we can identify factors that should affect the significance of a control weakness and that should enter into any cost/benefit analyses. In evaluating the significance of a control weakness, management should consider the following attributes:

The adverse consequences that could result from the control weakness

The potential exposure to those adverse consequences

The chance of an adverse consequence actually occurring

The likelihood of an actual adverse consequence being detected on a timely basis

Qualitative factors, not otherwise classified.

If all of those attributes are considered for each control weakness, the evaluator or management, as appropriate, should be able to assess the benefit that would be achieved by eliminating a weakness, that is, the risk that would be avoided if the control were in place and operating. The system evaluator would use those attributes to determine (1) the areas where attention should initially be concentrated; (2) the level of testing appropriate to determine whether a control is effective; and (3) the level of management to which to report a control weakness. Management would use those attributes to determine (1) whether to correct the control weakness; (2) whether the company is in compliance with the Foreign Corrupt Practices Act if the weakness is not corrected; and (3) whether to mention the uncorrected weakness in a public report on internal accounting control.

Each attribute cannot be considered and scored separately. For example, in the next section, four possible consequences of an internal control weakness are considered. From a risk evaluation point of view, none of the four *per se* is more or less important than any other. For compliance with the Foreign Corrupt Practices Act, none of the first three *per se* is more or less important than any other. Only when the other attributes, such as potential exposure and chance of occurrence, are used to quantify the possible consequences of control weaknesses can the benefits from correcting control weaknesses be assessed.

Possible Consequences of Control Weaknesses

Internal controls should prevent or detect the following consequences:

Misappropriation of assets. This includes theft by employees, management, or individuals not associated with the enterprise. Assets can be misappropriated because of inadequate separation of duties or the absence of custodial devices such as controlled access to storage areas. Misappropriation of assets by employees or management assumes an attempt will be made by the perpetrator to cover up the loss by deliberately misstating the accounting records.

Deliberate accounting or reporting errors, not associated with misappropriation of assets. This includes errors to disguise management performance, such as delaying sales (either actual or reported sales) until the start of a contest period and leveling output reports by creating a "kitty" for bad months.

Accidental accounting or reporting errors. These could occur at any stage in the processing of information.

Reduced operating efficiency. This is the result of an operational, rather than accounting, control weakness. It can occur in the form of excessive costs or the loss of potential revenue, both in the short run and in the long run.

Potential Exposure to Adverse Consequences

The preceding section discussed what could possibly go wrong because of a control weakness. The magnitude of what could go wrong is dependent on the potential exposure to each adverse consequence over a particular time period, such as a year. For example, if inadequate control of over-the-counter sales of merchandise for cash could lead to misappropriation of cash, the system evaluator and management should determine how often such sales occur and their average value. Thus, the expected volume of transactions passing through a control each year and the average value of those transactions provide a measure of the maximum potential misappropriation, error, or loss of income that could result from a control weakness over the year. Since the disciplinary controls discussed in Chapter 2 (supervision, separation of duties, and custodial arrangements) often operate on groups of transactions rather than individual transactions, the volume and total value of transactions passing through a disciplinary control may be quite large. Consequently, the potential exposure from a disciplinary control weakness may be greater than the exposure from a weakness in a basic control.

Secondary or indirect adverse financial consequences of control weaknesses could result from violating statutes or the rules of regulatory agencies. Those consequences could be in the form of fines, penalties, injunctive actions, or other sanctions.

Chance of Adverse Consequence Actually Occurring

An internal control weakness means that an asset misappropriation, error, or operating inefficiency *could* occur; it does not mean that the adverse consequence *will* occur. Assets may be left unguarded, yet they may not be stolen. Supervision of accounting clerks may be lacking, yet errors may also be lacking because the clerks are competent and highly motivated. In evaluating the overall significance of the control weakness, the evaluator and management must consider the likelihood of the possible adverse consequence actually occurring.

The likelihood that possible asset misappropriations will actually occur depends largely on the liquidity and convertibility of the particular asset. Cash is more prone to misappropriation than are elephants. The likelihood that possible accidental errors will actually occur may depend on the complexity of the event or transaction being recorded and the amount of judgment needed in measuring and recording it. For operating inefficiencies, the actual or potential losses each year can sometimes be calculated; if so, determining the "chance of occurrence" would not be appropriate. For example, if inadequate operational controls exist over taking cash discounts on purchases, the system evaluator may be able to estimate the actual discounts lost each year based on a sample of transactions; the maximum potential loss each year could be calculated from the total value of purchases entitled to a discount.

Likelihood of Timely Detection of Misappropriations and Errors

Misappropriation of assets and accounting and reporting errors resulting from weaknesses in internal accounting controls could be detected before the transaction cycle is complete or before financial data are prepared.* Several factors may influence the possibility of detecting errors subsequent to their occurrence, including the effectiveness of supervision. In an effective system of internal control, supervision should detect breakdowns in basic control tasks. This suggests that some controls are more important than others, that is, there is a hierarchy of controls in which disciplinary controls outrank basic controls.

Moreover, many basic controls are interrelated. For example, if the controls over the completeness of recording purchase invoices break down, this could be detected by an investigation of unmatched records of goods received or by agreeing suppliers' statements to the accounts payable records. Similarly, customers may advise the company that shipments billed to them were not received, or salespersons may complain that commissions earned were not paid.

Errors resulting from weaknesses in controls over the completeness of transaction processing are often impossible to identify. While the salesperson in the above example may complain that commissions earned were not paid and thereby inform management of unrecorded sales, customers will rarely inform vendors on a timely basis of goods received but not billed. Thus, a weakness in a completeness control is more likely to lead to undetected errors than a weakness in a control over the authorization or validity of transactions.

Management's "style" and skills may affect its ability to detect errors. If supervisors responsible for an activity are expected to review disaggregated data concerning that activity (for example, time charged to each job in a job order cost system or exception reports of transactions of high monetary value or of transactions that do not conform to established norms), a conscientious review of those data may reveal intentional or unintentional errors in accounting for labor costs. (A manager's ability to detect errors is reduced as the data reviewed become more aggregated.)

Qualitative Attributes of Control Weaknesses

To varying degrees, the factors that determine the significance of a control weakness discussed above can be quantified; those that follow cannot. Yet they must be considered by both the system evaluator and management in determining the appropriate response by each to an internal control weakness. Among the additional factors are:

---

*This discussion is inapplicable to weaknesses in operational controls. An operating inefficiency cannot be "reversed" after the weakness is discovered. For example, a lost discount for prompt payment cannot be recovered if the loss is subsequently discovered.

The enterprise's unwillingness to tolerate certain kinds of errors in any amount, possibly because of the effect of even small errors on the enterprise's image. For example, a small error in a customer's account in a brokerage house might cast sufficient doubt on the effectiveness of the firm's accounting system to lead to the loss of the customer.

The belief that higher standards of care and integrity should apply to higher levels of management. A control weakness that allowed a deliberate overstatement of one salesperson's expense account by $1,000 might not be considered very significant; a similar weakness that permitted the president to overstate an expense account by the same amount might be considered reportable to the board of directors.

Related to other qualitative factors, the degree of embarrassment from disclosure of a misappropriation or error resulting from a control weakness. This could be affected by past unfavorable publicity related to similar control weaknesses.

Aspects of internal control that the audit committee has expressed specific interest in, such as the effectiveness of the internal audit department or of certain operational controls.

Relationship to Traditional Materiality Criteria

The concept of "materiality" of an internal accounting control weakness as viewed by the CPA differs from the concept of "significance" as viewed by a system evaluator or by management. In an audit environment, a weakness in internal accounting control is "material" if the errors or misappropriations that could result from it could make the financial statements misleading. In the environment of evaluating internal accounting controls, the concept of materiality is replaced by the concept of significance, which can be determined only within the context of management's philosophy of control. The ultimate judgment of the significance of a control weakness, i.e., whether it should be corrected, must be management's, not the evaluator's and not the independent auditor's. We believe, for example, that if the independent auditor is asked to comment on the enterprise's internal accounting controls, the comments should be related to the *process* by which management determines whether to correct control weaknesses, not to the decisions themselves.

INTEGRITY CONTROL WEAKNESSES IN COMPUTER SYSTEMS

All of the attributes that influence the level of significance of a control weakness in a non-computer system also apply in a computer system. In addition, however, the evaluator should consider the effect of weaknesses in integrity controls on the programmed procedures or data elements at risk. These are the programmed procedures and data in each application control objective that are not checked in detail by the user. Weaknesses in the different areas of integrity controls may have different effects on the programmed procedures and data, as follows:

1. Weaknesses in implementation controls may cause new or revised systems to function incorrectly. Often, the errors are imbedded in the system and the erroneous processing will continue until the error is identified and corrected.

2. Weaknesses in program security controls may allow unauthorized changes to be made in the systems, i.e., changes can be made that are not subject to the normal implementation controls covered in item 1 above. The company may not be sure which systems have been changed. These weaknesses increase the risk of misappropriation of the company's assets and the risk of accounting errors.

3. Weaknesses in computer operations controls generally mean that random errors may occur in the system. While some errors, such as those in standing data, may have a lasting effect, the main effect of such weaknesses is similar to that of weaknesses in a non-computer system, i.e., most processing will be correct but occasionally an error may occur. This contrasts with the continuous errors arising from the implementation control weaknesses in item 1 above.

4. Weaknesses in data file security controls may allow unauthorized changes to be made in the data. The time taken to discover these unauthorized changes will depend largely on the structure of the application controls. Some errors in transaction data may be discovered fairly quickly, for example, through the operation of control accounts or the mailing of statements. Errors in standing data usually take longer to detect. Weaknesses in data file security controls combined with weaknesses in program security controls increase the risk of undetectable misappropriation of assets and accounting errors. Weaknesses in data file security controls coupled with weaknesses in the application controls over the continuity of data also increase the chances of undetected errors.

5. Weaknesses in system software controls do not have a direct effect on the applications. Such weaknesses may, however, mean that system software relied on for the proper functioning of the controls described in items 1 to 4 above is not appropriate. As a result, one or more of the controls described above may be weak.

PRELIMINARY EVALUATION OF SIGNIFICANCE OF POTENTIAL CONTROL WEAKNESSES

To decide whether the control system is operating effectively, management should theoretically determine the effectiveness of all parts of the system. Testing the effectiveness of every control in every cycle, however, may not be feasible because the commitment of time and resources would be excessive. Also, management may want to undertake the formal evaluation in stages. It thus becomes important to identify the areas of high risk to management so that the review can be initially concentrated where the likelihood of significant weakness is greatest. This can be done, prior to performing functional (or compliance) tests, by assessing the potential for finding a significant weakness in the control system. The factors to be considered are the same as those that enter into the judgments made after the control system has been evaluated and weaknesses have been found. At this point, however, those factors are being used to identify *potentially* significant control weaknesses preliminary to any actual compliance testing. The identification is solely for the purpose of deciding where to concentrate the initial effort.

LIMITATIONS OF INTERNAL CONTROL EVALUATIONS

Neither an internal control system nor a review of that system can achieve ultimate perfection. Not only do cost/benefit relationships affect the design and review of a control system, but there are inherent limitations that must be recognized in considering both the system and its evaluation.

Authoritative auditing literature notes the limitations inherent in any accounting control system:

> In the performance of most control procedures, there are possibilities for errors arising from such causes as misunderstanding of instructions, mistakes of judgment, and personal carelessness, distraction, or fatigue. Furthermore, procedures whose effectiveness depends on segregation of duties obviously can be circumvented by collusion. Similarly, procedures designed to assure the execution and recording of transactions in accordance with management's authorizations may be ineffective against either errors or irregularities perpetrated by management with respect to transactions or to the estimates and judgments required in the preparation of financial statements. In addition to the limitations discussed above, any projection of a current evaluation of internal accounting control to future periods is subject to the risk that the procedures may become inadequate because of changes in conditions and that the degree of compliance with the procedures may deteriorate.*

Many of these same factors are applicable to the evaluation process. Human frailties do exist; evaluators may not be completely independent of personnel operating the system being evaluated; the evaluation may subsequently be affected by changes in the system. In the final analysis, the formal review process can give an enterprise considerable, but not absolute,

*SAS No. 1, paragraph 320.34.

comfort about the system and the evaluation. Both the concept of reasonable assurance discussed earlier and the inherent limitations noted above prevent absolute assurance.

POLICIES AND PROCEDURES FOR ORGANIZING AND IMPLEMENTING AN INTERNAL CONTROL EVALUATION

In view of the need to comply with the Foreign Corrupt Practices Act and the likelihood of public reporting on the adequacy of systems of internal accounting control, management must have assurance that the company's control system meets the appropriate objectives. Not only must the internal accounting control system be sufficient to achieve its objectives; management's system for evaluating internal accounting controls must also be sufficient to provide the necessary assurance about the adequacy of the controls.

Managing an internal control evaluation is no different in principle from managing any other endeavor; the same basic rules apply. Decisions must be made, policies adopted, and procedures installed to achieve a successful evaluation program. The decisions, policies, and procedures must address communications problems, implementation issues, and cost/benefit measurements. In addition, decisions must be made about the total audit function—how the internal and external auditors will cooperate in evaluating internal controls. The material that follows represents a sound way for management to meet its responsibilities under the Act and any attendant reporting requirements.

Before a company's management plans its evaluation program to meet those responsibilities, it must create an environment conducive to the evaluation. A key element in that environment is the existence of policies and procedures covering both the internal control system and the evaluation. Policies and procedures are therefore needed in the following areas:

1. Establishing internal control objectives;
2. Implementing those objectives;
3. Maintaining internal controls;
4. Reviewing the internal control system in the field;
5. Reporting weaknesses in internal controls to the appropriate levels of management;
6. Communicating these policies and procedures to appropriate personnel.

The following sections address each of those areas. To demonstrate a reasonable attempt to comply with the Act, management should be sure that all steps in the review process and all decisions made, together with the rationale, are well documented in writing.

Establishing and Implementing Internal Control Objectives

At the outset, top management must define its philosophy of control. This includes some notion of the risks that it is willing to take in terms of asset loss and accounting errors. The next step is to create rules, i.e., policies and procedures, for establishing and implementing internal controls. The rules of good management in this area are the same as elsewhere: policies and procedures for establishing internal controls must address activities within the same functional areas as operating policies and procedures.

For example, management should establish and communicate to appropriate personnel, policies and procedures related to the objectives of internal control and the Foreign Corrupt Practices Act. In addition to addressing substantive issues such as corporate conduct, financial planning and control, adequacy of documentation, and proper recordkeeping, the policies and procedures should cover how they will be communicated. Similarly, policies and procedures are needed in matters related to the personnel aspects of maintaining and monitoring internal accounting controls. Thus, policies and procedures should address such matters as selecting and training the system evaluation team, delegating authority within that team, and assigning responsibility to various groups, such as the internal auditors and the entity's CPAs, including oversight by the audit committee of the board.

Those policies and procedures should point out that management's interests in internal control go beyond the literal requirements of the Act. Management's interests require that rules, of an operating nature, be established to enhance the economy and efficiency of both the internal accounting control system and the evaluation. Because they are operating rules, they need the support of top management as well as of accounting personnel.

Maintaining Internal Controls

The objectives of policies for maintaining, or monitoring, the control system are to provide systematic responses to errors when they occur, to changed conditions, and to new types of transactions. Control maintenance policies require procedures, decisions, documentation, and subsequent audit.

Procedures are needed in such areas as specifying how the conditions noted above will generate new or amended documentation of the accounting system. Procedures must also address the manner in which new types of transactions that do not fit into the existing internal control system are identified and accepted as such and how the required new controls are established.

In addition, procedures are needed to detect and respond to errors in processing transactions. These include procedures for determining the cause and frequency of errors, reporting them to the appropriate level of management, and determining whether there is a significant control weakness. Decisions are then necessary to determine whether a control weakness should be corrected. The entire detection, reporting, and decision-making process should be documented, using standardized forms as appropriate; it will subsequently be audited by the internal and/or external auditors. This systematic approach to maintaining the internal control system will generate a catalogue of every possible type of error.

The maintenance function should be accomplished principally by the operation of the system itself. The disciplinary controls, particularly supervision and segregation of duties, should ensure that the system is operating as planned. In addition, employees' awareness that adherence to company policies and procedures will be monitored is an important element of the overall control environment.

User Common File. Control maintenance is enhanced by a high level of cooperation and interchange of information between the system evaluators, usually the internal auditors, and the external auditors. A device known as a "user common file" is useful in achieving such cooperation and exchange. The user common file contains systems flowcharts, internal control questionnaires, internal control maintenance policies and procedures, auditors' reports on control weaknesses, and lists of exceptions found. Both the internal and external auditors develop the file, since both groups participate in systems reviews on a continuing basis. Duplication of effort can be avoided by making the file available to appropriate persons associated with the audit function, both internal and external. Our experience has shown that the user common file enhances cooperation between and coordination of the internal and external audit functions, and that it can lead to economies in the cost of the total audit function.

The Field Review

The concepts and procedures described in this book can fulfill a variety of management needs, particularly providing a basis for demonstrating compliance with the Foreign Corrupt Practices Act and possible future reporting requirements. We also believe that the suggested procedures are extremely flexible and can be implemented in many different ways to evaluate both accounting controls and operational controls of an accounting and financial nature. This gives management considerable discretion in determining how much of its internal control system it wishes to evaluate, the degree of detail it wishes to go into in performing the evaluation, the personnel to make the evaluation, and the method of reporting.

The adaptability of the approach is an important feature because management in different companies has different objectives in making an evaluation, and thus needs different levels of testing to gain reasonable assurance that the specific objectives are met.

The policy document referred to earlier should also cover field reviews of the control system. Items to be covered include:

1. The format for documenting the system. Preferably, this should follow the approach used by the external auditors, to permit the creation of a user common file.

2. Who should prepare the systems documentation. This should preferably be done by accounting people in the field according to instructions issued by the system evaluator and approved by both field and corporate management.

3. The relationships among the several groups who will participate in the review: local management, the internal auditors, the external auditors, corporate management, and the audit committee. One technique for assuring the cooperation of local management, as well as assuring that the proper perspective is maintained when control weaknesses are found, is to create control maintenance committees at the local level. Their function is to apply the analytical techniques the enterprise has adopted for evaluating the significance of control weaknesses and determining whether they should be corrected.

4. Who should review the documentation of the system and test compliance with it. Preferably, this should be done by the system evaluators, normally the internal auditors, who may have to be trained so that a uniform approach will be followed by both the internal and external auditors, and the attendant benefits realized.

5. The staffing of the evaluation, presumably in the internal audit department. This requires policies and procedures regarding (a) the level of audit activity, (b) coordination and planning between internal and external auditors, and (c) whether audits are directed at operational as well as accounting controls. (See item 7 below.)

6. Whether to obtain representations from local management. The purpose of the representations should be to help in identifying management's perceptions of control weaknesses; an overall assessment of control quality should not be requested.

7. The coverage of the review, that is, whether it should be limited to internal accounting controls or should include operational controls that can conveniently be evaluated at the same time or at little additional cost. Because of the legal implications of complying with the Act, companies will want to define internal accounting control narrowly. That should not discourage management, however, from extending the review to include accounting-related operational controls, such as the budgeting system.

8. The completeness of the review, that is, whether all accounting control systems for all cycles at all sites should be reviewed or whether a less inclusive review should be made, at least in the first year. An alternative to

performing a complete review in one year is to identify the more significant areas, review those first, and leave the other areas for subsequent years. After the initial reviews are completed, a decision may be made that subsequent reviews should be done on a cycle basis, for example, every three to five years.

9. The specific procedures to be followed. This issue involves the broad question of the overall evaluation approach to be used, and also the narrower question of the depth of the review of each control system, for example, whether functional, i.e., compliance, testing will be done. The decision to functionally test will depend in large part on the level of assurance management wants. Management can obtain some assurance merely by relying on the operation of disciplinary controls, particularly supervision.

10. Requirements regarding the party to whom the system evaluator's findings will be reported. (The contents of this report are discussed in Chapter 7.)

Since many of the above decisions will significantly affect the cost and timing of the evaluation, management will have to establish priorities so that efforts can be concentrated where the need is greatest. The priorities should be determined primarily on the basis of risk evaluation; the highest priority should be given to those parts of the internal accounting control system where the risk of error or loss of assets is greatest because of potential control weaknesses. Management will also want to consider the additional benefits from a review of internal controls, beyond those directly associated with risk avoidance, in setting its priorities. Those additional benefits are considered later in this chapter.

Reporting Control Weaknesses

Policies, and particularly procedures, must be formulated for ranking control weaknesses for purposes of correcting and reporting them. The ranking system should recognize the possibility that a weakness that appears insignificant at one location may, because of its pervasiveness throughout the organization, be of great significance for the enterprise as a whole. A weakness of that type requires the attention of top management. Similarly, any weakness or problem in management's strategic planning for the review of controls and the subsequent identification, ranking, correcting, and reporting of control weaknesses is of the highest importance and should be so treated. Other factors affecting the significance of control weaknesses were suggested earlier in this chapter.

Policies are needed to specify who should be informed of control weaknesses and who should be informed of management's response to them. All control weaknesses or breakdowns should ordinarily be reported to some appropriate level of management, even those that do not affect the financial statements. For example, a control may require the monthly reconciliation of the payroll bank accounts. If the reconciliation for April was not performed, a control breakdown occurred and should be reported. This is appropriate even though the May reconciliation, if it was done, would have revealed and permitted the correction of any April errors. As discussed earlier, the question "To whom should it be reported?" would be answered based on the significance of the control weakness, but it should be reported to someone. Also, as discussed in greater detail in Chapter 7, a policy is needed for the type of report to be made to the audit committee.

Communicating With Appropriate Personnel

Corporate management should develop a policy of communicating to local management the enterprise's responsibilities under the Foreign Corrupt Practices Act. Local management should also be informed how the enterprise will plan, perform, and monitor the review.

Communication upward is also important. A control device is necessary to ensure that decisions made at the local level fit into the company's overall internal control plan.

An Action Plan for the First-Year Review

The program described above is the basis for a review of internal controls that may well take more than one year to complete. Many companies will want to consider performing the evaluation over a three- to five-year period, and then using a three- to five-year cycle for future reassessments. A plan of action that recognizes the need for a continuing evaluation of internal controls should be formulated, communicated, and implemented as soon as possible. Our suggestions for that action plan include:

1. Initiate the user common file described earlier.
2. Communicate the company's responsibilities for compliance with the Foreign Corrupt Practices Act to all levels of management.
3. Disseminate information on how the company plans to meet those responsibilities.
4. Create control maintenance committees at the various locations, including headquarters.
5. Obtain and review reports on internal control made over the past three years by both the internal and external auditors.
6. Determine whether changes in accounting controls recommended previously have been acted on.
7. Report uncorrected control weaknesses from prior years to the appropriate control maintenance committee.
8. Instruct the external auditors to report all control weaknesses or breakdowns encountered, even those without audit significance.

9. Develop policies and procedures in each of the areas discussed earlier.
10. Communicate those policies and procedures to the appropriate personnel.
11. Report the results of the internal control review to the appropriate levels of management and to the audit committee.

Providing Reasonable Assurance of Compliance

If the above program is implemented, management can have reasonable assurance, taking cost/benefit concepts into account, of the company's compliance with the Act, even though not all internal accounting controls are assessed in the first year. That assurance is based on the establishment of the evaluation system, including policies and procedures for all aspects of the review, and on the review of several internal accounting control systems, which provides some assurance regarding the operation of other systems.

In future years, control maintenance committees, working with both the internal and external auditors, will follow through on recommended control modifications. Each control system will be periodically reviewed, and a system for detecting and reporting errors will be in place and operating continuously.

Staffing the Evaluation

Decisions about the deployment of resources require the exercise of judgment concerning the high risk areas that should receive top priority. Only management has the knowledge of the business and the familiarity with overall corporate objectives that are necessary to make those decisions. Therefore, the most efficient and effective way for a company to undertake a formal assessment of its internal control is to do the job itself. Outsiders, particularly independent auditors, can help management to ask the right questions, but outsiders usually cannot perform the review at as low a cost and with as many benefits as company personnel.

There is another advantage of using company personnel to conduct the evaluation. Those who operate the controls—from receiving clerks to accounts payable supervisors—are more likely to cooperate and provide assistance if the system evaluators are company personnel. Moreover, the more familiar the evaluators are with the day-to-day operations of the business, the more knowledge they will have of operational as well as accounting controls. We ordinarily recommend that the evaluation be extended to include both types of controls.

The internal auditors are the logical personnel to staff a program in most organizations. In any event, it is advisable to define clearly, as early as possible, the role of the personnel who will perform the evaluation. Written statements should be prepared covering general responsibilities, independence, ethics, standards of performance, training, and competence of the evaluation team. This should include a statement concerning the extent of access to company functions, records, property, and personnel. The people who conduct the evaluation must be fully trained in the conceptual approach; failure to understand the theory will lead to a tendency to perform by rote and the consequent inability to spot errors. A periodic quality control review of the adequacy of the evaluation effort (including staffing requirements, quality of work, and planning) is desirable.

Additional Benefits From Internal Control Evaluations

Apart from present and future legal or regulatory requirements, the evaluation process will further management's goals of economical, effective, and efficient operations. For example:

The evaluation process generates flowcharts of transaction flows and internal control questionnaires. These are effective communication devices for personnel actually running the system, especially if both accounting and operational controls are reviewed. During one formal evaluation, personnel at the sites requested the flowcharts and internal control questionnaires, and several stated that, for the first time, they had gained an understanding of how their jobs fitted into the system.

The company personnel who operate the system will often have worthwhile ideas for improving it. Their knowledge and expertise can be tapped in the course of the interviews that are part of the evaluation process.

Educational tools, some of which are discussed in subsequent chapters, can be developed to assist local managers in understanding and implementing necessary controls in their operations on a uniform basis.

The understanding of transaction flows gained by the internal auditors makes their subsequent work more effective and efficient.

A formal review can be especially helpful in an overall systems development program since it can be used at individual sites to identify excessive control procedures, more efficient control procedures, and procedures required to eliminate a lack of control.

The documentation resulting from the evaluation can also form an important part of management's information system and the basis for a feedback mechanism to the audit committee.

Systems documentation produced by internal auditors may reduce the cost of the annual audit by expediting and reducing the work of the external auditors. A user common file of that documentation, accessible to both the internal and the independent auditors, can be created.

Assuring an Effective Program

Essential to the success of an evaluation of the system of internal control are the support of senior management and a clear understanding of the objectives of the evaluation, including adequate communication of the importance of the program and its results.

Senior Management Support. The most important ingredient of a successful program is the active support of senior management. Chief operating and financial officers must communicate the importance of the evaluation program to all personnel involved in the operation of the internal control system. When a program is being designed, senior management should meet with personnel responsible for planning and implementing it. Requiring regular progress reports will underline management's concern. In the initial stages of implementation, it is effective for senior management to arrange and attend a presentation for senior operating and financial personnel, outlining the purpose and nature of the evaluation. A follow-up letter to all personnel involved and presentations at local sites should stress the importance of internal controls; this will enhance the operation of the system even before any evaluation procedures are initiated. Later on, interest should be maintained through regular communications from senior management about evaluation results, including recognition, through prizes and awards, of individuals who have contributed useful suggestions for improving the system.

Evaluation Objectives. As with most undertakings, clear delineation and communication of objectives are essential. Primary objectives are demonstrating compliance with government requirements and reducing risks of various types. Secondary objectives are the other possible benefits previously discussed. Management should carefully appraise its objectives and requirements before it initiates a program and budgets time and personnel. For this reason, management may want to conduct a pilot study to gain a better understanding of the features it would like to have in its program and of the qualifications and abilities of personnel needed to perform evaluations. A pilot study will also provide a starting point for developing budgets.

Certain preparatory procedures will enhance the quality of a company's evaluation. For example, where internal auditors will perform the work, it is useful to map out the details of entry and exit meetings with local management, advance material to be collected at each site (e.g., the data necessary for the preliminary evaluation of potential control weaknesses), and structured interview procedures to be used during the evaluation. A clear communication of evaluation objectives is necessary to enable each of the subsequent steps to succeed.

4

Evaluating the System: The Preliminary Phase

This chapter and Chapter 5 detail the formal methodology for reviewing and evaluating a system of internal control. The preliminary steps are elaborated below; performing the actual evaluation is discussed in Chapter 5; the methodology is applied to the payments and time cycles in Chapter 6; and reporting on internal control is covered in Chapter 7.

OBTAINING AN UNDERSTANDING OF THE SYSTEM

The evaluation will be facilitated by as much advance planning and preparation as possible. The system evaluator should identify and obtain information available in advance, including a list of internal control reviews made recently, perhaps over the past three years, by the company's internal auditors, CPAs, or others, and the results of those reviews. Lists of work that is performed on a continuing basis by the accounting department and is directed at detecting and correcting errors would also be useful. Insight into potential problem areas can be gained from a review of errors corrected over a recent thirty-day period. This would also be the appropriate time to request a listing of the approximate number of transactions of each type that occur over some time span, such as a month. All of this information will be helpful when the evaluator begins to obtain an understanding of the system.

The first formal step in obtaining that understanding is to identify and flowchart all transaction types at each site being evaluated.* Transaction types must be identified before the interviews discussed below can be planned effectively and the flowcharts prepared. A transaction is defined as a series of business activities related to an exchange involving money, goods, or services, or to any other change in an asset or liability that results in an accounting entry. Transactions are of different types, and require separate flowcharts, when the controls applied to one transaction vary from the controls applied to another transaction.

The system evaluator must obtain and record an understanding of the system of controls over each type of transaction for each cycle at each site to be evaluated. Knowledge of the system is usually obtained primarily through interviews with those who operate it, along with documents such as organization charts, company flowcharts, and procedures manuals. The interview is fundamental to obtaining an understanding of the enterprise, its business, and its controls. Interviewing requires knowing oneself and being able to deal with people effectively—being able to ask meaningful questions and to secure meaningful answers. The acquisition of proper interviewing skills is one of the most important nontechnical requirements for a reviewer. While extensive formal training in interview techniques is usually not necessary, some time should be devoted to this in training the system evaluator. We have included extensive suggestions on planning and conducting interviews in the section that follows, primarily because experience has shown us that interviewers frequently need this kind of advice.

To evaluate a computer system effectively, the system evaluator must have a general understanding of the principles of computers and computer processing. This understanding includes some knowledge of the basic units of a computer configuration, their interrelationship, the nature of computer processing from input to output, the concepts of programming, and

---

*See the discussion on page 49 for steps that should be taken by an evaluator who is not familiar with the system being evaluated.

the functions of the operating system. Depending on the evaluator's background, those topics may have to be included in the evaluator training program.

Planning the Interview

Responsibility for the proper conduct of all interviews should rest in one person, who should then delegate part of the interviewing authority to subordinates, with the proper retention of control.

Factors bearing on the selection of the interviewer include:

The job level of the person being interviewed. Senior executives should be interviewed by more experienced personnel.

Prior experience with the interviewee. Evasive interviewees call for experienced interviewers.

The existence of actual or potential problems in a particular area that are known or suspected as a result of past reviews or a preliminary assessment of control weaknesses. This situation requires a more experienced interviewer.

The complexity of the system. A complex standard cost system or an integrated EDP system, for example, may call for an interviewer experienced in both interviewing and the technical area.

The probable length of each interview, which depends on the number of questions to be asked and on the responses obtained, should be estimated. A single interview should not exceed one hour, if possible, so that the interviewer can retain the information gained. A break in the interview enables the interviewer to digest what has been learned, and allows the interviewee to return to regular duties.

In scheduling the interview, adequate time should be allowed for recording the results. Recording should take place immediately after the interview so that the interviewer can integrate the new information with what is already known.

Appointments must be made for interviews, which should be scheduled for times when the individuals to be interviewed are engaged in their normal activities. Since time must be blocked out in advance, the interviewer must keep appointments.

The person directly responsible for a particular function should be the one interviewed. In a smaller company, this will be the person who performs the function; in a larger company, it may be the first-level supervisor, such as the accounts payable supervisor.

An interview should not be conducted with an ''absentee'' executive.

For example, unless the company is small and the controller is a "hands-on" type, it would be inappropriate to deal with the controller, who may provide answers to "how it should be done" instead of "what is actually being done." On the other hand, the controller may be the appropriate person to interview if an overall understanding of the system is desired.

The questions to be asked should be formulated in advance: the interview will proceed more quickly and there will be less need for follow-up interviews to obtain relevant information that was overlooked in the initial interview. It is frequently possible to identify in advance the volume, size, and types of transactions passing through a particular control, as well as some idea of the types and amount of errors that may occur. This knowledge provides helpful information for formulating questions.

The interviewer should obtain in advance, perhaps from other staff members, as much information as possible about the personal characteristics of the individual to be interviewed. The interviewer may learn, for example, that the person is quite busy and does not like to engage in "small talk."

The interviewer should give thought to the contributions the interviewee may have made to the enterprise. The employee may have been responsible for parts of the system being reviewed and may take pride in them. Pride in the work accomplished and the contributions made to the system may encourage the interviewee to make further suggestions for improvement. The interviewer should be sure to give the person credit for any suggestions reported.

Conducting the Interview

Although the interviewer does not need to be professionally trained to obtain information effectively from an interview, the following practices should be helpful:

Inform the interviewee as to the reason and purpose of the interview;
Attempt to establish rapport;
Emphasize positive behavioral factors;
Choose vocabulary carefully during the interview.

Most people being interviewed want to know the reason for the interview, why they were selected, how the information obtained will be used, and whether they will be informed about the outcome. Those questions should be anticipated and dealt with early in the interview; the answers can provide positive motivation for reliable responses. If the relevance of the interview is not clear or the questions asked do not seem to relate to the purpose stated, barriers may be created. The interview will proceed more smoothly if the respondent is assured that an interview, not an audit, is being conducted. This can be accomplished in part by the interviewer's commitment to share any recommendations with the appropriate employees before the system review is completed.

The interviewer should provide the necessary motivation to continue the interview. If the person interviewed identifies with the interviewer (enjoys the interaction), or sees the interviewer as a source for some desired change, there will be a higher motivation to respond. On the other hand, the interviewee may be unwilling to give certain information that is potentially threatening or embarrassing, or may be unable to remember certain information. An inability to respond may also result from repressed envy or hostility. The better the interviewer's understanding of the psychological factors at work in the interview, the greater the ability to minimize or control negative forces. If the interviewer can see the world as the respondent sees it, through his or her particular experiences and background, there will be greater understanding in the communication process.

The interviewer should consider the security, or lack thereof, of the individual being interviewed. If a department has a reputation for being involved in difficulties and if there has been a history of rapid turnover of supervisors, the present supervisor may evidence a lack of security. Thus, it may be necessary for the interviewer to offer a measure of comfort and reassurance.

The behavior of both parties can act as positive or negative forces in the interview. The interviewer's role is to maximize the forces that enhance communication and at the same time reduce or eliminate the negative forces or barriers. Behavioral factors include: physical, vocal, and listening and feedback behavior.

Physical behavior includes eye contact, facial expressions, and mannerisms. A pleasant and relaxed appearance creates an easy and comfortable atmosphere. Initial impressions, conveyed in the first thirty to sixty seconds, can importantly affect the remainder of the interview. Therefore, in most interviews some time should be spent in establishing rapport. Such physical mannerisms as a ''dead fish'' handshake or a steady stare can create uncomfortable or stressful situations. For some people, gum chewing and cigarette smoking may be serious irritations. Taking notes during the interview may increase or decrease motivation. To some people, it may be a sign that the interviewer is listening and that what they are saying is important; to others, it may be threatening. Since physical factors are magnified in the interview, the interviewer should be particularly aware of personal characteristics and mannerisms as well as other potentially distorting environmental influences.

Vocal communication entails a pleasant voice tone, audibility, articulation, and projection of interest. Most people prefer a certain naturalness and spontaneity. Negative vocal factors, which can create barriers, include speaking too fast or too slowly, a brisk or impersonal speaking manner in which little interest or enthusiasm is projected, mumbling and overarticulate speech. Although physical and vocal communication are important, perhaps the most important trait, which can overcome both physical and vocal limitations, is conveying to the interviewee the feeling of a personal and genuine interest.

Listening and feedback behavior concerns the interviewer's sensitivity and willingness to respond to the different cues given by the interviewee. Does the interviewer listen to and try to understand the person being interviewed or simply conduct a monologue? Restating a response or statement in one's own words so that the interviewee can hear what has been said is an effective listening technique. It gives a feeling of being listened to and also improves the accuracy of the interchange. Sometimes a person needs help in expression; a good interviewer should make certain that ample time is given for answering a question and that the respondent is encouraged to express personal thoughts. The interviewer should be quick to sense when the respondent wants to express or elaborate on a particular point but may be unable to do so without some prodding or help. Some areas may be difficult to discuss, or there may be some question of their appropriateness. The good interviewer will sense those difficulties and try to create an atmosphere conducive to free discussion. The interviewer should be flexible enough to adjust and modify the interview in light of the responses, yet make certain that the objectives of the interview are met.

Because note taking may have negative behavioral consequences for the person interviewed or may impede the smooth flow of the interview, recording of answers should be kept to a minimum. One method of taking notes consists of drafting an "outline" that describes three factors:

The action that triggers the operation;
The operation itself;
The next step and the distribution of a form created by the operation.

For example, a portion of the interview notes, utilizing an "outline," for a clerk who is involved with the purchasing function might look like this:

PURCHASE ORDER CLERK

(1) Receives purchase requisition

(2) Types purchase order with four copies:

(3) Original————Vendor
    Copy #1————Receiving clerk
    Copy #2————Cost clerk
    Copy #3————Filed numerically
    Copy #4————Filed by date to be received

If several operations result from the same "trigger" action, they should be recorded in chronological order of performance. Abbreviations should be used whenever possible; transfers should be indicated by arrows. This is an informal document, and the interviewer is the only one who needs to understand it. However, it would be both good business judgment and a courteous gesture to give the interviewee a chance to see and comment on the information before it is finalized.

The vocabulary (word choices) used by the interviewer can be a major problem in the communication process. Words must be shared; that is, they must be understandable to both parties in the interview. If the interviewee is unfamiliar with certain terms or concepts, the interviewer should take the lead in establishing a frame of reference. For example, the interviewer may refer to the process of accounting for the numerical sequence of prenumbered documents as a completeness control, while the interviewee refers to it as "the number control." The interviewer would be well advised to refer to the process as the number control. Sometimes the interviewer may have to increase the vocabulary used, to include words familiar to the respondent. The words chosen should motivate communication; they should not be beyond the interviewee's vocabulary level and yet should not appear to be oversimplified.

Another aspect of word choice is making sure that any appropriate distinctions in terminology are made and understood. For example, if the person being interviewed is responsible for both domestic and export sales, which are processed differently and thus are different transaction types, the interviewer should ensure that the question and the answer deal with the same particular transaction, e.g., domestic sales.

Sometimes including in a question a reference to possible extenuating circumstances indicates a nonjudgmental attitude and increases the likelihood of getting an accurate response. For example, assume that the person who accounts for the numerical sequence of receiving reports does not follow up on all missing numbers. To which of the following questions is that person more likely to give an accurate answer? "Do you follow up on all the missing numbers?'' or ''I can see that you're very busy. Do you always have a *chance* to follow up on all the missing numbers?'' Ordinarily, the second question will be answered more accurately.

Types of Questions

The basic types of questions are:

Open-ended
Direct
Closed
Yes–No
Probes
Restatement

Open-ended questions are broad and basically unstructured; they simply establish the topic and allow the answer to be structured as the interviewee sees fit. They convey that the interviewer is interested in personal feelings and help to reveal a frame of reference, attitudes, and a value system. Open-ended questions establish good rapport and help maintain good communication. Their degree of openness varies. For example:

Tell me about the company's accounting system.
What is the accounting system for purchases?
How do you process invoices for purchases of raw materials?
How do you process invoices for purchases of steel?

Although these questions are all open-ended, they are successively limited in their degree of openness. Because open-ended questions cannot be answered ''yes'' or ''no,'' the answers given reveal the respondent's perceptual field and allow the interviewer to gain an insight into the respondent's frame of reference.

Many interviewing situations demand direct information. Once rapport has been established, certain questions should be asked directly. Direct questions ask for explanations or further expansion on a particular point—they call for a specific reply on a specific topic. The following are examples of direct questions:

How often is the bank account reconciled?
How do you ensure that all goods shipped are billed to customers?

Closed questions are a form of direct question that greatly narrows the range of possible responses. The closed question is appropriate when the objective is to lead the interviewee to identify with a certain attitude or perception, or to express agreement or disagreement with a stated viewpoint. For example:

Do you value inventory by the first-in, first-out; average; last-in, first-out; or specific identification method?

Why don't you account for the numerical sequence of shipping advices?

If the question is not threatening, it is usually easily answered (see the first question in the pair above). If, however, it is threatening, it may not be answered directly and can create barriers (see the second question above). The use of closed questions assumes that (1) the interviewer has substantial knowledge of the respondent's information level, (2) there are a limited number of known frames of reference, which are clearly presented in the question, and (3) the interviewee has information or an opinion on the matter. Since closed questions assume considerable knowledge, they should be used with caution. When the objective is to force the respondent to consider or think through several factors or alternatives before coming to a conclusion, a series of closed questions can be used effectively. In these cases, the interviewer should determine that all the assumptions of closed questions are met.

"Yes–no" questions are an extreme form of closed question and allow virtually no latitude of response except "yes," "no," or possibly, "I don't know." This sort of question is often used by the inexperienced interviewer. While it is useful for the purpose of filling out forms and obtaining specific facts, it also tends to limit the amount of information obtained. Since the "law of least effort" usually operates, the respondent answers only what is asked. Even if some additional information is volunteered, the interviewer, whose concentration is likely to be directed at formulating more questions, is apt to pay little attention.

A major problem of the yes–no question is that it may become an interrogation resembling the "third-degree" type of questioning. The tendency to ask questions in rapid order often causes a defensive reaction rather than frank, honest answers. Short-answer questions should be used to get needed factual data and should be interspersed into the interview as needed. Any masses or fast sequence of yes–no questions should generally be avoided.

Probes are used to stimulate discussion and obtain more information. They motivate the interviewee to enlarge on, clarify, or explain reasons behind what has been said and thereby to communicate more fully. Probes are ways of following up on partial or superficial responses by directing the interviewee's thinking to further aspects of the topic under discussion. Some examples of probes are:

How do you mean?
Could you give me an example of what you mean?
I'd like to know more about your thinking on that.
What do you have in mind when you say that?
Why do you think that is so?
Could you tell me more about that?
Why do you feel that way?
Do you have any other reasons for feeling as you do?
Is there anything else that may be affecting the situation?

Probing is necessary to obtain specific, complete responses. Some respondents have difficulty putting their thoughts into words, or their answers may be unclear or incomplete; others may want to hide information they feel would be unacceptable to the interviewer. Probes can be used after any question to direct thinking to further aspects of the topic. For example:

INTERVIEWER:	[open-ended question] How do you process invoices for purchases of raw materials?
CHIEF ACCOUNTANT:	Poorly.
INTERVIEWER:	[probe] Why do you say that?
CHIEF ACCOUNTANT:	We don't have any idea of whether we got what we paid for.

The purposes of restatement are to check the interviewer's understanding of what the respondent has said and to let the person hear what has been said as encouragement to go on speaking, examining, or looking deeper into the question. Restatement communicates the thought, "I am listening to you very carefully—so carefully, in fact, that I can restate what you have said. I am doing so now because it may help you to hear yourself through me so that you may absorb your statement and consider its impact, if any, on you. For the time being, I am keeping myself out of it." Often, the most effective method of restating is to repeat the part of what has been said that the interviewer feels is most significant and worth having the interviewee hear again. To continue with the previous example:

| INTERVIEWER: | [probe] Why is that? |
| CHIEF ACCOUNTANT: | Joe has no control over those guys and they never make out a receiving report anymore. |

INTERVIEWER: [restatement] The receiving clerks never make
                      out receiving reports and the suppliers' invoices
                      are paid anyway?

CHIEF ACCOUNTANT: That's the problem. We owe so much money we
                      have to pay before the goods are shipped. And
                      we're laying off nonproduction people to save
                      money.

INTERVIEWER: [restatement] There are significant accounts
                      payable to the trade that are past due and some
                      of the company's accounting controls are not
                      being followed in order to save money?

When using the restatement technique, the interviewer should not state personal views. Rather, the restatement technique shows that the interviewer, without making a commitment or judgment, understands the respondent's point of view. It also enables the respondent to hear his or her own logic, possible biases, and assumptions that may be based on false fears and doubts. Restatement should have a positive effect on the interviewee because it demonstrates that the interviewer is listening and trying to understand what is being said. Like all good things, however, restatement can also be overdone, resulting in an artificial and affected communication situation.

Interviewing for Error Rates

Chapter 3 discussed the usefulness of identifying areas where the likelihood of significant internal control weaknesses is greatest, before deciding whether to evaluate the controls in a particular cycle at a specific location. A knowledge of those areas may similarly be useful after deciding to evaluate the controls in a particular cycle but before deciding to perform functional tests on specific controls. The object is to help management to identify "hot spots" so it can order its priorities. Therefore, the interview should be designed to elicit information about the potential weaknesses in the system.

The information that will be most useful in the preliminary evaluation of the likelihood of control weaknesses centers around the nature of the risk and the potential exposure to it. The risks described in Chapter 3 included misappropriated assets, deliberate and accidental errors, and reduced operating efficiency. The potential exposure to those risks depends largely on the value and volume of transactions subject to a particular control. Consequently, the interviewer should seek information about the types of errors that occur and their frequency.

The interviewer should be aware of several factors in formulating the questions asked to elicit that information:

Terms such as "errors" and "error rates" should be avoided since they will put the interviewee on the defensive.

In many cases, information about error rates may be imprecise and incomplete.

Often, the only feedback obtainable may relate to the *types* of errors rather than the *frequency* of errors, but even that is useful information.

Although it would be preferable to record error rates by types, information about the *total* rate of *all* errors taken together is also useful.

Frequently, questions will elicit information about error rates in processes performed *prior* to those performed by the person being interviewed. Occasionally, they may elicit data about processes performed *subsequent* to those performed by the interviewee. Often this appears to be the most fruitful source of such information.

Some errors are more important than others. As a result, the interviewer should spend more time in identifying the error rate for certain types of errors. For example, if the error type would permit conversion of corporate assets or would not be caught and corrected at a subsequent point in the internal control system, further inquiry may be warranted.

Possible questions follow:

1. *How could the task be done more easily or better?* There are two aspects to this question. First, it will frequently identify ways to improve efficiency and control. Second, responses will often indicate whether errors are widespread and the type of errors involved. The information can then be pursued further.

2. *What kinds of things cause you to take extra time in processing documents?* This question can elicit information on two possible sources of errors: first, those that come through the processing sequence to the interviewee; and second, those that are identified further along in the processing flow and are sent back to be rectified.

3. *What is the most common mistake that you see in documents that you process?* While this question can be used to identify types of errors, it is more general and is designed to prompt the respondent to consider what errors are encountered on the job. Obviously, the interviewer should not stop here, but should use the response as a basis for pursuing further information. (A follow-on question might be: "Do any others come to mind?")

4. *Are documents ever returned to you after they have been processed further?* This question can be used to initiate a discussion of what kinds of errors are returned to the interviewee. It will also identify personnel further along in the processing flow who can be queried about errors.

5. *Why do you think people keep making the same mistake?* This may identify possible improvements and provide a better appreciation of the frequency of the error.

6. *Do you keep track of errors that you correct?* This may provide information about the type and quantity of errors.
7. *Do you communicate mistakes that you find back down to the field?* If the answer to this question is "no," the respondent may identify the person who does make such communications, and that person may be a useful source of information. If no communication is made, the interviewer may have uncovered a major problem area.

The interviewer should also try to identify procedures in effect that might be useful in determining error rates, such as:

1. *Computer rejects.* If error runs are made, or if input is frequently returned from the computer processing section, there may be a record of error types.
2. *Manual listings.* In addition to information elicited in question 6 above, the interviewer may find listings of documents returned for additional information or correction. For example, there may be a list of requisitions returned to the field because proper approval was not indicated.
3. *Budget variance analysis.* A form of control over errors may exist as part of the investigation of budget variances. Personnel performing such investigations may be a useful source of information about the types and extent of errors found.

As noted above, a great deal of the information will not be precise and may consist of impressions that are rather subjective. Whenever possible, ask personnel to give a percentage estimate. This will provide some "order of magnitude." For example, if somebody says there is "probably only a 2 per cent to 5 per cent error rate," the interviewer gains a different appreciation of the range of the problem than if the respondent says there is "a 10 per cent to 15 per cent chance that the stuff will be wrong." When personnel do not feel that they can give a percentage estimate, try to capture a general impression of the extent of error (for example, "appears to be low frequency of error," or "may be frequent errors").

RECORDING THE UNDERSTANDING: FLOWCHARTING THE SYSTEM

The understanding of the system obtained from interviews should be properly documented and recorded, and flowcharting is generally the recommended method. This section describes the procedures for flowcharting that the authors prefer. It is not concerned with alternative methods of recording the understanding, such as narratives, which in some cases may be used. Flowcharting imposes a discipline on the system evaluator; it also promotes efficiency and uniformity in describing the internal control system. Moreover, flowcharts are more readable than narratives, and this improves communication among those involved in the administration and evaluation of the system. We have repeatedly asked people skeptical about flowcharting to prepare a flowchart from their own narrative description of a system. In every case the skeptics conceded that their inability to complete the flowchart resulted from inadequacies in their narratives.

Flowcharting Guidelines

Flowcharts are actually transaction flowcharts; they identify all significant procedures that pertain to a specific transaction processing system. Flowcharting can be applied to most systems, regardless of size. Nevertheless, there will be rare situations (e.g., when major changes in the system are expected to occur or when control procedures tend to be nonexistent) when it may be more efficient for system evaluators to prepare succinct narrative explanations of their understanding of the system. When narratives are used, care should be exercised to insure that they contain the same information concerning the system that flowcharts would contain. The reasons for using narratives and the approval of supervisory personnel should be documented.

The flowcharts should include all procedures that have significant accounting control implications. The technique recommended in this book also permits the integration of operational controls into the flowcharts. Alternatively, if it is more efficient, operational controls may be included in narratives supplementing the flowcharts. Decisions relating to whether operational controls are to be reviewed and the extent of documentation necessary to conduct such a review must be made prior to beginning the system review.

When flowcharts are used, their preparation or updating is regarded as an integral part of the internal control evaluation process. The person who obtains (or updates) the understanding of the system and the related controls should record the understanding; the help of specialists may be required in flowcharting more complex computer systems. Flowcharts should be reviewed by supervisory personnel and by those who operate the system. Elsewhere in this book, we have stressed the usefulness of a user common file and noted that the systems flowcharts are a major part of its contents. Since the user common file serves both the internal auditors and the CPAs, and since both groups of auditors participate in the review process, care should be taken that the flowcharting techniques used are common to both groups. Accordingly, both groups might usefully participate in the flowchart review.

The flowcharting technique that we recommend has been designed specifically to depict control procedures so that the system evaluator can determine which procedures are significant for purposes of meeting the internal control objectives of a system. Thus, the flowcharts should meet the following criteria:

1. Procedures should be shown in sequence, including procedures performed in the computer department. Processing of transactions moves along a vertical line on the chart, called the main flowline.
2. All copies of pertinent documents should be explained and accounted for.
3. The maintenance of files and the preparation of reports with control significance should be shown.
4. The flow of documentation among the various departments of the business should be shown.
5. The title or position and, where practicable, the name of the person performing the procedures should be shown.
6. Estimates of the number of transactions of each type and dollar amounts processed, together with the error rate experienced, should be shown.

An example of a flowcharting worksheet form is found in Exhibit 4. Complete instructions for the preparation of flowcharts are provided in Appendix A.

In view of the specialized purpose of this flowcharting technique, flowcharts previously prepared by the company may not be acceptable. It may, however, be appropriate to arrange for accounting and management personnel to prepare the needed flowcharts, provided they are familiar with the prescribed flowcharting technique. This will help to achieve their participation and hence their cooperation in the evaluation; it will also keep costs down. If flowcharts prepared by others are utilized, the system evaluator should be satisfied that the flowcharts are fully comprehensible, that they are suitable for the purposes intended, and that they can be adequately cross-referenced to the evaluator's other flowcharts. If the system evaluator prepares the flowcharts, copies should be given to accounting and management personnel; they may find the flowcharts useful for their own purposes, or the system evaluator may want to ask them to confirm the accuracy of the flowcharts.

Flowcharts should be reviewed and updated at scheduled intervals, preferably annually. When changes are necessary, the system evaluator may either draw new charts or correct the old charts. A complete redrawing of flowcharts normally is not necessary unless they have been entirely superseded or their legibility has become impaired. If the flowchart pages merely require changes, photocopies of the old charts should be prepared so that there is a record of the procedures in force at a particular date. Control should be maintained over all corrections or changes made on flowcharts.

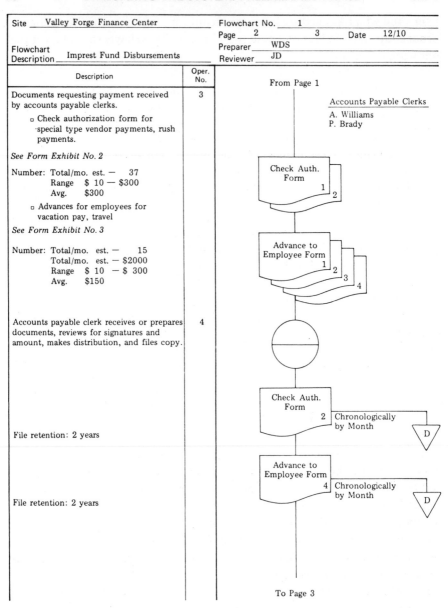

Site	Valley Forge Finance Center	Flowchart No.	1
Flowchart Description	Imprest Fund Disbursements	Page 2 3 Date 12/10
		Preparer WDS
		Reviewer JD

Description	Oper. No.
Documents requesting payment received by accounts payable clerks.	3
□ Check authorization form for ·special type vendor payments, rush payments.	
See Form Exhibit No. 2	
Number: Total/mo. est. — 37 Range $ 10 — $300 Avg. $300	
□ Advances for employees for vacation pay, travel	
See Form Exhibit No. 3	
Number: Total/mo. est. — 15 Total/mo. est. — $2000 Range $ 10 — $ 300 Avg. $150	
Accounts payable clerk receives or prepares documents, reviews for signatures and amount, makes distribution, and files copy.	4
File retention: 2 years	
File retention: 2 years	

From Page 1

Accounts Payable Clerks
A. Williams
P. Brady

Check Auth. Form
1
2

Advance to Employee Form
1
2
3
4

Check Auth. Form
2 Chronologically by Month D

Advance to Employee Form
4 Chronologically by Month D

To Page 3

Exhibit 4.   Example of Flowcharting Worksheet Form.

Supporting documentation pertaining to the recording of the understanding (e.g., copies of filled-in forms, copies of or extracts from pertinent procedures manuals) should be cross-referenced to and filed with the flowcharts.

Flowcharting Technique

Good flowcharting technique involves the preparation of one flowchart for each transaction processing system or major part thereof. It features a "main flowline" illustrating the flow of processing and the documents involved. The flowline runs from the beginning to the end of each system, starting with the inception of transactions and ending with their recording in the books of account.

We have adopted a standard set of flowcharting symbols, most of which are familiar to persons who utilize flowcharts. We have also adopted a standard format for flowchart working papers, which is illustrated in a specimen form in Appendix A.

Flowcharts should not be unnecessarily elaborate. It is not necessary to flowchart in detail every process applied to every copy of every document. The information should be confined to what is essential to an understanding of the significant aspects of the system and the controls incorporated therein. Particular attention should be given to showing the linkage of the flow of principal documents through the whole system so that the flowcharts will provide a suitable basis for carrying out transaction reviews (discussed below). Frequently, processing functions for transaction types become commingled as transactions proceed through the control system. When that occurs, one flowchart should end, and a notation should be made that the processing flow from this point on can be found in the flowchart for another (designated) type of transaction.

With respect to computerized systems, the company's electronic data processing (EDP) personnel may use an adaptation of a flowchart that shows the sequence of computer runs, together with representations of the inputs and outputs. Those charts may be particularly useful in obtaining an initial understanding of a new computer application, but would not be a substitute for the kinds of flowcharts described in this chapter and in Appendix A, unless they meet the prescribed criteria.

The system evaluator should adopt a standard form that provides for signing off in connection with the preparation or updating of flowcharts and performance of the related transaction reviews; there should also be space for evidencing review of the flowcharts. A specimen, filled-in form is included in Appendix A.

Overview Flowcharts. If a system is especially complex, people other than the original preparer of the charts may find it difficult to obtain from the detailed flowcharts a broad view of the flow among the various departments of the business. In those limited circumstances, it may be useful to prepare an "overview flowchart" to serve as a summary or index to the detailed flowcharts. The overview flowchart represents the organization of the processing system and depicts the sources of information, general nature of the procedures followed, and results of that processing. The overview flowchart does not contain transaction flowlines and is thus not a substitute for a transaction flowchart.

This very condensed representation, however, may be helpful in providing a broad view and a quick grasp of the nature of the transaction processing, to allow the evaluator to assess the potential significance of the relationship between information and reports. An overview flowchart may be helpful to the evaluator's preliminary understanding of the linkage between processing activities, for example, the linkage between the computer and user department activities. As the evaluator gains experience with the enterprise's systems, the need for these preliminary schematic representations diminishes, and time can probably be saved by moving directly to the transaction flowchart.

Flowcharting Computer Systems

An important aim when flowcharting systems with computerized operations is to integrate the computer and non-computer parts of the system into a single flowchart. This is achieved easily with the flowcharting method described here. The flowline moves on the flowchart into, through, and out of the computer department at the appropriate stages. As far as possible, the same flowcharting conventions and symbols are used to illustrate the processing in both computer and non-computer departments. Additional symbols are, of course, required for devices unique to computer systems, such as tape and disc files, but these are readily understandable.

The flowcharts and narratives recording the computer parts of a system should be as simple as possible. This facilitates understanding by nontechnical readers and highlights the important operations. Various aids to simplification are discussed in the following paragraphs.

Programmed Procedures.* Programmed procedures can be recorded with the same symbols used for operations and controls performed by people. Often, the method used in a program to perform a particular operation or control will have to be described, for example, the way in which a sales order is tested for credit status. This can be done by inserting a cross-reference on the flowchart to the detailed program documentation or to a narrative description attached to the flowchart.

The level of detail in which programmed procedures are flowcharted

---

*The reader is reminded that this and other computer-related terms are defined and discussed in Chapter 2.

should ordinarily be limited to that necessary for understanding the overall flow of processing. Since the flowcharts need not include the individual instructions in a computer program, they will not provide the detailed information necessary for a complete understanding of the logic of the construction of individual programs. When the system evaluator is analyzing the integrity controls related to the development of new programs, that detailed information will be needed. Ordinarily it will be available in the documentation related to the development of new programs. In addition, if the evaluator is seeking a level of understanding of the program sufficient to permit the design of computer software to be used in performing validation tests, as would be necessary for an audit, more detailed program information, requiring computer expertise, will be needed.

Standing Data Amendments.   Procedures relating to amendments of standing data are usually difficult to incorporate in the flowcharts dealing with the processing of the related master files. Accordingly, it is preferable to prepare separate flowcharts for these procedures.

Rejection Procedures.   Rejections normally arise at the edit and updating stages of processing. If the company has standard procedures for identifying, investigating, correcting, and resubmitting rejections, those procedures are normally flowcharted only once. Thereafter, when rejections arise, a reference to the rejection flowchart is made on the main flowchart. In many cases, however, rejection procedures are not standardized and should be flowcharted for each application.

Periodic Controls.   Control procedures that are carried out only periodically and separately from the normal processing of data, such as control account reconciliations, are often flowcharted separately. A cross-reference can be entered at the most suitable point on the flowcharts.

Integrity Controls.   Integrity controls, while relevant to the consistency of processing, operate separately from the flow of data through the accounting system. Accordingly, they do not appear on the data flowline. Since the procedures are usually relevant to all accounting applications processed, they may be separately flowcharted.

CONFIRMING THE UNDERSTANDING: TRANSACTION REVIEWS

A transaction review is the process of tracing one transaction of each type through an accounting system to confirm the understanding of the system as recorded in the flowcharts. Normally, transaction reviews should be performed after the flowcharts have been prepared or updated. However, particularly in the case of simple systems, it may be more efficient to perform the transaction reviews and prepare the related documentation concurrently with obtaining or updating the understanding of the system and the preparation of the documentation thereof. The system evaluator who prepares or updates the flowcharts should generally perform the transaction reviews.

Selection of Transactions

As discussed earlier in this chapter, the distinction between types of transactions is based on the nature and method of control applied to the transactions. For example, if the procedures for recording and controlling domestic sales are the same as those for export sales, domestic and export sales are considered to be the same type of transaction. On the other hand, if some of the procedures followed for domestic sales differ from those followed for export sales, there are two different types of transactions.

Each type of transaction identified at the time the understanding was obtained and the flowcharts prepared should be subject to a transaction review. It will normally be desirable to select a transaction that has recently been completed. This general rule is, however, subject to the following additional considerations.

First, at various stages in the processing of a transaction, the pertinent documents may be held in a temporary file. Since the review will always be of a completed transaction, the pertinent documentation will not be in the temporary file. If the procedures for entering and/or removing the documents from the temporary file constitute a control procedure, the transaction review should also include a brief inquiry into those procedures.

Second, the system evaluator's interest in the system is ordinarily limited to the operation of the system at the time of the review. If there has been a change in the system during the year, however, the evaluator should consider obtaining an understanding of the prior system and performing transaction reviews of it as well as the current system. This is because the system review may be intended in part to provide support for the work of the independent auditors, who may be interested in the functioning of the system over the entire period covered by the financial statements. Enterprise management may also want evidence of the system's functioning throughout the entire year, to meet its responsibilities under the Foreign Corrupt Practices Act.

Nature of Transaction Reviews

Transaction reviews should cover each operation shown on the flowcharts. The review should include examining evidence that the operation was performed (if such evidence still exists), interviewing site personnel as to procedures followed, and reperforming, to the extent practicable, the procedures applied by them (e.g., comparing pertinent data shown on the supplier's invoice with the receiving report and purchase order). When carrying out transaction reviews, the system evaluator should be alert to the possibility that operations with internal accounting control significance may have been omitted from the flowcharts; if so, necessary additions should be made to the flowcharts.

The starting point for a transaction review may be at any stage in the flow where the type of transaction is readily identifiable. Depending on circumstances and the system evaluator's judgment, it may be most efficient to begin the transaction review in the middle of the flow of a transaction and work toward both its inception and its recording in a general ledger account; alternatively, a transaction may be selected from the general ledger and traced back to its inception, or selected at its inception and traced to its termination.

If individual types of transactions are combined during processing and subjected to common procedural and reporting controls from that point forward, only one example of the combined type need be traced through the subsequent controls. For example, differences in types of sales would have no significance after the different types of sales invoices have been entered in the sales journal.

Documentation

Often, more than one transaction type is dealt with in each flowchart. In that event, brief notes should be made setting out each transaction type and its identifying characteristics. A specimen working paper to illustrate this is shown in Appendix B.

Transaction review working papers should document the work performed. To minimize the time required to prepare transaction review working papers, the following techniques should be used:

1. The worksheet should preferably be prepared in a form that will accommodate several years' evaluations.
2. The worksheet should be prepared in columnar form with the numbers of the operations on the flowcharts listed on the left. It should not be necessary to narrate the operations to be reviewed since they should be apparent from the operations number cross-referenced from the flowchart. There may, however, be occasions when a particularly complex operation should be subdivided and explained in a narrative.
3. Columns of the worksheet should be used to identify the specific transactions reviewed and to record the several types of transactions that may be encompassed within a particular processing system.

Where the work performed is evident from the flowchart or narrative and from the document cross-references shown on the transaction review working papers, no further documentation is required. Where exceptions are noted, supplementary explanations should be provided.

The specimen transaction review working paper shown in Appendix B contemplates situations where the work performed should be apparent from the operations number cross-referenced from the flowchart or narrative. This design recognizes that the purpose of transaction reviews is to confirm the understanding as recorded in the flowcharts, and that transaction reviews do not constitute evidence that controls are operating as planned, as do functional tests. However, it may be desirable to include more information in the transaction review working papers so that the supervisory reviewer can gain a better understanding of the work performed. In those circumstances, it may be appropriate to supplement the worksheet with copies of documents examined or narratives, or to redesign the worksheet to allow for the presentation of greater detail.

Completion of a transaction review should be indicated in the space provided on the Record of Flowchart Preparation and Transaction Reviews (included in Appendix A).

Appraising Transaction Reviews

If the transaction reviews confirm the understanding of the system and that understanding has been correctly recorded in the flowcharts, no further work with regard to transaction reviews is necessary. If the transaction reviews indicate that the system was not correctly understood and recorded, the reviewer should ascertain the procedures in force, revise the documentation of the system accordingly, and note this in the working papers.

If site personnel contend that an exception revealed by the transaction review is an isolated instance, the system evaluator should perform a few additional reviews of the procedures giving rise to the exception, to determine whether the contention is correct before revising the flowcharts or narratives.

Transaction Reviews in Computer Systems

As noted earlier, the purpose of transaction reviews is to enable the evaluator to confirm the understanding of the system. The characteristics of most computer systems usually do not permit the tracing of a single transaction through the system, for reasons described below. As a result, transaction reviews *per se* are often not performed in computer systems. Instead, other techniques are used to achieve the same objective as a transaction review. Transaction reviews in a non-computer environment serve to inform the evaluator of steps in the transaction processing flow that are different from the description of the system obtained from interviews and enterprise documents. In a computer environment, where processing must be rigorously structured and documented in substantial detail, the evaluator can confirm the understanding by other means, for example, by reading the computer processing instructions.

Human Controls Using Visible Output. With some modifications, transaction reviews of controls over the non-computerized portion of the system are performed in a manner similar to that in a totally non-computerized system. There may be insufficient evidence to trace easily input transactions to output, or vice versa. If input transactions are batched or posted to a computer file, the batch, file, or total will be traced rather than the individual transactions. Lastly, the review of non-computerized controls cannot be regarded as complete until the programmed procedures have also been reviewed.

Programmed Procedures. Two problems are usually encountered in carrying out reviews of programmed procedures. First, as previously indicated, transactions are generally grouped into batches or files for computer processing. The results of the procedures applied to the group as a whole are usually reported, but complete evidence as to the effect of processing on each individual transaction may not be. A similar activity occurs in a non-computer environment when the character of the data processed changes from individual transactions to a group of transactions. Second, a particular programmed procedure may consist of one or more complex programs and involve several computer files. Each program may encompass many different logical paths (a hundred or so is not uncommon). Not all those paths will be of accounting significance, but an overall review may first be necessary to identify those that are. The discussion on pages 88 and 89 of the level of detail necessary for flowcharts of computer systems is relevant here as well. Evaluators should not lose sight of their task, namely, finding and evaluating controls.

As in non-computer systems, evaluators will look for evidence that may be used to confirm their understanding of programmed procedures. The following techniques may be helpful in meeting that objective:

To the extent practicable, examining evidence and reperforming programmed procedures by inspecting computer output such as computer-produced invoices, transaction listings, and reports, and comparing transaction output to transaction input; and

Reviewing the systems and program documentation. As a practical matter, a review of program documentation would be necessary for obtaining an understanding of the system, and would be done at that time rather than as part of the transaction review. In any computer system of reasonable size, an understanding of how the system works could not be conveyed to the evaluator without reference to the program documentation. Therefore, it is especially desirable that the same person obtain the understanding and carry out the transaction review. The completeness of program documentation is ascertained by reviewing the implementation controls rather than by tracing transactions through the system in particular computer applications.

Integrity Controls. The understanding of integrity controls is confirmed in a manner similar to the transaction review of application controls: the evaluator confirms the procedures carried out by computer department personnel and, where necessary, reviews the functioning of significant procedures carried out by software. Each aspect of integrity controls is discussed separately below.

Implementation Controls. The evaluator will normally need to select separate "system transactions" for developing new systems, changing existing ones, and preparing them for use. If implementation controls over new systems vary from system to system (e.g., because separate groups are responsible for the various systems), the evaluator should review each type of control. The review should include procedures incorporated into software, such as compilers and program library maintenance packages, and is carried out in the same way as the review of programmed procedures. The evaluator should also review the procedures that ensure that program documentation accurately reflects the actual operating system. Much of the evidence (e.g., systems specification change notices and program flowcharts) will be prepared by people in the computer department but some (e.g., source listings) will be computer-prepared.

Program Security Controls. Here the transaction review may include such "transactions" as jobs processed and pages of the console log (i.e., the log of computer operations). The job selected for processing can conveniently be the same one selected to review non-computerized accounting procedures (see above). Where many different transactions are being traced, however, it is necessary to trace only one job (or one job of each type if there is more than one type) through the operations. Software procedures requiring review will include aspects of the operating system (e.g., generation of the console log). Evidence will be limited to such items as processing schedules, problem reports, and console logs. Where evidence does not exist, appropriate inquiries should be made (e.g., as to differences in procedures on weekends).

Controls Over Access to Programs and Data Files.   It is necessary to review procedures controlling access to data files and program libraries. Controls over both files in use and files not in use, including custodial controls, should be reviewed. Evidence is limited to library issue records, console log reports of incorrect uses of passwords, and the like; therefore, some reliance must be placed on inquiries and interviews here as well.

5

Evaluating the System: The Questionnaire and Testing Phase

THE INTERNAL CONTROL QUESTIONNAIRE

To achieve a consistent approach to the study and evaluation of internal controls, an Internal Control Questionnaire (ICQ) and a Record of Control Weaknesses should be used. The purposes of those documents are to assist in evaluating internal controls as a basis for reporting weaknesses in the system, to provide a record of the work done, and for use in subsequent evaluations. Appendix C contains instructions for completing the questionnaire and record of control weaknesses, with a complete set of questions for the payments cycle, for both non-computer and computer systems.

Format of the Internal Control Questionnaire

The ICQ is divided into four sections, called "cycles." The first three relate to payments, production, and revenue, respectively, which represent the typical transactions of a business. The fourth section of the ICQ, called the "time cycle," relates to other events that occur periodically, as described in Chapter 2. The flowcharts that record the understanding of the underlying system should be used in completing the questionnaire.

Each section of the ICQ comprises a number of internal control objectives which should be achieved by the company's internal control procedures. Achievement of an objective means that a risk to which the enterprise would otherwise be exposed has been avoided by the use of appropriate controls. The emphasis on control objectives is intended to assist the system evaluator in obtaining a proper understanding of the purpose of the questions encompassed by the control objectives, and in identifying the specific control procedures used by the company for meeting the objectives of the control system. Listed under each objective are a number of questions that relate to individual accounting and operational controls. Each question is phrased so that it may be answered "Yes" or "No" and thereby indicate whether a control is present or absent. In addition, the questions that deal with disciplines over basic controls (see Chapter 2) have been identified to assist in determining the appropriate assessment of and corrective response to an indicated control weakness.

Internal accounting controls identified by "Yes" answers will be functionally tested if senior management has decided to include functional testing as part of the evaluation.* At the option of senior management, operational control questions may be completed and the related procedures tested by an operational review, described below. If the answer to a question is "No," it will not be possible to carry out a functional test of an internal accounting control or a review of an operational control since there is no control to test or review.

---

*See the discussion on page 107 regarding management's discretion in determining whether functional testing is appropriate.

The control objectives in the ICQ have been classified as follows:

1. *Standard control objectives.* These are objectives that apply to the common activities of most industrial and commercial undertakings and in respect of which relevant internal accounting and operational control questions are provided.
2. *Supplementary control objectives.* These relate to certain activities that may be sufficiently important in a particular industry or business to warrant a separate subsystem of processing and control, usually because the volume of transactions is relatively high. Although the standard control objectives usually cover those activities, the evaluator will probably find it easier to consider the controls over the subsystem separately. Certain supplementary objectives are listed at the end of each section of the ICQ, but these lists inevitably cannot be comprehensive, and other objectives may need to be formulated for a company that carries on unusual activities. See Appendix C for instructions regarding supplementary control objectives.

The existence of supplementary control objectives that may be used on an optional basis to tailor precisely the standardized ICQ format to the circumstances of a particular enterprise, together with the emphasis on objectives and controls rather than on procedures, permits the use of a standardized ICQ containing questions that are appropriate for all enterprises.

Standard Control Objectives

We have found it useful to translate the broad objectives of internal control, as described in Chapter 1, into standard "cycle-specific" control objectives. Meeting cycle-specific objectives requires that the related control tasks also be cycle-specific. Thus, the broad objective that *transactions* should be "executed in accordance with management's general or specific authorization" is translated in the payments cycle as *"purchases* should be initiated only on the basis of appropriate authorizations. . . ." (See page 136.) Similarly, the basic control operation of authorization—described in Chapter 2 as a comparison of a proposed transaction with plans, conditions, constraints, or general knowledge of what constitutes propriety, and a decision as to whether it is proper—is translated in the payments cycle in question form as: "Are all significant purchase commitments and changes thereto initiated only on the basis of appropriate written authorizations?" (See page 136.)

The flexibility provided by standard control objectives for each cycle makes the approach efficient for large companies with many different types of transactions in each cycle. In fact, it is difficult to conceive of an alternative; if control objectives and tasks were made specific for a given type of transaction, they would not be applicable to other transactions in the same cycle and would have to be revised every time a change took place in a particular type of transaction.

While control objectives and related questions are specified in the ICQ for each cycle, procedures for accomplishing the objectives are not. An important characteristic of the ICQ is that the focus is on accounting control over transaction flows by the accomplishment of control tasks, rather than on the presence or absence of a specific procedure.

This specification of control tasks, rather than detailed procedures, recognizes the variety of procedural responses to the performance of a control task. For example, the objective that "control should be established over all checks received" is met by a "Yes" answer to the question: "Are records prepared in detail of checks received when the mail is opened?" The detailed records could be a listing of payers and amounts or a photocopy of each check. Focusing on the control objective and task as related to each transaction flow, rather than on specific procedures, provides the flexibility needed to evaluate the effectiveness of internal control systems in varied environments and diverse industries. It also allows the evaluator of the system to identify the specific procedures used to meet each control objective without attempting to classify them as either accounting or operational controls, which is not practical in view of the overlapping between areas. (See the discussion in Chapter 1.)

The ICQ is oriented toward control objectives, and recognizes that a stated objective can be met by any one or more of various procedures. Also, not all control objectives are relevant to a particular company. For example, if the company does not make cash sales, the system evaluator should not evaluate the control objectives for cash sales. The evaluator should also consider devising additional control objectives related specifically to any significant activities not covered by the standard or supplementary control objectives.

Supplementary Control Objectives

Every enterprise or subdivision has activities that warrant separate subsystems of processing and control. Although those activities are theoretically covered by the standard control objectives, it is often easier to consider controls over them separately. Supplementary objectives for such activities are listed at the end of each section of the ICQ, but without corresponding questions.

An example of a supplementary control objective (from the revenue cycle) is that bills, acceptances, and notes receivable should be accurately recorded, as a basis for determining the outstanding amounts receivable, and adequately safeguarded prior to maturity. This objective might be applicable to any entity that has a relatively large number of such transactions. While the controls that apply in general to sale transactions also apply to sales for which notes are received, an entity with many such transactions would probably choose to develop a subsystem of processing and control for those transactions. This would be desirable because the authority to sell merchandise for notes may be limited to a few persons, the instruments received are negotiable and thus warrant special custodial arrangements, and specialized knowledge of terminology, law, and customs relating to this practice is required. Also, since interest revenue from these instruments may be very different from the bulk of its revenue transactions, the entity may also choose to include in its subsystem procedures and controls over such interest revenue. Similarly, while the more generalized objectives and questions from the ICQ could be applied to those transactions, usually the evaluator will choose to adopt supplementary control objectives for revenue transactions involving bills, acceptances, and notes receivable and the accrual and receipt of interest.

Computer Questions

Although the control objectives are the same regardless of how transactions are processed, there are differences in processing and control techniques between computer and non-computer systems. Accordingly, we have included portions of an example of a computer ICQ that contains alternative sets of questions for some control objectives as a means of recognizing those differences in computer systems commonly used. For other control objectives, the same set of questions applies to both non-computerized and computerized processing. (Thus, for example, control objectives 3, 7, 8, and 11 do not appear in the Payments Cycle Internal Control Questionnaire for Computer Systems because the questions for those control objectives are the same in both computerized and non-computerized systems.) This is because either there are insufficient differences in control techniques to warrant separate sets of questions, or the procedures relating to the control objectives are unlikely to be processed by computer. When any of the processing relating to a particular control objective is performed by computer, the evaluator should answer the questions in the computer ICQ for that control objective. The complete ICQ for any system that involves computer processing will thus be a combination of computer and non-computer questions; the combination will, of course, vary from system to system.

Integrity Controls.   As explained previously, computer systems include controls designed to ensure that the programmed procedures operate continuously and properly and that the security of data files is maintained. There is a separate section of the ICQ for evaluating integrity controls, reproduced in Appendix C. Under each control objective in the computer ICQ there is a question that requires the evaluator to list all programmed procedures relevant to that control objective that are not adequately controlled by user controls. The evaluator is then referred to the integrity controls section of the ICQ to determine whether the requisite procedures exist to assure the continued functioning of the programmed procedures. Similarly, for control objectives that include questions on data file security, the evaluator is first asked whether there are adequate user controls. If there are not, the evaluator is again referred to the section on integrity controls to determine whether they provide the necessary assurance.

Controls Over Standing Data.   The evaluator should assess controls over standing data whenever they are relevant to a control objective. It would be unwieldy to list all the questions relating to standing data each time they apply under the relevant control objective. Accordingly, the questions relating to standing data are listed separately in a standing data controls section of the ICQ, reproduced in Appendix C. A separate questionnaire is filled in for each file containing standing data. Under each control objective to which standing data controls apply, there is a question with respect to the overall adequacy of those controls.

Custodial Activities

Some enterprises have substantial custodial activities that do not conceptually fall under either a transaction cycle or the time cycle. These activities are usually (but not always) "off the books"; examples are trust departments of banks, securities held for customers by brokerage houses, goods held on consignment, inventories held for others by public warehouses, and the holding of collateral by lenders. Such custodial activities are often perceived as being unique to an industry, giving rise to the jargon "industry-specific." From a control viewpoint, however, these "safekeeping" activities are basically similar. While specific control procedures will vary not only from industry to industry but also from company to company, the control objectives and tasks pertaining to safekeeping activities are the same regardless of the industry in which the activity occurs.

Controls over assets held for others are essential. In fact, management's responsibility for assets entrusted to it by third parties may be greater than for resources provided by owners or creditors. With some notable exceptions, such as the safekeeping activities of brokerage houses, however, those controls are not always evaluated by management.

While "safekeeping" activities are often not explicitly covered by control objectives or tasks in the ICQ sections relating to transaction cycles, this can be easily done. For enterprises that engage in such custodial activities, controls can be designed and evaluated either as part of the time cycle or, if more efficient, as supplementary control objectives of the transaction cycles to which these activities most closely relate. Though this book does not cover specific procedures related to custodial activities (or, for that matter, any specific procedures), management should not ignore the relevant control objectives and tasks.

"Common" Control Objectives

The four broad objectives of internal control defined in professional literature and the Foreign Corrupt Practices Act apply generally. The standard control objectives in our approach have been designed for specific cycles, as described above. Our approach does not single out control objectives common to all cycles. We do not consider it useful for control evaluation purposes to identify such "common" control objectives because the cycle-specific objectives preclude the need for "common" objectives. Such "common" control objectives, however, could be inferred from the basic control tasks described in Chapter 2. Indeed, the notion might be quite useful in teaching about the nature of internal control. If a pattern is sought, it is readily found.

For example, the payments, production, and revenue cycles each include a standard control objective relating to the authorization of movements of inventory. A control objective in the payments cycle reads:

1. Purchases should be initiated only on the basis of appropriate authorizations and records of commitments should be maintained as a basis for:
   a. determining that transactions are executed in accordance with authorizations;
   b. establishing the amount of any provision required for losses arising from unfulfilled commitments.

A similar control objective in the production cycle is:

2. Control should be established over:
   a. issues from inventories of materials and supplies to production, and returns;
   b. charges to production for labor and overheads;

    c.   transfers from production to inventories of parts and finished products; as a basis, where required, for making entries in the inventory records.

Citing a control objective from the revenue cycle:

3.   Control should be established over goods shipped and services performed as a basis for:
    a.   making charges to customers for all such sales;
    b.   determining the amount of the related revenues that have not been entered as accounts receivable;
    c.   where required, making the related entries in the detailed inventory records.

Another example is the standard control objectives relating to the validity of recorded transactions. Control objectives in the payments, production, and revenue cycles, respectively, that relate to the validity of transactions are reproduced below:

1.   Invoices and related documentation should be properly checked and approved as being valid before being entered as accounts payable.
2.   All charges and credits should be checked and approved as being valid before being entered in the work-in-progress records.
3.   All charges and credits should be appropriately checked as being valid before being entered in the accounts receivable records.

Common Control Procedures

On the other hand, we have identified five frequently recurring "common control procedures," which are included in the Internal Control Reference Manual (Appendix D). This is efficient because the purpose of the Reference Manual is to explain the questions in the ICQ and give examples of procedures that might be used in meeting the objectives of the internal accounting control system. If the explanation of one question would essentially parallel that of another question, a common control procedure has been identified. To avoid repetition where this happens often, the Reference Manual refers the reader to the section that explains the common control procedures.

The common control procedures included in the manual are:

1. Control over completeness of processing;
2. Maintenance of subsidiary records supporting a control account;
3. Postings to inventory records;
4. Supervisory review and approval;
5. Checking of extensions and additions.

This is not a complete list; other common control procedures could be identified.

Format of the Reference Manual

The Reference Manual aids the system evaluator in completing the Internal Control Questionnaire and Record of Control Weaknesses, explained below. The structure of the Reference Manual as a separate document represents a compromise. The information in the manual could have been included in the ICQ. The idea for the manual was conceived as a means of reducing the bulk of the ICQ and making it a more useful working document. The Reference Manual is intended as a training aid that can later serve as a reference book. Experienced evaluators may refer to it only occasionally.*

In addition to providing explanations of ICQ questions and examples of control procedures, the manual indicates how each control objective in each cycle can be traced to one or more control objectives of the Foreign Corrupt Practices Act. Exhibit 5 compares the control objectives in the payments cycle ICQ to the requirements of the Act.

Note: The headings refer to the requirements of the Foreign Corrupt Practices Act, listed in the footnote on page 11. The numbers under the headings refer to the relevant control objectives in the payments cycle.

A	B(i)	B(ii)(I)	B(ii)(II)	B(iii)	B(iv)
1	1	1			
2		2	2		
3		3	3		
4	4	4	4		
5		5	5		
6	6	6	6	6	
7		7	7		
8	8	8	8	8	8
9	9	9	9	9	
10		10	10	10	10
11	11	11	11		
12		12	12		
13		13	13		

Exhibit 5.   Comparison of Required Elements of Internal Control Systems
With the ICQ.

---

*The Reference Manual has several volumes. Volume 1 includes the introduction (the appropriate portions of which have been incorporated into this book) and the common control procedures. The remaining volumes are organized by cycle and include the explanations of the individual questions in the ICQ. (The volume on *The Payments Cycle* is reproduced in Appendix D.)

Explanations in the Reference Manual of individual questions in the ICQ are organized as follows:

Question. The question, as it appears in the ICQ, is printed at the beginning of each explanation.

Purpose. Appears immediately following the question and explains the purpose of control procedures covered by the question.

What Constitutes Adequate Control Procedures? Sets forth procedures commonly found in practice and explains the impact of those procedures on the adequacy of the company's internal control. Where appropriate, cross-reference is made to the common control procedures section. The information is presented as follows:

If. Describes a typical situation or procedure.

Impact on Adequacy of Control. Explains the effect of ''If'' on the adequacy of the company's internal control.

Example. Illustrates the circumstances described in the first two columns.

Possible Errors and Audit Effect. Describes the usual effect of a ''No'' answer. The ''If'' line describes the control weakness that would exist if the question were answered ''No.'' The remaining information is set out in three columns, as follows:

Possible Errors in Financial Statements. Explains the errors that could be present in the financial statements as a result of the control weaknesses described in ''If.''

Example. Illustrates the errors that may be present as a result of the control weakness.

Effect on Audit Procedures. Describes the changes that would usually be made in auditing procedures as a result of the control weakness. This column assumes that if the control were present, audit procedures would be based on reliance on it, i.e., functional tests and early validation would be emphasized and year-end validation restricted to the maximum extent possible. While designed for audits by the enterprise's public accountants, this information may also be useful to the enterprise's internal auditors. Moreover, it gives management an idea of the audit costs associated with a control weakness, in addition to the cost of possible noncompliance with the Foreign Corrupt Practices Act.

Record of Control Weaknesses

The purpose of this form is to ensure that the system evaluator considers the *potential* effect of all control weaknesses identified through the completion of the ICQ on meeting the objectives of the internal accounting control system or on operational efficiency. All control weaknesses identified should be recorded on the form, which also provides a record that the control weaknesses have been discussed informally with, and considered for formal reporting to, senior management.

In using the record of control weaknesses, the system evaluator must indicate whether a particular weakness could result, directly or indirectly, in "material error." The term "material error" as used here indicates any potential error other than one that is patently trivial. As noted earlier, the evaluator must determine the level of significance of a control weakness for the purpose of reporting the weakness to the appropriate level of management and for management's subsequent analysis made to ascertain the appropriate corrective action, if any. (The factors influencing "significance" are not repeated here.) All material errors that could possibly result from control weaknesses should be indicated on the record of weaknesses; whether a potentially "material error," as defined above and included on the record of weaknesses, turns out to be "significant" is a decision that management will subsequently make.

Completion of the Questionnaire and Record of Control Weaknesses

Detailed instructions for the completion of the ICQ and the record of weaknesses are provided in Appendix C.

The questionnaire and record of weaknesses should be updated annually for all changes in internal accounting control procedures, unless the procedures have changed to such an extent that it is more practicable to complete new forms. The same method should be followed for updating as for the initial preparation. The forms should not be updated until the related flowcharts have been updated. When amendments are made, the date of amendment should be clearly indicated and the previous answer should remain legible so that the procedures in force at a particular date can be ascertained.

As indicated above, senior management usually decides whether the operational control questions should be completed. In making this decision, it has a number of available alternatives: complete all the questions annually, complete all the questions over a period of years, or complete only certain cycles or control objectives. As suggested earlier, operational controls can usually be reviewed at the same time as the accounting controls, at little additional cost.

Preferably, the same personnel who prepared or updated the related flowcharts should complete the questionnaire and record of weaknesses. (On the other hand, understandability of the flowcharts may be enhanced if the preparer knows that someone else must later use them to answer the questionnaire.) A responsible supervisory individual should be appointed to make an appropriate review to determine that the ICQ and record of weaknesses have been properly completed, including cross-references to the flowcharts. Particular attention should be paid to ascertaining whether all pertinent control objectives and related procedures have been identified and that "No" answers have been properly assessed. The completion/up-dating/review record (first page of each ICQ section) provides spaces for signatures of the various individuals to evidence the above work and contains instructions as to the completion of the spaces.

FUNCTIONAL TESTS AND OPERATIONAL REVIEWS

Functional (or compliance) tests and operational reviews provide evidence as to whether an internal accounting control or operational control procedure identified by a "Yes" answer to an ICQ question is operating as planned.

The purpose of the operational control review differs from that of functional testing of internal accounting controls. An operational review may identify opportunities for system and operational improvements; a breakdown in an internal accounting control may indicate that the objectives of the internal accounting control system are not being met, which may be evidence of possible noncompliance with the Foreign Corrupt Practices Act.

Application and Scope

A decision to carry out functional tests or operational reviews is a matter of management discretion. If the evaluation indicates that the system as planned includes adequate segregation of duties and supervision, management may decide not to test or review, but to rely on those disciplinary controls. Supervision over accounting activities is an example of a disciplinary control. Management might decide to forgo functional testing and rely on the role of the supervisor who, among other things, can be assigned the responsibility for ascertaining that controls are operating to the extent prescribed and periodically testing the controls to be sure that personnel understand the duties they are expected to perform and are continually carrying them out. A review of accounting corrections to see that the cause of errors has been diagnosed and appropriately remedied is a common form of supervision.

Other sources of assurance that may reduce the need to test or review are the absence of significant required accounting adjustments in past periods and the reports of evaluations made by the company's CPAs. On the other hand, management may wish to test or review the system as a basis for further assurance that it is operating as planned. Management may also decide to test or review some, but not all, controls included in the evaluation. The same factors that influence the decision to include or exclude one or more areas from the overall evaluation (see Chapter 3) also influence the decision not to carry out functional tests or operational reviews of specific parts of the system.

Types of Functional Tests and Operational Reviews

Functional testing normally involves:

Examination of Evidence. Inspection of records, documents, reconciliations, reports, and the like, for evidence that a specific control appears to have been properly applied (e.g., by inspection of signatures or initials on a purchase invoice evidencing that the invoice was matched with a purchase order and record of goods received or by inspection of exception reports);

Reperformance. The repeating, either in whole or in part, of the work processes performed by employees (e.g., the matching of a purchase invoice with the corresponding purchase order and record of goods received); and

Observation. Watching the work process as it is performed by employees (e.g., control over counting and examining incoming goods and the physical security of inventory). This should be used only when it is the only means available.

These tests should not be confined solely to the inspection of signatures, references, and the like; the system evaluator should review the nature and reasonableness of the transactions recorded, observe generally the circumstances in which the operations are being carried out, and be alert to anything that appears to be out of the ordinary.

In some situations, observation is the only functional test that can be performed. In that situation, the system evaluator should bear in mind the possibility that the control may not be performed when no one is observing. Examination of action taken as a result of the application of controls, e.g., follow-up on exception reports listing short shipments of goods and/or defective items, is often a superior form of evidence of a control's existence.

Reviews of operational controls normally consist of examination of evidence. In the absence of a specific decision by management, operational controls generally should not be reperformed. (See the discussion starting on page 110.)

Categories of Controls To Be Tested or Reviewed

As noted in Chapter 2, internal controls can be divided into two categories:

1. Internal accounting controls, which may be further divided into two types:
   a. Basic controls—i.e., those controls that are necessary for the completeness and accuracy of the accounting records; and
   b. Disciplines over basic controls—i.e., those controls designed to ensure the continued and proper operation of basic controls and to safeguard assets.
2. Operational controls.

Basic Controls. Basic controls cover a wide range of checks and procedures. Typical examples are:

1. Checks on completeness (e.g., by means of sequential numbering of documents);
2. Matchings or comparisons of documents or figures;
3. Checks of additions, calculations, and extensions;
4. Controls over groups of transactions (e.g., by means of control accounts);
5. Controls over the recording of physical movements of goods.

Functional testing of basic controls should include both examination of evidence and reperformance; in some cases, observation may also be relevant. Complete reperformance may be impracticable. For example, in the case of a periodic agreement of accounts payable balances with the control account, reperformance might consist of testing the additions of the individual balances to arrive at the total and tracing a sample of individual balances from the ledgers to the listing and vice versa.

Disciplines Over Basic Controls. Disciplines over basic controls comprise:

1. Custodial arrangements, i.e.:
   a. The separation of the responsibilities for custody of assets and the related recordkeeping;
   b. Physical arrangements that prevent unauthorized access to assets or accounting records;
2. Adequate segregation of duties so that the work of one person checks that of another or prevents independent action by one party;
3. Adequate supervision of the work of persons involved in the operation of the basic controls. Supervision, often referred to as ''supervisory control,'' is normally carried out by more senior personnel and involves examination of evidence of the application of basic controls, spot checks of the proper application of basic controls, and/or scrutinies for reasonableness. ''Supervisory review and approval'' is one of the common control procedures discussed in the Reference Manual. (See Appendix D.)

Testing of controls relating to items 1 and 2 above involves observation and inquiry and/or examination of signatures and initials on documents and records. These tests should normally be carried out as part of the functional tests of the related basic controls, rather than as a separate operation.

Functional testing of the supervisory controls described in item 3 above, on the other hand, is based largely on the examination of evidence. The primary evidence will be the signature or initials of the person exercising the control on the relevant document or record. Careful attention should also be given to other evidence, such as exception reports or internal memoranda that indicate the disposition of unsatisfactory documents, or records that have been queried as a result of the supervisory control. The application of the supervisory control to current transactions may also be observed.

Complete reperformance of a supervisory control is often not possible, partly because the system evaluator does not have the knowledge and experience of the supervisor concerned, and partly because the nature and extent of the checks carried out by the supervisor may be a matter of discretion and may not be clearly evidenced. Reperformance should be limited to the tasks that are expected to be undertaken in the exercise of the supervisory control. It normally includes inspection of the supporting documentation that should have been examined by the person exercising the supervisory control and of evidence of prior checks that may have been required. The increased efficiency of using the same sample items for examination of evidence of basic controls should be borne in mind. Errors in the application of basic controls that were not detected by the supervisor may indicate that the related supervisory control is not being applied effectively.

Operational Controls. Operational controls deal with the efficient use of resources. Typical examples are:

1. Establishing an organization and policies to facilitate efficient operations;
2. Providing information necessary for effective decision making. Such information may relate to individual transactions (e.g., economic order quantities, technical performance specifications, routing instructions for use in purchasing), or to the general activities of a particular function (e.g., information as to sales by product, by customer, by region, etc., for use in the marketing function);
3. Establishing plans and procedures designed to promote operational efficiency (e.g., procedures for performing preventive maintenance, to limit machine downtime); and
4. Signalling departures from plans and targets as a basis for investigation and corrective action (e.g., determining the extent of compliance with the production schedules and the reasons for deviations).

Reviews of operational controls are usually based primarily on the examination of evidence. Such evidence may consist of the item that forms the basis for the control (e.g., an organization chart or policy manual); a report or worksheet (e.g., technical performance specifications for goods to be purchased); a document (e.g., a purchase order containing routing, delivery date required, and other instructions); or an exception report or internal memorandum indicating that the control is being applied.

Reperformance of an operational control often is not cost beneficial, primarily because a large amount of time may be required to reperform many operational controls. For example, the cost of taking the time to recalculate economic order quantities or checking the accuracy of routing instructions for purchased goods often exceeds the benefits, although the evaluator ordinarily will examine evidence that economic order quantities are used and that routing instructions are provided to purchasing personnel. Sometimes, however, evaluators will be able to reperform operational control procedures with a limited expenditure of time. For example, calculations may be reperformed to determine whether cash discounts on purchase invoices were appropriately taken.

Functional Tests in a Computer System

As in non-computer systems, the purpose of functional tests in computer systems is to provide evidence as to whether an internal accounting control procedure identified in the ICQ is operating as planned. However, because of the differences in controls in computer systems, as previously discussed, there are often differences in the techniques and extent of functional testing, which may require special skills on the part of the system evaluator.

The techniques for functional testing in computer systems are considered under the following categories:

Disciplines
User controls
Integrity controls
Programmed procedures

Tests of Disciplines.   Tests of supervisory controls in computerized systems are essentially the same as in non-computer systems. Tests of segregation of duties and custodial arrangements are normally carried out by the examination of signatures and initials on documents and records and by inquiry. It is not usually possible to carry out satisfactory reperformance tests on these disciplines.

The evaluator should examine evidence, for example, signatures and initials on reconciliations and exception reports, to confirm that the persons carrying out user controls are independent of computer operations personnel, that is, those responsible for system design, programming, and computer operating. The evaluator should also ascertain that suitable instructions for physical security have been distributed to EDP personnel and may examine evidence that the names of individuals, such as terminal operators, are consistent with the instructions. The computer department organization charts, written procedures, and job descriptions should be reviewed, to confirm that they provide for adequate segregation of duties, for example, among those involved in system development and maintenance, computer operating, and custody of data files, both during and outside the normal working day. In addition, where possible, work schedules, time reports, operator logs, and similar documentation should be examined, to confirm that individuals performing duties are authorized to do so.

Tests of User Controls.   Functional testing of user controls normally includes both examination of evidence and reperformance. Designing and carrying out tests should not be difficult because visible evidence of the operation of the relevant controls—for example, the agreement of control totals and the action taken on exception and rejection reports—is ordinarily available. It should be noted that because human action is required, complete reperformance may not be practicable where large volumes of data are involved. For example, if control is exercised by the reconciliation, through the use of a control register, of the totals of a number of individual batches with a subsequent total produced by the computer, reperformance might consist of checking the additions of a sample of batches and tracing the selected batch totals to the control register.

Tests of Integrity Controls.   The reviewer should functionally test the integrity controls that are carried out by people and should also be satisfied as to the appropriateness of a sample of system software procedures. A decision on how many, and which, system software procedures to test will be made in the light of the results of tests of the other integrity controls, particularly those over the implementation and security of system software. The same integrity controls may apply to both computer programs and data files. For example, both may be stored in the same physical library or both may be protected by the same software while on-line. If so, only one set of functional tests is required.

Functional testing of integrity controls that are carried out by people includes examination of evidence and reperformance. Many of the tests are similar to those for testing user controls, for example, the users' review of documentation supporting changes in computer programs. Other tests, such as those on the completeness controls over program changes, are similar to tests carried out in non-computer systems. Certain tests, for example, those of controls over the testing of newly developed procedures, are unique to integrity controls. Examination of evidence is particularly important in situations where reperformance is not appropriate; a systems description cannot be reperformed even though it may be reviewed for adequacy.

Various techniques are available to test the appropriateness of system software procedures. The technique selected will depend on the nature of the procedure being tested. For example, in testing cataloguing procedures, the use of test data and program code analysis may be suitable to establish that new or changed programs are functioning properly, thus confirming that they were satisfactorily catalogued. The use of test data and program code analysis is considered in greater detail later in this chapter.

The evaluator, in lieu of performing functional tests, may use computer programs that have been developed to validate the effectiveness of system software procedures. These include:

1. Programs that examine the company's production programs and, by comparing them with independently controlled copies, assist in confirming that authorized changes have been properly made or that unauthorized changes have not been made.
2. Programs that analyze and report defined items on the system log, which the reviewer can then compare with a report prepared by an individual.

The system software procedures for password protection can be conveniently tested by attempting to gain access to a data file or program from a terminal by using an invalid password. Before using such a technique, the evaluator should consider the possible effects both if the control operates properly and if it fails to operate.

Tests of Programmed Procedures.   Ordinarily, the reviewer achieves satisfaction as to the appropriateness and continued and proper operation of programmed procedures from the evaluation and functional testing of user and integrity controls. If the reviewer is unable to, or chooses not to, rely on user and integrity controls for this purpose, it will be necessary to test the operation of some or all programmed procedures. Accordingly, the evaluator should consider the likely error conditions and, because satisfaction is obtained through reperformance of the operation, the level of tests should take this into account.

The mere existence of visible evidence of computer activity is not a sufficient test of the continued and proper operation of programmed procedures. Accordingly, tests of those procedures are normally carried out in other ways, for example, by replicating the processing operation under controlled conditions and comparing the two sets of results. The visible evidence generated by a programmed procedure, for example, a list of missing receiving reports, can be tested for the correctness of what *is* listed by the computer. The printout by itself, however, gives the evaluator no knowledge about its completeness.

The principal techniques available to test programmed procedures include tests performed on visible evidence by people, the use of test data, program code analysis, and simulation using computer programs. The choice of technique is often governed by whether there is loss of visible evidence.

Loss of Visible Evidence.   In computer processing, the results of processing may not be printed out in detail. In the absence of such a printout, the reviewer cannot test the operation of programmed procedures by conventional means. There are two ways in which this difficulty can arise. First, totals and analyses may be printed out without supporting details, thus rendering it impossible to check the total or analysis without either obtaining those details or using specialized software. The second situation, although common, is less obvious. It is often impossible to establish by examining exception reports and rejection listings that all items that should have been reported or rejected have been properly treated. These two situations are commonly covered by the phrase "loss of audit trail." Unfortunately, this term implies that the means to check results by conventional tests should be available and that their absence is a failure in the system. This is not true; what matters is the adequacy of the controls. If the failure to print out constitutes a weakness in control, for example, if the contents of suspense files are not regularly printed out, the system is deficient and the evaluator is correct to draw this to the attention of management. But if the failure to print out does not represent a weakness, the evaluator should normally devise alternative techniques to test the operation of the programmed procedures. For these reasons, the term "visible evidence" is preferred to "audit trail."

Tests Performed on Visible Evidence by People.   Manual tests of programmed procedures can be performed if full visible evidence of the procedures is available. For example, if a complete listing of sales invoices is provided, it can be added up to confirm the sales total, or if debtors' statements show all transactions on individual accounts, postings thereto can be checked. Tests consist of repeating the work carried out by the program and verifying that the results are the same.

These tests can also be carried out if full visible evidence is not provided by the system but can be created in one of the following ways:

Re-assembling processed data so that they are in the same condition as when the programmed procedure was applied, for example, re-assembling batches of sales invoices to test the batch totals posted to the sales ledger control accounts;

Testing current data before they are processed by the computer, for example, testing the additions of batches before they are sent for conversion to test the establishment of a total used to control subsequent processing;

Selecting a small number of items from those submitted for processing and processing them in a separate run, for example, splitting a batch of 100 items into one of 90 items and one of 10 items, processing the 10 items separately, and agreeing the resultant computer-produced totals with pre-calculated results;

Requesting a special printout of items processed, for example, a listing of sales invoices included in a sales total produced by the computer.

Test Data. This technique consists of devising fictitious data and predicting the results that should be obtained if the programmed procedures operate properly. The data are processed against the operational programs and the actual results are checked against the predicted results. This technique is normally used where there is incomplete evidence available of how a programmed procedure operated and tests on visible evidence are either impracticable or inefficient. Test data are usually designed to test the operation of several programmed procedures within an application, for example, by processing fictitious orders to produce invoices, sales totals, and entries in inventory and accounts receivable ledgers. Specific tests may be necessary to confirm that the correct programs are used. Where the integrity controls have not been relied on, or where weaknesses or exceptions have been found, the evaluator may consider it advisable to be present during the running of the test data.

Program Code Analysis. Program code analysis comprises the examination of source listings of operational programs to determine that the relevant programmed procedures are present and logically coded. A high degree of technical skill is required to perform program code analysis. To verify that the coding on the source listing being examined is the same as that contained in the operational program actually used for processing, the reviewer has to be familiar with the program language used. If program code analysis is used, the reviewer must also be satisfied that the program code analyzed is actually used in a production environment.

Use of Computer Programs. The use of computer programs in testing programmed procedures is often referred to as *simulation*. The objective is to check that the programmed procedures are operating correctly by checking and agreeing figures produced by them with those produced by the reviewer's programs. Examples of the use of a computer program for testing programmed procedures include the examination of a sales invoicing file to verify the production of the company's sales analysis report, the examination of a file of numbered receiving reports to verify the production of a missing numbers report, and the examination and evaluation of a file of stock movements to verify the production of a stock evaluation and analysis report. Since the reviewer is concerned primarily with the programmed procedures, it is often unnecessary to duplicate exactly the precise and complete logic of those procedures. The reviewer's program may thus be less complicated.

One of the practical problems of simulation is that it is often difficult to simplify the logic of a complex program. In attempting to do so, the reviewer may arrive at different figures and have to spend time correcting his or her program logic or carrying out a reconciliation. Because of this potential problem, simulation is unlikely to be an efficient technique where the integrity controls have been tested and can be relied on, and only limited reperformance of programmed procedures is required. However, where the integrity controls cannot be completely relied on, simulation of the programmed procedures several times during the year may be a satisfactory alternative. Further, even though the evaluation of the integrity controls indicates that they are satisfactory, the reviewer may decide that it is more efficient to simulate programmed procedures several times during the year and reduce the reliance placed on the integrity controls.

Levels of Tests and Reviews

It is not possible to prescribe hard and fast rules for determining levels of tests (i.e., the number of items to be tested). The level to be selected in each case is a matter for judgment by management in the light of all relevant factors. The objective, however, should always be to test the minimum amount necessary to obtain reasonable assurance that a control is functioning properly.

All relevant factors should be taken into account in determining the appropriate levels of tests, e.g., the complexity of the transactions and experience on previous evaluations. The following points should be among those considered:

1. The frequency with which a control is performed; in general, the more frequently the control is performed, the higher the level of tests;
2. The levels of reperformance tests should be lower than those for examination of evidence;
3. In the case of controls involving groups of transactions, the levels of tests should be applied to the primary evidence of the control rather than to the

underlying individual transactions. For example, in the case of a monthly control over the completeness of sequentially prenumbered documents, functional testing might typically take the form of:

a. An examination of a few monthly reports of missing numbers to confirm that missing numbers appear to be identified and investigated;

b. Reperformance based on one or two reports; this would involve selecting a limited number of batches of documents, seeing that any missing numbers have been listed, and reviewing the results of the investigations.

Other relevant factors that may be considered are discussed in Chapter 3 under the heading "Ranking Control Weaknesses."

The need to spread tests throughout the period under review must be considered. The spreading of tests over different time periods is relevant to the levels of tests insofar as it is necessary to ensure that the number of items selected provides adequate representation of the population during the periods selected. At a minimum, the functional tests of the disciplines over basic controls should be spread. This is necessary to obtain assurance as to the consistent and proper operation of the underlying basic controls throughout the period under review. If the disciplines over basic controls appear to be operating properly, reperformance of the basic controls themselves can normally be restricted to one month or other period—usually, though not necessarily, the latest period available at the time of the test.

As with tests of internal accounting controls, it is not possible to prescribe hard and fast rules for determining levels of reviews (i.e., the number of items selected for review) of operational controls. The level to be selected in each case is again a matter of management judgment. The objective should be to review the minimum amount necessary to determine the apparent existence of the control; often the reviews may be limited to a few items. The levels of reviews of operational controls will generally be considerably lower than the levels of tests of accounting controls. This is because of the different purposes of functional tests and operational reviews, discussed earlier.

The levels of reviews of operational controls should be based primarily on the effort involved in performing a particular review procedure and the potential financial impact if the control is inoperative. Thus, if the additional time to review a control is small (as is normally the case when an operational control is reviewed in conjunction with the testing of a related accounting control), and the potential impact of a control breakdown is great, the level of review should be relatively high (but still lower than the level of test of the related accounting control). On the other hand, if the effort to review an operational control is great and the potential impact of a control breakdown is slight, it may not be necessary to perform any operational control reviews.

It is normally not necessary to spread reviews of operational controls throughout the period.

Levels of Tests in Computer Systems

Some guidelines that may be helpful in deciding on levels of tests for the various types of controls and procedures in computer systems are given below. As in non-computer systems, consideration should be given to spreading functional tests throughout the period under review to provide assurance of the consistent and proper operation of the controls.

Tests of User Controls. Normally, a test level comparable to that adopted in a non-computer system is appropriate if the frequency of operation of the control is similar.

Tests of Integrity Controls. *Implementation Controls.* It is usually appropriate to test the disciplinary control components of implementation controls for all new systems instituted in the period under review. If these tests are satisfactory, it will usually be sufficient to carry out tests on the basic control components for only a sample of the programmed procedures included in such systems. In choosing the sample, the reviewer should consider the following: the importance of the system and procedure, the effect if the control did not operate properly, and the likelihood that a breakdown in the procedure would be brought to light by the operation of other controls.

The level of tests applied to program changes should be comparable to that adopted in a non-computer system where the frequency of operation of the control is similar. The procedures will normally be similar for all systems. The evaluator should select both changes that relate to programmed procedures and changes that have only an operational effect, such as changes in print formats. The latter are tested to assure that unauthorized changes have not been made at the time of making a change in a print format. Also, an inappropriate change in a print format could affect a non-computer control.

Program Security, Computer Operations, and Data File Security Controls. These controls operate at all times; the frequency of their operation is not related to the volume of accounting data processed and in general depends on the number of programs run. It is often appropriate to select a level of tests comparable to that adopted in a non-computer system where the frequency of operation of the control is similar.

Tests of Programmed Procedures. The nature, extent, and timing of tests of programmed procedures are also largely a matter of judgment. The following factors should be taken into account, in addition to those applicable to non-computer systems:

1. The degree of reliance that can be placed on the integrity controls. If reliance on implementation controls is reduced, the evaluator should consider increasing the number of different programmed procedures tested. If reliance on program security or computer operations controls is reduced, the evaluator should consider whether to increase the number of times programmed procedures are tested and whether to spread the tests throughout the period under review.
2. The extent to which the results of processing are subsequently reviewed. A system that is subject to overall reconciliation of control totals is less susceptible to program error than a system in which transactions are generated by the computer in such a way that the total cannot be checked by people.

Selection of Items To Be Tested or Reviewed

Since the respective purposes of functional tests and operational reviews are to ascertain whether specific internal accounting controls are operating and specific operational controls are apparently in existence, no special emphasis need normally be placed, when examining evidence or carrying out reperformance, on selecting high-value items. Similarly, for this purpose, it is unnecessary to ensure that the items selected are representative of the various transactions processed through a control operation. The fact that otherwise similar basic controls are exercised by different people or in different locations does not alter that conclusion, provided, with respect to internal accounting controls, the basic control procedures are uniform and the system evaluator is satisfied that they are subject to the same supervisory controls.

Because functional tests and operational reviews are designed to test the operation and review the apparent existence of specific controls, they are concerned primarily with the flow of transactions through individual control points rather than through the system. Accordingly, different documents may be selected to verify different control points, i.e., it is not necessary, although it may sometimes be more efficient, to test or review related controls using the same documents.

Order of Performing Tests and Reviews

Internal accounting controls need not be tested in the order in which they appear in the ICQ. Supervisory controls are often tested before the related basic controls, and controls over groups of transactions before controls over the related individual transactions, because the results of tests of supervisory or group controls may determine, to some extent, the levels of tests to be applied to underlying controls. It is, however, equally acceptable to test the basic controls first, or the basic controls and the supervisory controls at the same time, if circumstances indicate this is more efficient.

Operational controls should be reviewed in whichever order is most efficient. Review of an operational control should be carried out in conjunction with the functional test of a related internal accounting control if this would enhance efficiency. For example, when performing operational reviews, the system evaluator normally determines whether routing and other instructions are on the purchase order and whether a cash discount was taken, simultaneously with testing the control over the matching of purchase orders with receiving reports and purchase invoices.

Departures and Breakdowns

All exceptions noted during functional tests and operational reviews are recorded on a Record of Control-Operation Exceptions (illustrated and described in Appendix E). When an exception is found (i.e., when a control is not being applied or is not evidenced), it is necessary to establish whether:

1. It is an ''isolated incident'' that need not be further considered, or
2. It indicates a departure from, or a breakdown in, the prescribed systems.

To find out whether item 1 applies, the first step is to ascertain why the exception arose. This may be done by inquiry and examination, or it may be necessary to extend the sample. Care should be taken to ensure that extension of the sample will assist in determining the nature and extent of the exception. If an exception represents a breakdown, the record of exceptions must note whether it has been corrected. If it has not been corrected, the notation on the form will be the basis for discussion with and a report to management.

If no exceptions are found as a result of the functional tests and operational reviews, this should be noted on a form titled Program and Record of Functional Tests and Operational Reviews (illustrated and described in Appendix E).

Functional Test and Operational Review Documentation

The documentation for functional tests and operational reviews should include, as a minimum:

1. A description of the tests and/or reviews performed;
2. A reference from each functional test and/or operational review to the related ICQ question number;
3. Identification of levels of tests and/or reviews;
4. Indication of periods tested and/or reviewed;
5. Identification of the evidence examined;
6. Identification of exceptions noted, if any, and their disposition; and
7. An indication that the work was completed, usually the initials of the person completing the work and the date of its performance.

All of this information should be included on the Record of Control-Operation Exceptions, on the Program and Record of Functional Tests and Operational Reviews, or in the related working papers. Detailed instructions regarding use of the forms are contained in Appendix E, which also includes specimen functional tests for many common internal accounting control techniques. These may be used where appropriate, in the manner described in the accompanying instructions.

6

Control Objectives and Tasks: The Payments and Time Cycles

This chapter illustrates the evaluation of internal controls in the payments cycle and discusses the control objectives of the time cycle.

THE PAYMENTS CYCLE

The paragraphs that follow describe many of the internal controls that are typically exercised over the acquisition of and payment for goods and services. The reader may wish to relate the material to the control objectives in the ICQ for the payments cycle, reproduced in Appendix C. The questions in the ICQ and the accompanying explanations in the related Reference Manual (Appendix D) may suggest additional controls beyond those discussed here.

Typical Transaction Systems and Internal Control

Every purchase of goods goes through about the same steps: determining needs; shopping for the best means of satisfying them and the best price; ordering the goods; receiving, inspecting, and accepting them; storing or using them; recording the transaction; and paying the invoice. Large or infrequent purchases of goods may be subject to special scrutiny, but the process is still basically the same. The same general process applies to purchases of services, although some steps are not relevant.

Determining Needs. The payments cycle starts when someone identifies a need, which may occur in several different ways. For example:

Raw material inventory replenishment needs may be determined by a person or automatically when stock on hand reaches a reorder point or when a bill of materials for a job order is prepared. Sometimes sophisticated computer programs identify needs by reference to records of quantities on hand or production orders and simultaneously execute some of the steps in the buying process, for example, selecting vendors and preparing purchase orders.

Needs for occasional goods and services are identified and described by the user, usually on a requisition form that has to be approved by the person (who may be the same as the user) responsible for authorizing the transaction.

The need for some services that are provided on a recurring basis by the same vendor, such as utilities, telephone, periodicals, or janitorial services, is usually determined initially and not redetermined until the end of the contract period.

Determining the need for certain other services, such as legal and auditing services, may be done without the existence of formal, specified procedures.

Needs for fixed assets are usually identified by engineers, planners, capital budgeters, or executives.

The purpose of control over requisitions is operational; it provides a means of collecting and documenting needed information so that requests can be efficiently processed. Requisitions may be prenumbered so that they are not lost. This may appear on the surface to be an accounting control, but it is not. The control task of authorization, which is where accounting control is initiated, takes place at a later stage in the processing. Approval of requisitions is usually exercised by a supervisor having responsibility for the type of purchase.

Strong controls over requisitioning are important to minimize the danger of overstocking—tying up cash and holding assets that may become obsolete or, less frequently, wasting cash through buying unnecessary services. Control can be exercised only by determining the optimum inventory level or purchase quantities and establishing them as the operational goal: examples are determination of economic order quantities and stock reorder points, and cost justification procedures for unusual expenditure requests.

Ordering. Preferred practice is to have a trained purchasing agent rather than personnel from user departments shop for sources, negotiate terms, and place orders. The separate purchasing function has become so well recognized as increasing the efficiency and effectiveness of a modern business that a purchasing department is considered essential for every enterprise of any significant size. Controls within the purchasing department comprise principally systemization through explicit, detailed procedures and supervision of purchasing personnel.

The purchasing department receives requisitions and establishes control over them. The handling of requisitions prior to actually placing purchase orders is a subject in itself—specialized skill or experience is needed for the most efficient grouping of items, concentration of orders to obtain volume discounts while also maintaining multiple sources of supply, effective bid solicitation, negotiating schedules for vendor production and storage prior to delivery, and all the other ramifications of getting the best possible prices and services. It is a skill easily neglected or abused, as the cost of inefficient purchasing is not separately measured and merely adds to the cost of items acquired.

The purchase order is the execution instruction that authorizes a vendor to deliver and bill on certain terms. It should be complete and specific as to delivery time, routing, and quality of materials as well as number and price; otherwise those terms are dictated by the supplier. The purchase order in well-organized systems also authorizes the receiving department to accept the goods described. Since the purchase order authorizes execution of transactions, control over the issuance of purchase orders is of great importance.

The accounting controls over purchase orders consist of some or all of the following:

Checking for completeness, for example, by prenumbering of purchase orders and subsequent accounting for all numbers.

Checking for accuracy, for example, by reviewing purchase order preparation, including data transcribed from requisitions and master files of data on vendors, prices, etc.; extensions and footings; and account distribution. That review can be mechanized in part: prices can be compared with standards or averages based on past experience, or purchase orders with small dollar amounts or routine characteristics can be mechanically passed for less detailed review.

Segregation of the functions of accounting and receiving so that they are independent of the purchasing function and of one another and can therefore serve as a control mechanism. Additionally, in some systems requisitioners receive copies of the purchase orders; their review for conformity with expectations constitutes a disciplinary control.

Some specialized goods and services cannot be handled by a purchasing department because the technical and performance requirements are too esoteric, or in some cases cannot be specified in advance. Such purchases must be negotiated directly between the ultimate user and the vendor. That situation is likely to be a persistent and sometimes highly sensitive problem for most companies because of the conflict between overall organizational, operational, and fiscal control, which calls for a centralized purchasing function, and the desires of individual users, almost all of whom are likely to believe that they can get better quality and service by dealing directly with vendors. Deciding where to draw the line between operational autonomy and organizational efficiency varies from company to company, but even in extreme situations some specialized services are allowed to bypass the purchasing function. In those cases, adequate accounting control is provided by requiring agreements to be in writing, checking on the receipt of goods, and requiring the user to approve the invoices.

Receiving, Inspecting, and Accepting.   Most enterprises receive a volume and variety of goods and are required to give written evidence of receipt of them on delivery; thus, companies must have an organized means for doing so, even if it consists only of informal instructions to the persons who are likely to accept delivery. The receiving function should be organized to serve control purposes and in most modern businesses it is. In companies engaged in production and distribution, the volume of receiving is so large that the receiving function is carried out in a specially organized department separate from the requisitioning, purchasing, and accounting departments.

The receiving function should inspect goods for conformity with specifications on purchase orders. Quantities should be verified by counting, weighing, or measuring. Some systems provide for omitting quantities from the copy of the purchase order sent to the receiving department, to improve the likelihood of independent verification or count of quantities; other companies believe this technique is inefficient or easily bypassed. One way to discover a failure to record part of a receipt is the subsequent follow-up of differences between the receiving report and the vendor's invoice or purchase order. In the process of verifying quantities, the receivers should also verify quality of goods insofar as possible, including freedom from shipping damage. If laboratory or technical analysis of the goods is necessary to verify quality, having a sample analyzed and subsequently distributing reports of the results are an extension or subroutine of the receiving function. In some cases, determining that the quality of goods meets expectations requires specialized technical skills and is assigned to an appropriately staffed inspection department.

Receipt and acceptance of a shipment must be reported to the purchasing and accounting departments, usually through copies of the receiving report identifying the vendor, date received, quantity of goods received and their condition, and sometimes the carrier.

Receiving is primarily a physical rather than a data processing function, and thus controls within the function are largely supervisory. Segregation of the receiving function from those of ordering and accounting also enhances the discipline of the system.

Sometimes services and, less frequently, goods do not arrive through the receiving department but are sent directly to the location where they will be used. While formal procedures may be prescribed for users to originate receiving reports, more often the vendor's invoice for the service or goods is forwarded to the user for approval and acknowledgment of receipt.

Storing or Using. Once received, goods must be forwarded to the appropriate location. In most companies the volume of receipts requires locating the facilities for storage of purchased goods close to the receiving department. Controls over storage and issuance of purchased goods are also covered in the payments cycle. The requisitioning department should compare the goods physically received with its file copy of the original requisition. Some systems call for forwarding evidence of that comparison to the accounting department before the invoice is approved for payment.

Recording. An asset or expense and the related liability are most often recorded in the accounts on the basis of a vendor's invoice for goods or services. Sometimes detailed inventory records are posted from the receiving report when it is forwarded to the accounting department, while the control accounts are posted later. Authorization for recording can be routinized: a clerk can be authorized to record invoices that are validated, that is, properly approved by an authorized representative of the requisitioning department, or invoices that match related purchase orders and receiving reports as to quantities, prices, and other terms.

Failure to establish control over vendors' invoices early in the process is a common control weakness that can have especially negative consequences if many invoices must be routed for approval to operating personnel whose main interests are directed elsewhere. Unless the flow of invoices can be controlled, it is advisable to establish documentation and numerical control by some means such as immediate entry in an invoice or a "pre-voucher" register listing the vendor's name, amount of the invoice, voucher number assigned, and department to which forwarded.

Once invoices have been authorized, the recording process consists of, first, recording the correct amount in the proper account and period, and second, correctly summarizing and posting the records. A clerk should check the arithmetic on the invoices, either by recomputing it or comparing it with purchase orders to verify the amount. The accounting distribution must be double-checked and entered (sometimes an initial entry is made on the purchase order). A clerk should also check that invoices are recorded in the proper period.

Supervision over the clerical processes of authorization and recording is exercised by review and approval of transactions by a responsible, knowledgeable individual. Invoices should be approved by supervisors prior to drawing checks for payment; a further review of supporting documents takes place when the check is signed.

Summarization and posting can consist of manual entry in a voucher register from which totals are posted to ledgers, or conversion of invoice data to machine or computer input. In either event, control over the completeness of processing is provided by double-checking the entry or conversion, by comparing batch or control totals, or by checking the footings. Assigning numbers to the invoices early in the recording process, subsequently accounting for the sequence of numbers, and periodically reviewing open files of items awaiting processing also serve as completeness controls over the omission of items from the recording process.

Discipline over the summarizing and posting process is provided primarily by supervisory review of reconciliations, trial balances, and open file follow-up. Segregating the duties of those who prepare vouchers, approve them, post the detailed inventory and accounts payable records, maintain control accounts, and make the reconciliations and follow-up also enhances discipline.

Payment. Accounting controls over the cash disbursements process are organized to provide all practicable and reasonable assurance that no unauthorized payments are made, accurate records are made of each payment, and unclaimed items are adequately identified, controlled, and ultimately cancelled. Operational controls should be organized to ensure that all liabilities are paid on time.

Basic controls to prevent unauthorized payments consist of requiring valid support for all requests for payment plus various measures, such as cancellation, to prevent reprocessing of documents a second time. Persons who prepare checks should not have conflicting duties, such as originating requests for payment. Signed checks should be mailed by the signer or processed in a way that makes them inaccessible to the persons who authorize payment; unissued checks should be safeguarded; authorizing documents should be cancelled after they have been used; the final approving authority, usually the signer of the check, should have evidence of the authorization, propriety, and processing of supporting documents.

Even if the number of employees is limited and the same person performs duties that are by nature incompatible from an internal control viewpoint, some benefit can be derived by involving the supervisor in the processing. For example, sometimes the same person records and draws checks to pay vendors. In this situation, the supervisor who signs the checks should require that all supporting evidence accompany the checks presented for signature and should see that someone is assigned to cancel the supporting documents and mail the checks directly to the vendors.

Operating control requires that all acknowledged liabilities be paid in time to take advantage of cash discounts, minimize controversy with suppliers, and maintain the enterprise's credit rating. Control over timely payment is provided by periodic reviews of files of unmatched receiving reports and invoices and the aging of open accounts payable.

Complete and accurate recording of payments is controlled by maintaining the numerical sequence of unused checks, maintaining a detailed check register, accounting for the numerical sequence of checks entered in the register, and comparing paid checks returned by the bank with the check register as part of the periodic reconciliation of cash in bank accounts. After appropriate inquiry into the reasons for long outstanding checks, they should be cancelled, payment stopped at the bank, and the accounts adjusted to record the items as accounts payable.

Discipline over the cash disbursements process is provided by the check signer's review of supporting documentation, and by supervisory review of bank reconciliations and follow-up of unmatched items in holding files, the accounts payable trial balance, and bank statements.

Payrolls.   Payroll processing is the one function that is most likely to be similar from one organization to another. Over the years, payroll systems have become highly organized and generally well controlled. The payroll transaction system, theoretically the same as for purchase transactions, differs importantly in practice. The functions of requisitioning and purchasing labor frequently have less significance than they do for other items because control is focused on receipt of services, recording, and payments. Another feature of this function is the withholding of amounts to cover various types of employee obligations, for example, taxes and insurance premiums, and the payment of accumulated amounts. The following paragraphs describe the controls to be expected in a typical payroll transaction processing system.

Authorization of the purchase of labor occurs, in many cases, with the approval of time and production reports. Authorization to employ and pay should be prepared independently of the immediate user (employer or supervisor) and of those responsible for preparing the payroll. Preferred modern practice is to lodge that responsibility in the personnel department, which hires employees and in the process creates records authorizing employment at a particular job or in a particular department, the rate of pay, and payroll deductions. The personnel department should also be responsible for originating termination notices. The validity of payroll transactions is controlled by using and accounting for the sequence of prenumbered employment and termination notices, and by personnel department review and approval of recorded payroll data.

Authority to pay and evidence of receipt or performance of services should be produced in the form of time reports or clock cards, which should be controlled first by supervisory review and approval. If pay is based on production rather than time, as in piece work or commissions, the quantity basis should be similarly approved and reconciled to available production or sales data that are under accounting control. Control is also facilitated by comparison of payroll costs to standards or budgets or by reconciliation to production cost or job order records.

The computation of pay can be simple or exceedingly complex; it can be done manually or in a fully mechanized way. In any event, the controls consist basically of double-checking the computation (including the rates used) or control totals derived from a separate calculation of the aggregate amount. The self-interest of employees and their ready access to the personnel department also act to limit the risk of underpayment. Normally the risk of overpayment is reduced by limit checks, for example, specifying the maximum amount of a payroll check.

Accounting distribution for financial purposes is not ordinarily difficult to control because the wages of most employees are charged to the same account from one period to another. Accounting distribution for detailed cost accounting systems may call for allocation of pay among cost centers; in those cases, control is usually exercised by the use of control totals. The accuracy of the allocation may be checked by the investigation of differences revealed by variance analysis.

The computation of payroll deductions is governed either by statute (in the case of payroll taxes) or contract (union agreement, group insurance contract, or agency agreements with charitable organizations or credit unions). The authorization to make deductions from an individual's pay is given by the employee and is ordinarily obtained by the personnel department. Cumulative records of deductions are required for each employee, and the posting to the cumulative records acts as a control total for comparison to the amounts withheld from each payroll. Control over payments of withheld amounts is similar to control over payments of accounts payable.

Payment of net pay is usually by check, most often prepared as an integral part of the computation procedure. Segregation of duties related to payroll disbursements made by check should be the same as over other cash disbursements. If the checks are distributed rather than mailed, it is important to segregate duties. For example, employees' checks should be distributed by persons who do not have responsibility for approving the payroll.

Cash payrolls, once common, are becoming a rarity, primarily because of the additional costs required in maintaining control over currency and the increasing availability of personal banking. The handling of cash payrolls can be turned over to specialized contracting agencies. If a cash payroll is handled by the company, each payroll should be accounted for on an imprest basis. The required denominations of currency and coin should be pre-tallied; preparation of pay envelopes should consume all the currency drawn for that purpose, and the pay envelopes should be totalled after preparation for balancing to the imprest total.

Pay envelopes should be controlled until turned over to employees in exchange for signed receipts. The pay should be distributed by persons without conflicting duties. The signed receipts and unclaimed pay envelopes should be promptly reconciled when the distribution is complete. Unclaimed amounts should be listed at once, kept under control, and returned to cash if unclaimed within a short period of time.

In most organizations, the recognized advantages of separation of duties are not difficult to achieve. In the accounts payable system, the duties of purchasing, receiving, recording, and paying are separated as a matter of operational logic and efficiency as well as good accounting control. Similarly in the case of payroll, the duties of the personnel and accounting departments are separated, and the person who approves payrolls is independent of both departments.

Returns, Credits, and Claims.   Every claim due an enterprise, either because goods were returned or because something about the purchase was unsatisfactory and an allowance was negotiated, is an asset equivalent to a receivable. It is important therefore that claims be controlled. That is easier said than done, however, because some claims are likely to be non-routine, infrequent, and random, thus making them difficult to systematize.

Returns have to be prepared for shipping back to the vendor, and thus the shipping department should have a routine for originating controlled notification to the accounts payable and purchasing departments at the time items are returned. Control can be exercised through a subsystem similar to that used in controlling sales. Control of freight claims can usually be similarly achieved.

Claims for allowances, adjustments, and occasional returns that are not subject to the above procedures should be subject to a procedure for notifying the accounting and purchasing departments of a dispute or claim found to be due. Since no effective means exist for controlling compliance with that type of routine, periodic inquiry of all knowledgeable people throughout the company should be made as to the existence of outstanding claims or allowances which should be compared with what has been recorded.

Internal Control in Computer Systems

What follows is a summary of the processing procedures employed in a computer environment for four components of the payments cycle: order processing, goods received processing, accounts payable processing, and payments to creditors. This summary also discusses how control is achieved through a combination of approval of data entered in the system, use of approved programs and operating procedures, and the investigation and follow-up of exceptions printed out by the computer.

Order Processing.   Purchase orders are either input or initiated by the computer. The computer typically initiates orders, using an approved program, by comparing the stock balance with a pre-established minimum stock level held as standing data on the inventory file. Sometimes the computer will calculate a value of orders input, or initiated, by reference to prices input or price data held on a controlled master price file. Orders input, or initiated and printed by the computer, will be written to a computer file called a pipeline file, which is a temporary record that normally holds only transaction data, such as outstanding purchase orders. A record of transactions can be produced for, among other uses, the control purposes described below.

Open orders remain on the pipeline file until matched with the details of goods received. The pipeline file is read periodically and information on orders that have been outstanding for a predetermined period and have not been filled is printed out. If values are recorded for orders, the value of outstanding purchase commitments can be summarized and printed out. Printouts should be reviewed periodically to identify vendors who are not meeting delivery schedules. This review and follow-up may also reveal goods received but not recorded.

Goods Received Processing.   Properly approved goods received details are input and, if order processing is also by computer, matched with the order record on the pipeline file. When matched, it is usual for an indicator to be set on the record noting that the goods have been received. When order processing is not by computer, the approved goods received data are written to the pipeline file, and normally a summary record is produced for control purposes. The computer commonly calculates the value of goods received, if this has not already been done. Normally, this calculation is made by reference to prices held as standing data on a controlled master file.

Goods received data remain on the pipeline file until matched with the suppliers' invoice details (see below). At the time of matching, if the goods received are recorded at standard costs, the computer may calculate the price variance. Price variances should periodically be reported for review. The pipeline file is read periodically and goods received but not matched with suppliers' invoices (outstanding receipts) for a given period are printed out. This printout should also be reviewed and unmatched items investigated. The review and follow-up of these items is a control to identify unrecorded liabilities. If values are entered for goods received, the computer can calculate and print out the amount of the possible total accrued liability.

Accounts Payable Processing.   The accounts payable file, illustrated in Exhibit 6, is updated by both transaction data and standing data. The main types of transaction data are suppliers' invoices, adjustments, and details of cash paid. If goods received processing is by computer and suppliers' invoices are matched with goods received records, a facility for accepting invoices relating to items for which a receiving report is not prepared, for example, services, must be incorporated into the system. This can be achieved by including an indicator on the relevant invoices that the computer recognizes as an instruction to bypass the pipeline file, for example, of receiving reports, for those items. Those items should be printed out and investigated for validity and authorization.

Adjustments will always be necessary to correct mispostings revealed by user controls. They may also be needed for other purposes, for example, to facilitate quick payment of suppliers' invoices to ensure that allowable cash discounts are taken. An adjustment is then made to the accounts payable file to record the discount taken. Adjustments should be listed so they can be investigated and approved by an appropriate individual.

Payments to Creditors.   Any accounting system for purchasing may include computer involvement in the payment of creditors. This includes all instances in which the computer selects items for payment. As a result of the selection, the computer may produce:

1. Details from which checks are manually or mechanically prepared;
2. Checks for manual or mechanical signature; or
3. Pre-signed checks.

The computer also normally prints out remittance advices showing the details of payments. The usual selection criteria are date and, less frequently, discount indicators. The computer compares the dates on invoices with a date input as a constant and selects specified items, for ex-

Description	Number of Characters
Supplier details	
1 Supplier number	6
2 Supplier name	15
3 Date opened	6
4 Date last amended	6
5 Address line 1	20
6 Address line 2	20
7 Address line 3	20
8 Check limit	4
9 Terms	4
10 Value outstanding—credit	6
11 Value outstanding—debit	6
12 Payment due week 1	6
13 Payment due week 2	6
14 Payment due week 3	6
15 Payment due week 4	6
16 Check name	20
17 Bank code	10
18 Total value invoices year to date	8
19 Total value invoices previous years	8
	183

Description	Number of Characters
Transaction details—may be repeated 30 times	
20 Transaction type	2
21 Date of transaction	6
22 Transaction number	6
23 Order number	6
24 Invoice amount	8
25 Discount on invoice	4
26 Nominal ledger code	6
27 Stock reference number	8
28 Payment date	6
29 Payment indicator	1
	53

Exhibit 6.   Accounts Payable Ledger—File Layout.

ample, all invoices more than four weeks old. The computer may be programmed to recognize an indicator on invoices that means that a discount is available if payment is prompt. The computer may also be programmed to calculate discounts by reference to discount terms held as standing data. However, the processing of invoices by computer for early payment can be complex, and invoices of this nature are often diverted on receipt for separate manual payment. Manually produced checks may also be required for other purposes; the details of such payments would be input as adjustments. Manual preparation requires the controls described in the first part of this chapter.

The method by which details of cash paid are updated depends on whether items are selected for payment manually or by computer. If items are selected by people, the details of items paid have to be input and updated in the same manner as suppliers' invoices. The computer may select items based on either the account number alone or the account number, invoice number, and value. If the computer selects items for payment, the details are normally updated at the time of selection. The methods of selection were described above. Any manual changes to items selected are input and updated as adjustments and should be appropriately approved.

Suppliers' invoices and adjustments are summarized and categorized for posting to the general and cost ledgers. These summaries may be printed out or written to a file for direct input into a general ledger computer application. If the processing of the general and cost ledgers is integrated with accounts payable processing, updating may be simultaneous.

Amendments to standing data are needed to open and close suppliers' accounts and alter the various standing data files. The file layout in Exhibit 6 illustrates the wide variety of data that may be held and for which amendment routines may be necessary. A listing of standing data amendments is normally produced and should be reviewed for appropriateness and approved by a knowledgeable individual.

During updating of the accounts payable file, the computer normally summarizes the items or balances and produces information for control purposes. Details of balances and exception reports, for example, lists of debit balances, may also be produced. Exception reports should be reviewed and investigated.

Evaluation of Internal Control

As discussed earlier, the evaluation process is enhanced through the use of an Internal Control Questionnaire that specifies control objectives and related control tasks and an accompanying Reference Manual that explains the questions in the ICQ and describes the effects of accounting control weaknesses.

The portions of those two documents relating to control objective no. 1 in the payments cycle, for both non-computer and computer systems, are reproduced below. The remainder of the questionnaire and manual for the payments cycle is found in Appendices C and D. Each control objective in the questionnaire is followed by a series of questions; a "Yes" answer indicates the existence of a control, which, in the case of accounting controls, management may want to confirm by a functional test, and a "No" answer indicates the absence of a control. Questions in gray shading relate to operational controls. For each accounting control, the manual explains the purpose of the question, followed by a discussion of what constitutes adequate control procedures and the possible effects of the absence of the procedures.

NON-COMPUTER SYSTEMS ICQ

Control Objective

1. Purchases should be initiated only on the basis of appropriate authorizations and records of commitments should be maintained as a basis for:
   (a) determining that transactions are executed in accordance with authorizations;
   (b) establishing the amount of any provision required for losses arising from unfulfilled commitments.

Purchase Authorizations

QUESTION 1.1

Are all significant purchase commitments and changes thereto initiated only on the basis of appropriate written authorizations?

Purpose

To determine whether the company's system is such that significant purchase commitments are initiated only if supported by an appropriately approved authorization.

What Constitutes Adequate Control Procedures?

If	Impact on Adequacy of Control	Example
1. The company initiates *all* purchase commitments and changes thereto only on the basis of appropriate written authorizations,	Control is satisfactory because all purchase commitments are appropriately authorized.	All purchase orders are prepared from purchase requisitions authorized by departmental heads.

	Control will be adequate if:	The company requires authorized purchase requisitions for all purchases over $1,000. This policy has been approved by the vice president, operations and the controller.
2. Only purchase commitments over a specified monetary amount are authorized in writing,	(a) The specified amount has been approved by a responsible official;	
	(b) The specified amount is reasonable (if it is too high, significant purchase commitments may be made without appropriate authorization).	
3. Company initiates purchase commitments for goods only (i.e., not services) on the basis of appropriate written authorization,	The reviewer should evaluate the materiality of purchase commitments for services. It is unlikely that a material purchase commitment or loss thereon would arise from services.	Orders for maintenance services are oral, but these costs are payable monthly and are renegotiated at regular intervals.

Possible Errors in Financial Statements	Example	Effect on Audit Procedures
If: Significant purchase commitments are not authorized in writing,		
Because there is no control to ensure that all purchases are reviewed and authorized by a responsible official, the company may be committed to purchases at prices that will result in a loss or assets may be purchased in excess of requirements. As a result, net income may be overstated and liabilities (provision for losses) understated.	The purchase price in an authorized purchase commitment exceeds the current market price for that item. The resulting loss will result in an understatement of a liability for losses and an overstatement of net income if the correcting entry is not made.	1. When reviewing open purchase commitments for possible losses, the auditor should pay particular attention to commitments that were not appropriately authorized. 2. The auditor should consider this weakness in determining the extent of his review of slow-moving or obsolete inventory.

QUESTION 1.2

With respect to repetitively used articles, is there an attempt to reduce the volume of purchase authorizations by means of a systematic stocking program?

QUESTION 1.3

When there is a stocking program for repetitively used articles, are purchase authorizations initiated on a basis of one of the following techniques:

(a) calculations incorporating lead time and safety stock considerations;
(b) stock status ordering when availability reaches zero, or,
(c) period planning?

QUESTION 1.4

In deciding how much to buy, are economic order quantities calculated?

QUESTION 1.5

Do purchase authorizations indicate when material will be required?

QUESTION 1.6

Are purchase authorizations submitted to the purchasing agent with enough lead time so he can properly "shop the market"?

QUESTION 1.7

Do purchase authorizations contain technical and performance specifications so the purchasing agent knows exactly what to buy?

Purchasing Function

QUESTION 1.8

Does the purchasing function have:

(a) an organization chart;
(b) job descriptions;
(c) clear-cut buying assignments?

QUESTION 1.9

Is there a statement of purchasing policies which covers:

(a) corporate relationships, particularly buying responsibilities;
(b) competitive buying, source selection, and bidding;
(c) maintenance of multiple buying sources to protect the continuity of supply;
(d) rules on commitments and contracts;
(e) reciprocity;
(f) conflict of interest?

QUESTION 1.10

Where the purchasing function is decentralized, is there coordination as to what is bought at each location so that the various locations do not compete with each other and purchasing power is maximized?

QUESTION 1.11

Does the purchasing organization endeavor to bring purchasing power to bear via:

(a) nationwide buying contracts;
(b) blanket purchase commitments?

QUESTION 1.12

Does the purchasing agent actively solicit competitive bids from suppliers?

QUESTION 1.13

Are supplier negotiations facilitated by providing purchasing personnel with summaries of:

(a) commodity buying volumes;
(b) supplier buying volumes?

QUESTION 1.14

Does the purchasing agent participate in:

(a) standardization;
(b) value analysis;
(c) lease vs. buy analysis;
(d) negotiating options to purchase in lease agreements?

QUESTION 1.15

Does the purchasing agent have an orderly plan to insure the delivery of materials within the time specified on purchase commitments?

Does the purchasing agent maintain supplier evaluation files to determine the adequacy of suppliers' delivery, quality, and cost performances?

Initial Recording of Commitments

QUESTION 1.17

Are the purchase commitments referred to in 1.1 recorded in written form?

Purpose

To determine whether there is a record of purchase commitments that can be used in processing invoices and reviewing for possible losses.

What Constitutes Adequate Control Procedures?

If	Impact on Adequacy of Control	Example
1. All purchase commitments are recorded in written form,	Control is satisfactory.	All purchase requisitions are forwarded to a central purchasing department where a purchase order is completed and sent to the supplier. Retained copies of the purchase order serve as the company's record of purchase commitments.

If	Impact on Adequacy of Control	Example
2. Only purchase commitments over a specific monetary amount are recorded in writing,	Control will be adequate if: (a) The specified amount has been approved by a responsible official; (b) The specified amount is reasonable (if it is too high, significant purchase commitments may be made and not recorded); (c) Other controls indicate that all commitments over the specified amount are recorded.	(a) and (b) The company prepares purchase orders for all orders over $1,000. This policy has been approved by the controller. (c) In checking purchase invoices, the invoice clerk is required to check prices to approved purchase orders rather than price lists for all invoices that exceed $1,000. Invoices in excess of $1,000 for which purchase orders cannot be located are reported to the controller for follow-up.

Possible Errors in Financial Statements	Example	Effect on Audit Procedures
If: Purchase commitments are not recorded in written form,		
Income may be overstated and liabilities (provision for losses) may be understated. The company cannot determine if it is committed to purchase at more than current prices or in excess of requirements which may result in a loss to the company.	Because of a decline in raw material prices, the company has significant losses arising from firm purchase orders placed at a higher price.	In order to identify unrecorded purchase commitments at year-end, the auditor should: (a) Review the steps taken by management to identify significant purchase commitments;

(b) Request from major suppliers details of any purchase commitments outstanding as of year-end;

(c) Review selected invoices received after year-end for evidence of purchases at more than prevailing price in quantities in excess of current requirements, or of goods determined to be slow-moving or obsolete.

QUESTION 1.18

Do the commitment records state, insofar as is practicable:

(a) **quantities;**
(b) **prices;**
(c) **other relevant terms (e.g., discounts, freight terms)?**

Purpose

To determine whether the written commitments have sufficient detail to:

(a) Enable adequate checks to be made at a later date (e.g., checking of supplier's invoice);
(b) Facilitate the determination of any provisions for losses that may be required; and
(c) Determine, where appropriate, the amount of purchase commitments for disclosure in the notes to the financial statements.

143

What Constitutes Adequate Control Procedures?

If	Impact on Adequacy of Control	Example
The company's commitment records state quantities, prices and other relevant terms,	Control is satisfactory because data are available for subsequent accounting use.	Purchase orders include supplier's name and address, quantity ordered, price, and supplier's freight and discount terms.

Possible Errors in Financial Statements	Example	Effect on Audit Procedures
If: The commitment records do not state all the information set out in the question,		
1. Income may be overstated and liabilities (provision for losses) understated because losses inherent in certain commitments cannot be identified or recorded.	A purchase order is prepared with quantities only, although a unit price was also agreed. The price has declined since the order was placed.	The auditor should: (a) Request suppliers to report agreed prices for significant purchase commitments, particularly where there have been recent price declines; (b) Review suppliers' invoices received after year-end for indication of purchases at more than the prevailing price.
2. The company has no means of checking the validity of supplier's invoice prices with original commitments.	The purchase order includes quantities only.	In determining the extent of his lower of cost or market inventory tests, the auditor should keep in mind that the company is more likely to have overpaid for purchases in these circumstances.

Do the commitment records state, insofar as is practicable:

(d) **routing;**
(e) **sales tax returns;**
(f) **delivery dates and instructions;**
(g) **required testing procedures?**

QUESTION 1.19

Is the routing for purchase commitments furnished to the purchasing agent by qualified traffic personnel?

QUESTION 1.20

Are the commitments controlled in such a way that it can subsequently be established that they have all been accounted for (e.g., by sequential pre-numbering, by entry in a register or by establishment of batch totals)?

Purpose

1. To determine whether the company's procedures for recording purchase commitments are such that it *can* determine whether all such commitments have been accounted for. Thus, if the documentation for controlling them exists (e.g., purchase orders are pre-numbered), the auditor may be able to use it to reduce the amount of audit work otherwise required in situations where the company can, but does not, account for unmatched purchase commitments.

2. Note that the question is not whether commitments *are* in fact accounted for. Thus, if the documentation for controlling them exists (e.g., purchase orders are pre-numbered), the auditor may be able to use it to reduce the amount of audit work otherwise required in situations where the company can, but does not, account for unmatched purchase commitments.

What Constitutes Adequate Control Procedures?

This question deals with one of the controls over completeness of processing. Refer to the discussion under that heading on page 362, in Appendix D.

145

Possible Errors in Financial Statements	Example	Effect on Audit Procedures
If: It cannot subsequently be established that all transactions have been accounted for,		
Income may be overstated and liabilities (provision for losses) understated because losses inherent in certain purchase commitments cannot be identified or recorded.	Provisions for losses on open purchase commitments are based on unmatched purchase orders that are not pre-numbered. The company has removed all loss purchase orders from the open file and has not made the required provision.	The auditor should perform the procedures set out in Question 1.17.

Record of Unfulfilled Commitments

QUESTION 1.21

Are records maintained of commitments that have not been matched with receiving reports or equivalent records of goods or services received?

Purpose

1. To determine whether the company maintains adequate records of purchase commitments that have not been matched with receipts in order to determine the amount of unfulfilled commitments and any provision for losses arising therefrom.

2. Note that if Question 1.20 is answered "no," this question should also be answered "no."

3. Where sequentially pre-numbered forms are used, this question is inter-related with Question 1.22 and should be answered similarly. The records in Question 1.21 will not be adequate unless the control in Question 1.22 operates.

What Constitutes Adequate Control Procedures?

This question deals with one of the controls over completeness of processing. Refer to the discussion under that heading on page 362, in Appendix D.

Possible Errors in Financial Statements	Example	Effect on Audit Procedures
If: The company does not maintain adequate records of unmatched purchase orders,		
Income may be overstated and liabilities (provision for losses) understated because losses inherent in certain purchase commitments cannot be identified or recorded. (Same as Question 1.20.)	The company does not maintain a file of unmatched purchase commitments. Potential losses cannot be identified.	1. If the company does not control the transactions, but the documentation is such that the transactions could be controlled (e.g., documents are pre-numbered but not accounted for), the auditor may be able to use those records to determine whether there are any unmatched purchase orders at year-end. 2. If the auditor is not able to establish the missing control himself, or if it is more efficient not to do so, he should perform the procedures set out in Question 1.17.

QUESTION 1.22

Where sequentially pre-numbered forms or batch totals are used (1.20), are the numbers accounted for or the batch totals reconciled as part of the control procedure over unmatched commitments (1.21)?

Purpose

1. To determine whether all purchase orders have been accounted for when establishing the related entries for unmatched items. This question is inter-related with Question 1.21 and should be answered similarly.

2. The control question refers to batch totals; however, the use of this procedure to account for purchase commitments is not common in practice.

What Constitutes Adequate Control Procedures?

This question deals with one of the controls over completeness of processing. Refer to the discussion under that heading on page 362, in Appendix D.

Possible Errors in Financial Statements	Example	Effect on Audit Procedures
If: Sequentially pre-numbered forms are not accounted for,		
Income may be overstated and liabilities (provision for losses) understated because the company does not control transactions even though it is possible to do so. (Similar to Question 1.20.)	Pre-numbered purchase orders are filed by supplier rather than numerically. Unmatched documents can be removed without being detected.	The auditor should follow the procedures set out in Question 1.21.

148

QUESTION 1.23

Are unmatched commitments (1.21) reviewed on a regular basis, e.g., monthly, to determine the reasons for any that have not been matched within a reasonable period of time?

Purpose

Since unmatched purchase commitments outstanding beyond a reasonable period of time may indicate a breakdown in the matching procedures, the company should review them on a regular basis.

What Constitutes Adequate Control Procedures?

This question deals with one of the controls over completeness of processing. Refer to the discussion under that heading on page 362, in Appendix D.

Possible Errors in Financial Statements	Example	Effect on Audit Procedures
If: The unmatched commitments are not reviewed,		
Losses arising from purchase commitments may be overstated because purchase orders for completed transactions may not have been removed from the open file.	(a) The related invoice was paid, but the purchase order was not removed from the file. (b) The supplier's invoice was not forwarded to the accounting department because of a dispute, e.g., the price charged.	The auditor should either arrange for the company to institute the review procedure or perform it himself at year-end.

149

QUESTION 1.24

Is the review in 1.23 carried out by persons other than those who maintain the records of unmatched commitments (1.21)?

Purpose

To determine whether the review of unmatched purchase commitments can be relied upon because the reviewer has no incompatible duties.

What Constitutes Adequate Control Procedures?

This question deals with one of the controls over completeness of processing. Refer to the discussion under that heading on page 362, in Appendix D.

Possible Errors in Financial Statements	Example	Effect on Audit Procedures
If: The review is performed by the person who maintains the records of unmatched purchase commitments,		
Losses arising from purchase commitments may be overstated. (Same as Question 1.23.)	The recordkeeper's review reveals some purchase orders that he failed to remove upon receipt of goods and others with an uncertain status. He does not report or investigate them because he does not want his superior to know about them.	The auditor should reperform the review himself by either: (a) Performing an extensive review at an interim date with a lesser review at year-end; or (b) Performing an extensive review at year-end. This review should detect all invalid unmatched items, assuming records of unmatched purchase commitments are adequate. (Questions 1.21 and 1.22.)

QUESTION 1.25

Are the results of the procedures in 1.23 reviewed and approved by a responsible official?

Purpose

To determine whether such a review is performed. The review helps to ensure that the basic control is exercised regularly and effectively.

What Constitutes Adequate Control Procedures?

This question deals with the controls for supervisory review and approval. Refer to the discussion under that heading on page 374, in Appendix D.

Possible Errors in Financial Statements	Example	Effect on Audit Procedures
If: The supervisory control is absent,		
Losses arising from purchase commitments may be overstated because, in the absence of supervisory control, unmatched commitments may not be reviewed at all. (Similar to Question 1.23.)	The person performing the review learns that no follow-up action is taken by the supervisor. The person then stops performing the review.	To determine whether the related basic and division of duties controls have continued to operate properly, the auditor should perform the supervisory review at year-end. Refer to the common control procedure for supervisory review and approval (page 374) for guidance as to the procedures to follow.

151

COMPUTER SYSTEMS ICQ

Control Objective

1. Purchases should be initiated only on the basis of appropriate authorizations and records of commitments should be maintained as a basis for:
   a. determining that transactions are executed in accordance with authorizations;
   b. establishing the amount of any provision required for losses arising from unfulfilled commitments.

Purchase Authorization

1.1 Are all significant purchase commitments and changes thereto initiated only on the basis of appropriate written authorizations?
1.2 Are the purchase commitments referred to in 1.1 recorded in written form?
1.3 Do the commitments records state, insofar as is practicable:
   a. quantities;
   b. prices;
   c. other relevant terms (e.g., discounts, freight terms)?

Completeness of Input and Updating

Specify below the principal control that all details of purchase commitments and changes thereto are input to the computer and updated. If the principal control is:
   a. computer sequence check of serially numbered input documents, answer questions 1.4 to 1.9;
   b. agreement of manually established batch totals, specify totals used and answer questions 1.10 to 1.14.

Computer Sequence Check

1.4 Are there adequate controls to ensure that all transactions are recorded on a serially numbered document?
1.5 Is the method used in the program for the checking of numerical sequence appropriate (e.g., does accommodate changes in sequence and more than one sequence running at a time)?
1.6 Is a printout of missing documents produced at regular intervals (e.g., weekly)?
1.7 Is a total of accepted items accumulated by the computer during the sequence check run agreed to the total of items written to the purchase commitment file or, alternatively, are such totals carried through intermediate processing (including summarization of totals or changes in the totals used) so that it is established that all accepted input items are updated to the purchase commitment file?
1.8 Is the reconciliation of totals in 1.7 carried out manually or, alternatively, is the reconciliation carried out by the computer with adequate evidence of this check being printed out?

1.9 Are there adequate procedures for:
   a. investigation of missing documents (1.6);
   b. investigation and correction of differences disclosed by the update reconciliations (1.8)?

Batch Totals
1.10 Are there adequate controls to ensure that:
   a. a document is created for all purchase commitments;
   b. all documents are included in a batch;
   c. all batches are submitted for processing?
1.11 Are the totals of individual items accepted by the computer compared manually to pre-determined control totals or, alternatively, is such a comparison made by the computer with adequate evidence of the operation being printed out?
1.12 Are the totals in 1.11 agreed to the total of items written to the purchase commitment file or, alternatively, such totals carried through intermediate processing (including summarization of totals or changes in the totals used) so that it is established that all accepted input items are updated to the purchase commitment file?
1.13 Is the reconciliation of totals in 1.12 carried out manually or, alternatively, is the reconciliation carried out by the computer with adequate evidence of this operation being printed out?
1.14 Are there adequate procedures for:
   a. investigation and correction of differences disclosed by the input reconciliations (1.11);
   b. resubmission of all rejections;
   c. investigation and correction of differences disclosed by the update reconciliations (1.13)?

Disciplines Over Basic Input Completeness and Updating Controls
1.15 Are the following procedures either performed or checked by persons other than those involved in computer operations:
   a. investigation of missing documents (1.9(a));
   b. manual agreement of input totals (1.11);
   c. investigation and correction of differences disclosed by the input reconciliations (1.14(a));
   d. resubmission of all rejections (1.14(b));
   e. manual agreement of update totals (1.8, 1.13);
   f. investigation and correction of differences disclosed by the update reconciliations (1.9(b), 1.14(c))?
1.16 Are the results of the following procedures reviewed and approved by a responsible official:
   a. investigation of missing documents (1.9(a));
   b. manual agreement of input totals (1.11);
   c. investigation and correction of differences disclosed by the input reconciliations (1.14(a));

   d.   resubmission of all rejections (1.14(b));

   e.   manual agreement of update totals (1.8, 1.13);

   f.   investigation and correction of differences disclosed by the update reconciliations (1.9(b), 1.14(c))?

Accuracy of Input and Updating

1.17 Are there adequate controls to ensure that the following fields are accurately input and updated (e.g., batch totals, edit checks in program, reporting of nonmatched items):

   a.   quantity/value;

   b.   inventory/vendor reference fields;

   c.   date;

   d.   price?

1.18 Are there adequate procedures for:

   a.   the agreement of totals, where applicable;

   b.   investigation and correction of differences or exceptions?

1.19 Are the following procedures either performed or checked by persons other than those involved in computer operations:

   a.   agreement of totals, where applicable (1.18(a));

   b.   investigation and correction of differences or exceptions (1.18(b))?

1.20 Are the results of the following procedures reviewed and approved by a responsible official:

   a.   agreement of totals, where applicable (1.18(a));

   b.   investigation and correction of differences or exceptions (1.18(b))?

Computer Generated Orders

1.21 Are the methods used in the program to generate the commitments appropriate?

1.22 Is there an adequate check over the accuracy of the commitments generated (e.g., reasonableness check, manual review of generated commitments)?

1.23 Are the results of the check (1.22) reviewed and approved by a responsible official?

1.24 Is a total (specify total used) of generated items accumulated by the computer and agreed manually with a total of items written to the purchase commitment file or, alternatively, are the totals agreed by the computer with adequate evidence of this check being printed out?

1.25 Are there adequate procedures for investigation and correction of differences disclosed by the update reconciliation (1.24)?

1.26 Are the following procedures either performed or checked by persons other than those involved in computer operations:

   a.   manual agreement of update totals (1.24);

   b.   investigation and correction of differences disclosed by the update reconciliation (1.25)?

1.27 Are the results of the following procedures reviewed and approved by the responsible official:
  a. manual agreement of update totals (1.24);
  b. investigation and correction of differences disclosed by the update reconciliation (1.25)?

Authorization
1.28 If data are authorized prior to the establishment of the controls for completeness and accuracy of input (e.g., prior to establishment of batch control totals or recording on a sequentially numbered document), are there adequate controls (e.g., checking authorization after batch control totals are established or sequentially numbered documents created) to ensure that:
  a. no unauthorized alterations are made to authorized data during subsequent processing;
  b. unauthorized data are not added;
  c. all authorized items are included in subsequent processing?

Record of Unfulfilled Commitments
1.29 If the computer evaluates purchase commitments, review the answers to the standing data controls section as regards prices and vendors, where appropriate. Are there adequate controls over:
  a. where applicable, file creation;
  b. the authorization of amendments;
  c. the completeness of writing amendments to the file;
  d. the accuracy of writing amendments to the file;
  e. the maintenance of data on file?
1.30 Is the method used in the program for the calculation of value appropriate?
1.31 Are there adequate controls over the file holding details of outstanding purchase commitments to ensure that details of purchase commitments and changes thereto are completely and adequately maintained (e.g., manual control account)?
1.32 Is the method used in the program to match goods and, where applicable, services received to purchase commitments on file appropriate (e.g., does it flag or delete matched items)?
1.33 Is a printout of items outstanding for an unreasonable length of time (e.g., over one month) produced at regular intervals?
1.34 Are unmatched commitments (1.33) reviewed on a regular basis (e.g., monthly) to determine the reason for any which have not been matched?
1.35 Are the following procedures either performed or checked by persons other than those involved in computer operations:
  a. maintenance of the outstanding purchase commitments file (1.31);
  b. review of unmatched commitments (1.34)?
1.36 Are the results of the following procedures reviewed and approved by a responsible official:
  a. maintenance of the outstanding purchase commitments file (1.31);
  b. review of unmatched commitments (1.34)?

COMPUTER SYSTEMS ICQ (continued)

Programmed Procedures

1.37   List below the programmed procedures whose continued and proper operation is not assured by user controls.

In respect of the items listed above, review the answers to the integrity controls section. Are there adequate controls to ensure that:

    a.   appropriate programmed procedures are implemented in respect of:
       (i)   where applicable, new systems;
       (ii)   program changes;
    b.   unauthorized changes cannot be made to production programs;
    c.   programmed procedures are consistently applied?

Note: See Appendix C for sections of the computer ICQ on integrity controls and standing data controls.

THE TIME CYCLE

Coverage of the Time Cycle

With some exceptions, the time cycle deals with events caused by the passage of time rather than individual transactions. The events may trigger activity on a daily basis (such as transactions involving capital stock or debt), a monthly basis (such as reconciliation of bank balances), a quarterly basis (such as identification of obsolete inventory), or a yearly basis (such as year-end adjustments arising from physical inventory counts).* The control tasks in the time cycle are generally applied periodically to groups of transactions rather than each time an individual transaction occurs. For example, procedures are generally performed periodically to verify that all revenue due from investments is received.

Many control tasks in the time cycle are aimed at revealing accumulated errors. Bank reconciliations and physical inventory counts provide data that identify errors that have accumulated since the last reconciliation or count. Significantly, many control tasks in the time cycle require a comparison of accounting data in the books with evidence generated outside the books.

The time cycle also includes custodial activities, as noted in Chapter 5. Since custodianship of one's own securities is also required, controls over transactions in capital stock and debt are included in the time cycle.

---

* Enterprises that take physical inventory counts at one time during the year should have procedures for preparing adjustments to interim financial statements based on estimates.

Finally, the time cycle encompasses the reporting process, including controls over the adjusting and closing process, the preparation of trial balances, and the preparation of internal and external reports.

Evaluation of Internal Control

The control objectives in the time cycle are found in Exhibit 7. Control tasks and accompanying explanations are not reproduced for this cycle because of space limitations.

Several of the controls in the time cycle are operational, rather than accounting, controls. They relate to organizational arrangements and procedures that monitor performance of the accounting system through analysis and reporting of the results that it produces (e.g., internal financial statements and other reports to management).

I. Custodial Activities
  A. Procedures should exist to confirm the existence of assets and compare them to the accounting records. Those procedures should cover, for example:
    1. The accuracy of bank balances,
    2. The physical existence of inventories, including those held by or for others,
    3. The physical existence of property, plant, and equipment, including that held by or for others, and
    4. The physical existence of investment securities, including those held by or for others.
  B. Procedures should exist to prevent the unauthorized use of assets no longer on the books but which may have value, such as accounts receivable written off and fully depreciated property, plant, and equipment that has been removed from the property ledger.
  C. Accurate records should be maintained for outstanding capital stock and debt obligations, and transactions in respect thereof should be under accounting control.
II. Valuation Activities
  A. Costs attributable to inventories should be accurately determined.
  B. Procedures should exist for identifying all investments, receivables, and inventories for which provisions for loss may be required.
III. Reporting Activities
  A. All valid general ledger entries, and only those entries, should be accurately recorded. Procedures should exist for:
    1. Processing all entries,
    2. Ensuring the validity of non-recurring transactions,
    3. Maintaining subsidiary ledgers, and
    4. Preparation of trial balances.
  B. All financial reports (both internal and external) should be prepared accurately and on a consistent and timely basis.

Exhibit 7.   Control Objectives in the Time Cycle.

Internal audit may provide an additional level of discipline over basic control tasks through its appraisal of the functioning of management policies, including controls. The internal audit function, as a "super" control, should itself be evaluated as part of the overall evaluation of internal control. Control objectives relating to the organization, work, and effectiveness of the internal audit function are not included in the time cycle because, as noted in Chapter 2, no formal mechanism for evaluating internal audit presently exists. Until guidelines (which are under study at the time of this writing) for evaluating the internal audit function are developed and achieve acceptance, reviews of internal audit will require tailor-made programs for a self-evaluation or an evaluation by some external group, such as the company's CPAs.

7

Reporting on Internal Control

On completing an internal control evaluation, and on an ongoing basis even before the review is finished, the system evaluator should report the findings to various levels of management for their consideration and decisions about weaknesses to be corrected. Management in turn should report on the evaluation project and its results to the board of directors or audit committee.* Furthermore, management and the board may want to inform the public about the status of the company's internal controls, and perhaps about the evaluation process, in the annual report to stockholders. There is also a strong possibility that companies registered with the SEC may be required to report publicly on their compliance with the Foreign Corrupt Practices Act, which deals in part with internal accounting controls. Finally, the requirement in SAS No. 20, "Required Communication of Material Weaknesses in Internal Accounting Control," calling for CPAs to report material internal accounting control weaknesses to management may be expanded to call for public reporting on those controls.

REPORTING CONTROL WEAKNESSES WITHIN THE COMPANY

The evaluator should be given guidance by senior-level management, with the approval of the board of directors, on the content of reports on the

---

*In the subsequent discussion, the term "board of directors" or "board" should be understood to refer to either the full board or its audit committee.

evaluation, to whom they should be addressed, and who should receive copies. This requires a decision by management and the board on who should have the authority to respond to findings of control weaknesses and who should be responsible for reviewing those responses.

An appropriate policy might be to assign initial responsibility for responding to the evaluator's findings to management at the site at which the control weakness occurs. If, however, the same weakness occurs at more than one site, the response should be made by the next higher level of management. Under this policy, control weaknesses that are pervasive would be reported to senior-level management; weaknesses affecting only one plant, at the other extreme, would be reported to plant management. Copies of all findings should go to a committee established by senior-level management to oversee the internal control evaluation. That committee should also receive copies of responses to the evaluator's findings and should review the decisions made. Alternatively, the level of management to which findings are reported could be based on the "significance" of the control weaknesses, as discussed in Chapter 3.

For each finding reported, the evaluator should identify the system, the type of transaction, the control weakness, the volume of transactions passing through the control, the value of those transactions, and, if functional testing was done, the frequency of errors. The description of each control weakness identified should include (1) what could go wrong, that is, the possible adverse consequence; (2) the likelihood of the possible adverse consequence actually occurring; (3) the implications of that consequence to the company; and (4) the estimated incremental cost of correcting the weakness through alternative courses of action. Management should formulate a policy for the content of reports on responses to the evaluator's findings. They should describe the action taken, that is, the changes in control that were made, if any, and the reasons for that action.

A policy is also needed for the type of report to be made to the audit committee. One possibility is to inform the audit committee about the organization and performance of the review of internal control and the system for identifying, ranking, correcting, and reporting control weaknesses. The report might include a table showing, for each location and each level of significance, the number of weaknesses found, the number of weaknesses corrected, and the number of weaknesses reported for which management determined that no additional control was justified; the report might also contain an example of how the review, reporting, and decision-making system works. Management's strategy for dealing with business risk, which underlies decisions to correct or not to correct a control weakness, should also be brought to the committee's attention. In addition, the entire list of control weaknesses in all categories should be made available, so that the committee will have the option of pursuing particular items if it wishes.

Management should be sure that the audit committee is informed about both the objectives of the system of internal control and the process established for monitoring and maintaining it. The audit committee should be made aware that the overall objective of internal accounting control is to prevent errors from occurring in the first place and to detect those that cannot be prevented. The audit committee should also be reminded of the concept of reasonable assurance, that is, that some level of error is acceptable, and of the fact that the primary responsibility for the evaluation effort is management's. In its communications to the audit committee, management should indicate the extent to which it is supervising both the ongoing evaluations by lower-level personnel and the more formal periodic reviews that may have been made by the company's internal and external auditors.

THE IMPETUS FOR PUBLIC REPORTING

Pressure is growing for a published assessment, at least by publicly traded companies, of an enterprise's system of internal accounting controls. While it may be premature to speculate on the precise form and content of representations about internal control, and even though not everyone views a requirement for public disclosure as an unmitigated blessing, few would challenge a guess that public representations about internal control are inevitable. Many responsible corporate officers believe, however, that reports on their companies' internal accounting controls provide no substantive benefit to stockholders or other readers.

The Cohen Commission, on the other hand, has urged that corporations, or official bodies such as the SEC if necessary, require a company's chief financial officer or other representative of management to present a report with the financial statements. That report would contain, among other things, an "assessment of the company's accounting system and controls over it, including a description of the inherent limitations of control systems and a description of the company's response to material weaknesses identified by the independent auditor."* Under the Cohen Commission proposal, the report by management would be reviewed by the independent auditor.†

---

*Commission on Auditors' Responsibilities, *Report, Conclusions, and Recommendations.* (New York: American Institute of Certified Public Accountants, 1978), pp. 76–77.
†*Ibid.,* p. 80.

The Cohen Commission suggested the following language regarding internal accounting controls that management might use in its report:

> The company maintains an accounting system and related controls to provide reasonable assurance that assets are safeguarded against loss from unauthorized use or disposition and that financial records are reliable for preparing financial statements and maintaining accountability for assets. There are inherent limitations that should be recognized in considering the potential effectiveness of any system of internal accounting control. The concept of reasonable assurance is based on the recognition that the cost of a system of internal control should not exceed the benefits derived and that the evaluation of those factors requires estimates and judgments by management. The company's system provides such reasonable assurance. We have corrected all material weaknesses of the accounting and control systems identified by our independent auditors . . . [or, We are in the process of correcting all material weaknesses . . . ; or, We have corrected some of the material weaknesses but have not corrected others because . . .].
>
> The functioning of the accounting system and related controls is under the general oversight of the board of directors [or the audit committee of the board of directors]. The members of the audit committee are associated with the company only through being directors. The accounting system and related controls are reviewed by an extensive program of internal audits and by the company's independent auditors. The audit committee [or the board of directors] meets regularly with the internal auditors and the independent auditors and reviews and approves . . . their findings.*

The Cohen Commission reporting format may be inappropriate because it fails to state explicitly that some risks are deliberately borne by the enterprise and that only management is in a position to determine those risks, subject to oversight by the board of directors, in light of enterprise objectives. Also, the Cohen Commission's language does not acknowledge management's ongoing obligation to supervise the continued and proper operation of controls. Lastly, the suggested report implies an expanded role for independent auditors, without acknowledging the limitation of their ability to identify material weaknesses.

The Financial Executives Institute has taken the position that "a statement of management responsibility for financial statements, tailored to fit individual company circumstances, can be a significant step in improving communication to users by providing a convenient vehicle for management to discuss matters which bear on the quality of its financial information."† Among other subjects, the FEI recommended that a management report include the following:

---

*Ibid., pp. 79–80. This book discusses the report by management only insofar as internal control is concerned. Other aspects of the report are currently under consideration by committees of both the Financial Executives Institute and the American Institute of Certified Public Accountants.

†"Letter to FEI Members from C. C. Hornbostel." (New York: Financial Executives Institute, October 5, 1978.)

A discussion of management responsibility for maintaining internal control systems and an atmosphere or environment in which administrative and accounting controls can be effective, including among other things:

Communication of established written policies and procedures;
Careful selection and training of qualified personnel;
Organizational arrangements that provide appropriate delegation of authorities and segregation of responsibilities; and
A program of internal audits and appropriate follow-up by management.

Management's assessment of the effectiveness of the internal accounting control system.*

The FEI "Guidelines" stress communicating to stockholders the techniques that can be used to manage an activity. They do not discuss management's role as the assessor of business risk or its task of setting the course for the corporate ship; instead, they focus on the procedures that will be used to hold the ship on course once the journey begins.

The AICPA has appointed a committee to consider guidelines for a management report. The Auditing Standards Board of the AICPA is studying the question of auditor involvement, either directly or indirectly (through association with the management report), with reports on the quality of internal controls. While it will undoubtedly take some time before all of the important issues are finally resolved, the trend toward publishing information about internal controls will not await those resolutions.

SUGGESTED CONTENT OF A REPORT ON INTERNAL CONTROL

There is a danger that any statement about an enterprise's internal controls will be misunderstood by the public. This is particularly true if the language used to convey the overall assessment of the system does not adequately explain the cost/benefit trade-off implicit in the concept of reasonable assurance. The AICPA has for several years taken the position that the public's misunderstanding of such a report can be reduced "by adopt-

---

*Guidelines for Preparation of a Statement of Management Responsibility for Financial Statements. (New York: Financial Executives Institute, 1978.) An earlier draft, contained in a June 6, 1978 letter to members, substituted the following language for the first item: "Management responsibility for maintaining a system of internal accounting controls designed to provide reasonable assurance as to the integrity of the financial records and the protection of assets."

The FEI recommended that the following subjects also be discussed in a management report: management's responsibility for financial reporting, the independent public accountants' responsibility, the responsibilities of the board of directors (and its audit committee), and other matters such as changes in auditors, corporate conduct policies, corporate social responsibilities, and the significance of any uncertainties.

ing a reporting format that describes in reasonable detail the objectives and limitations of internal accounting control'' and the evaluation of it.

The following language from the AICPA Statements on Auditing Standards suggests a type of disclosure that meets those requirements and that, with appropriate wording and stylistic changes, would also be suitable for inclusion in a management report on internal control:

> The objective of internal accounting control is to provide reasonable, but not absolute, assurance as to the safeguarding of assets against loss from unauthorized use or disposition, and the reliability of financial records for preparing financial statements and maintaining accountability for assets. The concept of reasonable assurance recognizes that the cost of a system of internal accounting control should not exceed the benefits derived and also recognizes that the evaluation of these factors necessarily requires estimates and judgments by management.
>
> There are inherent limitations that should be recognized in considering the potential effectiveness of any system of internal accounting control. In the performance of most control procedures, errors can result from misunderstanding of instructions, mistakes of judgment, carelessness, or other personal factors. Control procedures whose effectiveness depends upon segregation of duties can be circumvented by collusion. Similarly, control procedures can be circumvented intentionally by management with respect either to the execution and recording of transactions or with respect to the estimates and judgments required in the preparation of financial statements. Further, projection of any evaluation of internal accounting control to future periods is subject to the risk that the procedures may become inadequate because of changes in conditions and that the degree of compliance with the procedures may deteriorate.*

The precision in expression achieved in the foregoing is obtained at a considerable sacrifice of comprehensibility.

Reports by management on internal controls should be tailored to the specific company and circumstances. They should not contain language that is true but cryptic, bland, and meaningless, or inconclusive and uninformative. We recommend as a foundation for reports on internal control, a combination of the positive assurances provided by the Cohen Commission model, the coverage suggested in the FEI "Guidelines," and the explicit statement of the limitations of an internal control system contained in the auditing literature. A specific recommendation is presented below, after a review and analysis of current practices.

AN ANALYSIS OF CURRENT REPORTING ON INTERNAL CONTROL

A review by the authors of published annual reports for 1977 revealed numerous and varied references to internal controls or internal accounting

---

*Statement on Auditing Standards No. 1, paragraph 640.12. (New York: American Institute of Certified Public Accountants, 1973.)

controls. Neither the absolute number of such references nor the percentages that they bear to various reporting populations are meaningful, because we made no attempt to control the population subject to review or to select randomly the reports reviewed. We can state, however, that approximately 60 instances were found of companies' referring to internal control in some manner somewhere in their annual reports.

The variety of language, location, authorship, and degree of association on the part of the company's CPAs indicates that no single method of reporting on internal control has become dominant. Companies will have to resolve the following issues, unless the SEC or some other authoritative body prescribes a uniform reporting format:

1. Where should the report appear? Comments on internal control were found:
   a. In a note to the financial statements titled, among others:
   Responsibility for Financial Statements
   Audit Committee
   Audit Committee, in the Summary of Significant Accounting Policies
   Audit Committee Activities

   In almost all of the examples reviewed, when mention was made of internal control in a note to the financial statements, it was solely in the context of audit committee activities and contained no description of the strength or adequacy of either the control system itself or of the process for evaluating the system.
   b. In the financial review section (not part of the audited financial statements) under the following headings:
   Audit Committee
   Responsibility for Financial Statements
   Financial Responsibility
   Untitled
   c. On the same page as the auditors' report.
   d. In the management discussion section titled, among others:
   Our Management Resources
   Financial Controls
   Management
   Audit Committee
   The Role of Outside Directors: Audit Committee
2. Who should make the report? The annual reports examined contained reports by controllers, financial vice-presidents, presidents, chief operating officers, chief executive officers, audit committees, audit committee chairmen, board chairmen, and sometimes two people together (such as the president and the chairman).
3. Should the independent auditor be associated with comments on the adequacy of the control system?
   If the commentary on internal control is part of the financial statements, as it is when the report is in the form of a note to the financial statements, the in-

dependent auditor will be associated with it, unless the note is marked "unaudited."*

As noted earlier, when mention was made of internal control in a note to the financial statements, it was generally in the context of audit committee activities and contained no description of the strength or adequacy of the system or of the process for evaluating it. In those cases, auditor association with the financial statements did not include association with any substantive aspects of internal control or of the evaluation process. †

4. If management or the board of directors reports on internal control in a separate statement that is not part of the financial statements, how should the report be titled? Examples found included the following:

Report of Management
Financial Responsibility
Responsibilities for Integrity of Data
Financial Statements
Responsibility for Financial Statements
Management's Responsibility for Financial Statements
Management's Responsibility for Financial Reporting
Responsibilities for Preparation of Financial Statements

Many of the comments on internal control in annual reports followed, to varying degrees, the language suggested in the FEI "Guidelines" noted above.** None of the reports reviewed specifically discussed management's responsibility for maintaining "an atmosphere or environment in which administrative and accounting controls can be effective," as suggested in the second set of FEI "Guidelines." One company stated, however, that "the cornerstone of the system is a business ethics policy which requires employees to maintain the highest ethical standards in their conduct of Company affairs." Several reports addressed the general internal control objectives of providing "reasonable assurance as to the integrity of the financial records and the protection of assets," as suggested in the first draft of the FEI "Guidelines" but deleted from the later draft.

---

*If the report on internal control is not part of the financial statements, the independent auditor could still choose to be associated with it. Auditor association may also be required by the SEC in the future.

†In one case, however, a note to the financial statements, not marked "unaudited," stated that "management maintains formal policies and procedures that are consistent with high standards of accounting and administrative practices which are regularly communicated to all levels of the organization." The auditors rendered a standard, two-paragraph "clean opinion." Several banks presented an independent accountants' report on internal control (following the AICPA Statements on Auditing Standards, with the prescribed negative assurance). In those cases, the annual report contained no management representations on internal control.

**The discussion that follows is limited to the FEI "Guidelines" related to internal controls. As noted earlier, the FEI recommended that other matters be discussed in the management report.

A number of reports also encompassed some or all of the items suggested by FEI for inclusion in the discussion of management responsibility for internal controls: communication of policies and procedures, selection and training of personnel, delegation of authority and segregation of duties, and a program of internal audits. Several companies introduced the concepts of reasonable assurance, costs and benefits, and inherent limitations of control systems. It may be significant that those concepts are not included among the items in the FEI's "Guidelines" for management's discussion of internal controls.

The language used in "management's assessment of the effectiveness of the internal accounting control system" included such descriptions as: "highly developed," "strong," "sufficient to provide reasonable assurance . . . ," "consistent with high standards of accounting and administrative practices," "designed to provide reasonable assurance," "high level," "adequate to prevent . . . ," "practical and effective," and "designed to assure that . . . ." As noted below, however, while a number of the "assessments" gave the impression of conveying some degree of assurance about the system, on closer inspection they were devoid of any content.

Our review of present reporting practices revealed some pitfalls that management would be well-advised to avoid. Practices that we believe are inappropriate include:

1. The use of negative assurance. Authoritative auditing literature contains language designed to avoid a judgment by the independent auditor on the adequacy of internal controls; however, that is no reason for a similar absence of a positive statement by management. Outsiders, including the independent auditor, cannot and should not make this judgment; management can and should as part of its responsibilities for reporting on its stewardship over assets entrusted to it by investors and creditors. Accordingly, we believe that a statement by management or the board, for example, that "nothing of a material adverse nature [about the accounting and financial aspects of the company] has come to our attention" provides less information to stockholders than they deserve.

2. The use of words and phrases that describe a condition that cannot be present. For example, one company speaks of "the highest quality and integrity" of "its accounting, administrative procedures and reporting practices." "Integrity" is a human characteristic not possessed by accounting or administrative procedures or reporting practices.

3. The use of language that appears to be descriptive of the quality of the control system but on closer inspection may convey goals rather than results. For example, one company states that "management believes a high level of internal control is maintained by the selection and training of qualified per-

sonnel, by the establishment and communication of accounting and business policies and by an effective internal audit system.'' One interpretation of that statement is that it is a statement of management's philosophy of what constitutes a good internal control system.

4. The use of language by management rather than by the independent auditor that associates the latter with the assessment of internal controls. For example, one company made the statement that ''the corporation's independent public accountants regularly appraise these internal control procedures...''; another that the auditors ''evaluate the effectiveness of our internal accounting control systems.'' Another company, with a ''clean opinion'' from its CPAs, states in the notes to the financial statements (not marked ''unaudited'') that ''management maintains formal policies and procedures that are consistent with high standards of accounting and administrative practices . . . .'' Statements such as those do not indicate the extent to which the external auditors' review of internal accounting controls went beyond that needed for the purposes of auditing the financial statements. The reader can only assume that the independent auditors read those comments, extended their procedures beyond those required by generally accepted auditing standards, and agreed with the statement by management. If these assumptions are true, perhaps the readers' needs would have been better served if the auditors had provided their own comments. At the very least, the absence of reported comments by the auditors implies that they did not have any. Management may, of course, make these statements if they are true. However, management then has the responsibility to report any material adverse comments the auditors may have made; this may be a good argument for not starting the practice.

A MODEL REPORT BY MANAGEMENT ON INTERNAL CONTROL

What follows is a suggested model report by management on internal control that combines the strengths and avoids the weaknesses of the various proposed and actual reports. In particular, the report describes the procedures that management employed to reach its conclusions. The disclosures included in the model should be thought of as minimal; additional matters could be reported on, as long as the pitfalls noted in the preceding section are avoided. The model report is limited to commentary on internal controls; this could be included in the more comprehensive report by management suggested by the Cohen Commission and already presented by several companies. Accompanying the model report is a commentary explaining the rationale behind each of the assertions.

Model Management Report on Internal Control

The Company maintains a system of internal accounting control designed to provide reasonable assurance that assets are safeguarded against loss from unauthorized use or disposition and that financial records are reliable for preparing financial statements and maintaining accountability for assets.

> *This explains management's responsibility for internal accounting control and defines the term. The reference to "reasonable assurance" implies the need for management to exercise sound business judgment.*

The Company augments this system through its operating policies and procedures which, among other things, ensure that it employs qualified personnel and appropriately delegates authority to carry on the Company's business, with suitable segregation of responsibilities.

> *This introduces the notion of the conditions of control; it suggests that the system of internal accounting control is similar to other management control systems.*

Internal accounting controls are intended to prevent errors and to detect on a timely basis errors that do occur.

> *This briefly describes the purpose of accounting controls. Errors include accidental errors as well as irregularities.*

There are inherent limitations in the effectiveness of any system of control because it comprises both controls and personnel who apply them. Human errors can result and controls can be circumvented or deliberately overridden.

> *This warns the reader that no system is infallible and that controls can be overridden.*

As a result, the determination of the extent of control needed for particular risks is dependent on the concept of reasonable assurance, which recognizes that the cost of control should not exceed the benefits derived. That determination requires estimates and judgments by company management.

> *This explains that the concept of reasonable assurance requires an evaluation of risks and of the costs and benefits of reducing or eliminating those risks, and that this evaluation must be made by management.*

The Company reviews and evaluates the control system and compliance with it by integrating into the system an extensive degree of management supervision, and through periodic internal audits carried out by Company employees. In addition, our independent auditors also evaluate certain internal accounting controls as part of their examination of the Company's financial statements.

This describes the three broad techniques of monitoring the system, namely, ongoing supervision, internal audits, and reviews by external auditors as part of their examination of the financial statements. Reference to the internal auditors would not be made if the company does not have an internal audit function.

All of the findings of these examinations are reviewed by management and considered in initiating corrective action.

This indicates that management has retained the responsibility for assessing costs and benefits of correcting control weaknesses found through the monitoring process.

Based on its evaluation, management believes that no significant control weaknesses exist and that the internal accounting control system in use provides reasonable assurance that assets are safeguarded and that the financial records are reliable.

This is a clear expression of opinion on the reasonableness of the system in meeting its objectives and again suggests the notion of reasonable, rather than absolute, assurance.

APPENDICES

Preparation of Flowcharts

INTRODUCTION

Flowcharts express procedures in graphic form and thus facilitate comprehension and communication of information. Flowcharts enable the system evaluator to identify particular control features of the system and to direct attention to how those controls meet the objectives of an internal accounting control system.

Flowcharts should meet the following criteria:

1. Procedures should be shown in sequence.
2. All copies of pertinent documents should be explained and accounted for.
3. The maintenance of files and the preparation of reports with control significance should be shown.
4. The flow of documentation between the various departments of the business should be shown.
5. The title or position and, where practicable, the names of the persons performing the procedures should be shown.

The flowcharting technique described below, which is designed to meet these criteria, is an adaptation of standard flowcharting approaches to the special needs of the internal control system evaluator. It identifies records, files, and reports; describes operations and related documents in the sequence of processing; and guides the system evaluator through all the processing steps leading to the disposition of copies of documents with internal accounting control significance.

Three major points should be kept in mind:

1. The flow of transactions through a specific system must be charted step by step.
2. All relevant information relating to the transactions, such as completeness of documentation, establishment of control totals, and review of open files, should be recorded so that the related questions in the Internal Control Questionnaire can be properly answered.
3. Clarity and simplicity of presentation are important.

Flowcharts should reflect all significant internal accounting controls. If operational controls related to a transaction processing system are also evaluated, they may be integrated within the flowcharts and may also be flowcharted. For example, the part of the payments system flowchart describing control procedures in the purchasing function may describe such operational control procedures as the solicitation of competitive bids from vendors, providing purchasing agents with summaries of buying volumes by commodity and by vendor, and the maintenance of vendor evaluation files.

Information necessary for the preparation or updating of flowcharts is usually obtained by inquiring of persons at each site as to procedures followed, and by reviewing procedure manuals. Particularly in updating flowcharts, such inquiries can often be made concurrently with performance of transaction reviews.

GENERAL INSTRUCTIONS

This flowcharting technique requires the preparation of a separate flowchart for each transaction processing system or major part thereof. The processing and the documents involved are shown sequentially on a "main flowline." The symbols shown in this Appendix should be used.

A standard format has been adopted for flowchart work papers. This format, which is illustrated in a specimen form on page 175, should be followed.

FLOWCHARTING WORKSHEET FORM

Client _____ Flowchart No _____

Flowchart

Page _____ of _____ Date _____

Description _____

Preparer _____

Reviewer _____

Description	Oper No	

Flowcharting Worksheet Form

A standard form has been designed for signing off in connection with the preparation or updating of flowcharts and performance of the related transaction reviews. The form also contains space for evidencing review of the flowcharts. A specimen, filled-in form is shown below.

Preparation/updating of flowcharts (F) and performance of transaction reviews (TR)

No.	Description of System	F	TR	Done By	Reviewed By	F	TR	Done By	Reviewed By	F	TR	Done By	Reviewed By
	Flowchart	**19**		Prepared/Updated*		**19**		Prepared/Updated*		**19**		Prepared/Updated*	
	PAYMENTS. CYCLE:												
1	RAW MATERIALS	✓	✓	Jones	Strong								
2	ADVERTISING	✓	✓	Jones	Strong								
3	OTHER	✓	✓	Jones	Strong								
4	PRODUCTION CYCLE	✓	✓	BWhite	Strong								
	REVENUE CYCLE:												
5	EXPORT	✓	✓	BWhite	Strong								
6	DOMESTIC	✓	✓	BWhite	Strong								

* Place ticks (✓) in columns provided.

Record of Flowchart Preparation and Transaction Reviews

Flowcharts should be prepared in pencil. Preparation time should be commensurate with the expected benefits. Accordingly, excessive time should not be spent on charts expected to have only limited usefulness.

Each flowchart should have a separate flowchart number. The individual pages of each chart should be numbered sequentially.

Flowcharts should be reviewed and updated at scheduled intervals, preferably annually; a complete redrawing of flowcharts normally is not necessary, unless the underlying procedures have been superseded or the legibility of the charts has become impaired as a result of previous amendments. If flowcharts require amendment, photocopies of the old charts should be taken before changes are made, so that there is a permanent record of the systems reviewed in the past. Supporting documentation, such as copies of or extracts from accounting procedure manuals and filledin specimen forms of documents, should be cross-referenced to, and filed with, the flowcharts.

Except in simple accounting systems, it is often impracticable to prepare one flowchart covering an entire system. For example, separate flowcharts may be required for the purchase of goods, the purchase of services, and the computation and payment of wages, if all three are significant and the control procedures are different for each. If common procedures are applied at some point, only one flowchart is needed after that point. For example, a system that involves sales of finished goods for cash and a leasing operation may both conclude with the same cash receipts procedures.

Minor deviations from the system may be explained either in the space provided in the flowcharts for narrative or, if necessary, in separate notes, so that the flowcharts are not unnecessarily complicated. This procedure can be used where different transaction types are involved. For example, if purchases of goods and purchases of services are processed similarly except for initial authorization, both types of transactions may be covered in the same flowchart and the deviation explained in the narrative column.

The flowcharts should show the complete path of each type of transaction from its inception to its termination. A transaction can be defined as a series of business activities related to an exchange involving money, goods, or services or to any other change in an asset or liability that should result in an accounting entry. For example, all of the activities that result in the recording of a purchase of a raw material in the accounts are part of a transaction. Those activities would normally include preparing a purchase requisition, preparing and mailing a purchase order, recording receipt of the goods, matching the supplier's invoice with the record of goods received and purchase order, approving the supplier's invoice for payment, paying the supplier (including, where applicable, preparing, signing, and mailing checks), recording the purchase in the appropriate asset or expense account, recording the liability and subsequent cash disbursement in the appropriate accounts, and controlling the foregoing documents before and during the related processing activities (e.g., controls over unmatched receiving reports and controls to ensure that all approved suppliers' invoices are recorded properly). Transactions are of different types when the controls applied to one transaction vary from the controls applied to another transaction. For example, if purchases of raw materials are processed and controlled in the same manner as purchases of office supplies, then those purchases represent only one type of transaction. On the other hand, if purchases of raw materials are processed and controlled differently from purchases of office supplies, those purchases represent two types of transactions.

In distinguishing among types of transactions, emphasis should be placed on differences in controls. The fact that otherwise similar transactions are processed by different people, or in different locations, does not in itself mean that they are different types; if the control procedures are uniform and there is reason to believe that they are adequately supervised, the transactions can be considered to be the same type.

Flowcharts and/or narratives should show posting to the general ledger; this helps to trace the flow of transactions into the accounting records and ensures that all principal documents in the system have been included.

Brief narrative descriptions of most of the operations appearing on the flowcharts should be shown on the left side of the flowchart. Where appropriate, the narrative should include authority limits, explanations of how controls are evidenced, and the frequency of operation of the control; descriptions should be sufficient to enable a reader to understand the nature of processing and related controls. In addition, all available information about the extent of transaction flows (number of transactions, total and average amount, error rates in transaction processing, etc.) should also be recorded. If such information is not regularly available at sites, requesting in advance that sites develop such data would be advisable. This information will be extremely useful in evaluating the potential effect of any control weaknesses identified. The format for entering this information on the flowchart is illustrated on pages 191–94.

Operation numbers for each process should be shown in a separate column to the right of the narrative description, i.e., to the left of the main flowline.

To avoid clutter, the system evaluator may describe in narrative form control procedures that are performed periodically rather than as part of transaction processing; an example of such periodic processing is the monthly balancing of account details to a control account. Conversely, if such periodic processing tends to be quite detailed, the evaluator may prepare separate flowcharts.

If a separate flowchart is used to show the details of a particular operation, or if the narrative required is so lengthy that it does not fit on the flowchart page, the operation shown on the flowchart should be referenced to the underlying detail with a single numbered symbol.

The system evaluator should decide whether to start a separate page when the processing flow enters a new department. If relatively few operations are involved, more than one department may be shown on a page. Alternatively, the use of separate pages may be advantageous so that the pages can be sorted by department and all activities within a particular department brought into perspective. (The pages should be re-sorted into the actual processing sequence before being filed.)

In addition to flowcharting on the basis of types of transactions, the system evaluator may wish to prepare an optional "overview flowchart." These optional charts should be prepared where the systems are complex and where it is believed that a broad view of the flow among the various departments of the business will be useful to the evaluator and a reviewer. In essence, the overview flowchart is a summary of, and an index to, the detailed flowcharts; it is described in greater detail later in this Appendix.

In addition, when visiting a new site or obtaining an understanding of a new application, the system evaluator may find it helpful at the start of his review, that is, before detailed charts are prepared, briefly to sketch an outline of the system.

PROCESSING SEQUENCE

Organizational Units

All areas of responsibility in a system are assigned a distinct organizational unit name. An organizational unit may vary from a large department, e.g., sales department, to one individual, e.g., credit manager. The area of responsibility should be shown when the flow of transactions passes from one organizational unit to another, e.g., from the purchasing department to the accounting department. This can be done by drawing a horizontal line, or using a separate page, and entering the name of the new organizational unit.

The description of the organizational unit and the title and, if desired, the name of the person in charge are placed on each page on the right side of the flowchart (Example 1).

Description	Oper. No.		Accounting Dept. Chief Accountant (A. Name)

Example 1

As already discussed, in simple systems new organizational units may be introduced in the middle of a page. The new organizational unit should be described on the right side under the horizontal line. If the flowline continues on a second page, the name of the organizational unit should be repeated at the top of the page.

Operation or Process

Symbols:

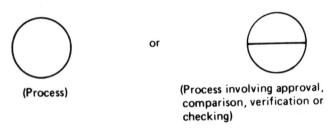

(Process)   or   (Process involving approval, comparison, verification or checking)

These symbols indicate processing. They must be numbered in the appropriate column, in the order in which the activity occurs within the transaction processing system. The symbols always appear on a flowline.

As indicated above, a horizontal line in the processing symbol indicates an approval, comparison, verification, or checking routine. If errors detected are cleared by the person performing the step, this fact need not be mentioned in the narration and the correction process need not be charted. If the correction involves re-routing the documentation, the correction routine should be flowcharted or narrated, as appropriate.

The description/narrative and operation number columns should be filled in opposite the operation symbol. Descriptions should be complete but concise (Example 2).

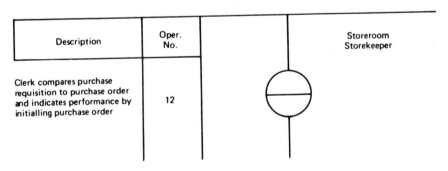

Description	Oper. No.			Storeroom Storekeeper
Clerk compares purchase requisition to purchase order and indicates performance by initialling purchase order	12			

Example 2

If the process creates a document, the document symbol only, as discussed subsequently, appears on the main flowline; it is not necessary to show an operation symbol. However, the operation is assigned its own number. If the activity involves a Yes/No decision, the diamond symbol described below is used in lieu of the operation symbol. Again, a separate operation number is assigned.

Main Flowline

Processing within an organizational unit moves along a vertical line called the main flowline (Example 3).

Description	Oper. No.		Accounts Payable Disbursements Supervisor
Clerk checks mathematical accuracy of invoice and indicates performance on audit stamp	14		
Clerk indicates accounting distribution of invoice	15		

Example 3

Symbols for documents or other information media involved in processing appear on the main flowline, as described below, when the documents are created or received. The documents are presumed to flow along with the processing from department to department until their disposition is indicated. File/storage symbols and connector symbols, discussed subsequently, indicate the permanent or temporary removal of media from processing. Only documents that are germane to the function being described should normally remain on the main flowline.

If the nature of the documents or media remaining on the main flowline might not be evident to the reader, the symbols or a narrative description, surrounded by brackets, may be shown on the main flowline as a reminder. This technique is sometimes referred to as "ghosting" (Example 4).

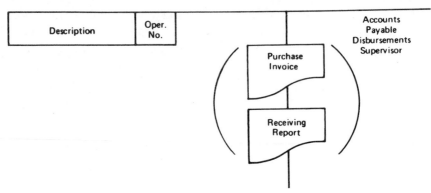

Example 4

When the flowline continues on a second page, appropriate references are entered at the bottom of the first page and top of the second page.

Decision and Branching

Symbol:

Over $10? → Yes

No

This symbol represents a point at which alternative procedures are flowcharted. Processing along the main flowline is suspended until the branch condition has been accommodated. If alternative processing is significant and/or extensive, a separate flowchart should be considered (Example 5).

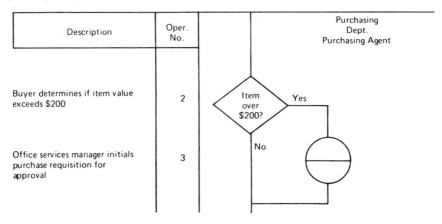

Example 5

MEDIA

A symbol for information media appears on the main flowline when the media are prepared or received and reappears when they are distributed, filed, or disposed of. If origin coincides with disposition (with no intervening processing) the symbol need not be repeated.

Document

Symbol: 1)

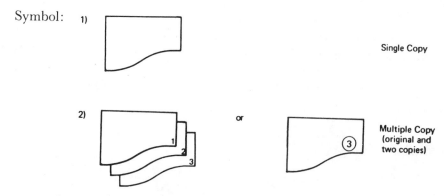

Single Copy

Multiple Copy (original and two copies)

This symbol is used to designate items such as a purchase order, requisition, invoice, voucher, etc. The name of the document is inserted in the symbol. (See below.)

Multiple copy overlapping symbols may be used when more than one copy of a document is prepared and distributed. Alternatively, the number of copies may be indicated by a circled number placed within the single document symbol. When it is desirable to show disposition, the copies for which disposition is indicated are shown separately and identified by number. Each copy having accounting significance should be followed from its origin to its disposition.

If a document (single or multiple copy) is numbered serially for accounting control purposes, the letter "N" should be placed in the upper right corner of the document symbol. This alerts the system evaluator to numerical control aspects (Example 6).

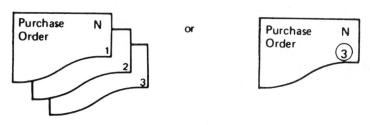

Example 6

Report/Book

Symbol:

This symbol represents a report, journal, book, register, computer listing, or similar document; it may be machine printed or completed by hand. Its title is inserted in the symbol. The symbol usually represents self-contained output media (e.g., a complete listing of selling prices) which may be used as input for other processing (e.g., pricing customers' invoices).

Machine Tape

Symbol:

This symbol depicts a continuous machine-printed paper tape such as a "control" or "proof" tape from an adding or posting machine.

Paper Tape

Symbol:

This symbol represents a single data file contained on a strip or coil of perforated paper tape used in conjunction with electronic data processing.

Magnetic Tape

Symbol:

This symbol is used in conjunction with electronic data processing. A single symbol represents one or more reels or cassettes of tape containing a single data file.

Magnetic Disk

Symbol:

Price
List

This symbol is used in conjunction with electronic data processing to represent a single data file contained on one or more disk packs. A separate symbol is used for each data file although a single disk can hold more than one data file.

Punched Card

Symbol:

Sales

This symbol is used in conjunction with electronic data processing. A single symbol represents one or more punched cards containing a single data file.

INFORMATION FLOW AND DISPOSITION

Referral Line

Symbol:

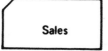

This symbol is used to indicate referral to information, such as reviewing a file to obtain information, or posting information. The referral line leads to a symbol depicting the media and content of the reference source. That source does not "travel" with the main flowline but remains in physical custody of or is accessible to the organizational unit indicated (Example 7).

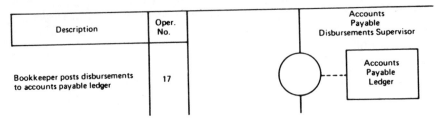

Description	Oper. No.		Accounts Payable Disbursements Supervisor
Bookkeeper posts disbursements to accounts payable ledger	17		Accounts Payable Ledger

Example 7

Document Distribution Line

Symbol:

The movement of all documents and other information media follows the main flowline from one organizational unit and process to another. The movement of information media to or from the main flowline is indicated by a horizontal document distribution line attached to the document or other media symbol.

Information media leaving or entering the system from outside or from an organizational unit not charted are shown with the origin or disposition explained on a horizontal line. An arrowhead denotes movement. Documents may be brought onto the main flowline from either the left or right. Normally, document disposition is to the right (Example 8).

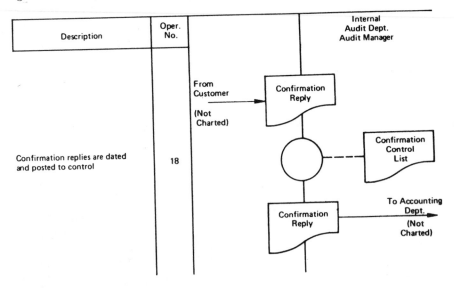

Description	Oper. No.		Internal Audit Dept. Audit Manager
Confirmation replies are dated and posted to control	18	From Customer (Not Charted) → Confirmation Reply · Confirmation Control List · Confirmation Reply → To Accounting Dept. (Not Charted)	

Example 8

If a document or other media come from or are sent to another organizational unit, the media symbol appears on the main flowline at the points at which the media enter or leave the processing. Connector symbols, cross-referenced as described below, are drawn at the end of the document distribution line (with arrowheads) to or from the media symbols on the main flowline. If the media are stored without immediate or further processing, the symbol on the main flowline carries a document distribution line connected with a file/storage symbol, as discussed later, to indicate that disposition (Example 9).

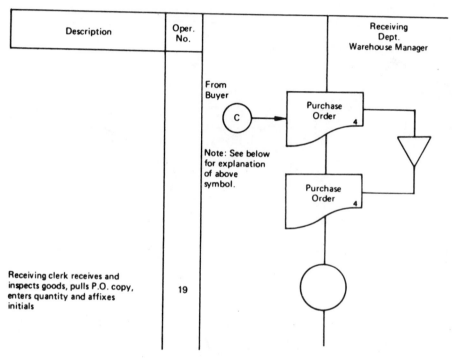

Example 9

Connector

Symbol:

The connector symbol is used in sets of two, one at each point being indexed. Each of the pair of symbols contains the same unique identification letter of the document distribution line.

Connector symbols are used to cross-reference the continuation of a horizontal document distribution line. The horizontal distribution line joins the connector and the document or other media symbol. The page reference may be noted beside corresponding connectors, particularly those that do not appear on adjacent pages. The name of the organizational unit of destination or origin should be written above the horizontal distribution line (Example 10).

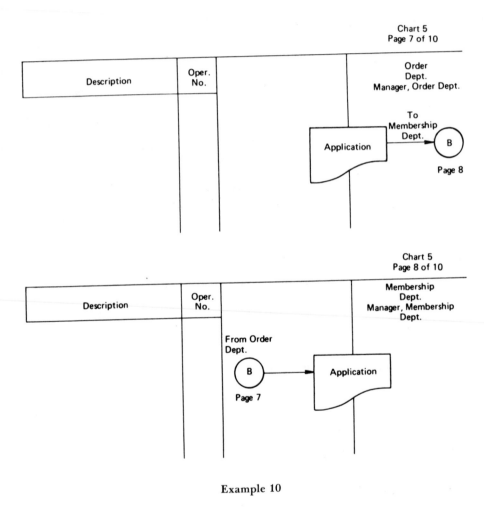

Example 10

References between narratives or other working papers and flowchart pages may cite the flowchart operation number in addition to the page.

File/Storage

Symbol:

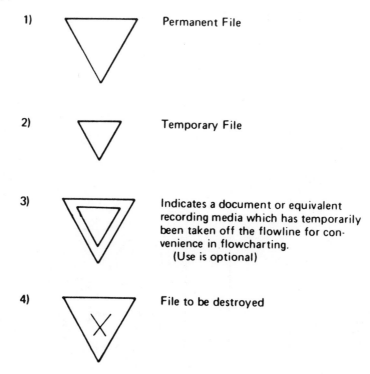

1)   Permanent File

2)   Temporary File

3)   Indicates a document or equivalent recording media which has temporarily been taken off the flowline for convenience in flowcharting.
(Use is optional)

4)   File to be destroyed

A letter designation is used to indicate the manner of filing:

A — Alphabetic

N — Numeric

D — Date

S — Sundry (to be specified)

The file/storage symbol is used to indicate that a document or other information media that have left the main flowline (via a horizontal document distribution line) are being held in the custody of the organizational unit under which the symbol appears.

The filing of information media is depicted by placing the appropriate file symbols at the end of the horizontal document distribution line drawn from the media symbol on a main flowline. The retrieval and restoration of a document or other media to the main flow of processing are shown in the same manner. The direction of movement is shown by arrowheads on the document distribution line or by entering the file/storage symbol from the top and leaving it from the bottom.

If a tape file is used in a process that creates a new (updated) replacement for the tape entering processing, that fact is reflected by a solid line connecting the media symbol and the operation symbol. The solid line is marked with arrowheads pointing both right and left to mark the withdrawal and supersession of the original tape and the return of the updated tape. It is usually not necessary to show the tape library as a separate organizational unit, but the system evaluator should record the tape library procedures on a separate working paper. A tape file that supplies data but does not result in a replacement tape should be shown with a referral line (Example 11).

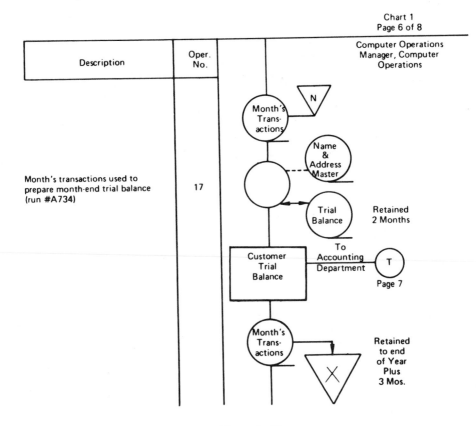

Example 11

ILLUSTRATIVE FLOWCHART

The flowchart in Example 12 illustrates a segment of a manufacturing company's payments system. The inclusion of operational controls, which is optional, is also illustrated.

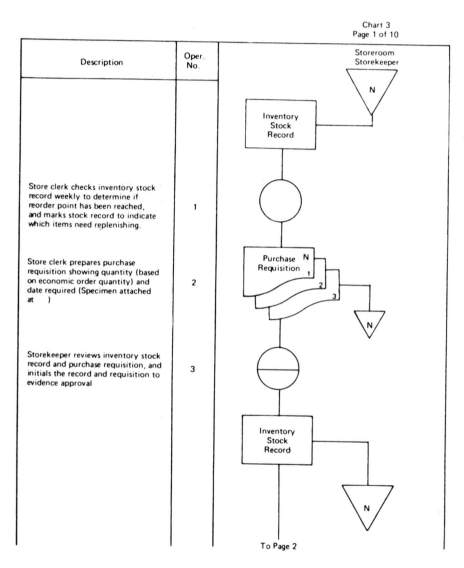

Example 12

Chart 3
Page 2 of 10

Description	Oper. No.	Purchasing Purchasing Manager
Assistant buyer determines if total cost of purchase will exceed $2500	4	
Assistant buyer refers to vendor evaluation reports, and records on purchase requisition those vendors considered	5	

Number : 150 per month
Amount: Total : $1,050,000
       Average : $ 7,000
       Range: $ 2,500 to
           $ 65,000

Assistant buyer selects three vendors and requests bids from them, noting the names on the purchase requisition	6	
Assistant buyer receives bids from vendors	7	
Assistant buyer evaluates bids, selects vendor, and marks bids "rejected" or "accepted "	8	
Assistant buyer determines if freight cost will exceed $50	9	
Assistant buyer reviews routing and mode of transportation with traffic department	10	
Assistant buyer records vendor name, price, and routing and mode of transportation on purchase requisition	11	
Typist prepares purchase order from purchase requisition (Specimen attached at)	12	

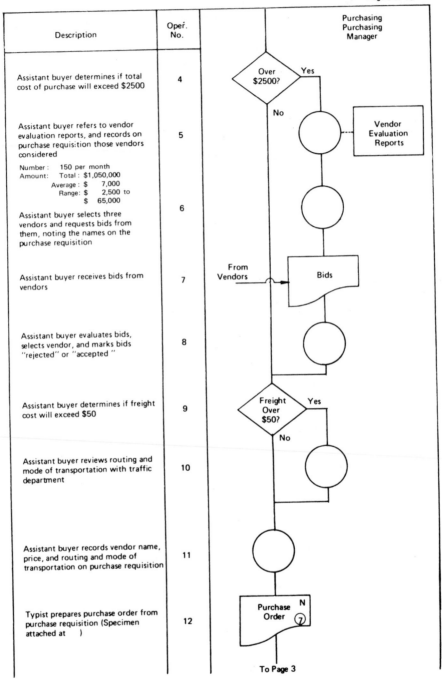

To Page 3

Example 12 (continued)

192

Chart 3
Page 3 of 10

Description	Oper. No.	Purchasing
Buyer reviews purchase order with purchase requisition and bids (where applicable) attached, and initials purchase order to evidence approval	13	
Buyer determines if total cost will exceed $5000	14	

Purchasing manager reviews purchase order with supporting documentation, and initials purchase order as evidence of approval
 	
Number : 100 per month
Amount : Total: $850,000
       Average: $ 8,500
       Range: $ 5,000 to
             $ 65,000
	15	

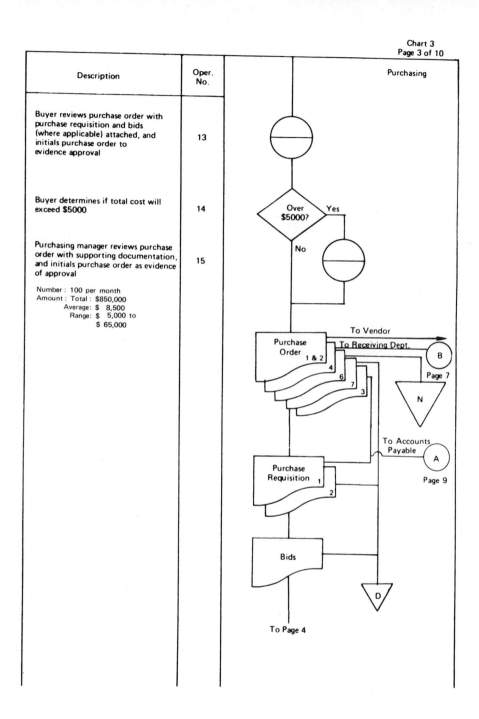

Example 12 (continued)

193

Chart 3
Page 4 of 10

Description	Oper. No.	Storeroom
		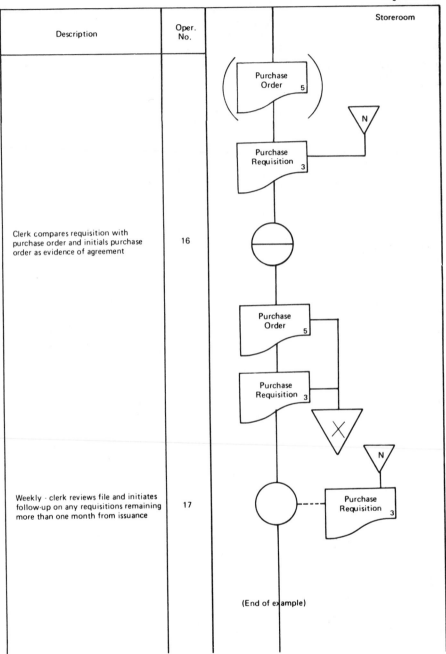
Clerk compares requisition with purchase order and initials purchase order as evidence of agreement	16	
Weekly · clerk reviews file and initiates follow-up on any requisitions remaining more than one month from issuance	17	

(End of example)

Example 12 (continued)

OVERVIEW FLOWCHARTS (OPTIONAL)

Purpose

Overview flowcharts provide an overall view of the flow among the various departments of a business and serve as an index to facilitate reference to detailed flowcharts and/or narrative descriptions of processing.

Major Features

The overview flowchart summarizes the detail appearing on the departmental flowcharts. Each column in the overview flowchart represents an organizational unit. All processing operations that occur during the passage of the main flow through an organizational unit are represented on the chart by a single operation symbol, cross-referenced to the detail appearing on the departmental chart.

Operation or Function

The range of numbers of the operations occurring in the organizational unit is inserted in the operation symbol. The bar indicating approval, etc., is not shown inside the circle symbol on overview charts (Example 13).

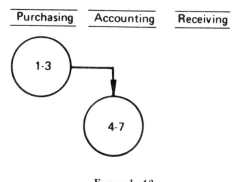

Example 13

Main Flowline

On the overview flowchart, the main flowline is drawn horizontally from one organizational unit to the next and down to the process symbol representing the consecutive operations in that department. Arrowheads are used to show direction. Just before the main flowline turns downward to the next process symbol, a document symbol is used to display only the principal documents (if any) entering the organizational unit at that point. Multiple copies and attachments are all depicted by the same single document symbol, and the title of the principal document is written inside the symbol. As shown in Example 14, the request document is shown as input to operations 11 and 12. This processing generates the order document which becomes input to the succeeding operations in another organizational unit.

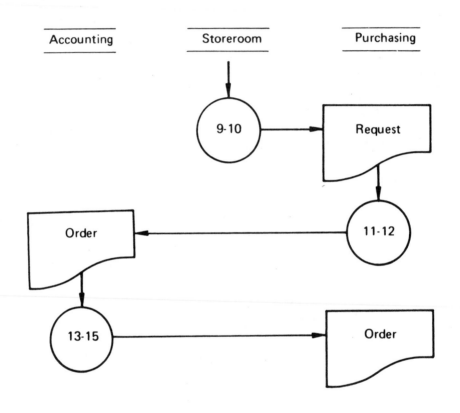

Example 14

Decision and Branching

On the overview flowchart, branching to other organizational units for processing of special cases is depicted by dual main flowlines. Titles of documents distinguish the main flow from the branching operations (Example 15).

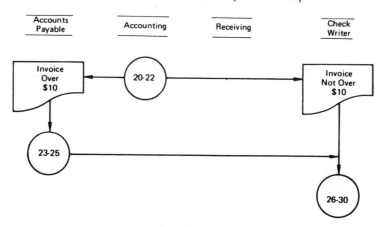

Example 15

(Note that operation #22 would have been represented on the departmental flowchart by a decision symbol.)

The distribution of information media is usually not shown on the overview flowchart, unless the media also serve as input, on the main flowline, to the next processing stage. Consequently, the outgoing media symbol does not appear under the unit of origin, and horizontal document distribution lines are superseded by the main flowline moving to another organizational unit. In Example 16, a copy of the purchase order is sent from the purchasing department to the receiving department, in addition to the copies accompanying the main flow.

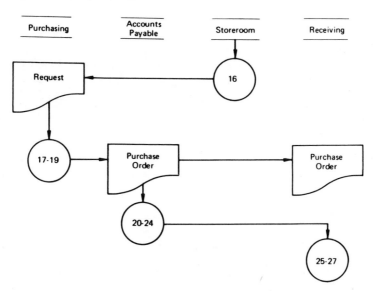

Example 16

Illustration

The flowchart shown in Example 17 illustrates the entire payments cycle from an overview point of reference. It summarizes the operations of the organizational units presented in the detailed flowchart illustration and gives an overview of the cycle.

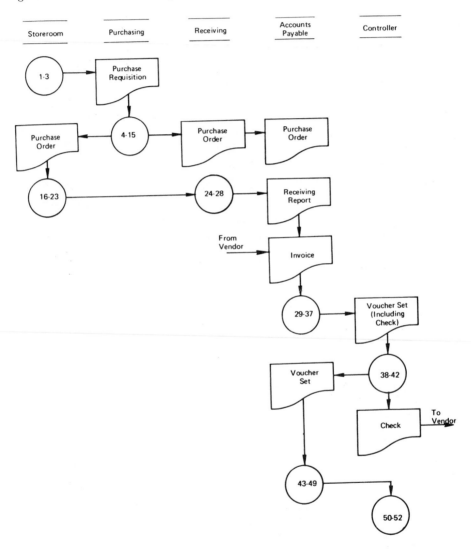

Example 17

B

Specimen Working Paper: Transaction Review— Payments Cycle

Identification of Transaction Types

Type I involves raw materials. An annual buying contract is negotiated, requiring the company to take down an aggregate tonnage, subject to periodic release. The contract includes a specific price, certain price protection clauses in case of declining prices, and cancellation clauses.

Type II involves production items other than raw materials. Specific purchase orders are issued for each transaction. Competitive bids are sought where aggregate cost is thought to exceed $1,000.

Type III generally involves non-production items such as office supplies, promotional materials, and the like. Department heads usually place orders with vendors by telephone. Materials are sent directly to the departments concerned; formal receiving reports are not used.

Type IV involves check requisitions. A check requisition is used where there is no vendor invoice, e.g., tax payments, transfers between bank accounts.

JOY CANDIES, INC.

Transaction Review—Payments Cycle—Flowchart Number 1

Flowchart Operation Number	1980 Documents Examined				1981 Documents Examined			
	Type I Raw Material Release	Type II Purchases Against P/Os	Type III Invoices Only	Type IV Check Requisition	Type I Raw Material Release	Type II Purchases Against P/Os	Type III Invoices Only	Type IV Check Requisition
1	Req 204	Req 223	N/A	N/A				
2	R 1570	N/A	N/A	N/A				
3	N/A	PO 10/3	N/A	N/A				
4	R 1570 (Copy 5)	PO 10/3 (Copy 5)	N/A	N/A				
5	(Copy 5)	N/A	N/A	N/A				
6	Note 1	Note 1	N/A	N/A				
7	N/A	N/A	VO 11-18	N/A				
8	VO 11-389	VO 11-390	N/A	N/A				
9	VO 11-389	VO 11-390	N/A	N/A				
10	VO 11-389	VO 11-390	N/A	N/A				
11	VO 11-389	VO 11-390	N/A	VO 11-1				
12	VO 11-389	VO 11-390	N/A	VO 11-1				
13	VO 11-389	VO 11-390	N/A	VO 11-1				
14	VO 11-389	VO 11-390	N/A	VO 11-1				
15	VO 11-389	VO 11-390	N/A	Note 2				
16	CK 11-1780	CK 11-3	CK 12-2	CK 11-340				
17	CK 11-1780	M	M	M				
18	CK 11-1780	M	M	M				
19	CK 11-1780	M	M	M				

Performed by: WS

Date: 10/11/80

M = Commingled for processing purposes. (Only one tested through the rest of the system.)

Notes: 1. Since the documents examined are no longer in the open files (flowchart operation number 6), we inquired into and observed procedures related to the open files and examined other documents on a test basis. 2. Type IV vouchers are approved by the accounting department supervisor, not by the chief accountant. Flowchart amended.

C

Internal Control Questionnaire

INSTRUCTIONS

1.   These instructions relate to the use of the Internal Control Questionnaire (ICQ).

The Extent to Which Internal Accounting Controls Should Be Evaluated

2.   The first step in completing the ICQ is to identify the internal accounting control objectives that should be achieved at each site. Any significant business activities not covered by the standard or supplementary control objectives in the ICQ should be identified, and additional control objectives devised to evaluate the control procedures related to such activities. Operational control procedures should be evaluated to the extent determined by senior management.

3.   Sometimes an activity to which a control objective relates is insignificant from an external audit viewpoint on the grounds that, in total,

the transactions and related assets or liabilities are not material to the financial statements. However, the Foreign Corrupt Practices Act may have changed the traditional audit materiality threshold (material when related to the financial statements taken as a whole). At this time, there is no clear guidance concerning the appropriate materiality threshold for an evaluation; thus, management, with the advice of legal counsel, will have to make individual decisions in this regard. The questionnaire is designed to allow management, if it chooses, to relate materiality to individual sites being evaluated. Doing this usually facilitates identification of problems at particular sites.

4.   All control objectives to be covered by the evaluation should be identified on the completion/updating/review record. Standard control objectives that are not applicable at a site and therefore are not to be covered should be identified separately on the record. The questions under those objectives should be removed from the questionnaire.

5.   To facilitate use of the supplementary control objectives (listed at the end of each ICQ section), columns are provided for recording:

     a.   Whether the activity covered by the objective is relevant to the business; and
     b.   If so, whether the procedures followed regarding the supplementary control objective are the same as those followed with regard to a standard control objective.

If a supplementary control objective is relevant and the same procedures are *not* followed, the supplementary control objective should be listed on the completion/updating/review record, i.e., the first page of the ICQ section.

Method of Answering ICQ Questions

6.   The information contained in the flowcharts should be used, as far as possible, in answering the ICQ questions relating to the control objectives that the system evaluator has decided are relevant. Normally, the ICQ should not be completed until:

     a.   The flowcharts have been prepared; and
     b.   The information in the flowcharts has been subjected to transaction reviews.

7.   All answers based on information included in the flowcharts should be referenced to the flowcharts in the column provided. Both the number of the flowchart and the number of the operation should be identified; for example, if the reference is to operation number 21 on flowchart number 3, it

should be stated as "3/21." Sometimes the reason for the answer to a question in the ICQ is not apparent from the related flowchart. In that event, the relevant facts underlying the answer should be reflected in the flowchart or, alternatively, an explanation should be noted in the ICQ.

8. Where the transactions relating to a control objective are processed by computer, all questions in the standard ICQ that are applicable should be answered. In addition, the internal control questionnaire for computer systems should be completed.

9. Each question in the ICQ has been phrased so that it may be answered "Yes" or "No" and thereby indicate, respectively, the presence or absence of a control procedure. The answer should be recorded by placing a check in either the "Yes" or "No" column, as appropriate. If a question does not apply to a specific site, this should be indicated by inserting "N/A" in the "Yes" column.

10. Explanations of individual questions and guidance for answering them are set out in the Internal Control Reference Manual. The system evaluator should refer to the Reference Manual when answering the questions, particularly where a judgment has to be made.

11. Often more than one control procedure relates to a question. In such cases, there is likely to be a principal control over the completeness and/or accuracy of processing as a whole, and one or more secondary control procedures covering parts of the processing only. The question should be answered based on the control on which the system evaluator intends to rely.

12. The questions in the ICQ do not normally ask whether the operation of a control has been evidenced (e.g., by signatures or initials on documents) because a control cannot be considered to be adequate from an evaluation viewpoint if it is not evidenced. It is therefore necessary to consider, where appropriate, whether such evidence exists and, if not, to answer the question "No," together with an explanation.

13. The questions in the ICQ that deal with disciplines over basic controls have been marked as follows:

C — Separation of responsibility for custody of assets and the related record-keeping and physical arrangements that prevent unauthorized access to assets or accounting records (Custodial).

D — Segregation of duties so that the work of one person checks that of another (Division of duties).

S — Supervision of the work of persons involved in the operation of the system of basic controls (Supervision).

Two distinct disciplines over basic controls have been grouped into one

(Custodial) for this purpose because the evaluator's response should be the same if either of those disciplines is not present. Questions that are not marked with a letter relate to basic controls. The questions that deal with operational controls are identified by italics and shading.

14.   Control procedures may vary according to types of transactions or between different locations. In these circumstances, the different procedures should be recorded either:

a. By identifying each procedure in the spaces provided under the questions for narrative explanations; or
b. Where the procedures differ substantially, by completing separate series of questions for the related control objective(s).

15.   As indicated above, it may be necessary to expand the answers to questions by narrative explanations. Accordingly, space has been left after each question for this purpose.

16.   The system evaluator should be alert to the possibility that occasionally the questions in the ICQ may not cover all control procedures relevant to the objective. In that event, additional questions will be needed.

17.   Individual questions are not provided for supplementary control objectives; however, the system evaluator should identify the control procedures relevant to achieving such objectives. The most effective manner of doing this may be to formulate questions appropriate to the objective. The questions should be recorded on the supplementary control objective evaluation sheets.

Assessment of Answers

18.   All internal accounting control procedures identified by "Yes" answers may then be functionally tested. See Appendix E for specimen functional tests. A "Program and Record of Functional Tests and Operational Reviews" (PRT) is generated in carrying out functional tests, and is cross-referenced to the ICQ via the column in the ICQ labeled "'Yes' Answers PRT Ref."

19.   A "No" answer means that a control weakness exists. All weaknesses should be entered on the Record of Control Weaknesses (RCW) in the manner explained in the following section of this Appendix. The column headed "'No' Answers RCW Ref." should be checked to indicate that this has been done.

20.   The system evaluator should consider whether, in light of his or her understanding of the system, there are any control weaknesses with

regard to supplementary control objectives. Any control weaknesses so determined should be identified in the space indicated on the evaluation sheets and entered on the RCW. A check should be placed in the column headed ''RCW'' to record that this has been done.

Abbreviations

21. A list of abbreviations used in the internal control questionnaire and related documents follows:

Abbreviation	Meaning
ICQ	Internal Control Questionnaire
C	Custodial control
D	Division of duties control
S	Supervisory control
RCW	Record of Control Weaknesses
PRT	Program and Record of Functional Tests and Operational Reviews
SCO	Supplementary control objective
RCE	Record of Control-Operation Exceptions

RECORD OF CONTROL WEAKNESSES

1. All control weaknesses identified during the preparation, updating, or review of the ICQ should be recorded on the Record of Control Weaknesses (''RCW,'' page 206). Separate RCW sheets or series of sheets should usually be prepared for each relevant section of the ICQ.

Internal Accounting Control Weaknesses

2. Columns 1 and 2 of the RCW are provided, respectively, to identify the numbers of the related ICQ questions (including those applicable to supplementary control objectives) and to explain the nature of the weaknesses and their possible effect on meeting internal accounting control objectives and/or efficiency of operations. Each weakness should be described in the context of the control objective to which it relates and an explanation should be given as to why and how the weakness could affect the financial statements and internal accounting control objectives. Guidance as to possible effects is contained in the Internal Control Reference Manual, which indicates for each question:

Record of Control Weaknesses

Company/Location _____ Page _____ of _____

ICQ Section _____

| ICQ Reference (1) | Nature of Weakness and Possible Effect on Internal Accounting Control and/or Efficiency of Operations (2) | Could a Material Error Arise? | | Notification of Weakness to Responsible Management | | |
		Yes/No (3)	Justification (4)	Informal Discussion with Site Management (Date) (5)	Report to Senior Management Yes (Date) No (6)	Response/Comments (If Applicable) (7)

a. The items in the financial statements that are directly related thereto; and/or

b. The possibility of major error in the financial statements, e.g., a loss may not be disclosed in the income statement or may be carried forward in the balance sheet as a fictitious asset or an understated liability.

3.   The system evaluator should next consider whether the weaknesses identified could give rise to material error. This decision must be made in the light of all the circumstances, including the number and size of the transactions affected and the existence of other control procedures that would detect a material error. The system evaluator should also consider whether a weakness could have a cumulative effect on a judgment relating to any other weakness, e.g., the absence of a proper capital expenditure authorization procedure combined with inadequate control over the coding of purchase invoices.

4.   If the evaluator decides, taking all the circumstances into account, that the weakness could not give rise to a material error, this decision should be recorded in column 3 of the RCW and the justification for it in column 4. Such weaknesses should be considered for reporting to senior management, as mentioned in paragraph 14 below.

5.   If the evaluator believes that a material error could arise, this possibility together with the justification for it should be recorded in columns 3 and 4.

6.   The information and conclusions recorded in columns 2, 3, and 4 should be discussed with site personnel to:

a. Identify any controls that were not apparent when the ICQ was completed;

b. Identify any other relevant factors that should be considered to place the weakness in proper perspective; and

c. Enable corrective action to be taken at the earliest opportunity.

The date of the discussion, the name and title of the personnel involved, and details of the discussion should be recorded in columns 5 and 7.

7.   When site personnel correct a potentially material weakness, the system evaluator should delay functional tests until after the weakness has been corrected. The evaluator should also consider the effect, if any, of the weakness on the operation of the internal accounting control system and the financial statements prior to its correction.

Operational Control Weaknesses*

8.   If operational control questions are answered, the RCW is prepared

---

*The following paragraphs may be applicable to internal accounting control weaknesses as well as operational control weaknesses.

in the manner described in paragraph 2 above and the following paragraphs of this section.

9.   The system evaluator should consider whether the operational control weaknesses identified could have implications for meeting the objectives of the internal accounting control system (see paragraphs 2 and 3 above). If it is decided that a weakness could give rise to a material error, this possibility, together with the justification for the decision, should be recorded in columns 3 and 4, and the procedures described in paragraphs 6 and 7 of this Appendix should be followed.

10.   To make the evaluator's report to management as meaningful as possible, the system evaluator should quantify, where practicable, the effect of a weakness in terms of revenue losses or cost increases. If that is not practicable, an effort should be made to determine the order of magnitude of the transactions or operations to which the control weakness relates. For example, if it is not possible to determine the revenue lost or additional costs incurred due to the failure to calculate economic order quantities, the system evaluator may comment on the total volume of purchases, purchased goods inventory, etc.

11.   Weaknesses can be evaluated in terms of monetary significance by analyzing the operational effects of failure to perform the control procedures. Considerations include:

a. The potential profitability significance of a control weakness; and
b. Dollarization of the effect of a control weakness.

12.   Operational control weaknesses should be evaluated with respect to materiality. If a weakness has only an insignificant effect on operations, it may be included in a miscellaneous section of, or an appendix to, the evaluator's report to management or excluded from the report altogether. However, all weaknesses should be discussed with site personnel for possible correction.

13.   Operational control weaknesses should be discussed to:

a. Identify any controls that were not apparent when the ICQ was completed;
b. Identify any other relevant factors that should be considered to place the weakness in proper perspective;
c. Gain assistance in dollarizing a finding or evaluating the means of dollarization; and
d. Enable site personnel to take appropriate corrective action at the earliest opportunity.

The date of the discussion, the name and title of the personnel involved, and details of the discussion should be recorded in columns 5 and 7.

Reporting Weaknesses

14.   All internal accounting control and operational control weaknesses recorded on the RCW should be considered for reporting to senior management. Column 6 of the RCW should be completed to provide a record of the dates on which weaknesses were reported or to document that it was not considered necessary to report them.

15.   When a weakness is subsequently rectified, this should be evidenced on the RCW by recording the date in column 7. The ICQ should be amended accordingly.

COMPLETION/UPDATING/REVIEW RECORD

Part 1. Completion/Updating of ICQ and RCW

1.   The space provided on the completion/updating/review record at the beginning of the ICQ should be signed and dated as evidence of the completion/updating of the ICQ and RCW by the individual who has carried out this work. This person should also indicate in the space provided for each control objective whether the computer (C) or non-computer (M) questions have been answered. Frequently all, or the majority of, the control objectives in a cycle will be evaluated by the same person; in such cases, they may be bracketed together with a single signature.

2.   If a standard control objective does not apply at a site, the record should so indicate and the control objective and related questions should be removed from the questionnaire.

3.   The lists of supplementary control objectives provide columns for recording whether the activity covered by the objective is relevant to the business and, if so, whether the procedures followed are the same as those followed with regard to a standard control objective. If a supplementary control objective is relevant and the same procedures are not followed, the supplementary control objective should be listed on the completion/updating/review record by inserting the number of the objective in one of the spaces prefixed ''S.''

Part 2. Review and Approval

4.   The spaces provided on each completion/updating/review record should be signed, to evidence the review and approval of the ICQ and RCW.

Completion/Updating/Review Record

Site _____

1. Completion/Updating of ICQ and RCW

Control Objective No.	Accounting Controls				Operational Controls	
	19__ Completed by	C or M*	19__ Updated by	C or M*	19__ Completed by	C or M*
1						
2						
3						
4						
5						
6						
7						
8						
9						
10						
11						
12						
13						
S						
S						
S						
S						
S						
S						
S						

*Indicate for each control objective whether the computer (C) or non-computer (M) questions have been answered.

2. Review and Approval

Reviewed by evaluator	19__	19__	19__
Approved by supervisor			

210

PAYMENTS CYCLE

The Internal Control Questionnaire for the payments cycle is reproduced on the pages that follow. The questionnaire for non-computer systems is shown on pages 212–54, and the questionnaire for computer systems on pages 261–342. A "Yes" answer indicates that a control exists; a "No" answer shows the absence of a control. Questions that deal with operational controls are identified via italics and shading.

NON-COMPUTER SYSTEMS

Control Objective

1. Purchases should be initiated only on the basis of appropriate authorizations and records of commitments should be maintained as a basis for:

   (a) determining that transactions are executed in accordance with authorizations;

   (b) establishing the amount of any provision required for losses arising from unfulfilled commitments.

Questionnaire	Flow-chart Ref.	Yes	No	"Yes" Answers PRT Ref.	"No" Answers RCW Ref.
Purchase Authorizations					
1.1 Are all significant purchase commitments and changes thereto initiated only on the basis of appropriate written authorizations?					
1.2 With respect to repetitively used articles, is there an attempt to reduce the volume of purchase authorizations by means of a systematic stocking program?					
1.3 When there is a stocking program for repetitively used articles, are purchase authorizations initiated on a basis of one of the following techniques: (a) calculations incorporating lead time and safety stock considerations; (b) stock status ordering when availability reaches zero; or, (c) period planning?					
1.4 In deciding how much to buy, are economic order quantities calculated?					

Questionnaire	Flow-chart Ref.	Yes	No	"Yes" Answers PRT Ref.	"No" Answers RCW Ref.
1.5 Do purchase authorizations indicate when material will be required?					
1.6 Are purchase authorizations submitted to the purchasing agent with enough lead time so he can properly "shop the market"?					
1.7 Do purchase authorizations contain technical and performance specifications so the purchasing agent knows exactly what to buy?					
Purchasing Function					
1.8 Does the purchasing function have: (a) an organization chart; (b) job descriptions; (c) clear-cut buying assignments?					

213

Questionnaire	Flow-chart Ref.	Yes	No	"Yes" Answers PRT Ref.	"No" Answers RCW Ref.
1.9 Is there a statement of purchasing policies which covers: (a) corporate relationships, particularly buying responsibilities; (b) competitive buying, source selection, and bidding; (c) maintenance of multiple buying sources to protect the continuity of supply; (d) rules on commitments and contracts; (e) reciprocity; (f) conflict of interest?					
1.10 Where the purchasing function is decentralized, is there coordination as to what is bought at each location so that the various locations do not compete with each other and purchasing power is maximized?					
1.11 Does the purchasing organization endeavor to bring purchasing power to bear via: (a) nationwide buying contracts; (b) blanket purchase commitments?					

Questionnaire	Flow-chart Ref.	Yes	No	"Yes" Answers PRT Ref.	"No" Answers RCW Ref.
1.12 Does the purchasing agent actively solicit competitive bids from suppliers?					
1.13 Are supplier negotiations facilitated by providing purchasing personnel with summaries of: (a) commodity buying volumes; (b) supplier buying volumes?					
1.14 Does the purchasing agent participate in: (a) standardization; (b) value analysis; (c) lease vs. buy analysis; (d) negotiating options to purchase in lease agreements?					
1.15 Does the purchasing agent have an orderly plan to insure the delivery of materials within the time specified on purchase commitments?					
1.16 Does the purchasing agent maintain supplier evaluation files to determine the adequacy of suppliers' delivery, quality, and cost performances?					

Questionnaire	Flow-chart Ref.	Yes	No	"Yes" Answers PRT Ref.	"No" Answers RCW Ref.
Initial Recording of Commitments					
1.17 Are the purchase commitments referred to in 1.1 recorded in written form?					
1.18 Do the commitment records state, insofar as is practicable: (a) quantities; (b) prices; (c) other relevant terms (e.g. discounts, freight terms); (d) routing; (e) sales tax terms; (f) delivery dates and instructions; (g) required testing procedures?					
1.19 Is the routing for purchase commitments furnished to the purchasing agent by qualified traffic personnel?					
1.20 Are the commitments controlled in such a way that it can subsequently be established that they have all been accounted for (e.g. by sequential pre-numbering, by entry in a register or by establishment of batch totals)?					
Record of Unfulfilled Commitments					
1.21 Are records maintained of commitments which have not been matched with receiving reports or equivalent records of goods or services received?					

Questionnaire	Flow-chart Ref.	Yes	No	"Yes" Answers PRT Ref.	"No" Answers RCW Ref.
1.22 Where sequentially pre-numbered forms or batch totals are used (1.20), are the numbers accounted for or the batch totals reconciled as part of the control procedure over unmatched commitments (1.21)?					
1.23 Are unmatched commitments (1.21) reviewed on a regular basis, e.g. monthly, to determine the reasons for any which have not been matched within a reasonable period of time?					
1.24 Is the review in 1.23 carried out by persons other than those who maintain the records of unmatched commitments (1.21)? (D)					
1.25 Are the results of the procedures in 1.23 reviewed and approved by a responsible official? (S)					

Control Objective

2. Control should be established over goods and services received as a basis for:

   (a) determining and recording the liability for goods and services received but not entered as accounts payable;

   (b) where required, posting the items to detailed inventory records.

Questionnaire	Flow-chart Ref.	Yes	No	"Yes" Answers PRT Ref.	"No" Answers RCW Ref.
Initial Recording of Receipt of Goods and Services 2.1 Are the following checked by suitable methods (e.g. by counting or weighing and inspecting goods received) and the results recorded at the time of their receipt for subsequent checking with the related invoices: (a) nature, quantity and condition of goods received (including property, plant and equipment and major supplies, e.g. fuel, stationery); (b) major services received (to the extent practicable)?					
2.2 Are procedures in effect to foster: (a) accurate weights (e.g. by periodically testing scales); (b) weighing routines that are not unduly expensive (e.g. by using statistical sampling)?					
2.3 Is there a statement of policy with respect to the acceptance or nonacceptance of over, or under, shipments?					

218

Questionnaire	Flow-chart Ref.	Yes	No	"Yes" Answers PRT Ref.	"No" Answers RCW Ref.
2.4 Are the results of the receiving routines (i.e. timeliness, quantities, quality) communicated to the purchasing agent without delay?					
2.5 Are the receiving records (2.1) controlled in such a way that it can subsequently be established whether all the related transactions have been accounted for (e.g. by sequentially pre-numbering receiving reports or by entering receipts in a register), in respect of: (a) goods (2.1(a)); (b) major services (2.1(b))?					
Liability for Unprocessed Invoices 2.6 Are there adequate records of goods and services received which have not been matched with the related suppliers' invoices, in respect of: (a) goods (2.1(a)); (b) major services (2.1(b))?					
2.7 Where sequentially pre-numbered forms are used (2.5), are all numbers accounted for as part of the control procedure over unmatched receipts (2.6), in respect of: (a) goods (2.1(a)); (b) major services (2.1(b))?					

Questionnaire	Flow-chart Ref.	Yes	No	"Yes" Answers PRT Ref.	"No" Answers RCW Ref.
2.8 Are unmatched records of goods and services received (2.6) reviewed on a regular basis, e.g. monthly, to determine the reasons for any such receipts which have not been matched within a reasonable period of time, in respect of: (a) goods (2.1(a)); (b) major services (2.1(b))?					
2.9 Is the review (2.8) carried out by persons other than those who maintain the records of unmatched items (2.6)? (D)					
2.10 Are the results of the procedures in 2.8 reviewed and approved by a responsible official? (S)					
2.11 Are there systematic procedures for determining on a regular basis the liabilities for major services received other than those checked by the procedures in 2.1(b) (e.g. telephone services, electricity, municipal taxes or rates, liabilities under leases)?					
2.12 Are the results of the procedures in 2.11 reviewed and approved by a responsible official? (S)					

Questionnaire	Flow-chart Ref.	Yes	No	"Yes" Answers PRT Ref.	"No" Answers RCW Ref.
Entries in Inventory Records					
2.13 Where required, are the records of goods received (2.1(a)) used to post quantities to detailed inventory records?					

221

Control Objective

3.   Control should be established over goods returned to and claims on suppliers as a
      basis for:

      (a)   obtaining credit for all such items;

      (b)   where required, posting the items to detailed inventory records.

Questionnaire	Flow-chart Ref.	Yes	No	"Yes" Answers PRT Ref.	"No" Answers RCW Ref.
Initial Recording of Returns and Claims 3.1 Are the following recorded for accounting control purposes at the time the goods are returned or the claims are first established for subsequent checking with the related credit notes: (a) quantities of goods returned to suppliers; (b) other claims made on suppliers (e.g. for short deliveries, freight claims, damaged goods not returned)?					
3.2 Are procedures in effect whereby costs are accumulated and determinations made to charge suppliers back for: (a) rework costs necessitated by defective goods; (b) significant freight incurred for defective goods returned?					

222

Questionnaire	Flow-chart Ref.	Yes	No	"Yes" Answers PRT Ref.	"No" Answers RCW Ref.
3.3 Are the records (3.1) controlled in such a way that it can subsequently be established whether the related transactions have all been accounted for (e.g. by sequentially pre-numbering claims forms or by entering claims in a register), in respect of: (a) goods (3.1(a)); (b) other claims (3.1(b))?					
Obtaining Credit for Returns and Claims 3.4 Are records maintained of goods returned and claims made which have not been matched with the related credit (or debit) memoranda in respect of: (a) goods (3.1(a)); (b) other claims (3.1(b))?					
3.5 Where sequentially pre-numbered forms are used (3.3), are the numbers accounted for as part of the control procedure over unmatched items (3.4), in respect of: (a) goods (3.1(a)); (b) other claims (3.1(b))?					

Questionnaire	Flow-chart Ref.	Yes	No	"Yes" Answers PRT Ref.	"No" Answers RCW Ref.
3.6 Are unmatched records of returns and claims (3.4) reviewed on a regular basis, e.g. monthly, to determine the reasons for any such claims which have not been matched within a reasonable period of time, in respect of: (a) goods (3.1(a)); (b) other claims (3.1(b))?					
3.7 Is the review (3.6) carried out by persons other than those who maintain the records of unmatched items (3.4)? (D)					
3.8 Are the results of the procedures in 3.6 reviewed and approved by a responsible official? (S)					
Entries in Inventory Records 3.9 Where required, are the records of goods returned (3.1(a)) used to post quantities to detailed inventory records?					

Control Objective

4. Invoices and related documentation should be properly checked and approved as being valid before being entered as accounts payable.

Questionnaire	Flow-chart Ref.	Yes	No	"Yes" Answers PRT Ref.	"No" Answers RCW Ref.
Detailed Checking of Documentation					
4.1 Are invoices for goods received checked as to: (a) quantities and conditions of goods received (to receiving records); (b) nature and quantities of goods ordered (to purchase orders); (c) prices and other terms (to purchase orders or suppliers' price lists)?					
4.2 Are invoices for services received compared with the underlying documentation (e.g. records of receipts (2.1(b)), completion reports, leases, records of meter readings) or, if such documentation is not available, approved by a responsible official?					
4.3 Are profitable cash discounts taken when available?					

Questionnaire	Flow-chart Ref.	Yes	No	"Yes" Answers PRT Ref.	"No" Answers RCW Ref.
4.4 Taking into consideration the availability of profitable cash discounts (4.3), are payment dates deferred until due dates?					
4.5 Are the following functions performed by separate individuals: (a) preparation of purchase orders; (D) (b) preparation of receiving records; (D) (c) checking of purchase invoices (4.1 and 4.2)? (D)					
4.6 Are credit (or debit) memoranda checked to confirm that: (a) they agree with the original record of the goods returned or claims made; (b) where applicable, the prices agree with the original invoice?					
4.7 Are the extensions and additions of invoices and credit (or debit) memoranda checked to an adequate extent?					
4.8 Do the invoices and credit (or debit) memoranda bear adequate evidence that the checking (4.1 to 4.7) has been carried out?					

Questionnaire	Flow-chart Ref.	Yes	No	"Yes" Answers PRT Ref.	"No" Answers RCW Ref.
Approval of Documentation					
4.9 Are invoices and credit (or debit) memoranda subject to final written approval by a responsible official prior to entry as accounts payable? (S)					
4.10 Are adjustments to suppliers' accounts properly documented?					
4.11 Are the adjustments and related documentation (4.10) reviewed and approved by a responsible official prior to entry in the accounts payable records? (S)					

Control Objective

5. All valid accounts payable transactions, and only those transactions, should be accurately recorded as accounts payable.

Questionnaire	Flow-chart Ref.	Yes	No	"Yes" Answers PRT Ref.	"No" Answers RCW Ref.
Accounting for All Transactions					
5.1 Is the system such (e.g. by sequential pre-numbering or the use of invoice registers) that all of the following documentation is accounted for and the amounts posted to the accounts payable control accounts: (a) purchase invoices; (b) credit (or debit) memoranda; (c) adjustments to suppliers' accounts?					
5.2 Is a review made on a regular basis, e.g. monthly, for any documents which have not been accounted for (5.1) within a reasonable period of time?					
5.3 Is the review (5.2) carried out by persons other than those who maintain the accounts payable control accounts or subsidiary records? (D)					
5.4 Are the results of the review in 5.2 reviewed and approved by a responsible official? (S)					

Questionnaire	Flow-chart Ref.	Yes	No	"Yes" Answers PRT Ref.	"No" Answers RCW Ref.
Control over Processing of Transactions					
5.5 Are totals for posting to a control account established over the following before they are passed to the persons who post them in the accounts payable subsidiary records: (a) purchase invoices; (b) credit (or debit) memoranda; (c) adjustments to suppliers' accounts?					
5.6 Is the system such that all the items posted to the control accounts (5.5) have been checked and approved in accordance with control objective 4?					
5.7 Are totals for posting to a control account established over cash documentation that affects suppliers' accounts before it is passed to the persons who post the accounts payable subsidiary records?					
5.8 Are the accounts payable subsidiary records maintained by persons other than those who: (a) check and approve documents in accordance with control objective 4; (D) (b) maintain the control account? (D)					

Questionnaire	Flow-chart Ref.	Yes	No	"Yes" Answers PRT Ref.	"No" Answers RCW Ref.
Reconciliation of Control Account					
5.9 Are the accounts payable subsidiary records reconciled periodically, e.g. monthly, with the control account?					
5.10 Are there adequate procedures for investigating differences disclosed by the reconciliations (5.9) before any adjustments are made?					
5.11 Are the reconciliations and investigation of differences (5.9 and 5.10) either performed or checked by individuals other than those who: (a) post the accounts payable subsidiary records; (D) (b) maintain the control account? (D)					
5.12 Are the results of the reconciliations and investigation of differences (5.9 and 5.10) reviewed and approved by a responsible official? (S)					
Agreement with Suppliers' Records					
5.13 Are the accounts payable subsidiary records periodically reconciled to suppliers' records (e.g. by comparison with suppliers' statements)?					

Questionnaire	Flow-chart Ref.	Yes	No	"Yes" Answers PRT Ref.	"No" Answers RCW Ref.
5.14 Is the procedure in 5.13 either performed or checked by persons other than those who: (a) post the accounts payable subsidiary records; (D) (b) maintain the control account? (D)					
5.15 Are the results of the reconciliations in 5.13 reviewed and approved by a responsible official? (S)					

Control Objective

6. Payments in respect of wages and salaries should be:

(a) made only to company employees at authorized rates of pay;

(b) where required, in accordance with records of work performed;

(c) accurately calculated.

Questionnaire	Flow-chart Ref.	Yes	No	"Yes" Answers PRT Ref.	"No" Answers RCW Ref.
Standing Payroll Data					
6.1 Are the following authorized in writing: (a) employees added to payrolls; (b) employees removed from payrolls; (c) rates of pay and changes in rates of pay; (d) payroll deductions other than compulsory deductions (specify below)?					
6.2 Do persons other than those who prepare the payrolls provide the authorizations required in 6.1? (D)					
6.3 Are there adequate controls designed to ensure that the payroll reflects all authorized standing data (6.1) and only such authorized data?					

Questionnaire	Flow-chart Ref.	Yes	No	"Yes" Answers PRT Ref.	"No" Answers RCW Ref.
Transaction Payroll Date					
6.4 If employees are paid on the basis of time worked:					
(a) is the payroll based on adequate time records;					
(b) where applicable, are the time records checked to supporting records of time spent (e.g., time charges to jobs);					
(c) is idle time reported and explained;					
(d) are time charges to jobs (6.4(b)) evaluated in terms of a yardstick or estimate;					
(e) are the time records (6.4(a)) approved;					
(f) do the time records (6.4(a)) indicate that overtime has been properly authorized?					
6.5 If employees are paid on the basis of output, are the payments based on output records that are reconciled with production records that are under accounting control (e.g. 20.8(c), 20.21)?					
6.6 If salaried or other employees not included in 6.4 or 6.5 are paid for overtime, is the payroll based on time records which indicate that overtime has been properly authorized?					
6.7 If employees receive commissions on sales, are the commissions based on sales records that are reconciled with sales (less, where applicable, returns) recorded in the books?					

Questionnaire	Flow-chart Ref.	Yes	No	"Yes" Answers PRT Ref.	"No" Answers RCW Ref.
Payroll Preparation					
6.8 Is there a check on the calculation of gross pay (e.g. by agreeing in total with predetermined control totals or with cost records, or by sufficient checking of individual amounts), in respect of: (a) employees paid for time worked (6.4); (b) employees paid for output (6.5); (c) employees paid for overtime (6.6); (d) employees paid commissions (6.7)?					
6.9 Is there a check on the calculation of payroll deductions (e.g. by agreeing in total with predetermined control totals or by sufficient checking of individual amounts)?					
6.10 Are the calculations and additions of payrolls and payroll summaries checked to an adequate extent?					
6.11 Do persons other than those who prepare the payrolls or payroll summaries check: (a) the calculations of gross pay (6.8); (D) (b) the calculations of payroll deductions (6.9); (D) (c) the calculations and additions of payrolls and payroll summaries (6.10)? (D)					
6.12 Do payrolls bear adequate evidence that the procedures in 6.8 to 6.11 have been completed?					

Questionnaire	Flow-chart Ref.	Yes	No	"Yes" Answers PRT Ref.	"No" Answers RCW Ref.
6.13 Are payrolls subject to the final written approval of a responsible official before they are paid? (S)					
Payments to Employees					
6.14 Do persons other than those who prepare the payrolls compare payroll checks, either individually or in the aggregate, with the payrolls? (D)					
6.15 If employees are paid in cash: (a) is cash withdrawn only for the net amount of the payroll; (C) (b) do persons other than those who prepare the payroll physically control cash until it is distributed to employees; (C) (c) are unclaimed wages promptly recorded and controlled by persons other than those who prepare the payroll? (C)					

235

Control Objective

7. Payroll deductions should be correctly accounted for and paid to the third parties to whom they are due.

Questionnaire	Flow-chart Ref.	Yes	No	"Yes" Answers PRT Ref.	"No" Answers RCW Ref.
Initial Control over Deductions					
7.1 Are all payroll deductions recorded in separate control accounts?					
Checking of Amounts to be Paid to Third Parties					
7.2 Are payments of payroll deductions to third parties agreed to the related payrolls?					
7.3 Is the procedure in 7.2 carried out by persons other than those who prepare the payrolls? (D)					

Control Objective

8. Reimbursements of imprest and similar funds (e.g. postage and other franking meters, payroll deduction stamps) should be made only for valid transactions.

Questionnaire	Flow-chart Ref.	Yes	No	"Yes" Answers PRT Ref.	"No" Answers RCW Ref.
Overall Control of Funds					
8.1 Are imprest and similar funds:					
(a) maintained at a reasonable balance in relation to the level of expenditure; (C)					
(b) under the custody of persons who do not have access to non-imprest funds; (C)					
(c) periodically verified and reconciled with the general ledger control account by a person other than the custodian (all funds, both imprest and non-imprest, in the custody of the same person being verified at the same time)? (D)					
Expenditures from Funds					
8.2 Are all disbursements from imprest and similar funds:					
(a) supported by adequate documentation;					
(b) approved where appropriate?					
8.3 In the case of cash funds, are there reasonable limits on:					
(a) the size of individual disbursements; (C)					
(b) the extent to which personal checks of employees are cashed; (C)					
(c) loans and advances (e.g. for wages) made from such funds? (C)					

Questionnaire	Flow-chart Ref.	Yes	No	"Yes" Answers PRT Ref.	"No" Answers RCW Ref.
Requests for Reimbursement of Funds 8.4 Are all reimbursements made on an imprest basis?					
8.5 Are requests for reimbursement accompanied by details of expenditures and supporting vouchers?					
8.6 Are the reimbursements approved by an official who is not the custodian of the funds? (S)					

Control Objective

9. Disbursements from bank accounts should be made only in respect of valid transactions.

Questionnaire	Flow-cnart Ref.	Yes	No	"Yes" Answers PRT Ref.	"No" Answers RCW Ref.
9.1 Has consideration been given to using bank drafts as a payment instrument?					
Control over Issue and Usage of Checks					
9.2 Are supplies of unissued checks properly safeguarded? (C)					
9.3 Is the system such that: (a) the usage of checks is accounted for by persons other than those who have custody of unissued checks (9.2); (C) (b) spoiled checks are under adequate control? (C)					
9.4 Are the results of the procedures in 9.3 reviewed and approved by a responsible official? (S)					

Questionnaire	Flow-chart Ref.	Yes	No	"Yes" Answers PRT Ref.	"No" Answers RCW Ref.
Preparation of Checks and Bank Transfers					
9.5 Are checks and bank transfers prepared by persons other than those who initiate or approve any documents which give rise to disbursements for:					
(a) payments of accounts payable (control objective 5); (D)					
(b) payrolls and payroll deductions (control objectives 6 and 7); (D)					
(c) reimbursements of imprest and similar funds (control objective 8)? (D)					
9.6 Are checks and bank transfers prepared only on the basis of evidence that the validity of the transactions has been confirmed in accordance with the company's procedures, in respect of:					
(a) payments of accounts payable (control objective 5);					
(b) payrolls and payroll deductions (control objectives 6 and 7);					
(c) reimbursements of imprest and similar funds (control objective 8)?					
9.7 Are checks and bank transfers for transactions which, because of their nature, do not pass through the normal approval procedures as referred to in 9.6, (e.g. purchase of investments, payment of dividends, repayment of debt) initiated only on the basis of proper documentation of the validity of the transactions?					

240

Questionnaire	Flow-chart Ref.	Yes	No	"Yes" Answers PRT Ref.	"No" Answers RCW Ref.
9.8 Is the documentation in 9.7 reviewed and approved in writing by a responsible official before checks and bank transfers are initiated? (S)					
Signing of Checks					
9.9 Are checks signed by officials other than those who approve transactions for payment in respect of: (a) payment of accounts payable (control objective 5); (C) (b) payrolls and payroll deductions (control objectives 6 and 7); (C) (c) reimbursement of imprest and similar funds (control objective 8); (C) (d) other payments (9.7)? (C)					
9.10 At the time of signing checks and bank transfers, does each signatory examine: (a) original supporting documents (e.g. invoices, payrolls, or imprest cash records) which have been checked and approved in accordance with the company's procedures (control objectives 4, 6, 7 and 8 and Question 9.7); (S) or (b) substitute documents (such as remittance advices or check requisitions) which provide adequate evidence of the validity of the related transactions? (S)					

Questionnaire	Flow-chart Ref.	Yes	No	"Yes" Answers PRT Ref.	"No" Answers RCW Ref.
9.11 Are the supporting documents effectively cancelled by, or under the control of, the signatories to prevent subsequent re-use? (C)					
9.12 If a mechanical check signer is in use, is there adequate control over the custody and use of the signer and the signature plates? (C)					
Control of Checks and Bank Transfers after Signing 9.13 After signing, are checks and bank transfers forwarded directly to the payees (or to the bank with the bank transfer lists) without being returned to the originators or others who are in a position to introduce documents into the cash disbursements system? (C)					
Comparison of Disbursements Records 9.14 Are all checks and individual bank transfers as listed in the disbursement records compared as to names, dates and amounts with transactions processed through the company's bank accounts, e.g. as part of the bank reconciliation procedures?					

Questionnaire	Flow-chart Ref.	Yes	No	"Yes" Answers PRT Ref.	"No" Answers RCW Ref.
9.15 Is the comparison (9.14) carried out by persons other than those who prepare checks and bank transfers or who can introduce documents into the disbursements system? (D)					

Control Objective

10. Accurate detailed records should be maintained of materials and supplies inventories.

Note: The answers to the following questions should normally cover the following (whether on the client's premises or in the hands of third parties):

(a) all purchased inventories (including items purchased for resale);

(b) manufactured parts and sub-assemblies in store, where they are accounted for by the client as part of purchased inventories rather than as finished products.

State below the client's inventory categories covered by the answers.

Questionnaire	Flow-chart Ref.	Yes	No	"Yes" Answers PRT Ref.	"No" Answers RCW Ref.
Validity of Entries in Inventory Records 10.1 Are all movements of inventories that result in postings to the detailed records required to be: (a) supported by prescribed accounting documentation; (b) properly approved?					
Accounting for All Documents 10.2 Is the system such that it can subsequently be established that all documentation has been accounted for and posted to the control accounts (e.g. by sequential pre-numbering of documents and/or batches or by reconciliation of records)?					

Questionnaire	Flow-chart Ref.	Yes	No	"Yes" Answers PRT Ref.	"No" Answers RCW Ref.
10.3 Is a review made on a regular basis, e.g. monthly, to determine the reasons for any documents which have not been accounted for and posted within a reasonable period of time?					
10.4 Is evidence that all documentation has been accounted for and posted to the control account (10.3) reviewed and approved by a responsible official? (S)					
Control over Record Keeping					
10.5 Are the detailed records maintained by persons other than the storekeepers? (C)					
10.6 Are totals for posting to the control accounts established over all documentation before it is passed to the persons who post the detailed records?					
10.7 Are the control accounts maintained by persons other than those who maintain the detailed records? (D)					

Questionnaire	Flow-chart Ref.	Yes	No	"Yes" Answers PRT Ref.	"No" Answers RCW Ref.
Reconciliation of Control Accounts					
10.8 Are the balances in the detailed records periodically reconciled with the control account balances?					
10.9 Are there adequate procedures for investigating differences disclosed by the reconciliations (10.8) before any adjustments are made?					
10.10 Are the reconciliations and investigation of differences (10.8 and 10.9) either performed or checked by individuals other than those who: (a) post the detailed records; (D) (b) are responsible for the physical custody of the stock; (C) (c) maintain the control account? (D)					
10 11 Are the reconciliations in 10.10 reviewed and approved by a responsible official? (S)					
Other Accounting Entries					
10.12 In cases where adjustments to the detailed records are required and amounts are not easily quantified (e.g. losses due to evaporation) do the methods used to determine such adjustments appear reasonable?					

Questionnaire	Flow-chart Ref.	Yes	No	"Yes" Answers PRT Ref.	"No" Answers RCW Ref.
10.13 Are separate general or subsidiary ledger accounts maintained for all adjustments to inventory valuations (e.g. for provisions, variances, adjustments arising on physical verification)?					
Physical Control					
10.14 Are areas where materials and supplies are held protected against access by unauthorized personnel? (C)					
10.15 Are all materials and supplies inventories physically verified at least annually, either by cycle or periodic counts?					

Control Objective

11. **Additions to and disposals of property, plant and equipment should be properly authorized.**

Questionnaire	Flow-chart Ref.	Yes	No	"Yes" Answers PRT Ref.	"No" Answers RCW Ref.

Authorization of Expenditures and Disposals
 	
11.1 Are formal written requests and authorizations required for the following (if appropriate, over a certain limit):
 	
  (a) individual property, plant and equipment additions;
  (b) individual property, plant and equipment disposals;
  (c) major maintenance or repair of property, plant and equipment;
  (d) expenditures on property, plant and equipment over the amount initially authorized?					

11.2 Do the above requests include:
 	
  (a) the reasons for the expenditures or disposals;
  (b) the estimated amount of expenditures?					

11.3 Where the expenditure is for the replacement of an existing asset, is the system such that the related retirement or disposal is accurately recorded in the accounts?					

Questionnaire	Flow-chart Ref.	Yes	No	"Yes" Answers PRT Ref.	"No" Answers RCW Ref.
11.4 Are the above requests authorized by the Board of Directors or, if amounts are under a specified limit, by designated officials?					
11.5 Are the actual expenditures compared with the authorized requests and approvals obtained for excess expenditures?					
Authorization of Capitalization of Expenditures 11.6 Is the allocation of expenditure between capital expenditures and charges to current operations approved as part of the authorization for the expenditure?					

Control Objective

12. Accurate records should be maintained of the cost and accumulated depreciation of property, plant and equipment.

Questionnaire	Flow-chart Ref.	Yes	No	"Yes" Answers PRT Ref.	"No" Answers RCW Ref.
Detailed Records 12.1 Are property, plant and equipment subsidiary ledgers maintained for the following classifications: (a) land and buildings; (b) leasehold improvements; (c) plant and machinery; (d) furniture, fixtures and fittings; (e) office equipment; (f) motor vehicles; (g) property, plant and equipment leased or loaned to third parties; (h) other property, plant and equipment (specify below)?					
12.2 Do the subsidiary ledgers provide the following details for each item: (a) adequate identification; (b) cost; (c) accumulated depreciation?					

Questionnaire	Flow-chart Ref.	Yes	No	"Yes" Answers PRT Ref.	"No" Answers RCW Ref.
12.3 Are the subsidiary ledgers posted regularly, e.g. quarterly, for: (a) cost of additions and disposals; (b) depreciation for the period?					
Reconciliation with General Ledger 12.4 Are the subsidiary ledgers balanced at least annually with the general ledger for: (a) cost; (b) accumulated depreciation?					
12.5 Are there adequate procedures for investigating differences disclosed by the reconciliations (12.4) before any adjustments are made?					
12.6 Are the results of the procedures in 12.5 reviewed and approved by a responsible official before any adjustments to the accounts are made? (S)					

251

Questionnaire	Flow-chart Ref.	Yes	No	"Yes" Answers PRT Ref.	"No" Answers RCW Ref.
Property, Plant and Equipment Leased or on Loan from Third Parties 12.7 Are suitable records maintained of assets leased or on loan from third parties?					
12.8 *Are options to purchase leased assets periodically reviewed by a responsible official to determine the appropriateness of exercising the option?*					

252

Control Objective

13. General ledger entries arising from the payments cycle should be accurately determined.

Questionnaire	Flow-chart Ref.	Yes	No	"Yes" Answers PRT Ref.	"No" Answers RCW Ref.
Classification of Expenditures 13.1 Is the coding of the following transactions for posting to general ledger accounts checked to an appropriate extent: (a) invoices and other supporting documentation related to the payment of accounts payable; (b) payrolls; (c) reimbursements of imprest and similar funds; (d) disbursements from bank accounts not covered in (a) to (c) above; (e) depreciation of property, plant and equipment?					
13.2 Is the coding (13.1) of the following transactions approved by responsible officials: (a) invoices and other supporting documentation related to the payment of accounts payable; (S) (b) payrolls; (S) (c) reimbursements of imprest and similar funds; (S) (d) disbursements from bank accounts not covered in (a) to (c) above; (S) (e) depreciation of property, plant and equipment? (S)					

Questionnaire	Flow-chart Ref.	Yes	No	"Yes" Answers PRT Ref.	"No" Answers RCW Ref.
Summarization of Expenditure					
13.3 Are there adequate controls (e.g. reconciliation of totals) to verify that the summaries which are used as a basis for making the general ledger entries are arithmetically accurate in respect of:					
(a) invoices and other supporting documentation related to the payments of accounts payable;					
(b) payrolls;					
(c) reimbursements of imprest and similar funds;					
(d) disbursements from bank accounts not covered in (a) to (c) above;					
(e) depreciation of property, plant and equipment?					
13.4 Are the summaries referred to in 13.3 approved by a responsible official before posting to the general ledger accounts? (S)					

SUPPLEMENTARY CONTROL OBJECTIVES — ICQ PAYMENTS CYCLE

Indicate whether each supplementary control objective is applicable and if applicable whether it is fully covered by the same control procedures as those recorded under the standard control objectives. Any supplementary control objectives which are applicable and are *not* covered by the standard control objectives should be recorded on the supplementary control objective evaluation sheet and entered on the cover sheet.

(Tick (√) as appropriate)

Objective No.	Objective	Applicable?		Same Procedures?	
		Yes	No	Yes	No
S-1	**Payments Not in the Routine Course of Business** Payments in connection with recurring transactions not directly related to the client's main business activities should be made only on the basis of adequate and valid documentation. (This objective is relevant only where a separate processing system is used for such transactions.)				
S-2	**Vacation Pay** Entitlements under vacation pay arrangements should be authorized and recorded: (a) so that only valid payments are made to employees; (b) as a basis for determining the outstanding liability.				
S-3	**Bonus and Profit Sharing Plans** Entitlements under bonus and profit sharing plans should be authorized and recorded: (a) so that only valid payments are made to employees; (b) as a basis for determining the outstanding liability.				

255

Objective No.	Objective	Applicable?		Same Procedures?	
		Yes	No	Yes	No
S-4	**Loans to Officers and Employees** All loans to officers and employees should be: (a) properly authorized; (b) under proper accounting control.				
S-5	**Postage** Where postage expenditure is of particular significance to the client (e.g. in mail order businesses), special steps should be taken to confirm that disbursements for such expenditure are valid.				
S-6	**Employees Advance Accounts** All advances for expenses made to employees and all claims recorded in the accounts for the reimbursement of expenses incurred should be valid.				
S-7	**Bills, Acceptances and Notes Payable** Bills, acceptances and notes payable should be: (a) accepted/drawn only in respect of valid transactions; (b) accurately recorded, as a basis for determining the outstanding liability.				

(Tick (√) as appropriate)

Objective No.	Objective	Applicable?		Same Procedures?	
		Yes	No	Yes	No
S-8	**Inventories Held on Behalf of Third Parties** Accurate records should be maintained of material and supplies inventories held on behalf of third parties (e.g. component parts or packaging materials supplied by customers) so as to: (a) enable such inventories to be identified separately from those owned by the company; (b) provide a basis for establishing the liability for any such goods not ultimately returned.				
S-9	**Returnable Containers** Returnable containers received from third parties which are charged to the company should be accurately recorded as a basis for determining the liability for any containers not returned.				
S-10	**Patents and Trade Marks, etc.** Accurate records should be maintained of the cost of patents and trade marks.				
S-11	**Accrued and Prepaid Expenses and Deferred Charges** General ledger entries in respect of accrued and prepaid expenses and deferred charges should be accurately determined.				

257

Objective No.	Objective	Applicable?		Same Procedures?	
		Yes	No	Yes	No
S-12	**Accrued Interest and Credit Charges** Accrued interest and other credit charges payable should be accurately calculated and accounted for in the correct financial periods.				
S-13	**Goods on Consignment** Accurate records should be maintained of goods received on consignment as a basis for establishing the liability for any such goods sold or used by the client.				
S-14					
S-15					

SUPPLEMENTARY CONTROL OBJECTIVE EVALUATION SHEET

(Attach to related ICQ Section)

Control Objective (State S.C.O. number and objective in full)		
Control Procedures (Describe precise nature (except to the extent clearly apparent from flowchart) and cross-reference to flowchart.)	Flowchart Ref.	PRT Ref.
Identify control weaknesses (state "None" where appropriate).		RCW
Continue on reverse side, if necessary		

Identify control weaknesses (state "None" where appropriate).	RCW

COMPUTER SYSTEMS

Control Objective

1. **Purchases should be initiated only on the basis of appropriate authorizations and records of commitments should be maintained as a basis for:**
   (a) **determining that transactions are executed in accordance with authorizations;**
   (b) **establishing the amount of any provision required for losses arising from unfulfilled commitments.**

Questionnaire	Flow-chart Ref.	Yes	No	"Yes" Answers PRT Ref.	"No" Answers RCW Ref.
Purchase Authorization					
1.1 Are all significant purchase commitments and changes thereto initiated only on the basis of appropriate written authorizations?					
1.2 Are the purchase commitments referred to in 1.1 recorded in written form?					
1.3 Do the commitments records state, insofar as is practicable: (a) quantities; (b) prices; (c) other relevant terms (e.g., discounts, freight terms)?					
Completeness of Input and Updating					
Specify below the principal control that all details of purchase commitments and changes thereto are input to the computer and updated. If the principal control is: (a) computer sequence check of serially numbered input documents, answer questions 1.4 to 1.9; (b) agreement of manually established batch totals, specify totals used and answer questions 1.10 to 1.14.					

Questionnaire	Flow-chart Ref.	Yes	No	"Yes" Answers PRT Ref.	"No" Answers RCW Ref.
Computer Sequence Check					
1.4 Are there adequate controls to ensure that all transactions are recorded on a serially numbered document?					
1.5 Is the method used in the program for the checking of numerical sequence appropriate (e.g., does it cater for changes in sequence and more than one sequence running at a time)?					
1.6 Is a print-out of missing documents produced at regular intervals (e.g., weekly)?					
1.7 Is a total of accepted items accumulated by the computer during the sequence check run agreed to the total of items written to the purchase commitment file or, alternatively, are such totals carried through intermediate processing (including summarization of totals or changes in the totals used) so that it is established that all accepted input items are updated to the purchase commitment file?					
1.8 Is the reconciliation of totals in 1.7 carried out manually or, alternatively, is the reconciliation carried out by the computer with adequate evidence of this check being printed out?					

Questionnaire	Flow-chart Ref.	Yes	No	"Yes" Answers PRT Ref.	"No" Answers RCW Ref.

1.9   Are there adequate procedures for:
    (a) investigation of missing documents (1.6);
    (b) investigation and correction of differences disclosed by the update reconciliations (1.8)?					

Batch Totals					

1.10   Are there adequate controls to ensure that:
    (a) a document is raised for all purchase commitments;
    (b) all documents are included in a batch;
    (c) all batches are submitted for processing?					

1.11 Are the totals of individual items accepted by the computer compared manually to pre-determined control totals or, alternatively, is such a comparison made by the computer with adequate evidence of the check being printed out?					
1.12 Are the totals in 1.11 agreed to the total of items written to the purchase commitment file or, alternatively, are such totals carried through intermediate processing (including summarization of totals or changes in the totals used) so that it is established that all accepted input items are updated to the purchase commitment file?					

Questionnaire	Flow-chart Ref.	Yes	No	"Yes" Answers PRT Ref.	"No" Answers RCW Ref.
1.13 Is the reconciliation of totals in 1.12 carried out manually or, alternatively, is the reconciliation carried out by the computer with adequate evidence of this check being printed out?					
1.14 Are there adequate procedures for: (a) investigation and correction of differences disclosed by the input reconciliations (1.11); (b) resubmission of all rejections; (c) investigation and correction of differences disclosed by the update reconciliations (1.13)?					
Disciplines over Basic Input Completeness and Updating Controls 1.15 Are the following procedures either performed or checked by persons other than those involved in computer operations: (a) investigation of missing documents (1.9(a)); (D) (b) manual agreement of input totals (1.11); (D) (c) investigation and correction of differences disclosed by the input reconciliations (1.4(a)); (D) (d) resubmission of all rejections (1.14(b)); (D) (e) manual agreement of update totals (1.8, 1.13); (D) (f) investigation and correction of differences disclosed by the update reconciliations (1.9(b), 1.14(c))? (D)					

Questionnaire	Flow-chart Ref.	Yes	No	"Yes" Answers PRT Ref.	"No" Answers RCW Ref.
1.16 Are the results of the following procedures reviewed and approved by a responsible official: (a) investigation of missing documents (1.9(a)); (S) (b) manual agreement of input totals (1.11); (S) (c) investigation and correction of differences disclosed by the input reconciliations (1.14(a)); (S) (d) resubmission of all rejections (1.14(b)); (S) (e) manual agreement of update totals (1.8, 1.13); (S) (f) investigation and correction of differences disclosed by the update reconciliations (1.9(b), 1.14(c))? (S)					
Accuracy of Input and Updating 1.17 Are there adequate controls to ensure that the following fields are accurately input and updated (e.g., batch totals, edit checks in program, reporting of non-matched items): (a) quantity/value; (b) inventory/vendor reference fields; (c) date; (d) price?					
1.18 Are there adequate procedures for: (a) the agreement of totals, where applicable; (b) investigation and correction of differences or exceptions?					

Questionnaire	Flow-chart Ref.	Yes	No	"Yes" Answers PRT Ref.	"No" Answers RCW Ref.
1.19 Are the following procedures either performed or checked by persons other than those involved in computer operations: (a) agreement of totals, where applicable (1.18(a)); (D) (b) investigation and correction of differences or exceptions (1.18(b))? (D)					
1.20 Are the results of the following procedures reviewed and approved by a responsible official: (a) agreement of totals, where applicable (1.18(a)); (S) (b) investigation and correction of differences or exceptions (1.18(b))? (S)					
Computer Generated Orders 1.21 Are the methods used in the program to generate the commitments appropriate?					
1.22 Is there an adequate check over the accuracy of the commitments generated (e.g., reasonableness check, manual review of generated commitments)?					
1.23 Are the results of the check (1.22) reviewed and approved by a responsible official? (S)					

Questionnaire	Flow-chart Ref.	Yes	No	"Yes" Answers PRT Ref.	"No" Answers RCW Ref.
1.24 Is a total (specify total used) of generated items accumulated by the computer and agreed manually with a total of items written to the purchase commitment file or, alternatively, are the totals agreed by the computer with adequate evidence of this check being printed out?					
1.25 Are there adequate procedures for investigation and correction of differences disclosed by the update reconciliation (1.24)?					
1.26 Are the following procedures either performed or checked by persons other than those involved in computer operations: (a) manual agreement of update totals (1.24); (D) (b) investigation and correction of differences disclosed by the update reconciliation (1.25)? (D)					
1.27 Are the results of the following procedures reviewed and approved by a responsible official: (a) manual agreement of update totals (1.24); (S) (b) investigation and correction of differences disclosed by the update reconciliation (1.25)? (S)					

Questionnaire	Flow-chart Ref.	Yes	No	"Yes" Answers PRT Ref.	"No" Answers RCW Ref.
Authorization					
1.28 If data is authorized prior to the establishment of the controls for completeness and accuracy of input (e.g., prior to establishment of batch control totals or recording on a sequentially numbered document), are there adequate controls (e.g., checking authorization after batch control totals are established or sequentially numbered documents raised) to ensure that: (a) no unauthorized alterations are made to authorized data during subsequent processing; (b) unauthorized data is not added; (c) all authorized items are included in subsequent processing?					
Record of Unfulfilled Commitments					
1.29 If the computer evaluates purchase commitments, review the answers to the standing data controls section as regards prices and vendors, where appropriate. Are there adequate controls over: (a) where applicable, file creation; (b) the authorization of amendments; (c) the completeness of writing amendments to the file; (d) the accuracy of writing amendments to the file; (e) the maintenance of the data on file?					
1.30 Is the method used in the program for the calculation of value appropriate?					

Questionnaire	Flow-chart Ref.	Yes	No	"Yes" Answers PRT Ref.	"No" Answers RCW Ref.
1.31 Are there adequate controls over the file holding details of outstanding purchase commitments to ensure that details of purchase commitments and changes thereto are completely and accurately maintained (e.g., manual control account)?					
1.32 Is the method used in the program to match goods and, where applicable, services received to purchase commitments on file appropriate (e.g., does it flag or delete matched items)?					
1.33 Is a print-out of items outstanding for an unreasonable length of time (e.g., over one month) produced at regular intervals?					
1.34 Are unmatched commitments (1.33) reviewed on a regular basis (e.g., monthly) to determine the reason for any which have not been matched?					
1.35 Are the following procedures either performed or checked by persons other than those involved in computer operations: (a) maintenance of the outstanding purchase commitments file (1.31); (D) (b) review of unmatched commitments (1.34)? (D)					

Questionnaire	Flow-chart Ref.	Yes	No	"Yes" Answers PRT Ref.	"No" Answers RCW Ref.
1.36 Are the results of the following procedures reviewed and approved by a responsible official: (a) maintenance of the outstanding purchase commitments file (1.31); (S) (b) review of unmatched commitments (1.34)? (S)					

Programmed Procedures
 	
1.37 List below the programmed procedures whose continued and proper operation is not assured by user controls.
 	
In respect of the items listed above, review the answers to the integrity control section. Are there adequate controls to ensure that:
(a) appropriate programmed procedures are implemented in respect of:
  (i) where applicable, new systems;
  (ii) program changes;
(b) unauthorized changes cannot be made to production programs;
(c) programmed procedures are consistently applied?					

Control Objective

2. **Control should be established over goods and services received as a basis for:**

(a) **determining and recording the liability for goods and services received but not entered as accounts payable;**

(b) **where required, posting items to detailed inventory records.**

Questionnaire	Flow-chart Ref.	Yes	No	"Yes" Answers PRT Ref.	"No" Answers RCW Ref.
Initial Recording of Receipt of Goods and Services					
2.1 Are the following checked by suitable methods (e.g., by counting or weighing and inspecting goods received) and the results recorded at the time of their receipt for subsequent checking with the related invoices: (a) nature, quantity and condition of goods received (including property, plant and equipment and major supplies, (e.g., fuel, stationery); (b) major services received (to the extent practicable)?					
Completeness of Input and Updating					
Specify below the principal control that all details of goods, and where applicable, services received are input to the computer and updated. If the principal control is: (a) computer matching with a file of purchase commitments placed, answer questions 2.2 to 2.5; (b) computer sequence check of serially numbered input documents, answer questions 2.6 to 2.11; (c) agreement of manually established batch totals, specify totals used and answer questions 2.12 to 2.16.					

Questionnaire	Flow-chart Ref.	Yes	No	"Yes" Answers PRT Ref.	"No" Answers RCW Ref.
Computer Matching					
2.2 Review the answers to control objective 1. Are the matching procedures adequate to ensure that details of goods and, where applicable, services received are input completely?					
2.3 Is a total of accepted items accumulated by the computer during the matching run agreed to the total of items written to the receipts file or, alternatively, are such totals carried through intermediate processing (including summarization of totals or changes in the totals used) so that it is established that all accepted input items are updated to the receipts file?					
2.4 Is the reconciliation of totals in 2.3 carried out manually or, alternatively, is the reconciliation carried out by the computer with adequate evidence of this check being printed out?					
2.5 Are there adequate procedures for: (a) investigation and correction of differences disclosed by the matching process (2.2); (b) investigation and correction of differences disclosed by the update reconciliation (2.4)?					
Computer Sequence Check					
2.6 Are there adequate controls to ensure that all transactions are recorded on a serially numbered document?					

Questionnaire	Flow-chart Ref.	Yes	No	"Yes" Answers PRT Ref.	"No" Answers RCW Ref.
2.7 Is the method used in the program for the checking of numerical sequence appropriate (e.g. does it cater for changes in sequence and more than one sequence running at a time)?					
2.8 Is a print-out of missing documents produced at regular intervals (e.g., weekly)?					
2.9 Is a total of accepted items accumulated by the computer during the sequence check run agreed to the total of items written to the receipts file or, alternatively, are such totals carried through intermediate processing (including summarization of totals or changes in the totals used) so that it is established that all accepted input items are updated to the receipts file?					
2.10 Is the reconciliation of totals in 2.9 carried out manually or, alternatively, is the reconciliation carried out by the computer with adequate evidence of this check being printed out?					
2.11 Are there adequate procedures for: (a) investigation of missing documents (2.8); (b) investigation and correction of differences disclosed by the update reconciliations (2.10)?					

273

Questionnaire	Flow-chart Ref.	Yes	No	"Yes" Answers PRT Ref.	"No" Answers RCW Ref.
Batch Totals					
2.12 Are there adequate controls to ensure that: (a) a document is raised for all goods and services received; (b) all documents are included in a batch; (c) all batches are submitted for processing?					
2.13 Are the totals of individual items accepted by the computer compared manually to pre-determined control totals or, alternatively, is such a comparison made by the computer with adequate evidence of the check being printed out?					
2.14 Are the totals in 2.13 agreed to the total of items written to the receipts file or, alternatively, are such totals carried through intermediate processing (including summarization of totals or changes in the totals used) so that it is established that all accepted input items are updated to the receipts file?					
2.15 Is the reconciliation of totals in 2.14 carried out manually or, alternatively, is the reconciliation carried out by the computer with adequate evidence of this check being printed out?					

Questionnaire	Flow-chart Ref.	Yes	No	"Yes" Answers PRT Ref.	"No" Answers RCW Ref.
2.16 Are there adequate procedures for: (a) investigation and correction of differences disclosed by the input reconciliations (2.13); (b) resubmission of all rejections; (c) investigation and correction of differences disclosed by the update reconciliations (2.15)?					
Disciplines over Basic Input Completeness and Updating Controls 2.17 Are the following procedures either performed or checked by persons other than those involved in computer operations: (a) investigation and correction of differences disclosed by the matching process (2.5(a)); (D) (b) investigation of missing documents (2.11(a)); (D) (c) manual agreement of input totals (2.13); (D) (d) investigation and correction of differences disclosed by the input reconciliations (2.16(a)); (D) (e) resubmission of all rejections (2.16(b)); (D) (f) manual agreement of update totals (2.4, 2.10, 2.15); (D) (g) investigation and correction of differences disclosed by the update reconciliations (2.5(b), 2.11(b), 2.16(c))? (D)					

Questionnaire	Flow-chart Ref.	Yes	No	"Yes" Answers PRT Ref.	"No" Answers RCW Ref.
2.18 Are the results of the following procedures reviewed and approved by a responsible official: (a) investigation and correction of differences disclosed by the matching process (2.5(a)); (S) (b) investigation of missing documents (2.11(a)); (S) (c) manual agreement of input totals (2.13); (S) (d) investigation and correction of differences disclosed by the input reconciliations (2.16(a)); (S) (e) resubmission of all rejections (2.16(b)); (S) (f) manual agreement of update totals (2.4, 2.10, 2.15); (S) (g) investigation and correction of differences disclosed by the update reconciliations (2.5(b), 2.11(b), 2.16(c))? (S)					
Accuracy of Input and Updating 2.19 Are there adequate controls to ensure that the following fields are accurately input and updated (e.g., batch totals, edit checks in programs, reporting of non-matched items): (a) quantity/value; (b) inventory/vendor reference fields; (c) price; (d) date?					
2.20 Are there adequate procedures for: (a) the agreement of totals, where applicable; (b) investigation and correction of differences or exceptions?					

Questionnaire	Flow-chart Ref.	Yes	No	"Yes" Answers PRT Ref.	"No" Answers RCW Ref.
2.21 Are the following procedures either performed or checked by persons other than those involved in computer operations: (a) agreement of totals, where applicable (2.20(a)); (D) (b) investigation and correction of differences or exceptions (2.20(b))? (D)					
2.22 Are the results of the following procedures reviewed and approved by a responsible official: (a) agreement of totals, where applicable (2.20(a)); (S) (b) investigation and correction of differences or exceptions (2.20(b))? (S)					
Liability for Unprocessed Invoices 2.23 If the computer evaluates details of goods and services received, review the answers to the standing data controls section as regards prices and vendors. Are there adequate controls over: (a) where applicable, file creation; (b) the authorization of amendments; (c) the completeness of writing amendments to the file; (d) the accuracy of writing amendments to the file; (e) the maintenance of the data on file?					
2.24 Is the method used in the program for the calculation of value appropriate?					

Questionnaire	Flow-chart Ref.	Yes	No	"Yes" Answers PRT Ref.	"No" Answers RCW Ref.
2.25 Are there adequate controls over the file holding details of outstanding goods and, where applicable, services received, so that such details are completely and accurately maintained and subject only to authorized adjustments (e.g., manual control account)?					
2.26 Is the method used in the program to match invoices to goods and, where applicable, services received appropriate (e.g., does it flag or delete matched items)?					
2.27 Is a print-out of items outstanding for an unreasonable length of time (e.g., over one month) produced at regular intervals?					
2.28 Are unmatched records of goods and, where applicable, services (2.27) reviewed on a regular basis (e.g., monthly) to determine the reasons for any such receipts which have not been matched within a reasonable period of time?					
2.29 Are there systematic procedures for determining on a regular basis the liabilities for major services received and payments to be made other than any checked by the procedures in 2.25 to 2.28 (e.g., telephone services, municipal taxes or rates, liabilities under leases, royalties, commissions)?					

Questionnaire	Flow-chart Ref.	Yes	No	"Yes" Answers PRT Ref.	"No" Answers RCW Ref.
2.30 Are the following procedures either performed or checked by persons other than those involved in computer operations: (a) maintenance of control over the outstanding goods and services received file (2.25); (D) (b) review of unmatched records of goods and, where applicable, services received (2.28); (D) (c) determination of liability for services not covered in 2.25 to 2.28 (2.29)? (D)					
2.31 Are the results of the following procedures reviewed and approved by a responsible official: (a) maintenance of control over the outstanding goods and services received file (2.25); (S) (b) review of unmatched records of goods and, where applicable, services received (2.28); (S) (c) determination of liability for services not covered in 2.25 to 2.28 (2.29)? (S)					
Entries in Inventory Records 2.32 Where required, are the records of goods received (2.1) used to post quantities to detailed inventory records?					

Questionnaire	Flow-chart Ref.	Yes	No	"Yes" Answers PRT Ref.	"No" Answers RCW Ref.
Programmed Procedures					
2.33 List below the programmed procedures whose continued and proper operation is not assured by user controls.					

In respect of the items listed above, review the answers to the integrity control section. Are there adequate controls to ensure that:
 (a) appropriate programmed procedures are implemented in respect of:
    (i) where applicable, new systems;
    (ii) program changes;
 (b) unauthorized changes cannot be made to production programs;
 (c) programmed procedures are consistently applied?					

Control Objective

4. Invoices and related documentation should be properly checked and approved as being valid before being entered as accounts payable.

Questionnaire	Flow-chart Ref.	Yes	No	"Yes" Answers PRT Ref.	"No" Answers RCW Ref.
Checking of Goods and Services Received					
Specify below whether invoices for goods and, where applicable, services received, are checked manually or by the computer as to:					
(a) quantities and condition of goods and services received;					
(b) nature and quantities of goods ordered;					
(c) prices and other terms.					
As to (a) above, if the checking is done by the computer, answer question 4.1 or, if the checking is done manually, answer questions 4.7 to 4.8.					
As to (b) above, if the checking is done by the computer, answer question 4.2 or, if the checking is done manually, answer question 4.9.					
As to (c) above, if the checking is done by the computer, answer questions 4.3 to 4.6 or, if the checking is done manually, answer question 4.10.					

Questionnaire	Flow-chart Ref.	Yes	No	"Yes" Answers PRT Ref.	"No" Answers RCW Ref.
Computer Checking					
4.1 Review the answers to control objective 2: (a) are there adequate controls to ensure that: (i) quantities of goods and services received have been accurately recorded and maintained on the file (2.2 to 2.31); (ii) unauthorized records are not added (2.25); (b) is the method used in the program to match quantities on invoices with goods and services received records appropriate (2.26); (c) are differences disclosed by the matching process adequately investigated and suitable action taken (2.28)?					
4.2 Review the answer to question 1.32. Is the method used in the program to match goods and services received to purchase commitments appropriate?					
4.3 If purchase invoices are checked by computer with a record of goods and services ordered and/or received for prices and other terms, review the answers to questions 2.25 to 2.31: (a) is the method used in the program to match invoices to goods and services received and goods and services received to purchase orders appropriate; (b) are there adequate controls to ensure that unauthorized records are not added to the relevant files?					

Questionnaire	Flow-chart Ref.	Yes	No	"Yes" Answers PRT Ref.	"No" Answers RCW Ref.

4.4   If invoice/credit memoranda prices are checked by computer with a standard price file:
(a) review the answers to the standing data controls section as regards prices. Are there adequate controls over:
   (i) where applicable, file creation;
   (ii) the authorization of amendments;
   (iii) the completeness of writing amendments to the file;
   (iv) the accuracy of writing amendments to the file;
   (v) the maintenance of the data on the files;
(b) is the method used in the program for matching appropriate;
(c) is suitable action taken on variances (e.g., items exceeding a predetermined tolerance are reported and investigated)?					

4.5 Are the procedures in 4.4(c) above performed or checked by persons other than those involved in computer operations? (D)					
4.6 Are the results of the procedures in 4.4(c) above reviewed and approved by a responsible official? (S)					
Manual Checking 4.7 Are invoices for goods and services received checked to receiving records as to quantities and condition of goods and services received?					

Questionnaire	Flow-chart Ref.	Yes	No	"Yes" Answers PRT Ref.	"No" Answers RCW Ref.
4.8 Are invoices for services received, other than those checked in 4.1 and 4.6 compared with the underlying documentation (e.g., completion reports, leases, records of meter readings), or if such documentation is not available, approved by a responsible official?					
4.9 Are invoices for goods and, where applicable, services received checked to purchase orders as to nature and quantity of goods ordered?					
4.10 Are invoices for goods and, where applicable, services received checked to purchase orders or suppliers' price lists as to prices and other terms?					
Checking of Extensions and Additions Specify below the method used for checking extensions and additions of invoices and credit memoranda. If the checking is done: (a) by the computer, answer questions 4.11 to 4.14; (b) manually, answer questions 4.15 and 4.16.					
Computer Checking 4.11 Is the method used in the program to check extensions and additions of invoices and credit memoranda appropriate?					

Questionnaire	Flow-chart Ref.	Yes	No	"Yes" Answers PRT Ref.	"No" Answers RCW Ref.
4.12 Is suitable action taken on differences disclosed by the checking in 4.11?					
4.13 Are the procedures in 4.12 above performed or checked by persons other than those involved in computer operations? (D)					
4.14 Are the results of the procedures in 4.12 above reviewed and approved by a responsible official? (S)					
Manual Checking					
4.15 Are the extensions and additions of invoices and credit (or debit) memoranda checked to an adequate extent?					
4.16 Do the invoices and credit (or debit) memoranda bear adequate evidence that the manual checking (4.7 to 4.10, 4.15) has been carried out?					
Other Checking					
4.17 Are credit (or debit) memoranda checked to confirm that: (a) they agree with the original records of the goods returned or claims made; (b) where applicable, the prices agree with the original invoice?					

285

Questionnaire	Flow-chart Ref.	Yes	No	"Yes" Answers PRT Ref.	"No" Answers RCW Ref.
4.18 Are the following functions performed by separate individuals: (a) preparation of purchase commitments; (D) (b) preparation of receiving records; (D) (c) checking of purchase invoices (4.7 to 4.10, 4.15); (D) (d) computer operations? (D)					
4.19 If invoices and credit (or debit) memoranda are checked manually are they subject to final written approval by a responsible official prior to entry as accounts payable? (S)					
Adjustments to Suppliers' Accounts 4.20 Are adjustments to suppliers' accounts properly documented?					
4.21 Are the adjustments and related documentation (4.20) reviewed and approved by a responsible official prior to entry in the accounts payable records? (S)					

Questionnaire	Flow-chart Ref.	Yes	No	"Yes" Answers PRT Ref.	"No" Answers RCW Ref.
Programmed Procedures					
4.22 List below the programmed procedures whose continued and proper operation is not assured by user controls.					

In respect of the items listed above, review the answers to the integrity control section. Are there adequate controls to ensure that:
(a) appropriate programmed procedures are implemented in respect of:
  (i) where applicable, new systems;
  (ii) program changes;
(b) unauthorized changes cannot be made to production programs;
(c) programmed procedures are consistently applied?					

Control Objective

5. **All valid accounts payable transactions, and only those transactions, should be accurately recorded as accounts payable.**

Questionnaire	Flow-chart Ref.	Yes	No	"Yes" Answers PRT Ref.	"No" Answers RCW Ref.
Accounting for and Control over Processing of All Transactions Specify below which of the following are input to update the accounts payable file: (a) purchase invoices; (b) credit (or debit) memoranda; (c) adjustments to suppliers' accounts; (d) details of cash payments; (e) other (specify).					
Completeness of Input and Updating Specify below, for each type of input, the principal control that all documents in (a) to (e) above are input to the computer and updated. If the principal control is: (a) computer matching with a file of goods received, answer questions 5.1 to 5.4; (b) agreement of manually established batch totals (specify totals used), answer questions 5.5 to 5.9; (c) computer sequence check of serially numbered input documents, answer questions 5.10 to 5.15; (d) checking of print-outs of items written to the accounts payable file, answer questions 5.16 to 5.19.					

Questionnaire	Flow-chart Ref.	Yes	No	"Yes" Answers PRT Ref.	"No" Answers RCW Ref.
Computer Matching					
5.1 Review the answers to control objective 2. Are the matching procedures adequate to ensure that invoices are input completely?					
5.2 Is a total of accepted items accumulated by the computer during the matching run agreed to the total of items written to the accounts payable file or, alternatively, are such totals carried through intermediate processing (including summarization of totals or changes in the totals used) so that it is established that all accepted input items are updated to the accounts payable file?					
5.3 Is the reconciliation of totals in 5.2 carried out manually or, alternatively, is the reconciliation carried out by the computer with adequate evidence of this check being printed out?					
5.4 Are there adequate procedures for: (a) investigation and correction of differences disclosed by the matching process (5.1); (b) investigation and correction of differences disclosed by the update reconciliations (5.3)?					
Batch Totals					
5.5 Are there adequate controls to ensure that: (a) a document is raised for each transaction; (b) all documents are included in a batch; (c) all batches are submitted for processing?					

Questionnaire	Flow-chart Ref.	Yes	No	"Yes" Answers PRT Ref.	"No" Answers RCW Ref.
5.6 Are the totals of individual items accepted by the computer compared manually to pre-determined control totals or, alternatively, is such a comparison made by the computer with adequate evidence of the check being printed out?					
5.7 Are the totals in 5.6 agreed to the total of items written to the accounts payable file or, alternatively, are such totals carried through intermediate processing (including summarization of totals or changes in the totals used) so that it is established that all accepted input items are updated to the accounts payable file?					
5.8 Is the reconciliation of totals in 5.7 carried out manually or, alternatively, is the reconciliation carried out by the computer with adequate evidence of this check being printed out?					
5.9 Are there adequate procedures for: (a) investigation and correction of differences disclosed by the input reconciliations (5.6); (b) resubmission of all rejections; (c) investigation and correction of differences disclosed by the update reconciliations (5.8)?					
Computer Sequence Check 5.10 Are there adequate controls to ensure that all transactions are recorded on a serially numbered document?					

Questionnaire	Flow-chart Ref.	Yes	No	"Yes" Answers PRT Ref.	"No" Answers RCW Ref.
5.11 Is the method used in the program for the checking of numerical sequence appropriate (e.g., does it cater for changes in sequence and more than one sequence running at a time)?					
5.12 Is a print-out of missing documents produced at regular intervals (e.g., weekly)?					
5.13 Is the total of accepted items accumulated by the computer during the sequence run agreed to the total of items written to the accounts payable file or, alternatively, are such totals carried through intermediate processing (including summarization of totals or changes in the totals used) so that it is established that all accepted input items are updated to the accounts payable file?					
5.14 Is the reconciliation of totals in 5.13 carried out manually or, alternatively, is the reconciliation carried out by the computer with adequate evidence of this check being printed out?					
5.15 Are there adequate procedures for: (a) investigation of missing documents (5.12); (b) investigation and correction of differences disclosed by the update reconciliations (5.14)?					

Questionnaire	Flow-chart Ref.	Yes	No	"Yes" Answers PRT Ref.	"No" Answers RCW Ref.
Checking of Print-Outs					
5.16 Are there adequate controls to ensure that all documents are submitted for processing (e.g., by checking against retained copy, by manual sequence check)?					
5.17 Is there a regular (e.g., monthly) review of source documents for unprocessed items?					
5.18 Is the method used in the program for the production of the print-out appropriate (e.g., does it contain details of items that have been written to the accounts payable file)?					
5.19 Are there adequate procedures for investigation and correction of differences disclosed by the checking?					

Questionnaire	Flow-chart Ref.	Yes	No	"Yes" Answers PRT Ref.	"No" Answers RCW Ref.
Disciplines over Basic Input Completeness and Updating Controls					
5.20 Are the following procedures either performed or checked by persons other than those involved in computer operations or in maintaining a manual accounts payable control account:					
(a) investigation and correction of differences disclosed by the matching process (5.4(a)); (D)					
(b) manual agreement of input totals (5.6); (D)					
(c) investigation and correction of differences disclosed by the input reconciliations (5.9(a)); (D)					
(d) resubmission of all rejections (5.9(b)); (D)					
(e) investigation of missing documents (5.15(a)); (D)					
(f) regular (e.g., monthly) review of source documents for unprocessed items (5.17); (D)					
(g) investigation and correction of differences disclosed by the checking of print-outs (5.19); (D)					
(h) manual agreement of update totals (5.3, 5.8, 5.14); (D)					
(i) investigation and correction of differences disclosed by the update reconciliations (5.4(b), 5.9(c), 5.15(b))? (D)					

Questionnaire	Flow-chart Ref.	Yes	No	"Yes" Answers PRT Ref.	"No" Answers RCW Ref.
5.21 Are the results of the following procedures reviewed and approved by a responsible official: (a) investigation and correction of differences disclosed by the matching process (5.4(a)); (S) (b) manual agreement of input totals (5.6); (S) (c) investigation and correction of differences disclosed by the input reconciliations (5.9(a)); (S) (d) resubmission of all rejections (5.9(b)); (S) (e) investigation of missing documents (5.15(a)); (S) (f) regular (e.g., monthly) review of source documents for unprocessed items (5.17); (S) (g) investigation and correction of differences disclosed by the checking of print-outs (5.19); (S) (h) manual agreement of update totals (5.3, 5.8, 5.14); (S) (i) investigation and correction of differences disclosed by the update reconciliations (5.4(b), 5.9(c), 5.15(b))? (S)					
Accuracy of Input and Updating 5.22 Are there adequate controls to ensure that the following fields are accurately input and updated (e.g., batch totals, edit checks in program, reporting of non-matched items): (a) value; (b) vendor reference?					
5.23 Are there adequate procedures for: (a) the agreement of totals, where applicable; (b) investigation and correction of differences or exceptions?					

294

Questionnaire	Flow-chart Ref.	Yes	No	"Yes" Answers PRT Ref.	"No" Answers RCW Ref.
5.24 Is the method used in the program for the updating of individual accounts appropriate?					
5.25 Are the following procedures either performed or checked by persons other than those involved in computer operations or in maintaining a manual accounts payable control account: (a) agreement of totals, where applicable (5.23(a)); (D) (b) investigation and correction of differences or exceptions (5.23(b))? (D)					
5.26 Are the results of the following procedures reviewed and approved by a responsible official: (a) agreement of totals, where applicable (5.23(a)); (S) (b) investigation and correction of differences or exceptions (5.23(b))? (S)					
Authorization 5.27 If data is authorized prior to the establishment of the controls for completeness and accuracy of input (e.g., prior to establishment of batch control totals or recording on a sequentially numbered document), are there adequate controls (e.g., checking authorization after batch control totals established or sequentially numbered document raised) to ensure that: (a) no unauthorized alterations are made to authorized data during subsequent processing; (b) unauthorized data is not added; (c) all authorized items are included in subsequent processing?					

Questionnaire	Flow-chart Ref.	Yes	No	"Yes" Answers PRT Ref.	"No" Answers RCW Ref.
Computer Generated Data—Payment Details					
5.28 Where the computer is programmed to generate checks on the basis of information held on file, review the answers to control objective 9. Are there adequate controls to ensure that only valid items are selected for payment and that the amount is accurately calculated (e.g., calculation of discount)?					
5.29 Is a total (specify total used) of generated items accumulated by the computer and agreed manually with a total of items written off the accounts payable file or, alternatively, are the totals agreed by the computer with adequate evidence of this check being printed out?					
5.30 Are there adequate procedures for the investigation and correction of differences disclosed by the update reconciliation?					
5.31 Are the following procedures either performed or checked by persons other than those involved in computer operations or in maintaining a manual accounts payable control account: (a) manual agreement of update totals (5.29); (D) (b) investigation and correction of differences disclosed by the update reconciliations (5.30)? (D)					

Questionnaire	Flow-chart Ref.	Yes	No	"Yes" Answers PRT Ref.	"No" Answers RCW Ref.
5.32 Are the results of the following procedures reviewed and approved by a responsible official: (a) manual agreement of update totals (5.29); (S) (b) investigation and correction of differences disclosed by the update reconciliations (5.30)? (S)					
Maintenance of the Accounts Payable File 5.33 Is an accumulation of the items on file regularly reconciled with a manual control account maintained by a user department or, alternatively, reconciled with a control record on file with adequate evidence of reconciliation being printed out?					
5.34 Where the reconciliation is carried out by the computer, is the brought forward total checked or, alternatively, are there adequate controls over access to data files (review the answers to section 4 of the integrity controls questions)?					
5.35 Are there adequate procedures for investigating differences disclosed by the reconciliations (5.33, 5.34) before any adjustments are made?					

Questionnaire	Flow-chart Ref.	Yes	No	"Yes" Answers PRT Ref.	"No" Answers RCW Ref.
5.36 Are the following procedures either performed or checked by persons other than those involved in computer operations or in maintaining a manual accounts payable control account: (a) manual agreement of totals (5.33); (D) (b) checking of brought forward total (5.34); (D) (c) investigation and correction of differences disclosed by the reconciliations (5.35)? (D)					
5.37 Are the results of the following procedures reviewed and approved by a responsible official: (a) manual agreement of totals (5.33); (S) (b) checking of brought forward total (5.34); (S) (c) investigation and correction of differences disclosed by the reconciliation (5.35)? (S)					
Agreement With Suppliers' Records 5.38 Are the accounts payable subsidiary records periodically reconciled to suppliers' records (e.g., by comparison with suppliers' statements)?					
5.39 Is the procedure in 5.38 either performed or checked by persons other than those who are involved in: (a) maintenance of a manual accounts payable control account; (D) (b) computer operations? (D)					
5.40 Are the results of the reconciliation in 5.38 reviewed and approved by a responsible official? (S)					

Questionnaire	Flow-chart Ref.	Yes	No	"Yes" Answers PRT Ref.	"No" Answers RCW Ref.
Programmed Procedures					
5.41 List below the programmed procedures whose continued and proper operation is not assured by user controls.					
In respect of the items listed above, review the answers to the integrity control section. Are there adequate controls to ensure that:					
(a) appropriate programmed procedures are implemented in respect of:					
(i) where applicable, new systems;					
(ii) program changes;					
(b) unauthorized changes cannot be made to production programs;					
(c) programmed procedures are consistently applied?					

Control Objective

6. **Payments in respect of wages and salaries should be:**
   (a) made only to company employees at authorized rates of pay;
   (b) where required, in accordance with records of work performed;
   (c) accurately calculated.

Questionnaire	Flow-chart Ref.	Yes	No	"Yes" Answers PRT Ref.	"No" Answers RCW Ref.
Standing Payroll Data					
List below the standing data fields used in the preparation of payrolls (e.g., rate of pay, deductions, employee number, commission rates) and state on which file these fields are recorded.					
Controls over Standing Payroll Data					
6.1 **In respect of each field listed above, are there adequate controls over:** **(a) where applicable, file creation;** **(b) the authorization of amendments;** **(c) the completeness of writing amendments to the file;** **(d) the accuracy of writing amendments to the file;** **(e) the maintenance of the data on the file?**					

Questionnaire	Flow-chart Ref.	Yes	No	"Yes" Answers PRT Ref.	"No" Answers RCW Ref.
Transaction Payroll Data					
6.2 If employees are paid on the basis of time worked: (a) is the payroll based on adequate time records; (b) where applicable, are time records checked to supporting records of time spent, either manually or by the computer (specify which); (c) are time records (6.2(a)) approved; (d) do the time records (6.2(a)) or payroll indicate that overtime has been properly authorized (e.g., reference to clock card or a computer produced exception report of abnormal time)?					
6.3 If employees are paid on the basis of output are the payments based on output records that are: (a) reconciled to production records that are under accounting control either manually or by computer (specify which); (b) properly approved (e.g., by reference to production records or a computer produced exception report of abnormal output)?					
6.4 If salaried or other employees not included in 6.2 and 6.3 above are paid for overtime, is the payroll based on time records which indicate that the overtime has been properly authorized (e.g., by reference to overtime records or a computer produced exception report of abnormal overtime)?					
6.5 Where the authorization in 6.2(d), 6.3(b) and 6.4 above is based on computer produced exception reports, are the methods used in the program to determine abnormal items appropriate?					

Questionnaire	Flow-chart Ref.	Yes	No	"Yes" Answers PRT Ref.	"No" Answers RCW Ref.
6.6 If employees receive commissions on sales, are the commissions based on sales records that are reconciled with sales (less, where applicable, returns) recorded in the books?					
6.7 Are the following procedures either performed or checked by persons other than those involved in computer operations: (a) checking of time records to supporting records of time spent (6.2(b)); (D) (b) approval of time records (6.2(c)); (D) (c) checking of payments to output records (6.3(a)); (D) (d) approval of output records (6.3(b)); (D) (e) approval of overtime for salaried or other employees not included in 6.2 and 6.3 (6.4); (D) (f) reconciliation of commissions with sales (6.6)? (D)					
Payroll Preparation **Completeness of Input and Processing** Specify below the principal control that all transaction payroll data is input to the computer and processed. If the principal control is: (a) computer matching with the employee record on the file, answer questions 6.8 to 6.10; (b) agreement of manually established batch totals (specify totals used), answer questions 6.11 to 6.13.					

Questionnaire	Flow-chart Ref.	Yes	No	"Yes" Answers PRT Ref.	"No" Answers RCW Ref.
Computer Matching					
6.8 Review the answers to 6.1. Are there adequate controls to ensure that only authorized employees are held on the file?					
6.9 Is the method used in the program to match the transaction payroll data with the employee record appropriate (e.g., to reject duplicate or unmatched input)?					
6.10 Are there adequate procedures for the investigation and correction of differences disclosed by the matching process (6.9)?					
Batch Totals					
6.11 Are there adequate controls to ensure that: (a) all documents are included in a batch; (b) all batches are submitted for processing?					
6.12 Are the totals of individual items accepted by the computer compared manually to pre-determined control totals or, alternatively, is such a comparison made by the computer with adequate evidence of the check being printed out?					

Questionnaire	Flow-chart Ref.	Yes	No	"Yes" Answers PRT Ref.	"No" Answers RCW Ref.
6.13 Are there adequate procedures for: (a) investigation and correction of differences disclosed by the input reconciliations (6.12); (b) resubmission of all rejections?					
Disciplines over Basic Input Completeness Controls 6.14 Are the following procedures either performed or checked by persons other than those involved in computer operations: (a) investigation and correction of differences disclosed by the matching process (6.10); (D) (b) manual agreement of input totals (6.12); (D) (c) investigation and correction of differences disclosed by the input reconciliations (6.13(a)); (D) (d) resubmission of all rejections (6.13(b))? (D)					
6.15 Are the results of the following procedures reviewed and approved by a responsible official: (a) investigation and correction of differences disclosed by the matching process (6.10); (S) (b) manual agreement of input totals (6.12); (S) (c) investigation and correction of differences disclosed by the input reconciliations (6.13(a)); (S) (d) resubmission of all rejections (6.13(b))? (S)					

Questionnaire	Flow-chart Ref.	Yes	No	"Yes" Answers PRT Ref.	"No" Answers RCW Ref.
Accuracy of Input					
6.16 Are there adequate controls to ensure that the following fields are accurately input (e.g., batch totals, edit checks in program, reporting of non-matched items): (a) hours; (b) employee numbers; (c) allowances; (d) inventory reference, where applicable?					
6.17 Are there adequate procedures for: (a) agreement of totals, where applicable; (b) investigation and correction of differences or exceptions?					
6.18 Are the following procedures either performed or checked by persons other than those involved in computer operations: (a) agreement of totals, where applicable (6.17(a)); (D) (b) investigation and correction of differences or exceptions (6.17(b))? (D)					
6.19 Are the results of the following procedures reviewed and approved by a responsible official: (a) agreement of totals, where applicable (6.17(a)); (S) (b) investigation and correction of differences or exceptions (6.17(b))? (S)					

Questionnaire	Flow-chart Ref.	Yes	No	"Yes" Answers PRT Ref.	"No" Answers RCW Ref.
Completeness and Accuracy of Payroll Processing 6.20 As regards the computer calculations of gross amounts due, deductions and net amounts due: (a) is the method used in the program for the calculation appropriate; (b) are there controls over the accuracy of the calculation (e.g., an exception report of abnormal pay)?					
6.21 Where input to the payroll is a cumulative file of transactions, is a total of accepted items accumulated during the input run?					
6.22 Is the total in 6.21 agreed to the total of items written to the payroll, or alternatively, is the total carried through intermediate processing (including summarization of totals or changes in the totals used) so that it is established that all accepted input items are updated to the payroll?					
6.23 Is the reconciliation of totals in 6.22 carried out manually or, alternatively, is the reconciliation carried out by the computer with adequate evidence of this check being printed out?					
6.24 Are there adequate procedures for the investigation and correction of differences disclosed by the payroll reconciliation?					

Questionnaire	Flow-chart Ref.	Yes	No	"Yes" Answers PRT Ref.	"No" Answers RCW Ref.
6.25 Are the following procedures either performed or checked by persons other than those involved in computer operations: (a) manual agreement to payroll totals (6.23); (D) (b) investigation and correction of differences disclosed by the payroll reconciliation (6.24)? (D)					
6.26 Are the following procedures reviewed and approved by a responsible official: (a) manual agreement to payroll (6.23); (S) (b) investigation and correction of differences disclosed by the payroll reconciliation (6.24)? (S)					
Authorization					
6.27 If data is authorized prior to the establishment of the controls for completeness and accuracy of input (e.g., prior to establishment of batch control totals or recording on a sequentially numbered document), are there adequate controls (e.g., checking authorization after batch control totals are established or sequentially numbered documents raised) to ensure that: (a) no unauthorized alterations are made to authorized data during subsequent processing; (b) unauthorized data is not added; (c) authorized items are not omitted from subsequent processing?					
6.28 Are payrolls subject to the final written approval of a responsible official before they are paid?					

Questionnaire	Flow-chart Ref.	Yes	No	"Yes" Answers PRT Ref.	"No" Answers RCW Ref.
Payments to Employees					
6.29 Do persons other than those involved in computer operations compare payroll cheques, either individually or in the aggregate, with payrolls? (D)					
6.30 Are the results of the procedures in 6.29 reviewed and approved by a responsible official? (S)					
6.31 If employees are paid in cash: (a) is cash withdrawn only for the net amount of the payroll; (C) (b) do persons other than those involved in the control and processing of payroll data physically control cash until it is distributed to employees; (C) (c) are unclaimed wages promptly recorded and controlled by persons other than those involved in the control and processing of payroll data? (C)					

Questionnaire	Flow-chart Ref.	Yes	No	"Yes" Answers PRT Ref.	"No" Answers RCW Ref.
Programmed Procedures					
6.32 List below the programmed procedures whose continued and proper operation is not assured by user controls.					

In respect of the items listed above, review the answers to the integrity control section. Are there adequate controls to ensure that:
(a) appropriate programmed procedures are implemented in respect of:
  (i) where applicable, new systems;
  (ii) program changes;
(b) unauthorized changes cannot be made to production programs;
(c) programmed procedures are consistently applied?					

Control Objective

9.   Disbursements from bank accounts should be made only in respect of valid transactions.

Questionnaire	Flow-chart Ref.	Yes	No	"Yes" Answers PRT Ref.	"No" Answers RCW Ref.
Control of Issue and Usage of Checks					
9.1 Are supplies of unissued checks properly safeguarded? (C)					
9.2 Is the system such that: (a) the usage of checks is accounted for by persons other than those who have custody of unissued checks (9.1); (C) (b) spoiled checks are under adequate control? (C)					
9.3 Are the results of the procedures in 9.2 reviewed and approved by a responsible official? (S)					
Selection of Items for Payment					
9.4 Review the answers under control objectives 5, 6 and 7. Are there adequate controls to ensure that only authorized items are held on the accounts payable and payroll files?					

Questionnaire	Flow-chart Ref.	Yes	No	"Yes" Answers PRT Ref.	"No" Answers RCW Ref.
9.5 Are appropriate methods used in the program: (a) to select items for payment (e.g., to produce cheques on desired date, to take advantage of cash discount, to prevent selection twice); (b) to carry out calculations (e.g., discount, summarization)?					
9.6 Are amendments to the computer-selected items for payment (e.g., to delay or accelerate payments) reviewed and approved by a responsible official?					
9.7 Is a total of items selected accumulated by the computer and agreed directly to the total of checks issued or the bank transfer or, alternatively, is the total agreed to the total of checks issued or the bank transfer after approval and resubmission of the listing of selected items?					
9.8 Where checks or supporting documents are produced by the computer, as regards the names, addresses and bank details of payees and discount terms, review the answers to the standing data controls section. Are there adequate controls over: (a) where applicable, file creation; (b) the authorization of amendments; (c) the completeness of writing amendments to the file; (d) the accuracy of writing amendments to the file; (e) the maintenance of the data on the file?					

Questionnaire	Flow-chart Ref.	Yes	No	"Yes" Answers PRT Ref.	"No" Answers RCW Ref.
9.9 Is the authorization and maintenance in 9.8 carried out by persons other than those who deal with: (a) payroll transaction data; (C) (b) accounts payable transaction data; (C) (c) imprest and similar funds? (C)					
Signing of Checks 9.10 Where checks are prepared on pre-signed forms: (a) are checks over a reasonable amount counter-signed by officials other than those who approve transactions for payment; (b) where appropriate (e.g., payrolls), is a limit as to the amount payable stated on the checks?					
9.11 Where the checks are manually signed or counter-signed, are the checks signed by officials other than those who are involved in computer operations and those who approve transactions for payment in respect of: (a) payment of accounts payable (control objective 5); (C) (b) payrolls and payroll deductions (control objectives 6 and 7); (C) (c) reimbursement of imprest and similar funds (control objective 8); (C) (d) other payments? (C)					
9.12 Where checks are manually signed, does the signatory review supporting documentation for large value items?					

Questionnaire	Flow-chart Ref.	Yes	No	"Yes" Answers PRT Ref.	"No" Answers RCW Ref.
9.13 If a mechanical check signer is in use, is there adequate control over the custody and use of the signer and the signature plate? (C)					
General					
9.14 Are the supporting documents effectively cancelled by, or under the control of, the signatories to prevent subsequent re-use? (C)					
9.15 Are checks and bank transfers for transactions which, because of special circumstances, do not pass through the normal approval procedures referred to in 9.4 to 9.13, initiated only on the basis of proper documentation of the validity of the transactions?					
9.16 Is the documentation in 9.15 reviewed and approved by a responsible official before checks and bank transfers are initiated? (S)					
Control of Checks and Bank Transfers after Signing					
9.17 After signing, are checks and bank transfers forwarded directly to the payees (or to the bank with the bank transfer lists) without being returned to the originators or others who are in a position to introduce documents into the cash disbursement system? (C)					

Questionnaire	Flow-chart Ref.	Yes	No	"Yes" Answers PRT Ref.	"No" Answers RCW Ref.
Comparison of Disbursement Records 9.18 Are all checks and individual bank transfers as listed in the disbursement records compared either manually or by computer (specify which) as to name or number, dates and amounts with transactions passed through the company's bank accounts (e.g., as part of the bank reconciliation procedures)?					
9.19 When done manually, is the comparison in 9.18 carried out by persons other than those: (a) involved in preparation of cheques and bank transfers or who can introduce documents into the disbursements system; (D) (b) involved in computer operations? (D)					
9.20 Are the results of the procedures in 9.19 reviewed and approved by a responsible official? (S)					

Questionnaire	Flow-chart Ref.	Yes	No	"Yes" Answers PRT Ref.	"No" Answers RCW Ref.
Programmed Procedures					
9.21 List below the programmed procedures whose continued and proper operation is not assured by user controls.					

In respect of the items listed above, review the answers to the integrity control section. Are there adequate controls to ensure that:
(a) appropriate programmed procedures are implemented in respect of:
   (i) where applicable, new systems;
   (ii) program changes;
(b) unauthorized changes cannot be made to production programs;
(c) programmed procedures are consistently applied?					

Control Objective

10. **Accurate detailed records should be maintained of materials and supplies inventories.**
Note: The answers to the following questions should normally cover the following (whether on the client's premises or in the hands of third parties):
(a) all purchased inventories (including items purchased for resale);
(b) manufactured parts and sub-assemblies in store, where they are accounted for by the client as part of purchased inventories rather than as finished products.
State below the client's inventory categories covered by the answers.

Questionnaire	Flow-chart Ref.	Yes	No	"Yes" Answers PRT Ref.	"No" Answers RCW Ref.
Validity of Entries in Inventory Records					
10.1 Are all entries input to the materials and supplies records: (a) supported by adequate documentation; (b) priced by reference to an appropriate source; (c) checked to an appropriate extent, e.g., relative to value; (d) properly approved, where applicable?					
Accounting for and Control over Processing of All Transactions					
Specify below which of the following are input to update the materials and supplies inventory files (specify whether in quantity and/or value): (a) file/documents of goods received; (b) file/documents of transfers to work-in-progress or finished products; (c) file/documents of goods shipped; (d) adjustments; (e) returns; (f) other (specify).					

Questionnaire	Flow-chart Ref.	Yes	No	"Yes" Answers PRT Ref.	"No" Answers RCW Ref.
Completeness of Input and Updating Specify below for each type of input the principal control that all files and documents in (a) to (e) above are input to the computer and updated. If the principal control is: (a) agreement of manually established batch totals (specify totals used), answer questions 10.2 to 10.6; (b) computer sequence check of serially numbered input documents, answer questions 10.7 to 10.12; (c) reliance on controls over the purchases application, answer questions 10.13 to 10.17; (d) reliance on controls over the work-in-progress application, answer questions 10.13 to 10.17; (e) reliance on controls over the sales application, answer questions 10.13 to 10.17.					
Batch Totals 10.2 Are there adequate controls to ensure that: (a) a document is raised for each transaction; (b) all documents are included in a batch; (c) all batches are submitted for processing?					
10.3 Are the totals of individual items accepted by the computer compared manually to pre-determined control totals or, alternatively, is such a comparison made by the computer with adequate evidence of the check being printed out?					

Questionnaire	Flow-chart Ref.	Yes	No	"Yes" Answers PRT Ref.	"No" Answers RCW Ref.
10.4 Are the totals in 10.3 agreed to the total of items written to the material and supplies inventories file or, alternatively, are such totals carried through intermediate processing (including summarization of totals or changes in the totals used) so that it is established that all accepted input items are updated to the material and supplies inventories file?					
10.5 Is the reconciliation of totals in 10.4 carried out manually or, alternatively, is the reconciliation carried out by the computer with adequate evidence of this check being printed out?					
10.6 Are there adequate procedures for: (a) investigation and correction of differences disclosed by the input reconciliations (10.3); (b) resubmission of all rejections; (c) investigation and correction of differences disclosed by the update reconciliations (10.5)?					
Computer Sequence Check 10.7 Are there adequate controls to ensure that all transactions are recorded on a serially numbered document?					
10.8 Is the method used in the program for the checking of numerical sequence appropriate (e.g., does it cater for changes in sequence and more than one sequence running at a time)?					

Questionnaire	Flow-chart Ref.	Yes	No	"Yes" Answers PRT Ref.	"No" Answers RCW Ref.
10.9 Is a print-out of missing documents produced at regular intervals (e.g., weekly)?					
10.10 Is a total of accepted items accumulated by the computer during the sequence check run agreed to the total of items written to the material and supplies inventories file or, alternatively, are such totals carried through intermediate processing (including summarization of totals or changes in the totals used) so that it is established that all accepted input items are updated to the material and supplies inventories file?					
10.11 Is the reconciliation of totals in 10.10 carried out manually or, alternatively, is the reconciliation carried out by the computer with adequate evidence of this check being printed out?					
10.12 Are there adequate procedures for: (a) investigation of missing documents (10.9); (b) investigation and correction of differences disclosed by the update reconciliations (10.11)?					
Reliance on Controls over the Purchases/ Work-in-Progress/Sales Application 10.13 Review the answers under control objectives 2, 3, 5, 21 and 31, as applicable. Are there adequate controls to ensure that all items are accurately input to the purchase/work-in-progress/sales application?					

Questionnaire	Flow-chart Ref.	Yes	No	"Yes" Answers PRT Ref.	"No" Answers RCW Ref.
10.14 Is the method used in the program to select and accumulate items relevant to the materials and supplies inventories application appropriate?					
10.15 Is a total of selected items accumulated by the computer during the selection run agreed to the total of items written to the materials and supplies inventories file or, alternatively, are such totals carried through intermediate processing (including summarization of totals or changes in the totals used) so that it is established that all accepted input items are updated to the materials and supplies inventories file?					
10.16 Is the reconciliation of totals in 10.15 carried out manually or, alternatively, is the reconciliation carried out by the computer with adequate evidence of this check being printed out?					
10.17 Are there adequate procedures for investigation and correction of differences disclosed by the reconciliation (10.16)?					

Questionnaire	Flow-chart Ref.	Yes	No	"Yes" Answers PRT Ref.	"No" Answers RCW Ref.
Disciplines over Basic Input Completeness and Updating Controls					
10.18 Are the following procedures either performed or checked by persons other than those involved in computer operations or in maintaining a manual materials and supplies control account: (a) manual agreement of input totals (10.3); (D) (b) investigation and correction of differences disclosed by the input reconciliations (10.6(a)); (D) (c) resubmission of rejections (10.6(b)); (D) (d) investigation of missing documents (10.12(a)); (D) (e) manual agreement of update totals (10.5, 10.11, 10.16); (D) (f) investigation and correction of differences disclosed by the update reconciliations (10.6(c), 10.12(b), 10.17)? (D)					
10.19 Are the results of the following procedures reviewed and approved by a responsible official: (a) manual agreement of input totals (10.3); (S) (b) investigation and correction of differences disclosed by the input reconciliations (16.6(a)); (S) (c) resubmission of rejections (10.6(b)); (S) (d) investigation of missing documents (10.12(a)); (S) (e) manual agreement of update totals (10.5, 10.11, 10.16); (S) (f) investigation and correction of differences disclosed by the update reconciliations (10.6(c), 10.12(b), 10.17)? (S)					

Questionnaire	Flow-chart Ref.	Yes	No	"Yes" Answers PRT Ref.	"No" Answers RCW Ref.
Accuracy of Input and Updating					
10.20 Are there adequate controls to ensure that the following fields are accurately input and updated (e.g., batch totals, edit checks in program, reporting of non-matched items): (a) quantity; (b) value; (c) inventory reference?					
10.21 Are there adequate procedures for: (a) agreement of totals, where applicable; (b) investigation and correction of differences or exceptions?					
10.22 Is the method used in the program for the updating of individual accounts appropriate?					
10.23 Are the following procedures either performed or checked by persons other than those involved in computer operations or in maintaining a manual materials and supplies control account: (a) agreement of totals, where applicable (10.21(a)); (D) (b) investigation and correction of differences or exception (10.21(b))? (D)					

Questionnaire	Flow-chart Ref.	Yes	No	"Yes" Answers PRT Ref.	"No" Answers RCW Ref.
10.24 Are the results of the following procedures reviewed and approved by a responsible official: (a) agreement of totals, where applicable (10.21(a)); (S) (b) investigation and correction of differences or exceptions (10.21(b))? (S)					
Computer Generated Data					
10.25 Are the methods used in the program to generate the data and related control record appropriate (e.g., minor physical count adjustments)?					
10.26 Is there an adequate check over the accuracy of the data generated (e.g., reasonableness check, manual review of generated data)?					
10.27 Are the results of the check (10.26) reviewed and approved by a responsible official? (S)					
10.28 Is a total (specify total used) of generated items accumulated by the computer and agreed manually with a total of items written to/off the materials and supplies inventories file or, alternatively, are the totals agreed by the computer with adequate evidence of this check being printed out?					

Questionnaire	Flow-chart Ref.	Yes	No	"Yes" Answers PRT Ref.	"No" Answers RCW Ref.
10.29 Are there adequate procedures for investigation and correction of differences disclosed by the update reconciliation?					
10.30 Are the following procedures either performed or checked by persons other than those involved in computer operations or in maintaining a manual materials and supplies control account: (a) manual agreement of update totals (10.28); (D) (b) investigation and correction of differences disclosed by the update reconciliation (10.29)? (D)					
10.31 Are the results of the following procedures reviewed and approved by a responsible official: (a) manual agreement of update totals (10.28); (S) (b) investigation and correction of differences disclosed by the update reconciliation (10.29)? (S)					
Authorization of Adjustments 10.32 If data is authorized prior to the establishment of the controls for completeness and accuracy of input (e.g., prior to establishment of batch control totals or recording on a sequentially numbered document), are there adequate controls (e.g., checking authorization after batch control totals are established or sequentially numbered documents raised) to ensure that: (a) no unauthorized alterations are made to authorized data during subsequent processing; (b) unauthorized data is not added; (c) all authorized items are included in subsequent processing?					

Questionnaire	Flow-chart Ref.	Yes	No	"Yes" Answers PRT Ref.	"No" Answers RCW Ref.
Maintenance of the Materials and Supplies Inventories File					
10.33 Is an accumulation of the items on file regularly reconciled with a manual control account maintained by a user department or, alternatively, reconciled with a control record on file with adequate evidence of reconciliation being printed out?					
10.34 Where the reconciliation is carried out by the computer, is the brought forward total checked or, alternatively, are there adequate controls over access to data files (review the answers to section 4 of the integrity controls questions)?					
10.35 Are there adequate procedures for investigating differences disclosed by the reconciliations (10.33, 10.34) before any adjustments are made?					
10.36 Are the following procedures either performed or checked by persons other than those involved in computer operations (D), in maintaining a manual material and supplies control account (D) or in maintaining physical custody of inventory (C): (a) manual agreement of totals (10.33); (b) checking of brought forward total (10.34); (c) investigation and correction of differences disclosed by the reconciliations (10.35)?					

Questionnaire	Flow-chart Ref.	Yes	No	"Yes" Answers PRT Ref.	"No" Answers RCW Ref.
10.37 Are the results of the following procedures reviewed and approved by a responsible official: (a) manual agreement of totals (10.33); (S) (b) checking of brought forward total (10.34); (S) (c) investigation and correction of differences disclosed by the reconciliations (10.35)? (S)					
Other Accounting Entries 10.38 In cases where adjustments to the detailed records are required and amounts not easily quantified (e.g., losses due to evaporation), do the methods used to determine such adjustments appear reasonable?					
10.39 Are separate general or subsidiary ledger accounts maintained for all adjustments to inventory valuation (e.g., for provisions, variances, adjustments arising on physical verification)?					
Physical Control 10.40 Are areas where materials and supplies are held protected against access by unauthorized personnel? (C)					
10.41 Are all materials and supplies inventories physically verified at least annually, either by cycle or periodic counts (control objective 51)?					

Questionnaire	Flow-chart Ref.	Yes	No	"Yes" Answers PRT Ref.	"No" Answers RCW Ref.
10.42 Are the procedures in 10.41 either performed or checked by persons other than those involved in computer operations? (D)					

Programmed Procedures

10.43 List below the programmed procedures whose continued and proper operation is not assured by user controls.

    In respect of the items listed above, review the answers to the integrity control section. Are there adequate controls to ensure that:
  (a) appropriate programmed procedures are implemented in respect of:
    (i) where applicable, new systems;
    (ii) program changes;
  (b) unauthorized changes cannot be made to production programs;
  (c) programmed procedures are consistently applied?

12. Accurate records should be maintained of the cost and accumulated depreciation on property, plant and equipment.

Questionnaire	Flow-chart Ref.	Yes	No	"Yes" Answers PRT Ref.	"No" Answers RCW Ref.
Records Maintained					
Specify below whether property, plant and equipment subsidiary ledgers are maintained manually or by the computer for the following classifications (specify which for each type and complete manual questions for records not maintained by computer): (a) land and buildings; (b) leasehold improvements; (c) plant and machinery; (d) furniture, fixtures and fittings; (e) office equipment; (f) motor vehicles; (g) property, plant and equipment leased or loaned to third parties; (h) other property, plant and equipment (specify below)?					
Detailed Records					
12.1 Do the subsidiary ledgers provide the following details for each item: (a) adequate identification; (b) the cost; (c) the accumulated depreciation; (d) date of purchase?					

Questionnaire	Flow-chart Ref.	Yes	No	"Yes" Answers PRT Ref.	"No" Answers RCW Ref.
12.2 Are the subsidiary ledgers regularly updated (e.g., monthly) in respect of: (a) cost of additions and disposals; (b) depreciation for the period?					
Accounting for and Control over Processing of All Transactions Specify below, which of the following are input to update the computer subsidiary ledgers: (a) files of additions from other applications; (b) manually prepared documents of additions; (c) manually prepared documents of disposals; (d) adjustments.					
Completeness of Input and Updating Specify below for each type of input the principal control that all property, plant and equipment transactions above are input to the computer and updated. If the principal control is: (a) agreement of manually established batch totals (specify totals used), answer questions 12.3 to 12.7; (b) computer sequence check of serially numbered input documents, answer questions 12.8 to 12.13; (c) reliance on controls over the purchases application, answer questions 12.14 to 12.18; (d) reliance on controls over the payroll application, answer questions 12.14 to 12.18; (e) reliance on controls over the work-in-progress application, answer questions 12.14 to 12.18.					

Questionnaire	Flow-chart Ref.	Yes	No	"Yes" Answers PRT Ref.	"No" Answers RCW Ref.
Batch Totals					
12.3 Are there adequate controls to ensure that: (a) a document is raised for each transaction; (b) all documents are included in a batch; (c) all batches are submitted for processing?					
12.4 Are the totals of individual items accepted by the computer compared manually to pre-determined control totals or, alternatively, is such a comparison made by the computer with adequate evidence of the check being printed out?					
12.5 Are the totals in 12.4 agreed to the total of items written to the property, plant and equipment file or, alternatively, are such totals carried through intermediate processing (including summarization of totals or changes in the totals used) so that it is established that all accepted input items are updated to the property, plant and equipment file?					
12.6 Is the reconciliation of totals in 12.5 carried out manually or, alternatively, is the reconciliation carried out by the computer with adequate evidence of this check being printed out?					

Questionnaire	Flow-chart Ref.	Yes	No	"Yes" Answers PRT Ref.	"No" Answers RCW Ref.
12.7 Are there adequate procedures for: (a) investigation and correction of differences disclosed by the input reconciliations (12.4); (b) resubmission of all rejections; (c) investigation and correction of differences disclosed by the update reconciliations (12.6)?					
Computer Sequence Check 12.8 Are there adequate controls to ensure that all transactions are recorded on a serially numbered document?					
12.9 Is the method used in the program for the checking of numerical sequence appropriate (e.g., does it cater for changes in sequence and more than one sequence running at a time)?					
12.10 Is a print-out of missing documents produced at regular intervals (e.g., weekly)?					
12.11 Is a total of accepted items accumulated by the computer during the sequence check run agreed to the total of items written to the property, plant and equipment file or, alternatively, are such totals carried through intermediate processing (including summarization of totals or changes in the totals used) so that it is established that all accepted input items are updated to the property, plant and equipment file?					

Questionnaire	Flow-chart Ref.	Yes	No	"Yes" Answers PRT Ref.	"No" Answers RCW Ref.
12.12 Is the reconciliation of totals in 12.11 carried out manually or, alternatively, is the reconciliation carried out by the computer with adequate evidence of this check being printed out?					
12.13 Are there adequate procedures for: (a) investigation of missing documents (12.10); (b) investigation and correction of differences disclosed by the update reconciliations (12.12)?					
Reliance on Controls over the Purchases/ Payroll/Work-in-Progress Applications 12.14 Review the answers under control objectives 2, 5, 6 and 21 as applicable. Are there adequate controls to ensure that all items are accurately input to the purchases/payroll/work-in-progress applications?					
12.15 Is the method used in the program to select and accumulate items relevant to the property, plant and equipment application appropriate?					
12.16 Is a total of selected items accumulated by the computer during the selection run agreed to the total of items written to the property, plant and equipment file or, alternatively, are such totals carried through intermediate processing (including summarization of totals or changes in the totals used) so that it is established that all accepted input items are updated to the property, plant and equipment file?					

Questionnaire	Flow-chart Ref.	Yes	No	"Yes" Answers PRT Ref.	"No" Answers RCW Ref.
12.17 Is the reconciliation of totals in 12.16 carried out manually or, alternatively, is the reconciliation carried out by the computer with adequate evidence of this check being printed out?					
12.18 Are there adequate procedures for investigation and correction of differences disclosed by the update reconciliation (12.17)?					
Disciplines over Basic Input Completeness and Updating Controls 12.19 Are the following procedures either performed or checked by persons other than those involved in computer operations or in maintaining a manual property, plant and equipment control account: (a) manual agreement of input totals (12.4); (D) (b) investigation and correction of differences disclosed by the input reconciliations (12.7(a)); (D) (c) resubmission of all rejections (12.7(b)); (D) (d) investigation of missing documents (12.13(a)); (D) (e) manual agreement of update totals (12.6, 12.12, 12.17); (D) (f) investigation and correction of differences disclosed by the update reconciliations (12.7(c), 12.13(b), 12.18)? (D)					

Questionnaire	Flow-chart Ref.	Yes	No	"Yes" Answers PRT Ref.	"No" Answers RCW Ref.
12.20 Are the results of the following procedures reviewed and approved by a responsible official: (a) manual agreement of input totals (12.4); (S) (b) investigation and correction of differences disclosed by the input reconciliations (12.7(a)); (S) (c) resubmission of all rejections (12.7(b)); (S) (d) investigation of missing documents (12.13(a)); (S) (e) manual agreement of update totals (12.6, 12.12, 12.17); (S) (f) investigation and correction of differences disclosed by the update reconciliations (12.7(c), 12.13(b), 12.18)? (S)					
Accuracy of Input and Updating 12.21 Are there adequate controls to ensure that the following fields are accurately input and updated (e.g., batch totals, edit checks in program, reporting of non-matched items): (a) cost; (b) depreciation rate; (c) identification and/or description; (d) date of purchase; (e) depreciation method; (f) salvage value?					
12.22 Are there adequate procedures for: (a) the agreement of totals, where applicable; (b) investigation and correction of differences or exceptions?					

Questionnaire	Flow-chart Ref.	Yes	No	"Yes" Answers PRT Ref.	"No" Answers RCW Ref.
12.23 Is the method used in the program for the updating of individual accounts appropriate?					
12.24 Are the following procedures either performed or checked by persons other than those involved in computer operations or in maintaining a manual plant, property and equipment control account: (a) agreement of totals, where applicable (12.22(a)); (D) (b) investigation and correction of differences or exceptions (12.22(b))? (D)					
12.25 Are the results of the following procedures reviewed and approved by a responsible official: (a) agreement of totals, where applicable (12.22(a)); (S) (b) investigation and correction of differences or exceptions (12.22(b))? (S)					
Depreciation					
12.26 In respect of depreciation rates, review the answers to the standing data controls section. Are there adequate controls over: (a) where applicable, file creation; (b) the authorization of amendments; (c) the completeness of writing amendments to the file; (d) the accuracy of writing amendments to the file; (e) the maintenance of the data on the file?					

Questionnaire	Flow-chart Ref.	Yes	No	"Yes" Answers PRT Ref.	"No" Answers RCW Ref.
12.27 Are the methods used in the program for the calculation of depreciation appropriate?					
12.28 Is a total (specify total used) of generated depreciation charges accumulated by the computer and agreed manually with a total of items written to the property, plant and equipment file or, alternatively, are the totals agreed by the computer with adequate evidence of this check being printed out?					
12.29 Are there adequate procedures for the investigation and correction of differences disclosed by the update reconciliation?					
12.30 Is the method used in the program for updating of individual accounts appropriate?					
12.31 Are the following procedures either performed or checked by persons other than those involved in computer operations: (a) manual agreement of update totals (12.28); (D) (b) investigation and correction of differences disclosed by the update reconciliation (12.29)? (D)					
12.32 Are the results of the following procedures reviewed and approved by a responsible official: (a) manual agreement of update totals (12.28); (S) (b) investigation and correction of differences disclosed by the update reconciliation (12.29)? (S)					

Questionnaire	Flow-chart Ref.	Yes	No	"Yes" Answers PRT Ref.	"No" Answers RCW Ref.
Maintenance of the Property, Plant and Equipment File					
12.33 Is an accumulation of the items on file regularly reconciled with a manual control account maintained by a user department or, alternatively, reconciled with a control record on file with adequate evidence of reconciliation being printed out?					
12.34 Where the reconciliation is carried out by the computer, is the brought forward total checked or, alternatively, are there adequate controls over access to data files (review the answers to section 4 of the integrity controls questions)?					
12.35 Are there adequate procedures for investigating differences disclosed by the reconciliations (12.33, 12.34) before any adjustments are made?					
12.36 Are the following procedures either performed or checked by persons other than those involved in computer operations or in maintaining a manual property, plant and equipment control account: (a) manual agreement of totals (12.33); (D) (b) checking of brought forward total (12.34); (D) (c) investigation and correction of differences disclosed by the reconciliations (12.35)? (D)					

337

Questionnaire	Flow-chart Ref.	Yes	No	"Yes" Answers PRT Ref.	"No" Answers RCW Ref.
12.37 Are the results of the following procedures reviewed and approved by a responsible official: (a) manual agreement of totals (12.33); (S) (b) checking of brought forward total (12.34); (S) (c) investigation and correction of differences disclosed by the reconciliations (12.35)? (S)					
Property, Plant and Equipment Leased or Loaned from Third Parties 12.38 Are suitable records maintained of assets leased or on loan from third parties?					

Programmed Procedures
 	
12.39 List below the programmed procedures whose continued and proper operation is not assured by user controls.
 	
In respect of the items listed above, review the answers to the integrity control section. Are there adequate controls to ensure that:
(a) appropriate programmed procedures are implemented in respect of:
  (i) where applicable, new systems;
  (ii) program changes;
(b) unauthorized changes cannot be made to production programs;
(c) programmed procedures are consistently applied?					

Control Objective

13. **General ledger entries arising from the payments cycle should be accurately determined.**

Questionnaire	Flow-chart Ref.	Yes	No	"Yes" Answers PRT Ref.	"No" Answers RCW Ref.
Classification of Expenditures					
13.1 Is the coding of the following transactions for posting to general ledger accounts checked to an appropriate extent: (a) invoices and other supporting documentation related to the payment of accounts payable; (b) payrolls; (c) reimbursements of imprest and similar funds; (d) disbursements from bank accounts not covered in (a) to (c) above; (e) depreciation of property, plant and equipment?					
13.2 Is the coding (13.1) of the following transactions approved by responsible officials: (a) invoices and other supporting documentation related to the payment of accounts payable; (S) (b) payrolls; (S) (c) reimbursements of imprest and similar funds; (S) (d) disbursements from bank accounts not covered in (a) to (c) above; (S) (e) depreciation of property, plant and equipment? (S)					

339

Questionnaire	Flow-chart Ref.	Yes	No	"Yes" Answers PRT Ref.	"No" Answers RCW Ref.
13.3 Are there adequate controls to ensure that the coding of the following transactions is accurately input (e.g., validity checks in program): (a) invoices and other supporting documentation related to the payment of accounts payable; (b) payrolls; (c) reimbursements of imprest and similar funds; (d) disbursements from bank accounts not covered in (a) to (c) above; (e) depreciation of property, plant and equipment?					
Summarization of Expenditures 13.4 Are there adequate controls to ensure that the following computer produced analyses are complete and accurate (e.g., manual or programmed reconciliations): (a) invoices and other supporting documentation related to the payment of accounts payable; (b) payrolls; (c) reimbursements of imprest and similar funds; (d) disbursements from bank accounts not covered in (a) to (c) above; (e) depreciation of property, plant and equipment?					
13.5 Is the method used in the program to categorize and summarize the following computer produced analyses appropriate: (a) invoices and other supporting documentation related to the payment of accounts payable; (b) payrolls; (c) reimbursements of imprest and similar funds; (d) disbursements from bank accounts not covered in (a) to (c) above; (e) depreciation of property, plant and equipment?					

Questionnaire	Flow-chart Ref.	Yes	No	"Yes" Answers PRT Ref.	"No" Answers RCW Ref.
13.6 Where the computer produced analyses are further categorized and/or summarized manually, are there adequate controls (e.g., reconciliation of totals) to ensure that the manual summaries are complete and accurate?					
13.7 Are the manual procedures in 13.4 and 13.6 either performed or checked by persons other than those involved in computer operations? (D)					
13.8 Are the analyses referred to in 13.4 and 13.6 approved by a responsible official before posting to the general ledger accounts? (S)					

Questionnaire	Flow-chart Ref.	Yes	No	"Yes" Answers PRT Ref.	"No" Answers RCW Ref.
Programmed Procedures					
13.9 List below the programmed procedures whose continued and proper operation is not assured by user controls.					
In respect of the items listed above, review the answers to the integrity control section. Are there adequate controls to ensure that: (a) appropriate programmed procedures are implemented in respect of: (i) where applicable, new systems; (ii) program changes; (b) unauthorized changes cannot be made to production programs; (c) programmed procedures are consistently applied?					

INTEGRITY CONTROLS

IMPLEMENTATION CONTROLS

Control Objective

70. Appropriate procedures should be effectively included in production programs, both when the system originally becomes operational and when changes are subsequently made.

Questionnaire	Flow-Chart Ref.	Yes	No	"Yes" Answers PRT Ref.	"No" Answers RCW Ref.
New Systems					
70.1 Are new systems reviewed and approved by responsible officials: (a) in the user departments; (b) in the data processing function?					
70.2 Are new systems adequately tested to ensure the proper operation of programmed procedures?					
70.3 Are the testing procedures either performed or checked by persons other than those involved in writing the programs? (D)					
Systems and Program Changes					
70.4 Are all systems and program changes, including immediate modifications, supported by appropriate written authorizations?					
70.5 Are program changes, including immediate modifications, adequately tested to ensure: (a) the proper operation of changed programmed procedures; (b) the proper effect on unchanged programmed procedures?					
70.6 Are the testing procedures either performed or checked by persons other than those involved in writing the program changes? (D)					

Questionnaire	Flow-chart Ref.	Yes	No	"Yes" Answers PRT Ref.	"No" Answers RCW Ref.
Cataloguing of New Systems and Program Changes					
70.7 Is the following documentation prepared prior to final acceptance of programs and program changes? (a) instructions for setting up and running the job; (b) instructions for user procedures?					
70.8 As part of the final acceptance procedures, does a responsible official review and approve: (a) the appropriateness and results of testing procedures; (S) (b) the instructions for setting up and running the job; (S) (c) instructions for user procedures; (S) (d) the date of implementation?					
70.9 Are there adequate controls to ensure that tested and approved programs are properly taken into production?					
70.10 Are the results of the cataloguing (70.9) reviewed and approved by a responsible official? (S)					
System Software					

70.11 In respect of the system software procedures relied on for the purposes of this control objective:
(a) are the system software procedures appropriate;
(b) review the answer to control objective 74. Are there adequate controls to ensure that:
  (i) appropriate system software is properly implemented;
  (ii) unauthorized changes cannot be made to system software?					

PROGRAM SECURITY CONTROLS

Control Objective

71. Adequate steps should be taken to ensure the security of programs.
Note: The answers to the following questions should normally cover all programs that are used or could be used to process data of accounting significance.
(This control objective does not cover the controls over the authorization of program modifications which are included within the scope of control objective 70.)

Questionnaire	Flow-chart Ref.	Yes	No	"Yes" Answers PRT Ref.	"No" Answers RCW Ref.
71.1 Are programs protected from unauthorized changes: (a) while loaded on the computer system; (b) at other times? (C)					
71.2 Are the results of the following reviewed and approved by a responsible official: (a) the procedures to protect programs while loaded on the computer system; (b) the procedures to protect programs at other times? (S)					

System Software
 	
71.3 In respect of the system software procedures relied on for the purposes of this control objective:
(a) are the system software procedures appropriate;
(b) review the answers to control objective 74. Are there adequate controls to ensure that:
  (i) appropriate system software is properly implemented;
  (ii) unauthorized changes cannot be made to system software?					

COMPUTER OPERATIONS CONTROLS

Control Objective

72. Computer operations procedures should be adequate to ensure that:
   (a) authorized programmed procedures are consistently applied; and
   (b) the correct data files are used.

Questionnaire	Flow-chart Ref.	Yes	No	"Yes" Answers PRT Ref.	"No" Answers RCW Ref.
Job Set-up					
72.1 Are there appropriately authorized job set-up instructions for: (a) each application; (b) system software?					
72.2 Are job control statements and parameters used in processing recorded and checked to ensure that they are in accordance with approved instructions?					
72.3 Are the results of the procedures in 72.2 reviewed and approved by a responsible official? (S)					
Operator Actions					
72.4 Are there appropriately authorized operating instructions dealing with the following: (a) where applicable, use of system software; (b) use of application programs; (c) restart and recovery procedures; (d) other standard operating procedures?					
72.5 Are there adequate controls to ensure that: (a) operators comply with operating instructions; (b) operator action in the following circumstances is appropriate and does not adversely affect the results of processing: (i) restart and recovery; (ii) unusual situations?					
72.6 Are the results of the procedures in 72.5 reviewed and approved by a responsible official? (S)					
Use of Correct Files					
72.7 Are there adequate controls to ensure that: (a) correct files are used; (b) where applicable, all volumes of a multi-volume file are used?					
72.8 Are the results of the procedures in 72.7 reviewed and approved by a responsible official? (S)					

Questionnaire	Flow-chart Ref.	Yes	No	"Yes" Answers PRT Ref.	"No" Answers RCW Ref.
System Software					

72.9 In respect of the system software procedures relied on for the purposes of this control objective:
(a) are the system software procedures appropriate;
(b) review the answers to control objective 74. Are there adequate controls to ensure that:
    (i) appropriate system software is properly implemented;
    (ii) unauthorized changes cannot be made to system software?					

DATA FILE SECURITY CONTROLS

Control Objective

73. Adequate steps should be taken to ensure the security of data files.

Questionnaire	Flow-chart Ref.	Yes	No	"Yes" Answers PRT Ref.	"No" Answers RCW Ref.
73.1 Are data files protected from unauthorized changes: (a) while loaded on the computer system; (b) at other times? (C)					
73.2 Are the results of the following reviewed and approved by a responsible official: (a) the procedures to protect data files while loaded on the computer system (73.1(a)); (b) the procedures to protect data files at other times (73.1(b))? (S)					

System Software
 	
73.3 In respect of the system software procedures relied on for the purpose of this control objective:
(a) are the system software procedures appropriate;
(b) review the answers to control objective 74. Are there adequate controls to ensure that:
   (i) appropriate system software is properly implemented;
   (ii) unauthorized changes cannot be made to system software?					

SYSTEM SOFTWARE

Control Objective

74. Controls should be established over system software to ensure that:
    (a) system software procedures are properly checked and approved as being appropriate before being implemented;
    (b) all appropriate modifications are properly implemented; and
    (c) system software is adequately safeguarded.

Questionnaire	Flow-chart Ref.	Yes	No	"Yes" Answers PRT Ref.	"No" Answers RCW Ref.
74.1 Are system software specifications and all changes thereto reviewed and approved by: (a) those responsible for the system software function; (b) those responsible for using the software?					
74.2 Are testing procedures adequate to ensure: (a) the proper operation of system software procedures; and (b) in the case of supplied software, the correct implementation of all approved options?					
74.3 Are the following prepared prior to final acceptance of the system software: (a) instructions for setting up and running the software; (b) instructions for using the software?					
74.4 As part of the final acceptance procedures, does a responsible official review and approve: (a) the appropriateness and results of the testing; (S) (b) the appropriateness of the instructions for setting up and running the software; (S) (c) the appropriateness of the instructions for using the software; (S) (d) the date of implementation?					
74.5 Are there adequate controls to ensure that tested and approved system software is properly taken into production?					
74.6 Where immediate modifications have to be made to a system bypassing normal procedures, are there adequate procedures to ensure that the changes are correctly made and approved?					

Questionnaire	Flow-chart Ref.	Yes	No	"Yes" Answers PRT Ref.	"No" Answers RCW Ref.
74.7 Are the results of the following reviewed and approved by a responsible official: (a) procedures to ensure that tested and approved system software is properly taken into operation (74.5); (S) (b) checks on immediate modifications (74.6)? (S)					
Security Controls					
74.8 Are there adequate controls to ensure that unauthorized changes cannot be made to system software?					
74.9 Are the procedures in 74.8 reviewed and approved by a responsible official? (S)					

STANDING DATA CONTROLS
(INSERT NAME OF MASTER FILE)

Note: A separate section should be completed for each master file when indicated in the body of the questionnaire.

Obtain a copy of the file layout, mark on it all standing data fields that have accounting significance.

Questionnaire	Flow-chart Ref.	Yes	No	"Yes" Answers PRT Ref.	"No" Answers RCW Ref.
File Creation					
Note: This question is only relevant to the audit of the accounting period during which the file was initially created.					
1. Are there adequate controls that all data fields of accounting significance are completely and accurately set up initially on the file (specify)?					
Authorization of Amendments					
2. Are all manually prepared amendments to standing data authorized by a responsible official? (S)					

351

Questionnaire	Flow-chart Ref.	Yes	No	"Yes" Answers PRT Ref.	"No" Answers RCW Ref.
3. If data is authorized prior to the establishment of the controls for completeness and accuracy of input (e.g., prior to establishment of batch control totals), are there adequate controls (e.g., checking authorization after batch control totals are established) to ensure that: (a) no unauthorized alterations are made to authorized data during subsequent processing; (b) unauthorized data is not added; (c) all authorized items are included in subsequent processing?					
Completeness of Writing Input Amendments to the File Specify below the principal control that amendments to standing data are completely written to the file. If the principal control is: (a) checking of print-outs of items written to the file, answer questions 4 to 7 below; (b) agreement of manually established batch totals, specify totals used and answer questions 8 to 12 below.					
Checking of Print-outs 4. Are there adequate controls to ensure that all documents are submitted for processing (e.g., by checking against retained copies; by manual sequence check)?					
5. Is there a regular (e.g., monthly) review of source documents for unprocessed items?					

Questionnaire	Flow-chart Ref.	Yes : No	"Yes" Answers PRT Ref.	"No" Answers RCW Ref.
6. Is the method used in the program for the production of the print-out appropriate (e.g., does it contain details of items that have been written to the master file)?				
7. Are there adequate procedures for the investigation and correction of differences disclosed by the checking?				
Batch Totals				
8. Are there adequate controls to ensure that: (a) a document is raised for each transaction; (b) all documents are included in a batch; (c) all batches are submitted for processing?				
9. Are the totals of individual items accepted by the computer compared manually to pre-determine control totals or, alternatively, is such a comparison made by the computer with adequate evidence of the check being printed out?				
10. Are the totals in 9 agreed to the total of items written to the master file or, alternatively, are such totals carried through intermediate processing (including summarization of totals or changes in the totals used) so that it is established that all accepted input items are updated to the master file?				

Questionnaire	Flow-chart Ref.	Yes	No	"Yes" Answers PRT Ref.	"No" Answers RCW Ref.
11. Is the reconciliation of totals in 10 carried out manually or, alternatively, is the reconciliation carried out by the computer with adequate evidence of this check being printed out?					
12. Are there adequate procedures for: (a) investigation and correction of differences disclosed by the input reconciliations (9); (b) resubmission of all rejections; (c) investigation and correction of differences disclosed by the update reconciliations (11)?					
Disciplines Over Basic Input Completeness and Updating Controls 13. Are the following procedures either performed or checked by persons other than those who deal with the related transaction data or are involved in computer operations: (a) regular (e.g., monthly) review of source documents for unprocessed items (5); (D) (b) investigation and correction of differences disclosed by the checking of print-outs (7); (D) (c) manual agreement of input totals (9); (D) (d) investigation and correction of differences disclosed by the input reconciliations (12(a)); (D) (e) resubmission of all rejections (12(b)); (D) (f) manual agreement of update totals (11); (D) (g) investigation and correction of differences disclosed by the update reconciliations (12(c))? (D)					

Questionnaire	Flow-chart Ref.	Yes	No	"Yes" Answers PRT Ref.	"No" Answers RCW Ref.
14. Are the results of the following procedures reviewed and approved by a responsible official: (a) regular (e.g., monthly) review of source documents for unprocessed items (5); (S) (b) investigation and correction of differences disclosed by the checking of print-outs (7); (S) (c) manual agreement of input totals (9); (S) (d) investigation and correction of differences disclosed by the input reconciliations (12(a)); (S) (e) resubmission of all rejections (12(b)); (S) (f) manual agreement of update totals (11); (S) (g) investigation and correction of differences disclosed by the update reconciliations (12(c))? (S)					
Accuracy of Input and Updating of Amendments to the File 15. Are there adequate controls to ensure that all data fields of accounting significance are accurately written to the file (e.g., detailed checking of print-outs of items written to the file; agreement of manually established batch totals; programmed reasonableness checks)?					
16. Are there adequate procedures for: (a) the agreement of totals, where applicable; (b) investigation and correction of differences or exceptions?					
17. Is the method used in the program for updating individual accounts appropriate?					

Questionnaire	Flow-chart Ref.	Yes	No	"Yes" Answers PRT Ref.	"No" Answers RCW Ref.
18. Are the following procedures either performed or checked by persons other than those who deal with related transaction data or who are involved in computer operations: (a) agreement of totals, where applicable (16(a)); (D) (b) investigation and correction of differences or exceptions (16(b))? (D)					
19. Are the results of the following procedures reviewed and approved by a responsible official: (a) agreement of totals, where applicable (16(a)); (S) (b) investigation and correction of differences or exceptions (16(b))? (S)					
Computer Generated Amendments to the File 20. Are the methods used in the program to generate the data and related control record appropriate?					
21. Is there a check over the accuracy of the data generated (e.g., reasonableness check, manual review of data)?					
22. Are the results of the check (21) reviewed and approved by a responsible official? (S)					

Questionnaire	Flow-chart Ref.	Yes	No	"Yes" Answers PRT Ref.	"No" Answers RCW Ref.
23. Is a total of the items in 21 accumulated by the computer and agreed manually with a total of items written to the file or, alternatively, are the totals agreed by the computer with adequate evidence of this check being printed out?					
24. Are there adequate procedures for the investigation and correction of differences disclosed by the update reconciliation?					
25. Are the following procedures either performed or checked by persons other than those involved in computer processing: (a) manual agreement of update totals (23); (D) (b) investigation and correction of differences disclosed by the update reconciliations (24)? (D)					
26. Are the following procedures reviewed and approved by a responsible official: (a) manual agreement of update totals (23); (S) (b) investigation and correction of differences disclosed by the update reconciliations (24)? (S)					

Questionnaire	Flow-chart Ref.	Yes	No	"Yes" Answers PRT Ref.	"No" Answers RCW Ref.
Maintenance of Standing Data on the File					
27. Are there adequate controls to ensure that standing data fields of accounting significance remain correctly stored (e.g., a suitable combination of controls over access to data files (see integrity controls section)); regular agreement by a user department of printed out totals with independently maintained control totals; and detailed checking by user departments on a cyclical basis of print-outs to source data?					
28. Is the file regularly examined to identify standing data requiring action (e.g., the provision of exception reports of prices not changed for over twelve months)?					
29. Are there adequate procedures for: (a) investigation of differences disclosed by the checking (27) before any adjustments are made; (b) investigation and correction of data requiring action (28)?					
30. Are the following procedures either performed or checked by persons other than those who deal with related transaction data or who are involved in computer operations: (a) manual agreement of totals (27); (D) (b) cyclical checking (27); (D) (c) investigation and correction of differences (29(a)); (D) (d) investigation and correction of data requiring action (29(b))? (D)					

Questionnaire	Flow-chart Ref.	Yes	No	"Yes" Answers PRT Ref.	"No" Answers RCW Ref.
31. Are the results of the following procedures reviewed and approved by a responsible official: (a) manual agreement of totals (27); (S) (b) cyclical checking (27); (S) (c) investigation and correction of differences (29(a)); (S) (d) investigation and correction of data requiring action (29(b))? (S)					

D

Internal Control Reference Manual

COMMON CONTROL PROCEDURES

Adequacy of Controls Over Completeness of Processing

1. Entering Transactions on Control Documents

2. Establishing Completeness of Unmatched Documents (or Entries)

3. Investigation of Unmatched Items

4. Investigation of Unmatched Items by Persons with No Incompatible Duties

Adequacy of Controls Over Maintenance of Subsidiary Records Supporting a Control Account

1. Establishing Control Totals Before Subsidiary Records Are Posted

2. Maintenance of Control Accounts and Subsidiary Records by Persons with No Incompatible Duties

3. Reconciliation of Subsidiary Records with Control Accounts

4. Investigation of Differences Disclosed by the Reconciliations

5. Investigation of Differences by Persons with No Incompatible Duties

Adequacy of Controls Over Posting Quantities to Detailed Inventory Records

1. Timeliness of Entries

2. Dating of Postings

3. Source of Postings

Adequacy of Controls for Supervisory Review and Approval

1. Official Responsible for Review and Approval

2. Procedures To Be Followed

Adequacy of Controls Over Checking of Extensions and Additions

1. Extent of Checking

2. Method of Checking

3. Evidence of Checking

Adequacy of Controls Over Completeness of Processing

1. The company's procedures for ensuring that all transactions entered on a company document (e.g., receiving report, shipping advice) have been included in the accounting records are an important part of its internal control.

2. Questions dealing with those procedures appear under many control objectives. Adequacy of control is discussed centrally in this section for convenience and to emphasize that similar control procedures may apply to different cycles and different control objectives.

3. The factors to be considered in this section are listed below and discussed in more detail in the following charts:
   a. Entering transactions on control documents (Item 1);
   b. Establishing completeness of unmatched documents (or entries) (Item 2);
   c. Investigation of unmatched items (Item 3);
   d. Investigation of unmatched items by persons with no incompatible duties (Item 4).

4. Controls to ensure that all transactions are entered on a control document are also important. However, because the relevant procedures vary from control objective to control objective, this subject is discussed under each applicable control objective.

[Note: The following material is designed to be read across the page.]

If	Impact on Adequacy of Control	Example
1. Entering Transactions on Control Documents: a. Pre-numbered documents are used (this is practicable only when the documents are prepared internally) and the following conditions are met: (i) Physical control is maintained over unissued documents, (ii) The documents are issued in numerical order, (iii) All series are controlled,	Control will be adequate if the company periodically (at least monthly) identifies missing documents in either of two ways: (i) Using a list of document numbers against which an appropriate cross-reference can be made for completed transactions. Voided documents should be so indicated on the list and should be retained intact by the company; (ii) Using a numerical file of document copies against which appropriate cross-references can be made for completed transactions.	Purchase invoice numbers are indicated on a list of receiving report numbers. Purchase invoice numbers are indicated on copies of receiving reports filed numerically.

If	Impact on Adequacy of Control	Example
b. Internally prepared documents are numbered as the transactions occur,	Control is not as good as when the documents are pre-numbered. However, control may be adequate if there are procedures to ensure that all documents are numbered and that they are numbered in sequence, i.e., there are no duplicate or missing numbers.	Bills of lading are numbered sequentially by the shipping clerk. The shipping supervisor ensures that there is a bill of lading for each shipment and that the numbers are sequential.
c. Externally prepared documents are numbered as received,	Control will be adequate if there are procedures to ensure that: (i) All documents are numbered immediately upon receipt; (ii) The documents are numbered sequentially, i.e., there are no duplicate or missing numbers; (iii) The documents are received in authorized locations.	The company uses the customer's order as its sales order. All customers' orders are received in the Sales Service Department and are numbered immediately upon receipt. The sales supervisor reviews the assigned numbers for numerical sequence.
d. Documents are numbered sometime after their receipt or the transaction occurs,	Control is not adequate because documents may be lost or misplaced between time of receipt or preparation and numbering. This may be compensated for by other controls.	Purchase invoices are not numbered until matched with receiving reports and purchase orders. However, control may be adequate if the company: (i) Has well-controlled purchase order and receiving report procedures; (ii) Reconciles recorded accounts payable balances with suppliers' statements monthly.

364

e. Transactions are entered in a register as they occur,

Control will be adequate if the appropriate cross-references to the completion of the transaction are indicated in the register, the pages in the register are appropriately controlled, and unauthorized alterations are guarded against. The register serves as a permanent record of all transactions and indicates how they were subsequently accounted for.

Invoices from suppliers are entered in a register upon receipt and are subsequently cross-referenced to the appropriate cash disbursement or voucher number. Register pages are pre-numbered in a permanently bound book and all entries are in ink. Corrections are initialled by the supervisor.

2. Establishing Completeness of Unmatched Documents (or Entries):

a. One (or more) of the controls described in 1–a, 1–b, 1–c, or 1–e above is in operation,

The company can establish adequate control over unmatched documents by reviewing, as appropriate:
  (i) The numerical control record or file;
  (ii) The register of entries.

The absence of a voucher number next to an entry in a register of goods received would indicate that the liability for that item had not been recorded.

b. Numerical control list, register or file is merely marked off when the transaction is completed, i.e., the appropriate cross-reference is not entered,

Control is not adequate because the control documents do not indicate the details of subsequent processing. The effectiveness of the supervisory review procedure is reduced because the supervisor cannot tell whether the items have been matched to valid documents.

A check mark, rather than the invoice number, is placed against shipping advices when the sales invoice is prepared. A check mark can be made even if a sales invoice is not prepared.

c. Files of unmatched documents are maintained,

The file, by itself, is not an adequate control since items may be improperly added or deleted from the file without detection.

If	Impact on Adequacy of Control	Example
	Control will be adequate if: (i) The items in the file are compared to the numerical control listings or registers to ensure that no items have been added to or deleted from the file in error; (ii) Unused and voided documents are examined periodically (e.g., monthly) to ensure that they have not been used inadvertently (or otherwise) to record transactions.	All receiving reports over 30 days old are thrown away. Comparison of the unmatched documents file to a numerical listing of unmatched receiving reports would detect this error. Shipping advices are used out of sequence to suppress the record for billing purposes.
d. Records of unmatched documents are to be considered adequate,	They should contain enough information to enable full details of transactions to be identified and any necessary journal entry to be prepared.	Copies of the documents constitute the file (either those that are "open" or a complete file with notations as to those that have been completed).

3. Investigation of Unmatched Items:

Note: Review of numerical control records or registers usually indicates that some transactions have not been completely processed. For accounting control procedures to be adequate, unprocessed transactions should be investigated periodically and necessary corrective action taken.

If	Impact on Adequacy of Control	Example
a. Client procedures to investigate unmatched items are to be considered adequate,	The person making the investigation should be satisfied that all unmatched items are forwarded to him.	Investigator checks the numerical sequence of processed documents and compares the missing numbers to the items being forwarded.
b. Long outstanding items are revealed by the investigation,	The investigator should discuss them with knowledgeable persons in the company, ex-	Correspondence with supplier re disputed item is examined.

...ex-amine relevant documentation and, where appropriate, discuss them with any concerned outside parties to establish the validity of "open" items.

c. Adjusting entries appear to be necessary,

The investigator should determine whether they have been made and, if not, arrange for them to be made.

Expense and liability should be recorded for unprocessed invoice for advertising services.

d. Malfunctioning controls are detected,

The investigator should report them to persons with appropriate authority to evaluate corrective action needed so that errors do not continue to occur.

Accounts payable clerk does not remove receiving report when purchase invoice is processed.

e. Items are unmatched because they represent new or changed transactions.

Appropriate procedures should be established to account for them.

Sales invoices to a new customer are not processed because an account number has not been established.

4. Investigation of Unmatched Items by Persons With No Incompatible Duties:

The same person maintains the records and investigates the unmatched items,

It is less likely that apparent errors will be investigated and brought to the attention of a responsible official.

(i) Having another person perform the investigation serves as a check on the recordkeeper's work;

The investigator notices additional items that should be on the list of unmatched items and takes the necessary corrective action.

(ii) The recordkeeper may be reluctant to report such items or take necessary corrective action if he believes that doing so might adversely affect his job.

The recordkeeper does not report all unmatched shipping advices because he has previously been criticized for not matching advices correctly.

Adequacy of Controls Over Maintenance of Subsidiary Records Supporting a Control Account

1. The company's procedures for maintaining control accounts and subsidiary records are an important part of its internal control.

2. Questions dealing with those procedures appear under many control objectives. Adequacy of control is discussed centrally in this section for convenience and to emphasize that similar control procedures may apply to different cycles and different control objectives.

3. The factors to be considered in this section are listed below and discussed in more detail in the following charts:

   a. Establishing control totals before subsidiary records are posted (Item 1);

   b. Maintenance of control accounts and subsidiary records by persons with no incompatible duties (Item 2);

   c. Reconciliation of subsidiary records with control accounts (Item 3);

   d. Investigation of differences disclosed by the reconciliations (Item 4);

   e. Investigation of differences by persons with no compatible duties (Item 5).

4. Checking of postings to subsidiary records has not been included because it is usually not done, or, if it is, it is not evidenced. Thus, we would not be able to rely on the control in any event. The reconciliation indicated above should ensure that, in total, all items have been posted to the subsidiary records. The accuracy of the postings will be determined by validation procedures on the individual balances.

If	Impact on Adequacy of Control	Example
1. Establishing Control Totals Before Subsidiary Records Are Posted:		
a. Totals for posting to the control account are not established before the details are passed to the persons who post the subsidiary records,	Control will be inadequate because items could be added to or deleted from the detailed transactions to be posted without such alterations being detected. (See note.)	Accounts receivable detail is lost during posting to the subsidiary records. (See note.)

Note: Control would be adequate if the completeness control is performed after the subsidiary records are posted. However, this would be an unusual and inefficient procedure.

368

b. Control totals are established at the same time that completeness controls are performed,	Control will be adequate because there is assurance that all items are included in the control total.	Accounts receivable control totals are established immediately after the numerical sequence of sales invoices is accounted for.
c. Persons establishing control totals retain records of the individual items in sufficient detail to permit independent verification of differences or exceptions arising in the maintenance of subsidiary records,	Control will be adequate because the reasons for differences or exceptions between control totals and detail totals can be identified.	The person establishing control totals for accounts receivable maintains tapes with customers' names and amounts.
d. Control totals are passed to persons maintaining subsidiary records,	Control may be inadequate since the subsidiary recordkeepers may "force" differences between the total of the items posted and the control total, rather than investigate any such differences.	An erroneous total was entered on a posting control form for accounts receivable.
e. This control is: (i) Absent,	Effectiveness of previous processing and completeness controls can be negated. (See note to a.)	Accounts receivable detail is lost during posting to the subsidiary records. (See note to a.)
(ii) Present,	It does not compensate for weaknesses in prior processing and completeness procedures because control will be maintained only over transactions that have been entered on company documents (not necessarily over all transactions that have occurred).	Goods shipped for which shipping advices were not prepared will not be identified by the operation of this control.

If	Impact on Adequacy of Control	Example
2. Maintenance of Control Accounts and Subsidiary Records by Persons With No Incompatible Duties:		
a. Same person maintains control account and subsidiary records,	Control is inadequate since: (i) He can cover up differences between the two records so they will not be properly investigated and corrected; (ii) He may be able to defraud the company by manipulating the subsidiary records.	Accounts payable subsidiary records are altered so that they agree with an erroneous balance in the control account. He inflates accounts payable subsidiary records that are the basis for making payments to suppliers.
b. Same person has custody of assets and maintains related accounting records,	Control is inadequate since he can suppress differences between assets actually on hand and the balances in the accounting records. He can adjust the accounting records to reflect amounts on hand.	Inventory recordkeepers have responsibility for custody of inventory.
c. Same person processes or approves transactions and maintains related accounting records.	Control would be inadequate since he could introduce and approve fictitious transactions and detection may be delayed.	Persons who check and approve purchase invoices also maintain accounts payable records.
3. Reconciliation of Subsidiary Records With Control Accounts:		
a. Reconciliations are performed,	Control is adequate since the accuracy of the posting to subsidiary records (in total, not by individual item) can be assured.	The reconciliation balances, indicating that the postings to the subsidiary records are correct.
b. Reconciliations are not performed,	Control is inadequate because errors or omissions of postings to subsidiary records will not be detected.	Debit adjustments are erroneously posted to accounts receivable subsidiary records as credits. These errors may not be detected until the reconciliation is done. (See note.)

Note: The accuracy of the control account is covered by other questions. However, the reconciliation process may reveal errors in the control account (as well as errors in the subsidiary records), e.g., adjustments not posted to the control account.

c. Reconciliations are performed regularly,

Control is adequate because errors will be detected on a current basis. The frequency may vary with the nature of the account and the volume of transactions.

(i) Cash, receivables and payables are reconciled monthly.
(ii) Fixed assets are reconciled quarterly.

d. Reconciliations are performed at the end of an accounting period,

Control is adequate because there is assurance that closing and adjusting entries have been processed properly in the subsidiary records.

Physical inventory adjustments arising from cycle counts are posted at month-end. The reconciliation is performed after that posting is completed.

e. Appropriate circumstances are present,

The reconciliation can be done other than at the end of the accounting period.

The company bills accounts receivable on a cycle basis and balances the subsidiary records against the control at that time.

4. Investigation of Differences Disclosed by the Reconciliations:

a. Differences are not investigated nor corrective action taken,

Control is inadequate because the reconciliation process is incomplete. It will not be known whether adjustments are required to the control account, subsidiary records, or both.

Differences between the inventory control account and subsidiary records are not investigated.

b. The investigations are to be considered adequate,

The investigator should examine supporting documentation and check postings to both the control account and the subsidiary records. Particular attention should be directed to "cut-off" problems, i.e., the posting of items to the control account and subsidiary records in different time periods.

If the reconciling items involve credit memoranda, the credit memoranda and, if appropriate, the supporting evidence (e.g., records of goods returned) should be examined.

If	Impact on Adequacy of Control	Example
c. Immaterial differences are not investigated,	Control is not adequate. The immaterial difference may be the net effect of two material items, one valid and one invalid.	A material posting error is offset by differences arising from poor cut-off procedures.
d. Adjusting entries appear to be necessary,	The investigator should determine whether they have been made and, if not, arrange for them to be made to ensure that the accounting records are correct.	Adjustments posted to accounts receivable subsidiary ledgers were erroneously omitted from the control account.
e. Malfunctioning controls are detected,	The investigator should report them to persons with appropriate authority to take corrective action needed so that errors do not continue to occur.	Credit memoranda are not posted on a timely basis.
f. Differences arise from new or changed transaction types,	They should be identified so that appropriate procedures can be established to account for them promptly.	Postings to subsidiary records for new customers are lagging because account numbers have not been assigned.
5. **Investigation of Differences by Persons With No Incompatible Duties:** a. Reconciliation and investigation procedures are performed by persons maintaining either the subsidiary records or the control account,	The reconciliation and investigation control will not, by itself, be adequate, because: (i) They could suppress or cover up errors to avoid adverse conclusions concerning their job performance; (ii) Suppression of errors eliminates (or delays) the taking of corrective action.	Fictitious explanations are reported for differences and reconciling items. Unmatched shipping advices are not investigated because of the fictitious explanations.

b. Reconciliation and investigation procedures are performed by persons responsible for custody of related assets,

Control would not be adequate because they could cover up differences between items on hand and those in the records by reporting fictitious explanations for the reconciling items.

Persons responsible for custody of inventory investigate differences between subsidiary records and control accounts for inventory.

Adequacy of Controls Over Posting Quantities to Detailed Inventory Records

1. The company's procedures for ensuring that entries to the detailed inventory records are made properly and on a timely basis are an important part of its internal control.

2. Questions dealing with those procedures appear under many control objectives. Adequacy of control is discussed centrally in this section for convenience and to emphasize that similar control procedures may apply to different cycles and different control objectives.

3. The factors to be considered in this section are listed below and discussed in more detail in the following charts:

   a. Timeliness of entries (Item 1);
   b. Dating of postings (Item 2);
   c. Source of postings (Item 3).

If	Impact on Adequacy of Control	Example
1. Timeliness of Entries: The entries are not made on a timely basis,	The control would not be adequate because: (i) The records will not reflect the actual balances on hand; (ii) Detailed records may not balance with the control account.	Records are posted two weeks after receipt of raw materials. The control account is posted currently but the detailed records are not.

If	Impact on Adequacy of Control	Example
2. Dating of Postings: Postings are dated as of the date entries are made, rather than the date of inventory movement,	The control would not be adequate because the records will not reflect the actual balances on hand.	Postings for inventory purchased in the last 10 days of one month are entered (and dated) in the following month. Details will not balance with the control account and adjustments of the control account to "actual" may be in error.
3. Source of Postings: a. Postings are made from the document used to record the inventory movement,	Control would normally be adequate since that document is ordinarily prepared on a timely basis and thus should assure that the detailed inventory records are current.	Postings for sales of finished goods are made from shipping advices.
b. Postings are made from other documents,	Control would ordinarily not be adequate since the other documents are often not prepared on a timely basis. Also, use of secondary documents introduces potential problems regarding their completeness and/or accuracy. Additional control procedures would be required to ensure their completeness and accuracy.	Postings for sales of finished goods are made from summaries of shipping advices.

Adequacy of Controls for Supervisory Review and Approval

1. The company's procedures for supervisory review and approval of documents and control procedures are an important part of its internal control. Supervisory controls include reviews of documents, reports, adjustments, entries, reconciliations, completeness, accuracy and numerous other control procedures in all cycles.

2. Questions dealing with those procedures appear under many control objectives. Adequacy of control is discussed centrally in this section for convenience and to emphasize that similar control procedures may apply to different cycles and different control objectives.

3. The factors to be considered in this section are listed below and are discussed in more detail in the following charts:

   a. Official responsible for review and approval (Item 1);

   b. Procedures to be followed (Item 2).

If	Impact on Adequacy of Control	Example
1. Official Responsible for Review and Approval: The official has sufficient knowledge of the underlying transactions and procedures,	Control is adequate because he can exercise the informed judgment required to recognize erroneous or otherwise inappropriate items or events.	The official who reviews and approves sales invoices is knowledgeable about the company's customers, products and prices.
2. Procedures To Be Followed: a. The official determines whether all appropriate checking procedures have been performed and that the documentation appears to be complete,	Control is adequate because he will detect any malfunctioning or absence of checking procedures.	The official who reviews and approves purchase invoices sees that all blocks on the voucher stamp have been signed and that receiving reports and purchase orders are attached.
b. The official determines whether all appropriate completeness controls are functioning,	Control is adequate because he will detect any malfunctioning or absence of completeness controls.	The official who reviews and approves physical inventory results assures that the accounting for all inventory tags has been properly performed.

If	Impact on Adequacy of Control	Example
c. The official determines that exceptions are properly disposed of,	Control is adequate because unresolved exceptions, as well as inappropriate adjustments or entries, will be corrected.	The official who reviews and approves bank reconciliations assures that reconciling items are appropriate, long outstanding items have been investigated and any required adjustments to the records are made.
d. The official determines whether the documents and/or procedures appear valid or appear to contain questionable items,	Control is adequate. If the supervisory review and approval is performed in a perfunctory manner, it will be ineffective.	The official who reviews and approves payrolls determines that amounts appear reasonable for individuals and in total.
e. The review and approval is performed in a timely manner,	Control is adequate because errors, malfunctioning controls, etc., will not go uncorrected for an undue length of time.	The official who supervises the review of unmatched documents does so shortly after the review is completed.
f. The official ensures that all documents requiring his review are presented to him,	Control is adequate since he will review all matters requiring his attention.	The official maintains a control list of the due dates of all reconciliations and completeness reviews for which he is responsible.

Adequacy of Controls Over Checking of Extensions and Additions

1. The company's procedures for checking extensions and additions are an important part of its internal control.

2. Questions dealing with those procedures appear under many control objectives. Adequacy of control is discussed centrally in this section for convenience and to emphasize that similar control procedures may apply to different cycles and different control objectives.

3. The factors to be considered in this section are listed below and are discussed in more detail in the following charts:

a. Extent of checking (Item 1);

b. Method of checking (Item 2);

c. Evidence of checking (Item 3).

If	Impact on Adequacy of Control	Example
1. Extent of Checking:		
a. The company checks all extensions and additions,	The company has adequate control procedures in this regard because all errors should be detected.	Company checks extensions and additions on all purchase invoices.
b. The company checks extensions and additions above (or below) a specified monetary amount,	Control may be adequate if the cut-off point is reasonable and approved by a knowledgeable official. If the cut-off point is such that most transactions are not checked, then control is not adequate.	Extensions and additions are checked on purchase invoices over $1,000. If most invoices are below $1,000, then control is not adequate.
2. Method of Checking:		
a. The company checks all extensions and additions individually,	The company has adequate control procedures in this regard because all errors should be detected.	Company checks individual extensions and additions on all purchase invoices.
b. The company checks extensions and additions on an overall basis for groups of documents,	The company may be able to exercise adequate control under appropriate circumstances.	Company prepares a number of sales invoices for the same product using a standard price. Multiplying aggregate quantities by the standard price and agreeing that amount to the total of the individual invoices serves as an adequate check on the extensions and additions of the individual invoices.

If	Impact on Adequacy of Control	Example
3. Evidence of Checking: a. The person performing the checking initials or signs the document,	Control is adequate because the person is identified and the procedure is evidenced.	Clerk signs off voucher stamp block indicating that extensions and additions have been checked.
b. The company's procedures provide that only amounts above (or below) a specified amount need be checked,	The documents should indicate on their face that the appropriate checking has been done.	Company checks extensions and additions over $1,000. Clerk places tick mark beside each item checked, and initials voucher stamp block.

Index to Questions

Index to Questions (continued)

Question Number	Discussion of Question	Common Control Procedure (If Applicable)
Control Objective 5 (cont'd)		
5.9	465	370
5.10	466	371
5.11	467	372
5.12	468	374
5.13	469	
5.14	471	
5.15	473	374
Control Objective 6		
6.1	473	
6.2	477	
6.3	478	
6.4	480	
6.5	483	
6.6	485	
6.7	487	
6.8	488	376
6.9	491	376
6.10	493	376
6.11	494	
6.12	495	376
6.13	497	374
6.14	498	
6.15	499	

Question Number	Discussion of Question	Common Control Procedure (If Applicable)
Control Objective 9 (cont'd)		
9.9	527	
9.10	529	
9.11	531	
9.12	532	
9.13	534	
9.14	535	
9.15	537	
Control Objective 10		
10.1	538	
10.2	541	363, 368
10.3	542	365
10.4	543	374
10.5	544	370
10.6	545	368
10.7	546	370
10.8	547	370
10.9	548	371
10.10	549	372
10.11	550	374
10.12	551	
10.13	552	
10.14	553	
10.15	555	

Control Objective 7

7.1	501	
7.2	502	
7.3	503	

Control Objective 8

8.1	504	
8.2	506	374
8.3	508	
8.4	510	
8.5	511	
8.6	513	374

Control Objective 9

9.2	514	
9.3	517	
9.4	519	374
9.5	520	
9.6	523	
9.7	524	
9.8	526	374

Control Objective 11

11.1	556	
11.2	558	
11.3	559	
11.4	561	
11.5	562	
11.6	563	

Control Objective 12

12.1	564	
12.2	566	
12.3	567	
12.4	569	370
12.5	570	371
12.6	570	374
12.7	571	

Control Objective 13

13.1	573	
13.2	574	374
13.3	575	
13.4	577	374

REFERENCE MANUAL
PAYMENTS CYCLE

QUESTION 1.1

Are all significant purchase commitments and changes thereto initiated only on the basis of appropriate written authorizations?

Purpose

To determine whether the company's system is such that significant purchase commitments are initiated only if supported by an appropriately approved authorization.

What Constitutes Adequate Control Procedures?

[*Note:* Throughout the Reference Manual, material following this heading is designed to be read across the page.]

If	Impact on Adequacy of Control	Example
1. The company initiates *all* purchase commitments and changes thereto only on the basis of appropriate written authorizations,	Control is satisfactory because all purchase commitments are appropriately authorized.	All purchase orders are prepared from purchase requisitions authorized by departmental heads.
2. Only purchase commitments over a specified monetary amount are authorized in writing,	Control will be adequate if: (a) The specified amount has been approved by a responsible official; (b) The specified amount is reasonable (if it is too high, significant purchase commitments may be made without appropriate authorization).	The company requires authorized purchase requisitions for all purchases over $1,000. This policy has been approved by the vice president, operations and the controller.

3. Company initiates purchase commitments for goods only (i.e., not services) on the basis of appropriate written authorization,

The reviewer should evaluate the materiality of purchase commitments for services. It is unlikely that a material purchase commitment or loss thereon would arise from services.

Orders for maintenance services are oral, but these costs are payable monthly and are renegotiated at regular intervals.

Possible Errors in Financial Statements	Example	Effect on Audit Procedures
If: Significant purchase commitments are not authorized in writing,		
Because there is no control to ensure that all purchases are reviewed and authorized by a responsible official, the company may be committed to purchases at prices that will result in a loss or assets may be purchased in excess of requirements. As a result, net income may be overstated and liabilities (provision for losses) understated.	The purchase price in an unauthorized purchase commitment exceeds the current market price for that item. The resulting loss will result in an understatement of a liability for losses and an overstatement of net income if the correcting entry is not made.	1. When reviewing open purchase commitments for possible losses, the auditor should pay particular attention to commitments that were not appropriately authorized. 2. The auditor should consider this weakness in determining the extent of his review of slow-moving or obsolete inventory.

QUESTION 1.17

Are the purchase commitments referred to in 1.1 recorded in written form?

Purpose

To determine whether there is a record of purchase commitments that can be used in processing invoices and reviewing for possible losses.

QUESTION 1.17 (*continued*)

What Constitutes Adequate Control Procedures?

If	Impact on Adequacy of Control	Example
1. All purchase commitments are recorded in written form,	Control is satisfactory.	All purchase requisitions are forwarded to a central purchasing department where a purchase order is completed and sent to the supplier. Retained copies of the purchase order serve as the company's record of purchase commitments.
2. Only purchase commitments over a specified monetary amount are recorded in writing,	Control will be adequate if: (a) The specified amount has been approved by a responsible official; (b) The specified amount is reasonable (if it is too high, significant purchase commitments may be made and not recorded); (c) Other controls indicate that all commitments over the specified amount are recorded.	(a). and (b). The company prepares purchase orders for all orders over $1,000. This policy has been approved by the controller. (c). In checking purchase invoices (see Question 4.1), the invoice clerk is required to check prices to approved purchase orders rather than price lists for all invoices that exceed $1,000. Invoices in excess of $1,000 for which purchase orders cannot be located are reported to the controller for follow-up.

Possible Errors in Financial Statements	Example	Effect on Audit Procedures
If: Purchase commitments are not recorded in written form,		
Income may be overstated and liabilities (provision for losses) may be understated. The company cannot determine if it is committed to purchases at more than current prices or in excess of requirements which may result in a loss to the company.	Because of a decline in raw material prices, the company has significant losses arising from firm purchase orders placed at a higher price.	In order to identify unrecorded purchase commitments at year-end, the auditor should: (a) Review the steps taken by management to identify significant purchase commitments; (b) Request from major suppliers details of any purchase commitments outstanding as of year-end; (c) Review selected invoices received after year-end for evidence of purchases at more than prevailing prices, in quantities in excess of current requirements, or of goods determined to be slow-moving or obsolete.

QUESTION 1.18

Do the commitment records state, insofar as is practicable: (a) quantities; (b) prices; (c) other relevant terms (e.g. discounts, freight terms)?

Purpose

To determine whether the written commitments have sufficient detail to:
(a) Enable adequate checks to be made at a later date (e.g., checking of supplier's invoice);

QUESTION 1.18 (*continued*)

(b) Facilitate the determination of any provisions for losses that may be required; and

(c) Determine, where appropriate, the amount of purchase commitments for disclosure in the notes to the financial statements.

What Constitutes Adequate Control Procedures?

If	Impact on Adequacy of Control	Example
The company's commitment records state quantities, prices and other relevant terms,	Control is satisfactory because data is available for subsequent accounting use.	Purchase orders include supplier's name and address, quantity ordered, price, and supplier's freight and discount terms.

Possible Errors in Financial Statements	Example	Effect on Audit Procedures
If: The commitment records do not state all the information set out in the question,		
1. Income may be overstated and liabilities (provision for losses) understated because losses inherent in certain commitments cannot be identified or recorded.	A purchase order is prepared with quantities only, although a unit price was also agreed. The price has declined since the order was placed.	The auditor should: (a) Request suppliers to report agreed prices for significant purchase commitments, particularly where there have been recent price declines; (b) Review suppliers' invoices received after year-end for indication of purchases at more than the prevailing price.
2. The company has no means of checking the validity of supplier's invoice prices with original commitments.	The purchase order includes quantities only.	In determining the extent of his lower of cost or market inventory tests, the auditor should keep in mind that the company is more likely to have overpaid for purchases in these circumstances.

QUESTION 1.20

Are the commitments controlled in such a way that it can subsequently be established that they have all been accounted for (e.g. by sequential pre-numbering, by entry in a register or by establishment of batch totals)?

Purpose

1. To determine whether the company's procedures for recording purchase commitments are such that it *can* determine whether all such commitments have been accounted for.

2. Note that the question is not whether commitments *are* in fact accounted for. Thus, if the documentation for controlling them exists (e.g., purchase orders are pre-numbered), the auditor may be able to use it to reduce the amount of audit work otherwise required in situations where the company can, but does not, account for unmatched purchase commitments.

What Constitutes Adequate Control Procedures?

This question deals with one of the controls over completeness of processing. Refer to the discussion under that heading on page 363, item 1.

Possible Errors in Financial Statements	Example	Effect on Audit Procedures
If: It cannot subsequently be established whether all transactions have been accounted for,		
Income may be overstated and liabilities (provision for losses) understated because losses inherent in certain purchase commitments cannot be identified or recorded.	Provisions for losses on open purchase commitments are based on unmatched purchase orders that are not pre-numbered. The company has removed all loss purchase orders from the open file and has not made the required provision.	The auditor should perform the procedures set out in Question 1.17.

QUESTION 1.21

Are records maintained of commitments which have not been matched with receiving reports or equivalent records of goods or services received?

Purpose

1. To determine whether the company maintains adequate records of purchase commitments that have not been matched with receipts in order to determine the amount of unfulfilled commitments and any provision for losses arising therefrom.

2. Note that if Question 1.20 is answered "no," this question should also be answered "no."

3. Where sequentially pre-numbered forms are used, this question is inter-related with Question 1.22 and should be answered similarly. The records in Question 1.21 will not be adequate unless the control in Question 1.22 operates.

What Constitutes Adequate Control Procedures?

This question deals with one of the controls over completeness of processing. Refer to the discussion under that heading on page 365, item 2.

Possible Errors in Financial Statements	Example	Effect on Audit Procedures
If: The company does not maintain adequate records of unmatched purchase orders,		
Income may be overstated and liabilities (provision for losses) understated because losses inherent in certain purchase commitments cannot be identified or recorded. (Same as Question 1.20.)	The company does not maintain a file of unmatched purchase commitments. Potential losses cannot be identified.	1. If the company does not control the transactions, but the documentation is such that the transactions could be controlled (e.g., documents are pre-numbered but not accounted for), the audi-

tor may be able to use those records to determine whether there are any unmatched purchase orders at year-end.

2. If the auditor is not able to establish the missing control himself, or if it is more efficient not to do so, he should perform the procedures set out in Question 1.17.

QUESTION 1.22

Where sequentially pre-numbered forms or batch totals are used (1.20), are the numbers accounted for or the batch totals reconciled as part of the control procedure over unmatched commitments (1.21)?

Purpose

1. To determine whether all purchase orders have been accounted for when establishing the related entries for unmatched items. This question is inter-related with Question 1.21 and should be answered similarly.

2. The control question refers to batch totals; however, the use of this procedure to account for purchase commitments is not common in practice.

What Constitutes Adequate Control Procedures?

This question deals with one of the controls over completeness of processing. Refer to the discussion under that heading on page 365, item 2.

QUESTION 1.22 (continued)

Possible Errors in Financial Statements	Example	Effect on Audit Procedures
If: Sequentially pre-numbered forms are not accounted for,		
Income may be overstated and liabilities (provision for losses) understated because the company does not control transactions even though it is possible to do so. (Similar to Question 1.20.)	Pre-numbered purchase orders are filed by supplier rather than numerically. Unmatched documents can be removed without being detected.	The auditor should follow the procedures set out in Question 1.21.

QUESTION 1.23

Are unmatched commitments (1.21) reviewed on a regular basis, e.g. monthly, to determine the reasons for any which have not been matched within a reasonable period of time?

Purpose

Since unmatched purchase commitments outstanding beyond a reasonable period of time may indicate a breakdown in the matching procedures, the company should review them on a regular basis.

What Constitutes Adequate Control Procedures?

This question deals with one of the controls over completeness of processing. Refer to the discussion under that heading on page 366, item 3.

Possible Errors in Financial Statements	Example	Effect on Audit Procedures
If: The unmatched commitments are not reviewed,		
Losses arising from purchase commitments may be overstated because purchase orders for completed transactions may not have been removed from the open file.	(a) The related invoice was paid, but the purchase order was not removed from the file. (b) The supplier's invoice was not forwarded to the accounting department because of a dispute, e.g., the price charged.	The auditor should either arrange for the company to institute the review procedure or perform it himself at year-end.

QUESTION 1.24

Is the review in 1.23 carried out by persons other than those who maintain the records of unmatched commitments (1.21)? (D)

Purpose

To determine whether the review of unmatched purchase commitments can be relied upon because the reviewer has no incompatible duties.

What Constitutes Adequate Control Procedures?

This question deals with one of the controls over completeness of processing. Refer to the discussion under that heading on page 367, item 4.

QUESTION 1.24 (continued)

Possible Errors in Financial Statements	Example	Effect on Audit Procedures

If: The review is performed by the person who maintains the records of unmatched purchase commitments,

Possible Errors in Financial Statements	Example	Effect on Audit Procedures
Losses arising from purchase commitments may be overstated. (Same as Question 1.23.)	The recordkeeper's review reveals some purchase orders that he failed to remove upon receipt of goods and others with an uncertain status. He does not report or investigate them because he does not want his superior to know about them.	The auditor should reperform the review himself by either: (a) Performing an extensive review at an interim date with a lesser review at year-end; or (b) Performing an extensive review at year-end. This review should detect all invalid unmatched items, assuming records of unmatched purchase commitments are adequate. (Questions 1.21 and 1.22.)

QUESTION 1.25

Are the results of the procedures in 1.23 reviewed and approved by a responsible official? (S)

Purpose

To determine whether such a review is performed. The review helps to ensure that the basic control is exercised regularly and effectively.

What Constitutes Adequate Control Procedures?

This question deals with the controls for supervisory review and approval. Refer to the discussion under that heading on page 374.

392

Possible Errors in Financial Statements	Example	Effect on Audit Procedures
If: The supervisory control is absent,		
Losses arising from purchase commitments may be overstated because, in the absence of supervisory control, unmatched commitments may not be reviewed at all. (Similar to Question 1.23.)	The person performing the review learns that no follow-up action is taken by the supervisor. The person then stops performing the review.	To determine whether the related basic and division of duties controls have continued to operate properly, the auditor should perform the supervisory review at year-end. Refer to the common control procedure for supervisory review and approval (page 374) for guidance as to the procedures to follow.

QUESTION 2.1

Are the following checked by suitable methods (e.g. by counting or weighing and inspecting goods received) and the results recorded at the time of their receipt for subsequent checking with the related invoices: (a) nature, quantity and condition of goods received (including property, plant and equipment and major supplies, e.g. fuel, stationery); (b) major services received (to the extent practicable)?

Purpose

1. To determine whether the goods or services have been received and are of appropriate quality before payment is made.

2. To establish for cut-off purposes the date on which the goods or services were received.

3. To establish records that will support claims if goods are lost or damaged in transit.

What Constitutes Adequate Control Procedures?

If	Impact on Adequacy of Control	Example
1. Company personnel check and record the nature, quantity and condition of all goods and services received at time of receipt,	Control is adequate because making the checks and creating the records provide a basis for preventing payment for items not in fact received or received in unacceptable condition.	A copy of the purchase order, with the quantities ordered blocked out, is sent to the receiving department. When the goods are received, their quantity and condition are checked and recorded on the purchase order copy.
2. The units in which the quantities are counted or checked differ from the units in which the quantities are billed,	Control over quantities received will be adequate if the different units of measure can be correlated.	Screws are ordered and billed by number of units. The receiving department weighs the screws upon receipt. The weight is converted to number of units by means of conversion charts.
3. Receiving personnel count some goods received but not others,	Control over quantities received may or may not be adequate, depending on the following factors: (a) The person who decides what should not be counted does not have incompatible duties. The decision should be based on the best interests of the company, not of the individual.	Examples of inadequate procedures: (i) Purchasing agent decides what should not be counted and arranges with supplier for those items to be short-shipped; (ii) Receiving clerk decides what should not be counted based on minimizing his work. As a result, significant receipts are not counted.

(b) High value items or those easily converted to an individual's use should be counted. The risk of loss through error or misappropriation is high for those kinds of items.

Receipts of expensive hand tools should be counted.

(c) All receipts should be compared to the shipping advice to determine that the shipment appears to be complete. This will detect any apparent errors in the items shipped or their condition.

Receiving department does not count or weigh goods received but compares number of cartons received to number of cartons per shipping advice.

(d) The goods counted represent a significant portion of the value of the company's receipts.

The company's procedures result in counting goods representing 90% of the value of goods received.

4. Quantities are not blocked out on the copy of the purchase order sent to the receiving department,

Control may not be adequate because the receiving department may not count the goods received.

Receiving clerk compares purchase order and packing slip and, if quantities are the same, enters that quantity without counting.

5. The company checks goods and services received but does not make a record,

Control is not adequate because there is no record for use in later processing or for supervisory review.

Receiving personnel check some receipts to packing slips but make no record of what was done.

6. The nature of the goods received requires that they meet certain standards,

Control will be adequate if there are procedures for performing inspections and reporting thereon.

(a) Printed circuits are mechanically examined for flaws that may not be detected by observation.

(b) Ores and concentrates are assayed for metal content.

7. Receiving personnel are not present where goods are received (e.g., job sites, customer locations),

Control will be adequate if there is alternative documentation that ensures receiving records are accurate.

Customer personnel sign for goods received and the customer accepts this documentation as support for billing to him.

QUESTION 2.1 (*continued*)

If	Impact on Adequacy of Control	Example
8. Possible compensating controls:		
(a) Company has an effective job order cost system,	This may be an adequate compensating control because the physical status of a job may indicate whether all material billed has been received.	Materials are ordered by job number. Job cost records are posted from suppliers' invoices after matching with purchase order. Comparison of physical status of job with job cost records indicates whether all materials billed have been received.
(b) Quantity of goods received is verified by an independent carrier,	This may be an adequate compensating control for both quantities received and date of receipt because an independent carrier can be expected to report correct quantities and dates.	Company receives flour by railroad and pays for it on a weight basis. The railroad independently weighs the flour and reports the weights and date of receipt on a bill of lading (waybill).
(c) Freight bills indicate the date the company received the goods and can be identified with particular invoices,	This may be an adequate compensating control for cut-off purposes but not for quantities. The date of receipt can be established, although the individual items cannot be identified.	The carrier's freight bill indicates supplier, invoice number and date received by the company. However, the contents are shown only as numbers of cartons.
9. The company does not record the receipt of services,	The company's internal control is probably not adequate because the receipt of most services can be recorded.	The company leases business equipment and pays the related invoices without checking them. As a result, the company does not realize that it is paying for equipment that it has not received.

Possible Errors in Financial Statements	Example	Effect on Audit Procedures

1. If: Goods received are recorded based on suppliers' documentation but are not checked as to quantity and description,

Possible Errors in Financial Statements	Example	Effect on Audit Procedures
(a) Inventory and income may be overstated. Additions to inventory will be based on suppliers' invoices, which may include items that were not received by the company.	A supplier invoices for 60 items but the company receives only 40 items. The company pays for 60 items and charges them to inventory.	Ordinarily a complete physical inventory at year-end should be taken by the company and observed by the auditor.
(b) Individual expense items (e.g., cost of sales) in the income statement may be misstated because the company may have paid for goods it did not receive.	The company discovers that it has paid for a significant amount of goods that were not received. The extent of the loss is disclosed in a note to the financial statements.	If the auditor wishes to determine whether, and to what extent, short-shipments have occurred (e.g., because disclosure is required in the financial statements or as a client service), he should consider the following procedures (recognizing that they may not be conclusive):
		(i) Where practicable, review or prepare a reconciliation in quantities of opening inventory, recorded purchases, recorded sales and closing inventories. Inventory that cannot be accounted for may indicate short-shipment of goods (this procedure will be effective only if all other inventory movement is under accounting control);
		(ii) If they contain sufficient detail as to quantities, compare freight bills with suppliers' invoices.

397

Possible Errors in Financial Statements	Example	Effect on Audit Procedures
(c) Accounts payable may be overstated because the company may record a liability for goods that were not received.	The company is billed and records a liability for 60 items, although only 40 items were received.	Since the company ordinarily cannot challenge suppliers' invoices if it does not count incoming goods, the auditor may not need to perform additional procedures with respect to accounts payable. If alternative supporting evidence does exist, e.g., freight bills or production department records, the auditor may wish to examine that evidence.

2. If: Goods received are recorded based on suppliers' documentation but are not checked as to condition and quality,

(a) Inventory and income may be overstated because the company may include damaged or substandard goods in inventory at full value.	A shipment of 100 items is paid for, of which 40 items were defective.	The auditor should: (i) Request the company to inspect goods on hand that have not been examined for condition and quality; (ii) Evaluate slow-moving goods more closely at year-end, requesting technical assistance where necessary. Goods may be slow-moving because they are not suitable for use in the company's operations; (iii) Consider whether absence of inspection of incoming goods affects the value of related work-in-progress and finished goods inventory or the amount of warranty reserves.

(b) Accounts payable may be overstated and/or the company may have an unbooked receivable for claims against the supplier or carrier.

The company has paid for items that are found to be defective and makes a claim against the supplier.

The auditor should review the results of the procedures in 2(a) above and determine if an appropriate claim has been made against the supplier or carrier for any damaged or defective goods.

3. **If:** Goods received are not recorded at the time of their receipt,

(a) Inventory and income may be misstated, i.e., either overstated or understated, because the date the goods were received cannot be determined:

(i) Income will be overstated if the goods are included in inventory (e.g., by count) before the receipt of the goods is recorded;

A shipment of 60 items is received in December. The goods are included in the inventory count at December 31 but the receipt of the goods is not recorded until January.

(ii) Income will be understated if the receipt of goods is recorded but the goods are not included in inventory.

Sixty items are received in January but are recorded as if received on December 31. The goods are not included in inventory because they were not on hand and thus were not counted.

With respect to inventory, the auditor should follow the procedures in 1(a) and (b) above.

QUESTION 2.1 (continued)

Possible Errors in Financial Statements	Example	Effect on Audit Procedures
(b) Accounts payable may be misstated because a proper cut-off for recording accounts payable cannot be established if a timely record of receipts is not made.	A supplier bills for 60 items received in December. The client may not record the receipt until January and, therefore, the payable is not recorded in December.	With respect to accounts payable, the auditor should: (i) Request the company to implement special cut-off procedures at the time of inventory taking and at year-end (if different), such as: (A) Record number(s) of the last receiving report(s) used; (B) Examine unused receiving reports to ensure that documents have not been used out of sequence; (C) Ensure that the last documents used are entered in the records prior to the physical inventory and at year-end. (ii) Consider performing and/or extending year-end confirmation of suppliers' balances and/or reconciliation of recorded liabilities with suppliers' statements, review of credit (debit) memoranda received (issued) in the following year and search for unrecorded liabilities.

4. **If:** Services received are not checked as to quality or completeness,		
Expenses in the income statement may be misstated because the company cannot determine if it has received the service for which payment will be made.	A company pays for a repair that was not done satisfactorily or was not done at all.	If the auditor wishes to determine whether, and to what extent, services have been paid for but not received (e.g., because disclosure is required in the financial statements or as a client service), he should consider examining alternative records (if any) that may indicate receipt of services, e.g., production department records of electricity consumed, advertising department records of brochures distributed. The auditor should recognize that these procedures may not be conclusive.

5. **If:** Services are not recorded at the time of their receipt,		
Accounts payable and expenses may be misstated because a proper cut-off for recording accounts payable cannot be established if a timely record of services received is not made.	A company is billed in January for a service received in December. The transaction is recorded in January because there is no record of when the service was received.	The auditor should: (a) Apply the procedures set forth in 4 above to determine whether services appear to have been accounted for in the proper period; (b) Apply the procedures set forth in 3(b)(ii) above to determine whether year-end liabilities are properly stated.

6. **If:** The lack of control over receipts extends to items of property, plant and equipment,		
The asset balances may be overstated because the company may have paid for and included in the asset accounts items that were not received.	The company is billed and pays for 4 drilling presses, although only 2 presses are received.	The auditor should inspect recorded property, plant and equipment additions over a specified amount to ensure that the items were received.

QUESTION 2.5

Are the receiving records (2.1) controlled in such a way that it can subsequently be established whether all the related transactions have been accounted for (e.g. by sequentially pre-numbering receiving reports or by entering receipts in a register), in respect of: (a) goods (2.1(a)); (b) major services (2.1(b))?

Purpose

1. To determine whether the company's procedures with respect to recording receipts of goods and services are such that it *can* determine whether all such receipts have been accounted for.

2. Note that the question is not whether the records *are* in fact accounted for. Thus, if the documentation for controlling them exists (e.g., receiving reports are pre-numbered), the auditor may be able to use it to reduce the amount of audit work that would otherwise be required in situations where the company can, but does not, account for the documents.

What Constitutes Adequate Control Procedures?

This question deals with one of the controls over completeness of processing. Refer to the discussion under that heading on page 363, item 1.

If: It cannot be subsequently established whether all receiving reports have been accounted for,

Possible Errors in Financial Statements	Example	Effect on Audit Procedures
1. Income and accounts payable may be misstated. There is no way of knowing whether all transactions have been recorded.	Receiving reports are not pre-numbered. Accounts payable entries are based on un-matched receiving reports. Missing reports will not be detected and will result in an understatement of accounts payable.	Inventory and accounts payable validation procedures should be performed at year-end, including: (a) Observation of a complete physical inventory;
2. Income and inventory may be misstated if a complete physical inventory is not	Goods received prior to an interim inven-tory date but not recorded until later are	(b) Requesting the company to establish special cut-off procedures for a speci-

402

taken at year-end because of possible cut-off errors at the earlier inventory date.

recorded twice by year-end—first by count at the interim inventory date and again when the receipt was processed.

fied period before and after year-end as set out in item 3(b) of Question 2.1;

(c) Confirmation with suppliers and/or reconciliation of unrecorded liabilities with suppliers' statements.

[*Note*: The "Possible Errors and Audit Effect" material ordinarily can be read across the page. However, in some cases, the last column describes the effect on audit procedures of all the weaknesses on the "IF" lines, rather than each individual weakness. In these cases, a vertical line, as shown above, appears between the second and third columns.]

QUESTION 2.6

Are there adequate records of goods and services received which have not been matched with the related suppliers' invoices, in respect of: (a) goods (2.1(a)); (b) major services (2.1(b))?

Purpose

1. To determine whether the company maintains adequate records of goods and services received that have not been matched with related invoices in order to record the related assets, expenses and liabilities on a timely basis.

2. Note that if Question 2.5 is answered "no," this question should also be answered "no."

3. Note that when sequentially pre-numbered forms are used, this question is inter-related with Question 2.7 and should be answered similarly. Also, when pre-numbered forms are used, the records in this question will not be adequate unless the control in Question 2.7 operates.

What Constitutes Adequate Control Procedures?

This question deals with one of the controls over completeness of processing. Refer to the discussion under that heading on page 365, item 2.

QUESTION 2.6 (*continued*)

Possible Errors in Financial Statements	Example	Effect on Audit Procedures
If: Records of unmatched receipts are not adequate,		
Income, inventory and accounts payable may be misstated. (Similar to Question 2.5.)	The company files unmatched receiving reports by vendor but has no control over those files. Unmatched receiving reports removed from the file will not be detected and will result in an understatement of accounts payable.	1. If the documentation is such that control can be established (e.g., pre-numbered receiving reports are used in sequence but are not accounted for), the auditor should determine if it would be efficient to establish control himself. He could visit the company at the time of inventory taking and at year-end, record the last receiving report number used, and examine unissued receiving reports for completeness, thus establishing a basis for satisfying himself as to cut-off.
		2. If the auditor cannot establish control over the receiving records or if the procedure described in 1 above is not efficient, then he should follow the procedures set out in Question 2.5.

QUESTION 2.7

Where sequentially pre-numbered forms are used (2.5), are all numbers accounted for as part of the control procedure over unmatched receipts (2.6), in respect of: (a) goods (2.1(a)); (b) major services (2.1(b))?

404

To determine whether all receipts have been accounted for when establishing the related entries for unmatched items. This question is inter-related with Question 2.6 and should be answered similarly.

What Constitutes Adequate Control Procedures?

This question deals with one of the controls over completeness of processing. Refer to the discussion under that heading on page 365, item 2.

Possible Errors in Financial Statements	Example	Effect on Audit Procedures
If: Pre-numbered receiving reports are not accounted for,		
Income, inventory and accounts payable may be misstated. (Similar to Questions 2.5 and 2.6.)	The company uses pre-numbered receiving reports but does not account for their numerical sequence. Missing documents are not detected on a timely basis.	The effect on audit procedures is similar to that described in Question 2.6.

QUESTION 2.8

Are unmatched records of goods and services received (2.6) reviewed on a regular basis, e.g. monthly, to determine the reasons for any such receipts which have not been matched within a reasonable period of time, in respect of: (a) goods (2.1(a)); (b) major services (2.1(b))?

Purpose

Since unmatched receiving reports outstanding beyond a reasonable period of time may indicate the need for adjustments to be made or the malfunctioning of other controls, the company should review them on a regular basis.

QUESTION 2.8 (*continued*)

What Constitutes Adequate Control Procedures?

This question deals with one of the controls over completeness of processing. Refer to the discussion under that heading on page 366, item 3.

Possible Errors in Financial Statements	Example	Effect on Audit Procedures
If: A regular periodic review is not completed,		
Accounts payable, assets and expenses may be misstated. Journal entries based on unmatched receiving reports may include transactions that are completed and have been accounted for.	An invoice for advertising brochures is paid but the receiving report is not removed from the file. The unmatched receiving report serves as the basis for an erroneous entry debiting advertising expense and crediting accounts payable.	1. The auditor should request the company to perform the review and assure himself that it was properly performed. 2. If the company does not perform the review, the auditor should at year-end either perform extended validation procedures (including confirmation of unmatched items) on the pertinent accounts (e.g., expenses, accounts payable and, possibly, inventory), or perform the review and investigation of unmatched records himself, whichever is more efficient.

QUESTION 2.9

Is the review (2.8) carried out by persons other than those who maintain the records of unmatched items (2.6)? (D)

Purpose

To determine whether the reviewer has incompatible duties, which would reduce the effectiveness of the review.

What Constitutes Adequate Control Procedures?

This question deals with one of the controls over completeness of processing. Refer to the discussion under that heading on page 367, item 4.

Possible Errors in Financial Statements	Example	Effect on Audit Procedures
If: The review is performed by the persons who maintain the records of unmatched receiving reports,		
Accounts payable, assets and expenses may be misstated. Journal entries based on unmatched receiving reports may include transactions that are completed and have been accounted for. (Same as Question 2.8.)	The review is made by the recordkeeper, who determines that a number of the unmatched items represent completed transactions. However, he does not report these items because he does not want to call attention to the errors he has made.	The auditor should reperform the review himself by either: (a) Performing an extensive review at an interim date, with a lesser review at year-end; or (b) Performing an extensive review at year-end. The review should detect all invalid unmatched items, assuming records of unmatched receipts are adequate. (Questions 2.6 and 2.7.)

QUESTION 2.10

Are the results of the procedures in 2.8 reviewed and approved by a responsible official? (S)

Purpose

To determine whether such a review is performed. This review helps ensure that the basic control is exercised regularly.

What Constitutes Adequate Control Procedures?

This question deals with the controls for supervisory review and approval. Refer to the discussion under that heading on page 374.

Possible Errors in Financial Statements	Example	Effect on Audit Procedures
If: The supervisory control is absent,		
Journal entries based on unmatched receiving reports may include transactions that are completed and have been accounted for because unmatched receiving reports may not be reviewed at all. (Similar to Question 2.8.)	The person performing the review learns that no follow-up action is taken by the supervisor. The person then stops performing the review.	To determine whether the related basic and division of duties controls have continued to operate properly, the auditor should perform the supervisory review at year-end. Refer to the common control procedure for supervisory review and approval (page 374) for guidance as to the procedures to follow.

QUESTION 2.11

Are there systematic procedures for determining on a regular basis the liabilities for major services received other than those checked by the procedures in 2.1(b) (e.g. telephone services, electricity, municipal taxes or rates, liabilities under leases)?

Purpose

To determine whether the liabilities for services received (other than those referred to in Question 2.1(b)) are recorded on a timely basis.

What Constitutes Adequate Control Procedures?

If	Impact on Adequacy of Control	Example
1. A specific individual(s) is responsible for ensuring that all liabilities are recorded,	The likelihood of liabilities not being recorded because of oversight is reduced.	The assistant chief accountant is responsible for making sure that all liabilities for services are recorded.
2. A checklist of major services is signed off as the various liabilities are recorded,	This provides further assurance that all necessary liabilities have been recorded.	See 1 above. One of the steps performed by the assistant chief accountant is to review the completed checklist.
3. Analytical reviews are performed of the relevant liability and related expense accounts,	The failure to accrue unbilled services will often be detected.	When reviewing a preliminary trial balance, the reviewer sees that rent expense and accrued rents are lower than a year ago. Investigation reveals that the monthly rental on the company's fleet of motor vehicles has not been accrued.

Possible Errors in Financial Statements	Example	Effect on Audit Procedures
If: The company's procedures for recording liabilities for services are not adequate,		
Expenses and accounts payable may be understated because the company may omit an accrual for a service received prior to year-end or may record the wrong amount.	(a) The monthly electricity bill is not accrued. (b) A liability is not recorded for unusual legal expenses. (c) The accrual for salesmen's commis-	The auditor should perform validation procedures at year-end, including: (a) A detailed review of account balances; (b) Searching for unrecorded liabilities over a longer period of time;

QUESTION 2.11 (*continued*)

Possible Errors in Financial Statements	Example	Effect on Audit Procedures
	sions is understated because it does not reflect a recent increase in commission rates.	(c) Examination of statements from and/or confirmation with creditors.

QUESTION 2.12

Are the results of the procedures in 2.11 reviewed and approved by a responsible official? (S)

Purpose

To determine whether such a review is performed. This review helps ensure that the basic control is exercised regularly.

What Constitutes Adequate Control Procedures?

This question deals with the controls for supervisory review and approval. Refer to the discussion under that heading on page 374.

Possible Errors in Financial Statements	Example	Effect on Audit Procedures
If: The supervisory control is absent,		
Expenses and accounts payable may be understated because the company may omit an accrual for services received prior to year-end or may record the wrong amount. (Same as Question 2.11.)	The person responsible for recording the liabilities learns that no follow-up action is taken by the supervisor. The person then does a less thorough job of determining that all liabilities are recorded.	The auditor should increase his validation procedures on accruals and other liabilities at year-end.

410

QUESTION 2.13

Where required, are the records of goods received (2.1(a)) used to post quantities to detailed inventory records?

Purpose

1. To determine whether the company uses the actual record of goods received to post quantities to the detailed inventory records.

2. This question should be answered "not applicable" if the company does not maintain detailed inventory records.

What Constitutes Adequate Control Procedures?

This question deals with the controls over posting quantities to detailed inventory records. Refer to the discussion under that heading on page 373.

Possible Errors in Financial Statements	Example	Effect on Audit Procedures
1. **If:** Copies of receiving reports are not used,		
(a) Entries may be made to the wrong inventory account or for the wrong quantity because errors are made in preparing the data used as a posting source. (See 2 below.)	Quantities received are transposed when the posting document is prepared.	(a) The auditor should consider whether it would be more efficient to: (i) Perform sufficient functional tests to satisfy himself as to the reliability of the company's procedures for preparing alternative posting media; or (ii) Perform validation tests on inventory at year-end.
(b) Entries may be posted in a month subsequent to the month of receipt because source data is not prepared or received on a timely basis. (See 3 below.)	There is a two-week delay in preparing the posting document.	(b) If the company takes a complete physical inventory prior to year-end, the auditor should satisfy himself that the

QUESTION 2.13 (*continued*)

Possible Errors in Financial Statements	Example	Effect on Audit Procedures
2. If: Errors are made in preparing posting sources (Item 1(a)),		alternative posting media have been prepared properly during the intervening period. He can do this either by performing functional tests of the procedures followed or by validating the accuracy of the alternative posting media.
(a) These errors should be discovered when physical inventories are taken because the items on hand will not agree with the detailed records.	Receipt of 10 items of Part 120 was posted to Part 102.	
(b) The monetary effect of posting the right quantities to the wrong inventory account will depend on the unit value differential, since quantity differences will offset.	If the unit value of Part 120 is $1.00 and Part 102 $1.50, then the monetary difference will be $5.00 (10 items at $.50).	
(c) The monetary effect of posting the wrong quantities to the right account will depend on the unit value of the item. Since there is no offsetting quantity error, the erroneous quantity and related unit value determine the monetary effect.	The receipt of 10 items of Part 120 is posted as 100 items. The monetary effect is $90.00 (90 items times $1.00).	
3. If: Posting quantities to detailed inventory records is not up-to-date (Item 1(b)),		
Adjustments to detailed records arising from physical counts will result in an overstatement of inventory and income, unless the detailed records are summarized at that time or the comparison takes into account the unposted receipts. Inventory (both	Twenty items of Part 120 are received in December but are not posted to the detailed inventory records until January. A physical count at December 31 reveals an overage of 20 items for Part 120. Debiting inventory and crediting cost of sales for $20	

412

general ledger and detailed records) will be debited twice for items subject to delayed posting, once in the normal course and once as a result of the adjustment arising from the physical count.

(20 items at $1.00) results in overstating inventory and income by that amount. This error will be detected if the detailed records are summarized and compared to the control account at the date of the count, so long as the receipt of the 20 items was recorded in the control account in December.

---

4. **If:** Postings from receiving records to the detailed inventory records are mis-dated,

Inventory and income may be misstated.

Postings to the detailed inventory records are dated as of the date of posting rather than the date of inventory receipt. Consequently, the detailed records reflect less goods than are on hand. If the inventory control accounts are adjusted to the detailed records, inventory and income will be understated. On the other hand, if differences between the physical inventory and the detailed records are adjusted to the control accounts, the amount of inventory loss will be understated and inventory and income will be overstated.

The auditor should request the company to implement a special cut-off procedure at the time of inventory taking and at year-end (if different), such as making sure that the last receiving documents used are entered in the records prior to physical inventory and at year-end. He should also fully test the adequacy of this procedure as it is performed. If the company does not implement the special cut-off procedure, the auditor should perform it himself.

QUESTION 3.1

Are the following recorded for accounting control purposes at the time the goods are returned or the claims are first established for subsequent checking with the related credit notes: (a) quantities of goods returned to suppliers; (b) other claims made on suppliers (e.g. for short deliveries, freight claims, damaged goods not returned)?

Purpose

1. To determine whether the initial recording of all goods returned or of other claims made on suppliers is done on a timely basis.

2. To determine whether the data recorded (quantity, description, short delivery, damage, etc.) is adequate for effective operation of subsequent controls.

What Constitutes Adequate Control Procedures?

If	Impact on Adequacy of Control	Example
1. There is a procedure to ensure that an accounting document has been prepared for all goods leaving the company's premises,	Control is adequate because the company has a basis for determining that all goods returned to suppliers have been recorded.	Gatekeepers check all goods leaving the premises to determine whether: (a) The appropriate documents accompany the goods; (b) The quantities agree with the documentation.
2. Company personnel record the description and quantity of goods returned or other claims made and the date thereof,	Control is adequate because all the necessary information is available for the complete and accurate processing of claims. (a) If the goods are rejected at the time of receipt and no receiving record is prepared and no returns or claim records will be required. To maintain a complete record, the receiving department should notify the accounting department that the shipment was rejected.	The receiving department stamps its copy of the purchase order "shipment rejected" and forwards it to the accounting department.

414

(b) If part of the shipment is rejected or a claim is established at the time of receipt, a separate record permitting identification of the supplier, the date, and the description and quantity of goods returned or the nature of the claim made (e.g., short deliveries, damaged goods) would constitute an adequate procedure.

The receiving clerk enters on a pre-numbered claim form the name of the supplier, date, description and quantity of goods rejected or short-shipped.

(c) An annotation on the receiving record (see Question 2.1) may constitute an appropriate record of goods returned or claims made at the time of receipt, if such returns and claims can be distinguished from receipts.

The receiving report has columns where short-shipments or rejected goods are noted.

(d) If goods are returned subsequent to their receipt, the appropriate information should be entered on a pre-numbered form.

For each shipment, the customer name, description of goods, shipping destination, shipment date and quantity of items shipped are entered on a pre-numbered shipping form by the shipping clerk.

3. The company returns goods from locations where company personnel are not present (e.g., at warehouses maintained by independent agents),

Control is adequate if the custodian can be held responsible for all shortages or inventory movement not reported to the company.

Independent sales agents receive and maintain inventories for the company's account. Claims are based on reports from the agent. The agreement makes the agent liable for all inventory shortages.

Possible Errors in Financial Statements	Example	Effect on Audit Procedures
1. **If:** Goods returned or other claims made are not adequately recorded as to quantity or description,		
Purchases, accounts payable and inventories may be misstated. The company	(a) Twelve items are returned but only ten recorded on the shipping document;	(a) Ordinarily a complete physical inventory at year-end should be taken by the

Possible Errors in Financial Statements	Example	Effect on Audit Procedures
cannot correctly determine the number or description of items returned to suppliers. If entries in detailed inventory records are made from claims records, such records will also be misstated.	the company may not receive credit for two items. If inventory records are posted from the returns or claims documents, ten items will be relieved from inventory, with the result that inventory will be overstated by two items. (b) Ten carburetors are returned but are recorded as ten carburetor repair kits. The company may not receive credit for the value of the more expensive carburetors. Detailed inventory records for carburetors will be overstated by ten units and those for repair kits understated by ten units.	company and observed by the auditor. (b) With respect to accounts payable, the auditor should consider performing and/or extending his year-end confirmation of suppliers' balances and/or reconciliation of recorded liabilities with suppliers' statements, review of credit (debit) memoranda received (issued in the following year and search for unrecorded liabilities. (c) If the auditor wishes to determine whether, and to what extent, claims have not been recorded (e.g., because disclosure is required in the financial statements or as a client service), he should consider the following procedures (recognizing that they may not be conclusive): (i) If the company maintains detailed inventory records, review unexplained inventory shortages resulting from physical inventories; (ii) Where practicable, review or prepare a reconciliation of opening inventory, recorded pur-

chases, recorded sales and closing inventory. This procedure may help to establish if all returns or claims have been recorded, since inventory that cannot be accounted for may indicate unrecorded returns or claims. (This procedure will be effective only if all other inventory movement is under accounting control.)

With respect to accounts payable, the auditor should consider the procedures discussed in item 1 (b) above.

---

2. **If:** Supplier identifcation is not adequately recorded,

Accounts payable and income may be overstated. Returns debited to accounts payable may not be realizable because:
(a) No supplier is identified so that a claim can be made; or
(b) The misidentified supplier will not grant the claim because the goods in question were not returned to him.

The company purchases identical items from a variety of suppliers. Suppliers routinely deliver goods and pick up returned goods at the company's warehouse. Receiving personnel frequently do not write down the supplier identification and it is not possible to correlate receiving records and purchase orders to find the missing information.

---

3. **If:** The date the goods were returned is not adequately recorded,

Accounts payable and inventories may be misstated because a proper cut-off for recording them cannot be established.

The date of the return is recorded as December 30 but goods were not returned until January 10.

The auditor should request the company to implement special cut-off procedures at the time of inventory taking and at year-end (if different), such as:
(a) Record number(s) of the last shipping document(s) used;

Possible Errors in Financial Statements	Example	Effect on Audit Procedures
		(b) Examine unused shipping documents to ensure they have not been issued out of sequence;
		(c) Ensure that the last documents used are entered in the records prior to the physical inventory and at year-end. He should fully test the adequacy of these procedures as they are performed. If the company does not implement such procedures, the auditor should perform them himself and should consider the procedures set forth in 1 above, particularly item (a) and the confirmation procedures mentioned in item (b).

QUESTION 3.3

Are the records (3.1) controlled in such a way that it can subsequently be established whether the related transactions have all been accounted for (e.g. by sequentially pre-numbering claims forms or by entering claims in a register), in respect of: (a) goods (3.1(a)); (b) other claims (3.1(b))?

Purpose

1. To determine whether the company's procedures for recording claims are such that it *can* determine whether they have all been accounted for.

418

2. Note that the question is not whether the records *are* in fact accounted for. Thus, if the documentation for controlling them exists (e.g., claim reports are pre-numbered), the auditor may be able to use it to reduce the amount of audit work otherwise required in situations where the client can, but does not, account for unmatched returns.

What Constitutes Adequate Control Procedures?

This question deals with one of the controls over completeness of processing. Refer to the discussion under that heading on page 363, item 1.

Possible Errors in Financial Statements	Example	Effect on Audit Procedures
If: Company procedures do not permit establishing that all the related transactions have been accounted for,		
1. Accounts payable may be overstated because records of claims are lost, misplaced or stolen and, therefore, are not processed. If the documents cannot be located, then accounts payable are probably properly stated, because a credit cannot be obtained if the supplier cannot be identified.	Claim reports are not pre-numbered. The accounts payable clerk destroys all claim reports for companies in which he has a financial interest. The missing reports are not detected.	1. The auditor need not extend his year-end validation procedures on payables because this weakness does not affect the accuracy of the liabilities recorded but rather the completeness of processing claims against suppliers. 2. With respect to year-end inventories, refer to Question 3.1, item 1(a). 3. With respect to transactions during the year, refer to Question 3.1, item 1(c).
2. Income and inventory may be overstated because the return of goods has not been recorded.	See 1 above. The claim report copies sent to the accounting department are also used to post the detailed inventory records. Since the copies are destroyed, the records are not posted and inventory is overstated.	

419

QUESTION 3.4

Are records maintained of goods returned and claims made which have not been matched with the related credit (or debit) memoranda in respect of: (a) goods (3.1(a)); (b) other claims (3.1(b))?

Purpose

1. To determine whether the company maintains adequate records of unmatched goods returned and claims forms so that it is possible to (a) determine whether charges are made to suppliers for all returns and claims, and (b) record the unmatched amounts to purchases, accounts payable and, possibly, inventories on a timely basis.

2. Note that if Question 3.3 is answered "no," this question should also be answered "no."

3. Note that when sequentially pre-numbered forms are used, this question is inter-related with Question 3.5 and should be answered similarly. Also, when pre-numbered forms are used, the records in this question will not be adequate unless the control in Question 3.5 operates.

What Constitutes Adequate Control Procedures?

This question deals with one of the controls over completeness of processing. Refer to the discussion under that heading on page 365, item 2.

If: Adequate records of unmatched items are not maintained,

Possible Errors in Financial Statements	Example	Effect on Audit Procedures
1. Accounts payable may be overstated because records of returns are lost, misplaced or stolen. If the documents can-	The company does not maintain a file of unmatched claim reports or any other record of uncompleted transactions. Credit	1. If the company does not maintain adequate records of unmatched claim reports but the documentation is such that

420

not be located, then accounts payable may be properly stated, because the payable must be paid if the claim cannot be documented. (Similar to Question 3.3.)

2. Income and inventory may be overstated because the returned goods have not been recorded. (Similar to Question 3.3.)

may not be received for the return of goods for which the claim reports are lost, nor are they likely to be detected later.

See 1 above. If detailed inventory records are posted from claim reports, the return will not be credited to inventory.

they could be controlled (e.g., pre-numbered claim reports are used in sequence but are not accounted for), the auditor should consider whether it would be efficient for him to establish control himself. He could visit the company at the time of the physical inventory count and at year-end, record the last document number(s) used (or the last entry(ies) in the register), and examine unissued documents for completeness, thus establishing a basis for satisfying himself as to cut-off.

2. If the auditor cannot establish control over the records or if the procedure described in 1 above is not efficient, he should follow the procedures set forth in Question 3.3.

QUESTION 3.5

Where sequentially pre-numbered forms are used (3.3), are the numbers accounted for as part of the control procedure over unmatched items (3.4), in respect of: (a) goods (3.1(a)); (b) other claims (3.1(b))?

Purpose

To determine whether all goods returned and claims made have been accounted for when establishing entries for unmatched items. This question is inter-related with Question 3.4 and should be answered similarly.

421

QUESTION 3.5 (*continued*)

What Constitutes Adequate Control Procedures?

This question deals with one of the controls over completeness of processing. Refer to the discussion under that heading on page 365, item 2.

Possible Errors in Financial Statements	Example	Effect on Audit Procedures
If: Sequentially pre-numbered forms are not accounted for,		
1. Accounts payable may be overstated because records of returns are lost, misplaced or stolen. If the documents cannot be located, then accounts payable may be properly stated, because the payable must be paid if the claim cannot be documented. (Similar to Question 3.3.)	Pre-numbered claim forms are filed by supplier rather than numerically. Unmatched claim forms can be removed without being detected.	The auditor should follow the procedures set out in Question 3.4.
2. Income and inventory may be overstated because the return has not been recorded. (Similar to Question 3.3.)	See 1 above. The claim forms are also used to post the detailed inventory records. Since the forms have been removed, the records are not posted and inventory is overstated.	

QUESTION 3.6

Are unmatched records of returns and claims (3.4) reviewed on a regular basis, e.g. monthly, to determine the reasons for any such claims which have not been matched within a reasonable period of time, in respect of: (a) goods (3.1(a)); (b) other claims (3.1(b))?

Purpose

Since unmatched records of goods returned or claims made outstanding beyond a reasonable period of time may indicate the need for adjustments to be made or a breakdown in the matching of claims records (e.g., with suppliers' credit memoranda—see Question 4.6), the company should review them on a regular basis.

What Constitutes Adequate Control Procedures?

This question deals with one of the controls over completeness of processing. Refer to the discussion under that heading on page 366, item 3.

Possible Errors in Financial Statements	Example	Effect on Audit Procedures
If: The unmatched records are not reviewed periodically,		
Accounts payable and cost of sales may be misstated.	Accounts payable are understated because the accounts payable clerk prepared credit memoranda but the claim report was not removed from the file. The unmatched report serves as the basis for an erroneous entry debiting accounts payable and crediting purchases (income).	1. The auditor should request the company to perform the review and assure himself that it was properly performed. 2. If the company does not perform the review, the auditor should at year-end either perform extended validation procedures (including confirmation of unmatched items) on the pertinent accounts (e.g., purchases, accounts payable and, possibly, inventory) or perform the review and investigation of unmatched records himself, whichever is more efficient.

QUESTION 3.7

Is the review (3.6) carried out by persons other than those who maintain the records of unmatched items (3.4)? (D)

Purpose

To determine whether the person reviewing unmatched records of goods returned or claims made has incompatible duties, thereby reducing the effectiveness of the review.

What Constitutes Adequate Control Procedures?

This question deals with one of the controls over completeness of processing. Refer to the discussion under that heading on page 367, item 4.

Possible Errors in Financial Statements	Example	Effect on Audit Procedures
If: The review is performed by the persons who maintain the records of unmatched claims,		
Accounts payable and cost of sales may be misstated. (Same as Question 3.6.)	The review is made by the recordkeeper who determines that a number of the unmatched items represent completed transactions. However, he does not report these items because he does not want to call attention to the errors he has made.	The auditor should reperform the review himself by either: (a) Performing an extensive review at an interim date, with a lesser review at year-end; or (b) Performing an extensive review at year-end. This review should detect all invalid unmatched items, assuming records of unmatched returns and other claims are adequate. (Questions 3.4 and 3.5.)

QUESTION 3.8

Are the results of the procedures in 3.6 reviewed and approved by a responsible official? (S)

Purpose

1. To determine whether the results of the review of unmatched reports of goods returned or claims made are reviewed and approved by a responsible official.

2. The existence of a supervisory review helps to ensure that the basic control is exercised regularly.

What Constitutes Adequate Control Procedures?

This question deals with the controls for supervisory review and approval. Refer to the discussion under that heading on page 374.

Possible Errors in Financial Statements	Example	Effect on Audit Procedures
If: The supervisory control is absent,		
Accounts payable and cost of sales may be misstated because, in the absence of a supervisory control, unmatched items may not be reviewed at all. (Similar to Question 3.6.)	The clerk performing the review and investigation observes that his work is not reviewed by the supervisor. Accordingly, the clerk stops performing those procedures.	The auditor should perform a supervisory review at year-end to determine whether the related basic and division of duties controls have continued to operate properly. Refer to the common control procedure for supervisory review and approval (page 374) for guidance as to the procedures to follow.

425

QUESTION 3.9

Where required, are the records of goods returned (3.1(a)) used to post quantities to detailed inventory records?

Purpose

1. To determine whether the company uses reports of goods returned to post quantities to detailed inventory records.
2. This question should be answered "not applicable" if the company does not maintain detailed inventory records.

What Constitutes Adequate Control Procedures?

This question deals with the controls over posting quantities to detailed inventory records. Refer to the discussion under that heading on page 373.

Possible Errors in Financial Statements	Example	Effect on Audit Procedures
1. **If:** Copies of claim reports are not used,		(a) The auditor should consider whether it would be more efficient to:
(a) Entries may be made to the wrong inventory account or for the wrong quantity because errors are made in preparing the data used as a posting source. (See 2 below.)	Quantities returned are transposed when the posting document is prepared.	(i) Perform sufficient functional tests to satisfy himself as to the reliability of the company's procedures for preparing alternative posting media; or
(b) Entries may be posted in a month subsequent to the month of return because source data is not prepared or received on a timely basis. (See 3 below.)	There is a two-week delay in preparing the posting document.	(ii) Perform validation tests on inventory at year-end.
		(b) If the company takes a complete physical inventory prior to year-end, the

426

auditor should satisfy himself that the alternative posting media have been prepared properly during the intervening period. He can do this either by performing functional tests of the procedures followed or by validating the accuracy of the alternative posting media.

2. **If:** Errors are made in preparing posting sources (Item 1(a)),

(a) They should be discovered when physical inventories are taken because the items on hand will not agree with the detailed records.

Return of 10 items of Part 120 was posted to Part 102.

(b) The monetary effect of posting the right quantity to the wrong inventory account will depend on the differences in unit value between the item returned and the one to which the posting was made, since the quantity differences will offset.

If the unit value of Part 120 is $1.00 and Part 102 $1.50, then the monetary difference will be $5.00 (10 items at $.50).

(c) The monetary effect of posting the wrong quantities to the right account will depend on the unit value of the item. Since there is no offsetting quantity error, the erroneous quantity and related unit value determine the monetary effect.

The return of 10 items of Part 120 is posted as 100 items. The monetary effect is $90.00 (90 items times $1.00).

3. **If:** Posting quantities to detailed inventory records is not up-to-date (Item 1(b)),

Adjustments to detailed records arising from physical counts will result in an understatement of inventory and income, unless the detailed records are summarized at that time or the comparison takes into account the unposted returns. Inventory (both general ledger and detailed records)

Twenty items of Part 120 are returned in December but are not posted to the detailed inventory records until January. A physical count at December 31 reveals a shortage of 20 items for Part 120. Debiting cost of sales and crediting inventory for $20 (20 items at $1.00) results in understating

QUESTION 3.9 (*continued*)

Possible Errors in Financial Statements	Example	Effect on Audit Procedures
will be credited twice for items subject to delayed posting, once in the normal course and once as a result of the adjustment arising from the physical count.	inventory and income by that amount. This error will be detected if the detailed records are summarized and compared to the control account at the date of the count, so long as the return of the 20 items was recorded in the control account in December.	

4. If: Postings from claim records to the detailed inventory records are mis-dated,

Inventory and income may be misstated.	Postings to the detailed inventory records are dated as of the date of posting rather than the date of inventory movement. Consequently, the detailed records show more goods than are on hand. If the inventory control accounts are adjusted to the detailed records, inventory and income will be overstated. On the other hand, if differences between the physical inventory and the detailed records are adjusted to the control accounts, the amount of inventory loss will be overstated and inventory and income will be understated.	The auditor should request the company to implement a special cut-off procedure at the time of inventory taking and at year-end (if different), such as making sure that the last claims documents used are entered in the records prior to physical inventory and at year-end. He should also fully test the adequacy of this procedure as it is performed. If the company does not implement the special cut-off procedure, the auditor should perform it himself.

428

QUESTION 4.1

Are invoices for goods received checked as to: (a) quantities and conditions of goods received (to receiving records); (b) nature and quantities of goods ordered (to purchase orders); (c) prices and other terms (to purchase orders and suppliers' price lists)?

Purpose

1. To determine whether suppliers' invoices have been checked as to validity of the quantities received and their condition, authorization for the purchase, and prices and other terms.

2. If the procedures described in 1 above are not carried out, payments could be made and invoices included in accounts payable that are erroneous or fraudulent.

What Constitutes Adequate Control Procedures?

If	Impact on Adequacy of Control	Example
1. The company checks all invoices to supporting documents,	Control is adequate because all errors made by suppliers should be detected.	Company checks all suppliers' invoices in detail because the savings exceeds the related costs.
2. Only invoices over a specified monetary amount are checked to supporting documents,	Control is adequate if the following conditions are met: (a) The specified amount is reasonable, i.e., it is not too high, and has been approved by a responsible official; (b) There is a reasonableness check of invoices less than the specified amount;	Control is not adequate in the following example. Company checks all suppliers' invoices over $1,000. However, invoices of less than $1,000 make up 75% of the monetary value of all purchases. Company can be defrauded if it makes no check at all of invoices that individually are small but that could be large on an aggregate basis.

429

QUESTION 4.1 (continued)

If	Impact on Adequacy of Control	Example
	(c) The company's procedures ensure that all invoices that should be checked, are checked.	See 2(a) above. As part of the supervisory review (Question 4.9), the responsible official makes sure that all suppliers' invoices over $1,000 have been checked.
3. The checking is done by persons familiar with the transactions and the company's procedures,	Control is adequate because the person should be able to identify apparent errors or irregularities.	The person checking suppliers' invoices for a manufacturing company has experience in the purchasing and operations departments.
4. Items purchased by the company require special technical or quality control review,	The person checking suppliers' invoices should be aware of these procedures and check to determine that they have been performed.	The company purchases complex items which should be subjected to quality control procedures before acceptance. The clerk performing the check determines that appropriate technical reports are received before processing the invoice.
5. The invoices and supporting documentation contain evidence of the checks that have been performed,	Control is adequate because there is greater assurance that the checks have been performed. In addition, there is a basis for the supervisory review to be performed.	(a) Clerks who match purchase orders and receiving reports to the suppliers' invoices sign a voucher block stamp indicating the completion of the checks. (b) The invoice clerks note matters queried and their final resolution.

Possible Errors in Financial Statements	Example	Effect on Audit Procedures
1. **If:** Invoices for goods received are not compared with receiving reports,		

430

(a) Audit procedures for year-end inventory balances depend on the company's method of accounting for inventories:

(i) If the company does not maintain detailed inventory records or if detailed inventory records are posted from suppliers' invoices, the company should take, and the auditor should observe, a complete physical inventory at year-end;

(ii) If the company maintains detailed inventory records that are posted from receiving reports, the inventory balance can be based on pricing and extending the quantities in the detailed records, providing:

(A) There are no control weaknesses involving detailed inventory records; and

(B) The results of the company's cycle counts, including investigation of differences, and the auditor's tests thereof are satisfactory.

The company is billed for 100 units but only 60 units were received. However, the company pays the invoice and debits inventory for the 100 units.

Inventory and income may be overstated because payment may be made for goods that were not received or were received in unacceptable condition.

Possible Errors in Financial Statements	Example	Effect on Audit Procedures
		(b) With respect to transactions during the year, the auditor's reaction depends on whether he needs to satisfy himself as to whether material losses have occurred as a result of this weakness (e.g., because such losses need to be disclosed in the financial statements or as a client service). If he wishes to so satisfy himself, the auditor should:
		(i) Consider performing the comparison himself for all or selected periods of the year;
		(ii) Obtain or prepare an overall reconciliation of opening and closing inventories, purchases and sales, and investigate any significant differences (in order for this procedure to be effective, sales and opening and closing inventories should be under good accounting control);
		(iii) Where applicable, review the results of cycle counts during the year.
		The auditor should recognize that these procedures may not be conclusive.

2. **If:** Invoices for goods received are not compared with purchase orders,

Inventory and income may be overstated because the company has paid for goods that it did not order (and thus presumably does not need) or for goods in excess of its needs. Either of these conditions can lead to obsolete or slow-moving inventory.

The company receives and pays for 100 items of part number 616, although it had ordered part number 661. The company cannot use part number 616 and can sell it for only 25% of cost.

The auditor should extend his year-end review for obsolete or slow-moving inventory.

3. **If:** Prices on suppliers' invoices are not checked to an appropriate source,

Inventory and income may be overstated because the company paid an excessive price for the goods. (While the price might be too low, this is much less likely to occur.)

The suppliers' invoice expresses the quantities in units but the price in dozens, thus causing the company to pay 12 times the proper amount.

(a) With respect to year-end inventory balances, the auditor should extend his tests of:
  (i) Prices used to cost the inventory;
  (ii) Net realizable value (lower of cost or market).

(b) With respect to transactions during the year, the auditor's reaction depends on whether he needs to satisfy himself as to whether material losses have occurred as a result of this weakness (e.g., because such losses need to be disclosed in the financial statements or as a client service). If he wishes to so satisfy himself, the auditor should:
  (i) Consider performing the check himself for all or selected periods of the year;

QUESTION 4.1 (*continued*)

Possible Errors in Financial Statements	Example	Effect on Audit Procedures
		(ii) Consider the results of the tests performed in (a) above and similar tests performed by the company. The auditor should recognize that these procedures may not be conclusive.

4. **If:** One or more of the above weaknesses is present,

Possible Errors in Financial Statements	Example	Effect on Audit Procedures
Accounts payable may theoretically be overstated because the company does not owe the amount billed by the supplier. However, since the company intends to pay the amount billed, in practical terms accounts payable is stated properly.	The supplier's invoice expresses the quantity per unit, but receives only 60 items. While the company in theory owes only $360, the recorded liability of $600 is more realistic since the company will pay that amount.	Unless requested to do so by the company, the auditor need not extend his validation procedures on accounts payable because of these weaknesses. However, see also 1(b) and 3(b) above.

5. **If:** One or more of the above weaknesses is present for the purchase of assets other than inventory,

Possible Errors in Financial Statements	Example	Effect on Audit Procedures
The respective assets and income may be overstated.	The company pays for a drill press although it had ordered a lathe. The company has no use for a drill press and writes it down to net realizable value.	The auditor should extend the relevant year-end validation procedures on the respective assets to include: (a) Inspecting significant additions (where Question 4.1(a) is answered "no"); (b) Examining purchase orders or otherwise satisfying himself that the asset

was wanted and can be used by the company (where Question 4.1(b) is answered "no");

(c) Checking price lists or other appropriate sources to determine whether the price paid was reasonable (where Question 4.1(c) is answered "no").

QUESTION 4.2

Are invoices for services received compared with the underlying documentation (e.g. records of receipts (2.1(b)), completion reports, leases, records of meter readings) or, if such documentation is not available, approved by a responsible official?

Purpose

1. To determine whether suppliers' invoices for services received are checked for validity.

2. If the procedure described in 1 above is not carried out, erroneous or fraudulent payments could be made.

What Constitutes Adequate Control Procedures?

If	Impact on Adequacy of Control	Example
1. The company applies the control to all invoices for services,	Control is adequate because all errors made by suppliers should be detected.	The company checks all suppliers' invoices in detail.
2. Only invoices for services over a specified monetary amount are checked to supporting documentation,	Control is adequate if the following conditions are met: (a) The specified amount is reasonable, i.e., it is not too high, and has been approved by a responsible official;	Control is not adequate in the following example. Company checks all invoices for services over $1,000. However, invoices less than $1,000 make up 75% of the monetary value of all services purchased.

435

QUESTION 4.2 (continued)

If	Impact on Adequacy of Control	Example
	(b) There is a reasonableness check of invoices less than the specified amount;	Company can be defrauded if it makes no check at all of invoices that individually are small but that could be large on an aggregate basis.
	(c) The company's procedures ensure that all invoices that should be checked, are checked.	See 2(a) above. As part of the supervisory review (Question 4.9), the responsible official makes sure that all invoices for services over $1,000 have been checked.
3. The checking or approving is done by persons familiar with the transactions and the company's procedures,	Control is adequate because the person should be able to identify apparent errors or irregularities.	The person checking or approving invoices for sales promotion expense is familiar with the company's sales promotion techniques.
4. The invoices and supporting documentation contain evidence of the checks that have been performed,	Control is adequate because there is no greater assurance that the checks have been performed. In addition, there is a basis for the supervisory review to be performed.	(a) Clerks who match purchase orders and completion records to the suppliers' invoices sign a voucher block stamp indicating the completion of the checks. (b) The invoice clerks note matters queried and their final resolution.

Possible Errors in Financial Statements	Example	Effect on Audit Procedures
If: Invoices for services received are not checked to underlying documentation or approved by a responsible official,		
1. Individual expense items in the income statement may be misstated.	An employee submits fictitious freight bills because he knows that freight bills are not	With respect to transactions during the year, the auditor's reaction depends on

checked. The result is that freight expense is overstated and fraud loss is understated.

2. Accounts payable may theoretically be overstated because the company does not owe the amount billed by the supplier. However, since the company intends to pay the amount billed, in practical terms accounts payable is stated properly.

whether he needs to satisfy himself as to whether material losses have occurred as a result of this weakness (e.g., because such losses need to be disclosed in the financial statements or as a client service). If he wishes to so satisfy himself, the auditor should consider performing the comparison himself for all or selected periods of the year. The auditor should recognize that these procedures may not be conclusive.

See 1 above. The company has accrued $20,000 related to fictitious freight bills. Since the company intends to pay the bills, the liability is proper, even though the company does not legally owe the money.

Unless requested to do so by the company, the auditor need not extend his validation procedures on accounts payable because of this weakness. See also 1 above.

QUESTION 4.5

Are the following functions performed by separate individuals: (a) preparation of purchase orders; (D) (b) preparation of receiving records; (D) (c) checking of purchase invoices (4.1 and 4.2)? (D)

Purpose

To determine whether the person checking the purchase invoices has incompatible duties, which would reduce the effectiveness of the checking procedure.

What Constitutes Adequate Control Procedures?

If	Impact on Adequacy of Control	Example
1. The same person prepares purchase orders and receiving records,	Control is not adequate because fictitious purchase orders and receiving records can be prepared and introduced into the system.	The person sends the company a fraudulent supplier's invoice and prepares fictitious purchase orders and receiving reports as supporting documentation.
2. The same person prepares the purchase orders and checks purchase invoices,	Control is not adequate because the person can enter an invalid price without fear of being detected when the invoice is checked.	The person enters an overstated price on the purchase order, checks the supplier's invoice and receives a portion of the overcharge from the supplier.
3. The same person prepares receiving reports and checks purchase invoices,	Control is not adequate because he can prepare a fictitious receiving report to support a fraudulent invoice. The person can also suppress the fact that no purchase order was prepared.	The person sends the company a fraudulent invoice and prepares a fictitious receiving report as supporting evidence. He explains the absence of a purchase order by writing on the invoice "telephone order."
4. The same person prepares purchase orders and receiving reports and checks purchase invoices,	Control is not adequate for the reasons mentioned in 1, 2 and 3 above.	See above.

Possible Errors in Financial Statements	Example	Effect on Audit Procedures
If: Invoices are checked by persons with incompatible duties,		
Inventory, other assets and income may be overstated, the company may incur losses	For various examples, refer to Questions 4.1 and 4.2.	Refer to Question 4.1 or 4.2, as appropriate.

through fraud or otherwise, and individual items in the income statement may be misstated. The errors that can arise are the same as those that may occur when invoices are not checked. (Similar to Questions 4.1 and 4.2.)

QUESTION 4.6

Are credit (or debit) memoranda checked to confirm that: (a) they agree with the original record of the goods returned or claims made; (b) where applicable, the prices agree with the original invoice?

Purpose

1. To determine whether internal debit memoranda (or suppliers' credit notes) are checked with the original claim made for validity of quantities and amounts.

2. If the procedure described in 1 above is not carried out, credits can be processed that are not in accordance with the claim made in either the quantity of items returned or the amount credited.

What Constitutes Adequate Control Procedures?

If	Impact on Adequacy of Control	Example
1. Debit memoranda (or suppliers' credit notes) are checked with the original record of goods returned or claims made and, where applicable, original invoices,	Control is adequate because any errors made in preparing the documents should be detected.	The company returns 50 items but is credited for only 25 items. This is discovered when the credit note is compared to the record of goods returned.

439

QUESTION 4.6 (*continued*)

If	Impact on Adequacy of Control	Example
2. The checking is done by persons other than those who prepared the original record of goods returned or claims made,	Control is enhanced because another person is involved in checking the validity of claims.	The assistant accountant compares all debit memoranda to the record of returned goods prepared by the shipping clerk.
3. The checking of debit memoranda is done by persons other than those who prepare them,	Control is adequate because another person is more likely to detect inadvertent errors than is the original preparer. In addition, deliberate errors will likely be detected.	The assistant accountant checks all debit memoranda prepared by the invoice clerk.

Possible Errors in Financial Statements	Example	Effect on Audit Procedures

A. Company's Entries Based on Suppliers' Credit Memoranda

1. **If:** Credit memoranda are not checked with the original records of returned goods or claims,

Inventory and income may be overstated because credit was not received for goods that were returned.	The supplier credits the company for 60 units when 100 units were returned. The company accepts the supplier's credit memorandum and credits inventory accordingly.	(a) Audit procedures for year-end inventory balances depend on the company's method of accounting for inventories: (i) If the company does not maintain detailed inventory records or if detailed inventory records are posted from suppliers' credit memoranda, the company should take, and the auditor should ob-

440

serve, a complete physical inventory at year-end;

(ii) If the company maintains detailed inventory records that are posted from records of returned goods, the inventory balance can be based on pricing and extending the quantities in the detailed records, providing:

(A) There are no control weaknesses involving detailed inventory records;

(B) The results of the company's cycle counts, including investigation of differences, and the auditor's tests thereof are satisfactory.

(b) With respect to transactions during the year, the auditor's reaction depends on whether he needs to satisfy himself as to whether material losses have occurred as a result of this weakness (e.g., because such losses need to be disclosed in the financial statements or as a client service). If he wishes to so satisfy himself, the auditor should:

(i) Consider performing the comparison himself for all or selected periods of the year;

Possible Errors in Financial Statements	Example	Effect on Audit Procedures
		(ii) Obtain or prepare an overall reconciliation of opening and closing inventories, purchases and sales, and investigate any significant differences (in order for this procedure to be effective, purchases, sales and opening and closing inventories should be under good accounting control);
		(iii) Where applicable, review the results of cycle counts during the year.
		The auditor should recognize that these procedures may not be conclusive.

2. **If:** Prices on credit memoranda are not checked to original invoices (where applicable),

Inventory and income may be overstated because the company did not receive proper credit for the returned goods. (While the price might be too high, this is much less likely to occur.)	The supplier's credit memorandum expresses the quantities in dozens but the price in units, thus crediting the company only 1/12 of the proper amount.	(a) With respect to year-end inventory balances, the auditor should extend his tests of:
		(i) Prices used to cost the inventory;
		(ii) Net realizable value (lower of cost or market).

(b) With respect to transactions during the year, the auditor's reaction depends on whether he needs to satisfy himself as to whether material losses have occurred as a result of this weakness (e.g., because such losses need to be disclosed in the financial statements or as a client service). If he wishes to so satisfy himself, the auditor should:

    (i) Consider performing the check himself for all or selected periods of the year;

    (ii) Consider the results of the tests performed in (a) above and similar tests performed by the company.

The auditor should recognize that these procedures may not be conclusive.

---

3. **If:** One or both of the above weaknesses are present,

Accounts payable may theoretically be overstated because the company has a claim against the supplier for credits due the company that have not been granted. However, since the company intends to accept the amount credited, in practical terms accounts payable is stated properly.

The supplier credits the company for 60 units at $6 per unit, although 100 units were returned. While the company in theory is entitled to an additional credit of $240 (40 units at $6 per unit), the company has accepted the lower amount and thus no additional credit should be recorded.

Unless requested to do so by the company, the auditor need not extend his validation procedures on accounts payable because of these weaknesses. However, see also 1(b) and 2(b) above.

QUESTION 4.6 (*continued*)

Possible Errors in Financial Statements	Example	Effect on Audit Procedures
B. Company's Entries Based on Company-Prepared Debit Memoranda		
4. If: The company's entries are based on debit memoranda that are understated,		
Inventory and income may be overstated. The errors that may occur are the same as when credit memoranda are not checked. (Similar to 1, 2 and 3 above.)	The clerk preparing the debit memorandum records 10 units returned instead of the 100 units actually returned. The error is not detected because his work is not checked.	Refer to 1, 2 and 3 above.
5. If: The company's entries are based on debit memoranda that are overstated,		
(a) Accounts payable will be understated by the full amount of excessive debit memoranda.	See 4 above. Using a unit price of $1, accounts payable is understated by $90.	The auditor should perform the more efficient of the following procedures: (i) Extended validation procedures of accounts payable at year-end, including confirmation with suppliers and checking validity of debit memoranda not yet accepted by the supplier; (ii) Checking the validity of all debit memoranda issued during the year.
(b) Inventory will be understated to the extent that the excessive debit memoranda have not been adjusted (e.g., as a result of physical counts).	See (a) above. Year-end inventory is based on physical count and thus is properly stated.	Refer to 1(a) and 2(a) above.
(c) Income will be overstated by the excess of (a) over (b).	Income is overstated by $90.	

444

QUESTION 4.7

Are the extensions and additions of invoices and credit (or debit) memoranda checked to an adequate extent?

Purpose

To determine whether the company's procedures ensure that invoices and credit (or debit) memoranda are arithmetically accurate.

What Constitutes Adequate Control Procedures?

This question deals with the controls over checking of extensions and additions. Refer to the discussion under that heading on page 376.

Possible Errors in Financial Statements	Example	Effect on Audit Procedures
If: The company does not check the extensions and additions of invoices and credit (or debit) memoranda,		
1. Long-term assets may be misstated, most likely overstated, because of arithmetic errors on the relevant invoices.	An invoice for five small trucks at $7,000 each is extended as $45,000, instead of $35,000.	The auditor should review the reasonableness of extensions and additions on significant purchases during the year.
2. Inventory may be misstated, most likely overstated, for the following reasons:		
(a) The total amount charged to the control account is overstated;	An invoice for 100 units at $1 per unit is extended as $1,000.	The auditor should determine that detailed records are priced, extended and summarized at year-end.
(b) Costs for inventory valuation purposes may be based on dividing total invoice amount by quantities.	See 2(a) above. A new unit cost of $10 ($1,000 ÷ 100 units) is established erroneously.	The auditor should extend year-end validation procedures on unit costs by examining price lists, etc.
3. Accounts payable may be misstated.	See 1 and 2(a) above.	The auditor should review the reasonableness of extensions and additions on items comprising the year-end account balance.

QUESTION 4.7 (continued)

Possible Errors in Financial Statements	Example	Effect on Audit Procedures
4. Expense items may be misclassified.	An invoice for advertising brochures totals $10,000, but should be $6,000. Advertising expense includes $4,000 that the company should not have paid.	With respect to transactions during the year, the auditor's reaction depends on whether he needs to satisfy himself as to whether material losses have occurred as a result of this weakness (e.g., because such losses need to be disclosed in the financial statements or as a client service). If he wishes to so satisfy himself, the auditor should consider performing the checks himself for all or selected periods of the year. The auditor should recognize that these procedures may not be conclusive.

QUESTION 4.8

Do the invoices and credit (or debit) memoranda bear adequate evidence that the checking (4.1 to 4.7) has been carried out?

Purpose

1. To determine whether there is evidence of the checks performed on invoices and credit (or debit) memoranda.

2. This question deals with whether there is evidence that the control procedures in Questions 4.1 to 4.7 have been performed. If any of the answers to those questions is "no," then this question should also be answered "no." If the answer to this question is "no," then the answer to the relevant question in 4.1 to 4.7 should be "no." A control exists only if there is evidence of its operation.

446

What Constitutes Adequate Control Procedures?

If	Impact on Adequacy of Control	Example
1. The persons performing the checks in Questions 4.1 to 4.7 initial the documents for work performed,	Control is adequate because there is adequate evidence of work performed.	Persons performing the work initial for work completed on a voucher block stamp designed for this purpose.
2. The use of tick marks is the only evidence of work performed,	Control is not adequate because the precise work done and the person performing it cannot be determined.	A number of tick marks appear on the invoices but there is no indication of their significance.

Possible Errors in Financial Statements	Example	Effect on Audit Procedures
If: There is inadequate evidence of checks performed,		
Since the concern is that there is no evidence of the checks performed, the possible errors are the same as when no check is made. (Same as Questions 4.1 to 4.7.)	Tick marks appear on the invoice but there are no initials or indication of work performed.	If the company does not evidence the checks performed, then the internal control procedures are not adequate and our audit response would be similar to "no" answers for Questions 4.1 to 4.7. Refer to Questions 4.1 to 4.7 for the effect on audit procedures.

QUESTION 4.9

Are invoices and credit (or debit) memoranda subject to final written approval by a responsible official prior to entry as accounts payable? (S)

Purpose

To determine whether the approval is performed. The approval helps to ensure that the basic control is operating regularly.

What Constitutes Adequate Control Procedures?

This question deals with the controls for supervisory review and approval. Refer to the discussion under that heading on page 374.

Possible Errors in Financial Statements	Example	Effect on Audit Procedures
If: Invoices and credit (or debit) memoranda are not approved by a responsible official,		
In the absence of a supervisory control, the checks may not be performed. Accordingly, the possible errors are the same as when the checks are not performed. (Same as Questions 4.1 to 4.7.)	The persons performing the checks in Questions 4.1 to 4.7 observe that the responsible official does not review their work and they stop making the checks.	Ordinarily, the auditor will find it more efficient to perform the supervisory review by extending his functional tests of the related disciplinary and basic controls. The other alternative is to perform the procedures set out in Questions 4.1 to 4.7, as appropriate.

QUESTION 4.10

Are adjustments to suppliers' accounts properly documented?

Purpose

To determine whether the company's control procedures ensure that all adjustments to suppliers' accounts are documented, thereby increasing the likelihood that they are valid.

What Constitutes Adequate Control Procedures?

If	Impact on Adequacy of Control	Example
The adjustments are supported by appropriate documentation,	Control is adequate.	(a) Reconciliation of suppliers' statements with recorded liability, together with explanations of reconciling items (e.g., unmatched receiving reports). (b) Letter from a supplier authorizing a "policy adjustment" because of late receipt of goods.

Possible Errors in Financial Statements	Example	Effect on Audit Procedures
If: Adjustments are not adequately documented,		
Expenses, assets and accounts payable may be misstated because invalid adjustments may be processed.	The company reduces a recorded liability to a supplier to agree with the supplier's statement. However, the company buys from two divisions of the supplier and the statement relates to only one division.	The auditor should review adjustments recorded during the year. If the undocumented adjustments are material, he should perform extended validation procedures on accounts payable at year-end.

QUESTION 4.11

Are the adjustments and related documentation (4.10) reviewed and approved by a responsible official prior to entry in the accounts payable records? (S)

Purpose

To determine whether the review and approval is performed. The review helps to ensure that the basic control is exercised regularly.

What Constitutes Adequate Control Procedures?

This question deals with the controls for supervisory review and approval. Refer to the discussion under that heading on page 374.

Possible Errors in Financial Statements	Example	Effect on Audit Procedures
If: Adjustments to suppliers' accounts and related documentation are not approved,		
Expenses, assets and accounts payable may be misstated because invalid adjustments may be processed. (Same as Question 4.10.)	The person making the adjustments observes that the responsible official does not review his work and therefore he processes fraudulent adjustments to suppliers with whom he has made a financial arrangement.	The auditor should increase the level of his functional tests on the control in Question 4.10 to obtain assurance of the satisfactory operation of the control.

QUESTION 5.1

Is the system such (e.g. by sequential pre-numbering or the use of invoice registers) that all of the following documentation is accounted for and the amounts posted to the accounts payable control accounts: (a) purchase invoices; (b) credit (or debit) memoranda; (c) adjustments to suppliers' accounts?

Purpose

To determine whether the company has adequate controls to ensure that all purchase invoices received, credit (or debit) memoranda issued and adjustments applied to suppliers' accounts are accounted for.

450

What Constitutes Adequate Control Procedures?

If	Impact on Adequacy of Control	Example
1. This question deals with two of the controls over completeness of processing. Refer to the discussion under that heading on page 363, items 1 and 2.		
2. The total amounts to be posted to the control account are established immediately after the completeness checks are made,	Control is adequate because all valid transactions will be included in the total. If the totals are established before or some time after the completeness checks are made, it is possible that valid items will be excluded from the control total.	The company makes the completeness checks on the second working day but does not establish the control totals until the fourth working day. A number of valid debit memoranda are removed on the third working day and thus are not recorded in the accounts.
3. The control totals are the source for posting to the control account,	Control is adequate because the appropriate posting source has been used.	The control totals determined when the completeness checks were made are forwarded to the general ledger bookkeeper for posting.

Possible Errors in Financial Statements

If	Example	Effect on Audit Procedures
1. **If:** Invoices for goods or property received are not accounted for,		
(a) Income and inventory may be overstated if a physical inventory is taken and all accounts payable are not recorded. Items will be included in inventory based on physical inventory counts and included again when the invoice is processed in a later period.	Goods are received and counted in October and included in the inventory account. When invoiced in November, they are included in book inventory again. Accordingly, income and inventory at December 31 will be overstated.	(i) If the company's method of accounting for inventory is such that overstatements can occur, ordinarily the company should take, and the auditor should observe, a complete physical inventory at year-end.

451

QUESTION 5.1 (*continued*)

Possible Errors in Financial Statements	Example	Effect on Audit Procedures
		(ii) If the following conditions are present, the auditor may conclude that a complete physical inventory at year-end is not required: (A) Company maintains well-controlled detailed inventory records; (B) Results of the company's cycle count procedures, including investigation of differences, are satisfactory; (C) The auditor has no other reason to believe that inventory balances are misstated (e.g., unexplained differences in reconciling opening and closing inventories with purchases and sales). The auditor should bear in mind that many of the above tests will be based on interim data and that his decision should be reconsidered based on data for the full year.

452

(b) Assets (including inventory) and accounts payable may be understated because the company cannot determine if all transactions have been accounted for.

Purchase invoices are sent to purchasing agent for approval of prices prior to recording and some are not returned to accounts payable on a timely basis. Any invoices held by the purchasing agent are not recorded.

The auditor should perform extended validation procedures on accounts payable at year-end, including the following:
(i) Confirm balances with suppliers and/or reconcile suppliers' statements with recorded liabilities;
(ii) Extend the period for the search for unrecorded liabilities.

2. **If:** Invoices for services are not accounted for,

Expenses and accounts payable may be understated because the company cannot determine if all transactions have been accounted for.

The expense and liability for an invoice for advertising expense are not recorded because the advertising manager is holding the invoice pending the resolution of a price dispute.

Refer to the procedures set out in 1(b) above.

3. **If:** Credit (or debit) memoranda are not accounted for,

The effect will be the opposite of that explained under 1 and 2 above.
(a) Income and inventory may be understated if a physical inventory is taken and all credit (or debit) memoranda are not recorded. This is because inventory will be reduced based on physical inventory counts and reduced again when the credit (or debit) memorandum is processed in a later period.

Because the related credit memorandum was misplaced, the company erroneously pays for 50 items that were returned to the supplier. Inventory will be understated under the following circumstances:
(a) The goods are returned before a physical inventory is taken;
(b) The books are adjusted to reflect the items actually counted;

Refer to the procedures set out in 1 above.

453

Possible Errors in Financial Statements	Example	Effect on Audit Procedures
	(c) The credit memorandum is processed in the next month in the regular manner, i.e., by a credit to inventory.	
(b) Assets (including inventory), expenses and accounts payable may be overstated because the company has not accounted for items to be charged back to a supplier.	Because the credit memorandum for items returned to the supplier was not accounted for, inventory and accounts payable will be overstated under the following circumstances: (a) The goods were returned after the physical inventory was taken; (b) The company has not paid the supplier's invoice.	
4. If: Adjustments to suppliers' accounts are not accounted for,		
Assets (including inventory), expenses and accounts payable may be misstated because the company cannot determine if all adjustments have been accounted for.	An adjustment for an overpriced invoice is not processed.	Refer to the procedures set out in 1 above.
5. If: Control totals are not established immediately after the completeness checks are made,		
The possible effect is the same as when no completeness checks are made, because the control totals may exclude valid items. (See items 1 to 4 above.)	The accounts payable clerk omits debit memoranda to selected suppliers when establishing the control total, but includes them when sending debit memoranda to	Refer to the procedures set out in 1 to 4 above, as appropriate. The effect on our audit procedures is the same as when no completeness checks are made.

the accountable documents clerk. When they are returned to the accounts payable clerk, he destroys the omitted debit memoranda before further processing.

6. **If:** Control totals are not the source for posting to the control account,

The control total has not served its purpose if it is not posted to the control account. (See items 1 to 4 above.)	The company establishes control totals in the appropriate manner, but amounts posted to the control account are derived from the postings to the subsidiary records.

Refer to the procedures set out in 1 to 4 above, as appropriate.

QUESTION 5.2

Is a review made on a regular basis, e.g. monthly, for any documents which have not been accounted for (5.1) within a reasonable period of time?

Purpose

1. Since purchase invoices, credit (or debit) memoranda and adjustments to suppliers' accounts that have not been accounted for in a reasonable period of time may indicate the need for adjustments to be made or the malfunctioning of other controls, the company should make this kind of review on a regular basis.

2. Similarly, if unaccounted for items are not reviewed for propriety, the effectiveness of the control described in Question 5.1 is reduced.

What Constitutes Adequate Control Procedures?

This question deals with one of the controls over completeness of processing. Refer to the discussion under that heading on page 366, item 3.

QUESTION 5.2 (*continued*)

Possible Errors in Financial Statements	Example	Effect on Audit Procedures
If: A regular review of unmatched items is not made,		
The possible errors are similar to those that may arise if the items are not accounted for. Refer to Question 5.1.	A sequence check of suppliers' invoices reveals numerous missing items. In most cases, the goods were received but a receiving report was not prepared. Accordingly, inventory or cost of sales and accounts payable are understated.	1. The auditor should perform the review at year-end and evaluate the unaccounted for items. 2. Alternatively, if more efficient, the auditor may perform the extended validation procedures described in Question 5.1.

QUESTION 5.3

Is the review (5.2) carried out by persons other than those who maintain the accounts payable control accounts or subsidiary records? (D)

Purpose

To determine whether the review of unaccounted for purchase invoices, credit (or debit) memoranda and adjustments to suppliers' accounts can be relied upon because the reviewer has no incompatible duties.

What Constitutes Adequate Control Procedures?

If	Impact on Adequacy of Control	Example
Persons who maintain the accounts payable control accounts or subsidiary records investigate unaccounted for items,	Control is not adequate because those persons may be able to cover up errors or differences in the accounts of which they are aware. They may also be able to increase erroneously the amounts due selected suppliers.	The person maintaining the subsidiary records omits certain debit memoranda from the records. He then reports fictitious explanations for these items when he investigates unaccounted for items.

Possible Errors in Financial Statements

	Example	Effect on Audit Procedures

If: The review is performed by the persons who maintain the accounts payable control accounts or subsidiary records,

Since the concern is that the recordkeepers will not make an appropriate review of missing items, the possible errors are the same as when no completeness check is made. Refer to Question 5.1.	The review is made by the person maintaining the subsidiary records, who determines that a number of the unmatched items represent valid transactions that have not been posted. However, he does not report these items because he does not want to call attention to the errors he has made.	The auditor should reperform the review himself by either: (a) Performing an extensive review at an interim date with a lesser review at year-end; or (b) Performing an extensive review at year-end. The review should detect all invalid unmatched items, assuming records of unmatched items are adequate. (Question 5.1.)

QUESTION 5.4

Are the results of the review in 5.2 reviewed and approved by a responsible official? (S)

Purpose

To determine whether such a review is performed. The review helps to ensure that the basic control is exercised regularly and effectively.

What Constitutes Adequate Control Procedures?

This question deals with the controls for supervisory review and approval. Refer to the discussion under that heading on page 374.

Possible Errors in Financial Statements	Example	Effect on Audit Procedures
If: The supervisory review is absent,		
The absence of a supervisory control could result in the basic control not being performed. Therefore, the possible errors are similar to those that can arise when no review of unaccounted for documents is made. Refer to Question 5.1.	The clerk performing the review of unaccounted for documents observes that his supervisor does not review his work. The clerk then stops making his review.	To determine whether the related basic and division of duties controls have continued to operate properly, the auditor should perform the supervisory review at year-end. Refer to the common control procedure for supervisory review and approval (page 374) for guidance as to the procedures to follow.

458

QUESTION 5.5

Are totals for posting to a control account established over the following before they are passed to the persons who post them in the accounts payable subsidiary records: (a) purchase invoices; (b) credit (or debit) memoranda; (c) adjustments to suppliers' accounts?

Purpose

If totals for posting to the control account are not established before the details are passed to the persons who post them in the accounts payable subsidiary records, then the control account will not serve its intended purpose, i.e., to act as a control over the processing of transactions in the subsidiary records. Items could be added to or removed from the detail of transactions to be posted without such alterations being detected.

What Constitutes Adequate Control Procedures?

This question deals with one of the controls over maintenance of subsidiary records supporting a control account. Refer to the discussion under that heading on page 368, item 1.

Possible Errors in Financial Statements	Example	Effect on Audit Procedures
If: Control totals are not established before the details are passed to persons who post the subsidiary records,		
Purchases, expenses and accounts payable may be:	The accounts payable clerk includes invoices related to a company in which he has a financial interest when posting the subsidiary ledgers.	1. With respect to year-end balances, the auditor should perform the procedures set forth in Question 5.1.
(a) Overstated because the persons maintaining the subsidiary records add unauthorized transactions to the items to be posted;		2. If payments to suppliers are based on subsidiary records rather than matched invoices, the auditor may wish to determine whether, and to what extent, fictitious payments have been made during the year, either as a client service or because disclosure of such amounts in
(b) Understated because the persons maintaining the subsidiary records delete authorized transactions from the items to be posted.	In order to inflate the company's earnings, the controller instructs the accounts payable clerk to delete valid invoices when posting the subsidiary ledgers.	

Possible Errors in Financial Statements	Example	Effect on Audit Procedures
		the financial statements is required. If so, he should consider the following procedures: (a) If the system permits (e.g., invoices are numbered on receipt), perform the control procedure himself, either for the entire year or for selected periods; (b) Make detailed comparisons of approved invoices with payments made to the supplier; (c) If practicable, review or prepare reconciliations of opening and closing inventories, purchases and sales, and investigate significant differences. This procedure will be effective only if there is adequate control over sales and opening and closing inventories. The auditor should bear in mind that these procedures may not be conclusive.

QUESTION 5.6

Is the system such that all the items posted to the control accounts (5.5) have been checked and approved in accordance with control objective 4?

Purpose

To determine whether the company's control procedures are such that only accounts payable transactions that have been checked and approved as valid are processed to the accounting records.

What Constitutes Adequate Control Procedures?

If	Impact on Adequacy of Control	Example
1. The person establishing the control totals ensures there is adequate evidence that the checks in Control Objective 4 have been completed,	Control is adequate because all documents to be processed are reviewed for evidence that the required company procedure has been performed.	The clerk establishing the control totals reviews all documents for evidence that checks have been performed and rejects any unchecked or inappropriately checked documents.
2. The person performing the check in 1 above has an adequate knowledge of the required company procedures,	Control is adequate because the person's review is meaningful.	The procedures in Control Objective 4 are documented in an accounting manual that is issued to all the accounting department staff.

Possible Errors in Financial Statements

	Example	Effect on Audit Procedures
If: The items posted to the control account are not reviewed to determine if they have been checked and approved in accordance with Control Objective 4,		

QUESTION 5.6 (*continued*)

Possible Errors in Financial Statements	Example	Effect on Audit Procedures
Purchases, expenses and accounts payable may be misstated. Invalid items may be posted and valid items may contain errors.	A fictitious invoice not approved by a responsible official may be processed, thereby erroneously increasing purchases and accounts payable.	1. With respect to year-end accounts payable balances, the auditor should: (a) Perform the procedures in Question 5.1, item 1(b); (b) Review the items making up the balance for evidence of proper approval and checking. 2. If payments to suppliers are based on subsidiary records rather than matched invoices, the auditor may wish to determine whether, and to what extent, fictitious payments have been made during the year, either as a client service or because disclosure of such amounts in the financial statements is required. If so, he should consider examining items posted to the control account for all or selected periods of the year for evidence of proper approval and checking. The auditor should bear in mind that these procedures may not be conclusive.

QUESTION 5.7

Are totals for posting to a control account established over cash documentation that affects suppliers' accounts before it is passed to the persons who post the accounts payable subsidiary records?

Purpose

1. To determine whether control totals for cash disbursements are established before forwarding the details to the persons who maintain the subsidiary records.

2. If this procedure is not followed, details of cash disbursements can be added to or removed from the detail to be posted without such alterations being detected.

What Constitutes Adequate Control Procedures?

This question deals with one of the controls over maintenance of subsidiary records supporting a control account. Refer to the discussion under that heading on page 368, item 1.

Possible Errors in Financial Statements	Example	Effect on Audit Procedures
If: Control totals are not established before the details are sent to persons who maintain accounts payable subsidiary records,		
Accounts payable, bank balances and income may be misstated because persons posting the subsidiary records may add or remove items before posting the details.	(a) The accounts payable subsidiary records include a necessary credit adjustment that does not appear in the control account. To cover up this difference, debits representing fictitious payments are posted to the subsidiary records but not to the control account. (b) Payments to certain suppliers are not recorded in the subsidiary records, so that the amounts may be paid again.	1. If the amount of the cash disbursements entry can be influenced by this control weakness, the auditor should perform extended validation procedures on cash and accounts payable at year-end. 2. With respect to year-end accounts payable balances, refer to Question 5.1, item 1(b). 3. With respect to transactions during the year, refer to Question 5.5, item 2(b).

463

QUESTION 5.8

Are the accounts payable subsidiary records maintained by persons other than those who: (a) check and approve documents in accordance with control objective 4; (D) (b) maintain the control account? (D)

Purpose

To determine whether the accounts payable subsidiary records are maintained by persons who have no incompatible duties, thereby helping to ensure that the records are maintained properly.

What Constitutes Adequate Control Procedures?

This question deals with one of the controls over maintenance of subsidiary records supporting a control account. Refer to the discussion under that heading on page 370, item 2.

Possible Errors in Financial Statements	Example	Effect on Audit Procedures
1. **If:** The person who maintains accounts payable subsidiary records also checks and approves the related supporting documentation,		
Expenses, assets and accounts payable may be misstated because the recordkeeper could authorize fictitious transactions to achieve a desired result in the accounting records (e.g., cover up errors or conceal unauthorized payments).	The recordkeeper checks and approves invoices from a fictitious supplier and then establishes an accounts payable ledger card for that supplier.	(a) With respect to year-end accounts payable balances, the auditor should: (i) Perform the procedures in Question 5.1, item 1(b); (ii) Examine the supporting documentation for the items making up the year-end balance. (b) If payments to suppliers are based on subsidiary records rather than matched invoices, the auditor may wish to determine whether, and to what extent, fic-

464

titious payments have been made during the year, either as a client service or because disclosure of such amounts in the financial statements is required. If so, he should consider examining the supporting documentation for disbursements made during all or part of the year. The auditor should bear in mind that these procedures may not be conclusive.

Refer to 1 above. In addition, the auditor should add the subsidiary ledgers at year-end and compare the total to the control account balance.

2. **If:** The person who maintains subsidiary records also maintains the control account,

Accounts payable may be misstated because the recordkeeper could cover up differences between the two records or defraud the company by manipulating subsidiary records.

Since he controls both records, he can "force" differences between them and alter one of them without detection.

QUESTION 5.9

Are the accounts payable subsidiary records reconciled periodically, e.g. monthly, with the control account?

Purpose

If the accounts payable subsidiary records and the control account are in agreement, there is some assurance that the period's activity has been posted correctly.

What Constitutes Adequate Control Procedures?

This question deals with one of the controls over maintenance of subsidiary records supporting a control account. Refer to the discussion under that heading on page 370, item 3.

QUESTION 5.9 (*continued*)

Possible Errors in Financial Statements	Example	Effect on Audit Procedures
If: The reconciliation is not performed regularly,		
Accounts payable and income may be misstated because errors in either the control account or the subsidiary ledger will not be detected.	A batch of invoices is posted to the control account but is not posted to the subsidiary ledger.	As validation procedures are normally tied to the subsidiary records, the auditor should perform the reconciliation at year-end to establish if the subsidiary records and the control account agree. This would include investigating any differences revealed by the reconciliation.

QUESTION 5.10

Are there adequate procedures for investigating differences disclosed by the reconciliations (5.9) before any adjustments are made?

Purpose

To determine whether the company's control procedures ensure adjustments are made to account balances only after adequate investigations of the differences have been performed.

What Constitutes Adequate Control Procedures?

This question deals with one of the controls over maintenance of subsidiary records supporting a control account. Refer to the discussion under that heading on page 371, item 4.

Possible Errors in Financial Statements

Example

Effect on Audit Procedures

If: The differences disclosed by the reconciliation are not investigated,

The reconciliation procedure is incomplete and the possible errors that could arise are the same as if the reconciliation was not performed. Refer to Question 5.9.

The company performs the reconciliation monthly but investigates only significant differences. However, a small difference is actually the net effect of a significant error that should be corrected and a significant valid reconciling item that need not be adjusted.

The auditor should investigate all differences disclosed by the year-end reconciliation.

QUESTION 5.11

Are the reconciliations and investigation of differences (5.9 and 5.10) either performed or checked by individuals other than those who: (a) post the account payable subsidiary records; (D) (b) maintain the control account? (D)

Purpose

To determine whether the reconciliations and investigations of differences are performed or checked by persons with no incompatible duties, thereby helping to ensure that they are done properly.

What Constitutes Adequate Control Procedures?

This question deals with one of the controls over maintenance of subsidiary records supporting a control account. Refer to the discussion under that heading on page 372, item 5.

QUESTION 5.11 (*continued*)

Possible Errors in Financial Statements	Example	Effect on Audit Procedures
If: Reconciliations and investigations are performed by persons with incompatible duties, and are not checked by someone else,		
The possible errors are similar to those that may arise if the reconciliations and investigations are not performed. Refer to Question 5.9.	The person who maintains the subsidiary records performs the reconciliation and conceals the differences in order to avoid criticism of his job performance.	The auditor should perform the more efficient and effective of the following procedures: (a) The procedures discussed in Question 5.9; or (b) If the results of the functional tests of Questions 5.9 and 5.10 are satisfactory and the supervisory control (Question 5.12) is effective, perform extended funcional tests of the controls covered by those questions.

QUESTION 5.12

Are the results of the reconciliations and investigation of differences (5.9 and 5.10) reviewed and approved by a responsible official? (S)

Purpose

To determine whether such a review is performed. The review helps to ensure that the basic control is exercised regularly and effectively.

What Constitutes Adequate Control Procedures?

This question deals with the controls for supervisory review and approval. Refer to the discussion under that heading on page 374.

Possible Errors in Financial Statements	Example	Effect on Audit Procedures

If: The supervisory control is absent,

In the absence of a supervisory control, the reconciliation may not be performed adequately or at all. Accordingly, the possible errors are the same as when no review is made. Refer to Question 5.9.

The person performing the reconciliation and investigation notes that the supervisor does not review his work in this regard. Accordingly, he decides to do these jobs only when time permits.

To determine whether the related basic and division of duties controls have continued to operate properly, the auditor should perform the supervisory review at year-end. Refer to the common control procedure for supervisory review and approval (page 374) for guidance as to the procedures to follow.

QUESTION 5.13

Are the accounts payable subsidiary records periodically reconciled to suppliers' records (e.g. by comparison with suppliers' statements)?

Purpose

To determine whether the liabilities recorded on the company's records agree with the corresponding amounts on the suppliers' records. This comparison provides a check on the accuracy of the company's processing of accounts payable.

What Constitutes Adequate Control Procedures?

If	Impact on Adequacy of Control	Example
1. The person performing the reconciliations ensures that the amounts in the subsidiary records agree in total with the control account,	Control is adequate because the reconciler will know that he is dealing with the total liability reflected in the company's accounts.	The reconciler adds the subsidiary records and notes that the total exceeds the control account balance. This difference is investigated and appropriate adjustments made.

QUESTION 5.13 *(continued)*

If	Impact on Adequacy of Control	Example
2. The reconciler investigates all differences revealed by the reconciliations and ensures that appropriate adjustments are made,	Control is adequate because the relevant balances will be properly stated. His investigations should include discussions with appropriate company officials and/or the supplier, and examination of relevant supporting documentation.	The balance on a supplier's statement exceeds the recorded liability by $5,000, which is said to represent goods returned in one month not credited by the supplier until the next month. To substantiate this, the reconciler examines the company's record of goods returned and the supplier's credit memorandum, paying attention to dates, description of the item and quantity.
3. The reconciler reports breakdowns in controls revealed by his investigations to persons who can take corrective action,	Control is adequate because the company's records will be more reliable in the future.	The balance on a supplier's statement exceeds the recorded liability. The company records liabilities based on receiving reports. Investigation reveals that receiving reports are not prepared for goods received during lunch hour or breaks. This breakdown in control is reported and corrected.

Possible Errors in Financial Statements	Example	Effect on Audit Procedures
If: The reconciliation is not performed regularly,		
Accounts payable and income may be misstated because it is less likely that any unrecorded liabilities will be detected.	Supplier's statement shows several outstanding invoices that the company has not recorded.	1. The auditor should consider the following factors before determining whether to expand his validation procedures:

470

(a) Adequacy of the company's internal controls over accounts payable;

(b) Volume of activity in accounts payable, both in total and with specific suppliers;

(c) Whether there is any information indicating that all accounts payable may not be recorded.

2. Dependent upon the results of the above considerations, the auditor may wish to:

(a) Reconcile balances with suppliers' statements or confirm them with suppliers;

(b) Extend the period for which he conducts the search for unrecorded liabilities.

QUESTION 5.14

Is the procedure in 5.13 either performed or checked by persons other than those who: (a) post the accounts payable subsidiary records; (D) (b) maintain the control account? (D)

Purpose

To determine whether the persons who reconcile accounts payable subsidiary records with suppliers' statements have no incompatible duties, thereby helping to ensure that the reconciliation is done properly.

QUESTION 5.14 (*continued*)

What Constitutes Adequate Control Procedures?

If	Impact on Adequacy of Control	Example
1. The person who posts the subsidiary records performs the reconciliations and investigations,	Control is not adequate because the person can conceal differences revealed by the reconciliation. These differences can result from either intentional or inadvertent errors.	The person posting the subsidiary records makes numerous errors. He does not report differences arising from these errors because he does not want to call attention to his mistakes.
2. The person who maintains the control account performs the reconciliations and investigations,	Control is not adequate because the person can conceal differences revealed by the reconciliations that relate to errors he has made in maintaining the control account.	In establishing the control total, the person maintaining the control account omitted several invoices from a supplier. This difference is revealed by the reconciliation but is suppressed so that the person's error will not be noticed.

Possible Errors in Financial Statements	Example	Effect on Audit Procedures
If: The persons who post the accounts payable subsidiary records or maintain the control accounts make the reconciliations and investigations,		
It is even less likely that any unrecorded liabilities will be detected or reported. (Similar to Question 5.13.)	Supplier's statement reflects outstanding invoices that the company has not recorded because of the person's carelessness.	Refer to Question 5.13 for the effect on audit procedures.

472

QUESTION 5.15

Are the results of the reconciliations in 5.13 reviewed and approved by a responsible official? (S)

Purpose

To determine whether such a review is performed. The review helps to ensure that the basic control is exercised regularly and effectively.

What Constitutes Adequate Control Procedures?

This question deals with the controls for supervisory review and approval. Refer to the discussion under that heading on page 374.

Possible Errors in Financial Statements	Example	Effect on Audit Procedures
If: The supervisory control is absent,		
There is no assurance that the reconciliations are done regularly or properly. Refer to Question 5.13.	Action is not taken with respect to adjustments required and control weaknesses identified as a result of the reconciliations because the supervisor is not aware of them.	Refer to Question 5.13 for the effect on audit procedures. In addition, the auditor may wish to perform a review similar to a supervisory review at year-end or to increase his functional tests of the reconciliation procedure.

QUESTION 6.1

Are the following authorized in writing: (a) employees added to payrolls; (b) employees removed from payrolls; (c) rates of pay and changes in rates of pay; (d) payroll deductions other than compulsory deductions (specify below)?

Purpose

To determine whether all changes to standing payroll data are formally authorized.

473

What Constitutes Adequate Control Procedures?

If	Impact on Adequacy of Control	Example
1. Details of hirings, terminations, changes in rates of pay and other key payroll data are authorized in writing,	Control is adequate because there is a permanent record of authorized payroll data.	All amendments to standing data are entered on a "payroll amendment form" that is approved by a responsible official.
2. Blanket pay rate increases are granted,	Control is adequate if the written document clearly indicates personnel included or excluded, thereby ensuring that only authorized and valid amendments are made.	The authorization for a 5% pay increase for production workers also states that it does not apply to warehouse personnel.
3. Noncompulsory payroll deductions are authorized in writing,	Control is adequate because deductions from employees' salaries cannot be made without their consent.	A voluntary savings deduction is authorized in writing by the employee.

Possible Errors in Financial Statements	Example	Effect on Audit Procedures
1. **If:** Standing data amendments (excluding payroll deductions) are not authorized in writing,		
(a) Payroll expenses may be misstated, most likely overstated. Instructions may be misunderstood if not in writing. If the employee is underpaid, he is likely to draw it to the company's attention; however, this is not a certainty if the employee is overpaid.	An oral instruction to increase production employee rates by 5% was misunderstood and *all* employees received a 5% increase.	(a) and (b) If the auditor wishes to determine whether, and to what extent, invalid payments have occurred (e.g., because disclosure is required in the financial statements or as a client service), he should consider the following procedures (recognizing that they may not be conclusive):

(b) Company funds may be misappropriated because the person preparing the payroll can enter invalid standing data amendments.

The payroll preparer enters a fictitious employee and takes the additional paycheck.

(i) Obtain retroactive authorization from the client for all standing data amendments for the year;

(ii) If retroactive authorization cannot be obtained, the auditor should consider the following procedures to establish whether the payrolls are valid:

(A) Attend a payroll distribution on a surprise basis, observing the procedures used for employee identification, and follow up on all unclaimed paychecks or envelopes;

(B) Examine alternative evidence of employees' existence (e.g., production records, salesmen's call reports);

(C) Compare rates of pay to alternative sources (e.g., union contracts, governmental requirements). Review unsubstantiated rates of pay with management;

(D) Compare the payroll tested in (A) to (C) above with the other payrolls for the period under review. Investigate any significant differences or

Possible Errors in Financial Statements	Example	Effect on Audit Procedures
(c) Inventory and other assets may be misstated because they include invalid payroll amounts.	Invalid labor costs are included in inventory.	unexpected similarities (e.g., where volume is seasonal and the work force should vary but this is not reflected in payrolls). The auditor's response depends on the company's method for valuing inventory: (i) If the company's system is such that excessive payments are charged to cost of sales (e.g., quantities are extended at appropriate standard costs), the auditor's inventory work is not affected; (ii) If the company's system is such that excessive payments remain in inventory (e.g., all production costs are charged to inventory without analyzing variances), the auditor should perform some extended validation procedures on inventory at year-end, e.g.: (A) Observe a complete physical inventory, unless quantities are under adequate accounting control;

(B) Test the summarization of inventories at standard or actual costs;
(C) Review analyses of variances (if available);
(D) Extend lower of cost or market tests.

(d) Accrued liabilities may be misstated because invalid amendments are made to the last payrolls in the fiscal year.	To improve earnings, the payroll accrual for December omits 25% of the employees who will be paid in January.	The auditor should compare the last few payrolls in the year with similar payrolls for earlier periods and investigate any significant differences. He should also review payroll expenditures in the new year for evidence of payments relating to the year under review.

2. **If:** Payroll deductions are not authorized in writing,

Liabilities may be understated if payroll deductions are made in error and the funds cannot be recovered from the person to whom payment was made.	The company erroneously deducts union dues from certain employees and pays the withheld amounts to the union. The union refuses to return the money and the company must reimburse the employees concerned.	The auditor should request the company to obtain the missing authorizations. If this is not done and the auditor believes that the amounts involved might be material (e.g., because of numerous complaints from employees), he should attempt to obtain the missing authorizations himself.

QUESTION 6.2

Do persons other than those who prepare the payrolls provide the authorizations required in 6.1? (D)

Purpose

1. To determine whether there is an adequate segregation of duties over the authorization of standing payroll data.

2. If the procedure described above is not carried out, fraudulent or invalid amendments to standing payroll data could be made.

What Constitutes Adequate Control Procedures?

If	Impact on Adequacy of Control	Example
Amendments to standing data are authorized in writing by an appropriate responsible official not involved in payroll preparation,	Control is adequate because amendments are authorized by persons other than the payroll preparers.	(a) All amendments to standing payroll data are authorized by the personnel director who has no accounting responsibilities. (b) The hiring and termination of and pay increases for production workers are approved by the plant superintendent.

Possible Errors in Financial Statements	Example	Effect on Audit Procedures
If: Standing payroll data is authorized by persons with incompatible duties,		
Refer to Question 6.1. The possible errors are the same as when the amendments are not authorized.	The chief payroll clerk provides the authorizations referred to in the questions.	Refer to Question 6.1.

QUESTION 6.3

Are there adequate controls designed to ensure that the payroll reflects all authorized standing data (6.1) and only such authorized data?

Purpose

1. To determine whether adequate controls exist over the maintenance and use of standing payroll data.
2. If the controls described above are not present, the payrolls may be based on invalid data.

What Constitutes Adequate Control Procedures?

If	Impact on Adequacy of Control	Example
1. Selected payroll amounts are compared to predetermined control totals established from copies of authorized standing data amendments,	Control is adequate because the comparison will detect the failure to process valid amendments, the erroneous processing of valid amendments and the processing of invalid amendments.	Copies of all payroll amendments are forwarded to an official not responsible for payroll preparation. A reconciliation of gross and net amounts for one payroll compared to the previous payroll is prepared by the payroll department and presented to the official. The official compares the reconciling items with approved documentary evidence.
2. Periodic checks of payrolls with employee history cards are made,	Control is adequate because any errors or omissions in the standing payroll data will be detected.	At irregular intervals, but at least four times a year, the personnel department compares all payroll data with employee standing history files.
3. The control totals and comparisons described in 1 and 2 above are established or performed by persons not responsible for payroll preparation or authorization of amendments,	Control is adequate because differences or errors are more likely to be identified and reported.	See 2 above. The comparison is made by persons not responsible for preparing standing data amendments or forwarding them to the accounting department.

Possible Errors in Financial Statements	Example	Effect on Audit Procedures
If: Adequate control does not exist,		
Refer to Question 6.1. The possible errors are the same as when standing data amendments are not authorized.	The payroll clerk adds fictitious employees to the payroll and also uses inflated rates of pay for certain employees. These frauds	Refer to Question 6.1.

QUESTION 6.3 (*continued*)

Possible Errors in Financial Statements	Example	Effect on Audit Procedures
	are not detected because there is no control to ensure that invalid standing data amendments are not processed.	

QUESTION 6.4

If employees are paid on the basis of time worked: (a) is the payroll based on adequate time records; (b) where applicable, are the time records checked to supporting records of time spent (e.g. time charges to jobs); (e) are the time records (6.4(a)) approved; (f) do the time records (6.4(a)) indicate that overtime has been properly authorized?

Purpose

To determine whether the company's control procedures are such that payments are made for wages and salaries only on the basis of appropriately approved and authorized time records.

What Constitutes Adequate Control Procedures?

If	Impact on Adequacy of Control	Example
1. The payroll is based on time records,	The company should have controls to ensure that the hours on which the payroll is based agree with the hours per the time records.	A batch total of hours from clock cards is established before the payroll is prepared. This total is then compared to the total hours on the payroll.

480

2. Time records are agreed with supporting records of time spent,	Control is adequate because there is an accuracy check on the time records used for payroll purposes.	Clock cards are compared with job cost cards completed by each employee.
3. All time worked is recorded and approved,	Control is adequate because there is a permanent record of hours worked and any invalid hours should be detected.	Time worked is recorded on clock cards that are approved by foremen or department heads.
4. Only overtime hours worked are approved,	Control is adequate because all non-standard payroll details are approved.	Overtime hours are approved by foremen or department heads.
5. Time worked is reported by exception only,	Control is adequate because all non-standard payroll details are approved.	An employee list is sent to each department at the beginning of each pay period and the foreman or supervisor reports only cases in which time worked deviates from a normal work week for people included on the list.
6. Time worked is not approved but the use of clock cards is adequately supervised,	This may be a compensating control over time worked.	Each clock card station is permanently supervised by a timekeeper.

Possible Errors in Financial Statements	Example	Effect on Audit Procedures
1. **If:** The company does not have adequate time records or does not maintain adequate control over existing time records,		
Refer to Question 6.1, item 1. The same kinds of errors can arise when there is no control over transaction data as when there is no control over standing data.	The payroll clerk pays an employee for 40 hours work even though the employee was absent for 3 days (24 hours) without permission.	(a) With respect to transactions during the year, if the auditor wishes to determine whether, and to what extent, invalid payments have occurred (e.g., because disclosure is required in the

Possible Errors in Financial Statements	Example	Effect on Audit Procedures
		financial statements or as a client service), he should consider the following procedures (recognizing that they may not be conclusive): (i) Obtain retroactive authorization from the company of all unauthorized or unsubstantiated payroll transaction data for the year; (ii) If retroactive authorization cannot be obtained, the auditor should consider the following procedures: (A) Compare payroll hours to alternative documents (e.g., production department records of time worked or output); (B) Compare payrolls throughout the year for evidence of consistency, unexpected fluctuations, and the like. Inquire into unusual situations identified. (b) With respect to year-end balances in inventory, refer to Question 6.1, item 1(c).

(c) With respect to year-end balances in accrued liabilities, refer to Question 6.1, item 1(d).

2. **If:** The company has adequate time records but does not ensure that the payrolls agree with those records,

See 1 above.	See 1 above.	The auditor should perform the most effective and efficient mix of the following procedures: (a) Extended comparison of hours per the payroll with hours per the time records; (b) The procedures described in 1 above.

QUESTION 6.5

If employees are paid on the basis of output, are the payments based on output records that are reconciled with production records that are under accounting control (e.g. 20.8(c), 20.21)?

Purpose

To determine whether payments for wages based on production are checked by reconciling to appropriate production records.

What Constitutes Adequate Control Procedures?

If	Impact on Adequacy of Control	Example
1. The total production paid for (as shown by the payrolls) is reconciled with production records (less, where applicable, rejects and scrap) that are under accounting control,	Control is adequate because the company is assured that employees are paid only for actual production.	A foreman reports quantities produced by each employee. The total quantities are reconciled to the production records that serve as the input to the finished goods inventory records.

If	Impact on Adequacy of Control	Example
2. Production records are maintained by persons not concerned with payroll preparation,	Control is adequate because an independent record of production output is maintained.	Production records are maintained by the factory production department.
3. The reconciliation (1 above) is performed by persons other than those who maintain production records or prepare payrolls,	Control is adequate because errors or differences are more likely to be identified and reported.	Output per the payroll records is agreed to the production records by the cost department.

Possible Errors in Financial Statements	Example	Effect on Audit Procedures
If: The company does not perform this reconciliation,		
1. Payroll expense may be misstated, most likely overstated, because the output paid for differs from the actual output. This can happen inadvertently or deliberately.	When preparing the payroll, the payroll clerk increases the production quantities reported by the production department for certain employees.	If the auditor wishes to determine whether, and to what extent, invalid payments have occurred (e.g., because disclosure is required in the financial statements or as a client service), he should consider the following procedures (recognizing that they may not be conclusive): (a) Compare production paid for per the payrolls with output per the production records, either for the entire year or for selected periods. This comparison will be more effective if the production records are under accounting control;

(b) Compare payrolls throughout the year for evidence of consistency, unexpected fluctuations, and the like. Inquire into unusual situations identified by the review.

Refer to Question 6.1, item 1(c).

(a) The auditor should compare the last few payrolls in the year with similar payrolls for earlier periods and investigate any significant differences.

(b) He should review payroll expenditures in the new year for evidence of payments relating to the year under review.

(c) Depending on the results in (a) and (b) above, and on whether the production records are under adequate accounting control, the auditor may wish to make the comparison himself for the last payroll(s) in the fiscal year.

2. Inventory and other assets may be misstated because they include invalid payroll amounts.

See 1 above. Invalid labor costs are included in inventory.

3. Accrued liability for payrolls may be misstated because the wrong production figures are used.

The accrued liability is understated because the foreman failed to report two days production in each of the last two weeks in the fiscal year.

QUESTION 6.6

If salaried or other employees not included in 6.4 or 6.5 are paid for overtime, is the payroll based on time records which indicate that overtime has been properly authorized?

Purpose

To determine whether overtime for such employees is paid only on the basis of appropriately authorized time records.

QUESTION 6.6 (*continued*)

What Constitutes Adequate Control Procedures?

If	Impact on Adequacy of Control	Example
Overtime is paid only on the basis of an appropriate authorization,	Control is adequate because unauthorized payments cannot be made.	Department heads authorize overtime by approving "overtime request" forms, which are sent to the payroll department as a basis for payment.

Possible Errors in Financial Statements	Example	Effect on Audit Procedures
If: Authorization or approval is not required for the payment of overtime,		
1. Payroll expense may be misstated, more likely overstated. Underpayments will normally be reported by the employees concerned. However, overpayments are less likely to be reported and may be the result of deliberate misstatement of time worked.	Overtime worked is recorded on an "overtime form." However, this form is not authorized and is forwarded by the employee to the payroll department.	(a) The auditor should review or determine the amount of overtime paid to such employees and its relative materiality. (b) If material, the auditor should follow the procedures in Question 6.4, item 1(a.)
2. That portion of the inventory costs represented by indirect expenses may be overstated. The company may carry forward invalid payroll costs in inventory.	Overtime worked by the production supervisor is not authorized. This time is allocated to indirect production overhead and included in inventory costs.	The auditor should review or determine the relative materiality of the amounts involved, and, if material, perform the procedures in Question 6.1, item 1(c).

If employees receive commissions on sales, are the commissions based on sales records that are reconciled with sales (less, where applicable, returns) recorded in the books?

Purpose

1. To determine whether payments for commissions based on sales are reconciled with the accounting records for sales.

2. If the procedure described in 1 above is not carried out, commission payments may be in error.

What Constitutes Adequate Control Procedures?

If	Impact on Adequacy of Control	Example
1. The total sales used in determining commissions are reconciled with sales (less, where applicable, returns) recorded in the books,	Control is adequate because the company is assured that employees are paid only for actual sales.	The accounting department prepares a listing of sales by salesman (including "no commission" sales) and agrees the total to the month's sales entry.
2. The reconciliation is performed or checked by persons with no incompatible duties,	Control is adequate because there is additional assurance that commissions have been paid on the appropriate amount of sales.	See 1 above. The reconciliation is reviewed and approved by the controller and the sales manager.

Possible Errors in Financial Statements	Example	Effect on Audit Procedures
If: The reconciliation is not performed adequately,		
1. Sales commission expense may be misstated: (a) Commissions may be paid twice on the same sales;	Certain territories are assigned to more than one salesman and, because of a programming error, all sales in those territories are credited for commission purposes	The auditor should request the company to perform the reconciliation retroactively for selected periods. He should test the reconciliation and determine the reason-

487

QUESTION 6.7 (continued)

Possible Errors in Financial Statements	Example	Effect on Audit Procedures
(b) Commissions may not be paid on valid sales.	to each salesman in the territory. This error is not detected because the reconciliation is not performed.	ableness of commission expense in relation to sales for the year.
2. Accrued liabilities for sales commissions may be misstated.	Because of a programming error, sales of certain new products have not been credited to the salesmen for commission purposes. This error was not detected because the reconciliation was not performed.	The auditor should compare the commission to sales ratios for the last few payrolls in the year with similar payrolls for earlier periods and investigate any significant differences. He should also review commissions in the new year for evidence of payments related to the year under review.

QUESTION 6.8

Is there a check on the calculation of gross pay (e.g. by agreeing in total with predetermined control totals or with cost records, or by sufficient checking of individual amounts), in respect of: (a) employees paid for time worked (6.4); (b) employees paid for output (6.5); (c) employees paid for overtime (6.6); (d) employees paid commissions (6.7)?

Purpose

To determine whether there are sufficient checks performed to ensure that the gross pay calculation is arithmetically correct.

What Constitutes Adequate Control Procedures?

If	Impact on Adequacy of Control	Example
1. Individual amounts are checked,	The common control procedure related to controls over checking of extensions and	

488

(Internal Control)	(Evaluation)	
	additions would be applicable. Refer to the discussion under that heading on page 376.	
2. Predetermined control totals are used: (a) A control total is established and compared with the payroll by persons other than the payroll preparers,	Control is adequate because there is assurance that gross pay has been accurately determined.	Clock card details are evaluated and a control total established by the timekeeping department before processing. This total is agreed with the actual payroll total by the chief accountant.
(b) A standard payroll total is established,	Control is adequate if differences are adequately explained.	A standard office payroll total is established, i.e., no overtime is paid. This total is agreed to the actual payroll for each period.
3. The gross payroll amount is agreed to the cost records,	The agreement should be performed by persons not involved with payroll preparation or the maintenance of the cost records, or should be reviewed and approved by a responsible official.	The gross amounts on the payroll are agreed to the cost records (which have been entered from job cost cards) by the chief accountant.

Possible Errors in Financial Statements	Example	Effect on Audit Procedures
If: There is no check on the calculation of gross pay,		
1. Payroll expense may be misstated, most likely overstated. This can happen either inadvertently or deliberately.	The payroll preparer knows that his gross pay calculations are not checked and thus makes deliberate errors, i.e., overstatements, for certain employees with whom he has made an arrangement.	If the auditor wishes to determine whether, and to what extent, overpayments have occurred (e.g., because disclosure is required in the financial statements or as a client service), he should consider the following procedures (recognizing that they may not be conclusive):

Possible Errors in Financial Statements	Example	Effect on Audit Procedures
		(a) Request the company to establish the procedure retroactively and then apply appropriate audit tests;
		(b) If the company does not perform the above, the auditor should:
		(i) Select sample payrolls and check, or test check, the gross pay calculations;
		(ii) Review the payroll expense for the period, and obtain explanations for any significant variations or fluctuations from the payrolls tested in (i) above and vouch with supporting documents.
2. Inventory and other assets may be misstated because the company may carry forward amounts that represent invalid payroll payments.	See 1 above. The deliberate overstatements of gross pay are included in inventory at year-end under the company's accounting system.	Refer to Question 6.1, item 1(c).
3. Accrued liability for payroll may be misstated.	Clerical errors result in an understatement of gross pay for the last pay period in the year. Complaints from employees are received after the books are closed and thus the adjustment is not processed.	The auditor should:
		(a) Compare the accrued payrolls with payroll(s) that he has tested (see 1(b)(i) above) and investigate any significant fluctuations;

(b) Review payrolls in the new year for evidence of payments relating to the year under review.

QUESTION 6.9

Is there a check on the calculation of payroll deductions (e.g. by agreeing in total with predetermined control totals or by sufficient checking of individual amounts)?

Purpose

To determine whether the company's procedures ensure the accuracy of the calculation of payroll deductions.

What Constitutes Adequate Control Procedures?

If	Impact on Adequacy of Control	Example
1. The calculation of individual amounts is checked,	The common control procedure related to controls over checking of extensions and additions would be applicable. Refer to the discussion under that heading on page 376.	Taxes to be withheld are based on a stated percentage of gross pay.
2. Predetermined control totals are used:		
(a) The control total is regularly updated for new employees, terminations and changes in amount of deductions,	The comparison of the total deductions as shown by the payrolls to the control total will be effective because the control total is reliable.	The control total is established from copies of payroll change forms.
(b) The comparison is made by persons with no incompatible duties,	Control is adequate because all errors or differences should be identified and updated.	The comparison is made by a person other than the payroll clerk and the person maintaining the control totals.

QUESTION 6.9 *(continued)*

Possible Errors in Financial Statements	Example	Effect on Audit Procedures
If: There is no check on the calculation of payroll deductions,		
1. Compulsory deductions: (a) If excessive amounts are withheld, there is probably no effect on the financial statements since any claim by the employee for overwithholding can usually be offset by a claim against the payee (e.g., the taxing authority) for overpayment.	The company withholds excessive taxes from employees. Upon discovering the error, the company reduces the withholdings to offset the error.	Usually, there is no effect on audit procedures for the reasons set forth in the first column.
(b) If insufficient amounts are withheld, the company may be contingently liable for the deficiency and penalties if the employees do not make the payments.	The company withholds insufficient income taxes and must pay any income tax lost by the taxing authority, plus penalties.	The auditor should make sufficient tests of compulsory deductions to satisfy himself that the company could not have a material liability as a result of such errors.
2. Voluntary deductions: If amounts withheld are in error, there is probably no effect on the financial statements since the matter usually involves an employee and an outside agency.	The company fails to withhold amounts for a voluntary savings plan.	Usually, there is no effect on audit procedures for the reasons set forth in the first column. However, the auditor should be alert to the fact that overwithholdings may be misappropriated. He should satisfy himself that voluntary withholdings are remitted to the payee intact in a timely manner (see Control Objective 7).

492

QUESTION 6.10

Are the calculations and additions of payrolls and payroll summaries checked to an adequate extent?

Purpose

To determine whether the company's procedures are such that the arithmetic accuracy of the payrolls and payroll summaries is assured.

What Constitutes Adequate Control Procedures?

This question deals with the controls over checking of extensions and additions. Refer to the discussion under that heading on page 376.

Possible Errors in Financial Statements	Example	Effect on Audit Procedures
1. If: The procedures in Question 6.8 do not ensure that total gross pay is correct,		
The same errors can arise as those discussed in Question 6.8.	The addition of the gross pay column is not checked.	Refer to Question 6.8.
2. If: The procedures in Question 6.9 do not ensure that total deductions are correct,		
The company may make erroneous payments to third parties if the payments are based on the payroll totals. If erroneous payments are made, the company will have an unrecorded asset or liability.	The company withholds union dues aggregating $2,000 from employees. Because of a clerical error, the payroll shows a total of $1,400 and that amount is paid to the union. The company has an unrecorded liability of $600.	The auditor should make sufficient tests of the additions of payroll deductions to satisfy himself that material errors have not arisen.
3. If: The arithmetic accuracy of net pay is not checked,		
Company funds may be misappropriated. The person preparing the payroll may deliberately misstate the net payroll total	The net payroll total is overstated by $1,000 by the payroll clerk who misappropriates the cash.	If the auditor wishes to determine whether, and to what extent, fraud may have occurred (e.g., because disclosure is required

QUESTION 6.10 (*continued*)

Possible Errors in Financial Statements	Example	Effect on Audit Procedures

which is the basis for the cash withdrawn to pay the payroll.		in the financial statements or as a client service), he should consider the following procedures (recognizing that they may not be conclusive):
		(a) Request the company to establish the procedure retroactively and then apply appropriate audit tests;
		(b) If the company does not perform the above, the auditor should:
		   (i) Select sample payrolls and check, or test check, the addition of the net pay column;
		   (ii) Review the payroll from period to period and obtain explanations for any significant variations or fluctuations from the base payrolls in (i) above.

QUESTION 6.11

Do persons other than those who prepare the payrolls or payroll summaries check: (a) the calculations of gross pay (6.8); (D) (b) the calculation of payroll deductions (6.9); (D) (c) the calculations and additions of payrolls and payroll summaries (6.10)? (D)

Purpose

To determine whether the persons performing the checks on the accuracy of the calculations have no incompatible duties, thereby ensuring that all errors detected will be reported.

What Constitutes Adequate Control Procedures?

If	Impact on Adequacy of Control	Example
Persons other than those who perform the initial calculations check those calculations,	Control is adequate because those persons are more likely to identify and report errors, whether deliberate or inadvertent.	The sales invoice clerk checks the various calculations made by the payroll clerk.

Possible Errors in Financial Statements

Possible Errors in Financial Statements	Example	Effect on Audit Procedures

If: Calculations are not checked by persons with no incompatible duties,

Refer to Questions 6.8 to 6.10, as appropriate. The possible errors that could arise are similar to those that might arise if the checks were not performed at all.	The payroll clerk performs all the payroll preparation duties and checks his own work. His checking is done in a perfunctory manner because he feels he made no mistakes during preparation.	The auditor should perform the more efficient of the following approaches: (a) Extended functional tests of the controls covered by Questions 6.8 to 6.10; (b) The procedures set forth in Questions 6.8 to 6.11, as appropriate.

QUESTION 6.12

Do payrolls bear adequate evidence that the procedures in 6.8 to 6.11 have been completed?

Purpose

To determine whether the checks performed are properly evidenced. If they are not, then Questions 6.8 to 6.11, as appropriate, should be answered "no."

What Constitutes Adequate Control Procedures?

If	Impact on Adequacy of Control	Example
1. The calculation of individual amounts is checked,	The common control procedure related to controls over checking of extensions and additions would be applicable. Refer to the discussion under that heading on page 376.	
2. Predetermined control totals are used,	Control is adequate if there is evidence that the relevant amounts have been compared and that reconciling items have been investigated.	The assistant accountant compares the control total to the payroll and initials the payroll as evidence that he has done this. He also initials the report explaining the reconciling items after he has reviewed it.

Possible Errors in Financial Statements	Example	Effect on Audit Procedures
If: There is no evidence that the control procedures have been applied,		
Refer to Questions 6.8 to 6.11, as appropriate. If there is no evidence of a control, then the control is not adequate for audit purposes and the possible errors are similar to when the checks are not performed.	Payrolls and payroll summaries are not initialled or otherwise marked as being checked as to calculations and additions.	Refer to Questions 6.8 to 6.11, as appropriate.

496

QUESTION 6.13

Are payrolls subject to the final written approval of a responsible official before they are paid? (S)

Purpose

To determine whether all payrolls are subject to final approval by a responsible official before payment, thereby ensuring that the related basic and disciplinary controls have continued to operate.

What Constitutes Adequate Control Procedures?

This question deals with the controls for supervisory review and approval. Refer to the discussion under that heading on page 374.

Possible Errors in Financial Statements	Example	Effect on Audit Procedures
If: Payrolls are not approved in writing by a responsible official,		
Refer to Questions 6.8 to 6.11. In the absence of a supervisory control, the checks may not be performed. Accordingly, the possible errors are the same as when the checks are not performed.	The persons performing the checks in Questions 6.8 to 6.11 observe that their work is not reviewed by anyone and they stop performing the checks.	To determine whether the related basic and division of duties controls have continued to operate properly, the auditor should perform the supervisory review at year-end and for selected periods during the year. Refer to the common control procedure for supervisory review and approval (page 374) for guidance as to the procedures to follow.

QUESTION 6.14

Do persons other than those who prepare the payrolls compare payroll checks, either individually or in the aggregate, with the payrolls? (D)

Purpose

1. An individual review by another person should ensure that the payroll checks are payable to the appropriate person and in the right amount.

2. An aggregate review will ensure that the total of the payroll checks agrees with the net payroll, thereby preventing excess cash being disbursed.

What Constitutes Adequate Control Procedures?

If	Impact on Adequacy of Control	Example
1. All individual payroll checks are compared to payrolls by persons other than the payroll preparers,	Control is adequate because a complete check will detect any inaccuracies.	The check signer agrees each check drawn with the payroll.
2. Persons other than the payroll preparers add the individual payroll checks and compare the total to the payrolls,	Control is adequate although not as good as that described in 1 above. It is acceptable because it will prevent excess cash being drawn. However, it will not detect overpayments offset by underpayments, although the underpayments will presumably be drawn to the company's attention.	Payroll checks are totalled and agreed with the total payroll amount by the check signer.

Possible Errors in Financial Statements	Example	Effect on Audit Procedures
If: The comparison is not completed,		
Company funds may be misappropriated because the person preparing the payrolls	Checks totalling $10,000 are drawn for a net payroll of only $9,000. The excess	The auditor should expand his audit tests to include:

498

may draw checks for more than the valid payroll amount.

$1,000 is misappropriated.

(a) The agreement of the payroll amount with the checks drawn in total for the year; or
(b) The extension of the level of functional tests to determine whether payroll checks agree with payroll amounts.

QUESTION 6.15

If employees are paid in cash: (a) is cash withdrawn only for the net amount of the payroll; (C) (b) do persons other than those who prepare the payroll physically control cash until it is distributed to employees; (C) (c) are unclaimed wages promptly recorded and controlled by persons other than those who prepare the payroll? (C)

Purpose

To determine whether the company has adequate control over cash used in cash payrolls.

What Constitutes Adequate Control Procedures?

If	Impact on Adequacy of Control	Example
1. Cash is withdrawn for the net amount of the payroll,	The risk of loss or misappropriation is reduced because: (a) Only the exact amount needed is withdrawn from the bank and kept on hand; (b) Any errors in filling pay envelopes will be detected if the cash is used up before all the envelopes are filled (or vice versa).	Upon receipt of an authorization from the treasurer, the bank delivers cash equal to the net amount of the payroll to the payroll cashier.

QUESTION 6.15 (continued)

If	Impact on Adequacy of Control	Example
2. The person who prepares the payroll does not have access to the payroll cash at any time (e.g., when filling pay envelopes),	Control is adequate. If he had access to the cash, the payroll clerk could steal cash equal to deliberate overstatements of the payroll.	The payroll clerk intentionally mis-adds the gross and net pay columns by $10,000, intending to steal $10,000 from the payroll cash without detection. His plan is foiled because he cannot get access to the cash.
3. There are unclaimed pay envelopes after the payoff is completed,	Control is adequate if they are promptly recorded and controlled by persons other than those who prepare the payrolls or provide payroll authorizations.	Unclaimed pay envelopes are given to the fixed assets clerk, who releases them to employees only upon presentation of proper identification.

Possible Errors in Financial Statements	Example	Effect on Audit Procedures
1. If: Cash is withdrawn for more than the net amount of the payroll,		
The company's funds may be misappropriated because the amount withdrawn will not function to limit the payments disbursed.	Cash is drawn on an estimate of the net payroll and any surplus should be redeposited. However, the pay clerk misappropriates the excess.	The auditor should reconcile cash withdrawn and redeposited with net payroll totals for the year or for selected periods. Any material variances should be investigated.
2. If: The person responsible for payroll preparation has access to cash,		
The company's funds may be misappropriated because the payroll clerk can add fictitious people to the payroll and collect the excess wages.	The payroll department originates standing data amendments. The cash for a fictitious employee is misappropriated while under control of payroll department.	The auditor should attend on a surprise basis the distribution of pay envelopes to employees, and follow up and validate unclaimed wages.

500

3. If: Unclaimed wages are controlled by payroll department personnel,

Refer to 2 above.	The cash for fictitious employees is misappropriated by the payroll clerk when returned unclaimed from the distribution.	The auditor should perform the procedures noted in 2 above.

QUESTION 7.1

Are all payroll deductions recorded in separate control accounts?

Purpose

1. To determine whether the company records payroll deductions in separate control accounts, thereby providing adequate segregation for identification and control purposes.

2. It should be noted that the procedures for determining the accuracy of payroll deductions have been evaluated as part of Control Objective 6.

What Constitutes Adequate Control Procedures?

If	Impact on Adequacy of Control	Example
Each type of payroll deduction is recorded in a separate control account that is regularly reconciled to the payrolls,	Control is adequate because the liabilities for deductions are properly segregated and identified for control over supporting records and payments.	Payroll deductions are recorded in separate control accounts that are reconciled to the payrolls monthly. The reconciliations are reviewed and approved by a responsible official.

Possible Errors in Financial Statements	Example	Effect on Audit Procedures
If: Separate control accounts are not maintained or are not regularly reconciled to the payrolls,		
The liability for amounts deducted may be misstated, because recording errors may not be detected. Reconciliation with supporting records would be hindered because control totals for different types of deductions would be combined.	Payroll deductions are credited to a single general ledger account with no subsidiary ledgers. Errors in the control account are not detected because reconciliations to the payrolls are not performed.	1. The auditor should request the company to segregate the balances at year-end and reconcile them to the related payrolls. He should then test the reconciliations. 2. If the company does not do this, the auditor should do it himself.

QUESTION 7.2

Are payments of payroll deductions to third parties agreed to the related payrolls?

Purpose

1. To determine whether payments of payroll deductions are based on the related payrolls.
2. If the control described above is not carried out, unexplained variances may build up in the control account or invalid payments may be made.

What Constitutes Adequate Control Procedures?

If	Impact on Adequacy of Control	Example
1. Payments of payroll deductions are agreed to the related payrolls,	Control is adequate because a check is performed on the accuracy and validity of the payment.	The related payrolls are presented to the official approving the payment.

2. Payments of payroll deductions are agreed to the control account balances,

Control is adequate if the control account balance is reconciled to the payrolls as of the payment dates. (See Question 7.1.)

A reconciliation of the control account balance with the related payrolls is presented to the official approving the payment.

Possible Errors in Financial Statements	Example	Effect on Audit Procedures
If: Payments are not agreed to the related payrolls,		
Invalid or incorrect payments may be made, which can result in misstatement of: (a) Expenses for the year; (b) The liability account at year-end.	The company pays third parties based on estimated deductions and does not make the necessary adjustments to reflect actual deductions.	The auditor should: (a) Perform the procedures set forth in Question 7.1; (b) Compare payments made during the year with the actual payrolls.

QUESTION 7.3

Is the procedure in 7.2 carried out by persons other than those who prepare the payrolls? (D)

Purpose

To determine whether the persons performing the agreement of the payment with the payroll records have no incompatible duties.

What Constitutes Adequate Control Procedures?

If	Impact on Adequacy of Control	Example
The person performing the agreement is not involved in the payroll preparation,	Control is adequate because that person is more likely to detect and report any errors that may be present.	The agreement is performed by the check signer.

503

QUESTION 7.3 (*continued*)

Possible Errors in Financial Statements	Example	Effect on Audit Procedures
If: The agreement is performed by persons involved in payroll preparation,		
Refer to Question 7.2. The possible errors that could arise are similar to those that may occur when the agreement is not performed.	The payroll clerk deliberately overstates the amounts due to certain third parties with whom he has made an arrangement. The overstatement is not detected because no one else compares the payments to the related payrolls.	The existence of incompatible duties has a similar effect on our audit procedures as though no check was performed. Refer to Question 7.2.

QUESTION 8.1

Are imprest and similar funds: (a) maintained at a reasonable balance in relation to the level of expenditure; (C) (b) under the custody of persons who do not have access to non-imprest funds; (C) (c) periodically verified and reconciled with the general ledger control account by a person other than the custodian (all funds, both imprest and non-imprest, in the custody of the same person being verified at the same time)? (D)

Purpose

To determine whether the company adequately controls imprest funds by limiting balances, appropriate segregation of duties and periodic verification.

What Constitutes Adequate Control Procedures?

If	Impact on Adequacy of Control	Example
1. Imprest funds are maintained at a reasonable level,	Control is adequate because the amount subject to misappropriation is held to the minimum practicable level.	The company's imprest funds are kept at a balance approximating one to two weeks' disbursements.

504

2. Custodian does not have access to other cash funds,

Control is adequate because the custodian is precluded from concealing shortages in one fund by using other funds.

Petty cashier has no other cash handling functions.

3. Imprest funds are periodically verified and reconciled with the general ledger by someone other than the custodian,

Control is adequate because the procedure reaffirms the integrity of the fund(s), would detect misappropriations and acts as a deterrent to fraud.

A person not responsible for the custody of the funds counts all the cash funds and reconciles the amounts to the accounting records. (All funds under the control of the same person should be verified at the same time to prevent the transfer of amounts between funds to cover deficiencies.)

4. The person performing the verification (see 3) establishes the authenticity of the non-cash items in the fund,

Control is adequate because he should detect any fictitious documents included in the fund to conceal a misappropriation.

(a) All checks are examined to establish that their dates are current, and are deposited under the control of the person performing the verification.

(b) Disbursements and their supporting documentation are examined to establish their validity (see Question 8.2).

Possible Errors in Financial Statements	Example	Effect on Audit Procedures
1. **If:** Imprest funds are not maintained at a reasonable level,		
(a) Cash and income may be overstated because disbursements from the fund are not recorded on a timely basis.	Company has a petty cash fund of $100,000 which is reimbursed only twice a year (at January 31 and July 31). Expenditures from August through December are not recorded until the following year.	Either the company or the auditor should count the fund at year-end, reconcile the balance to the general ledger and ensure that the disbursements are properly recorded.
(b) Cash and income may be overstated because part of the excessive balance has been stolen.	See (a). The custodian has stolen $50,000 from the petty cash fund.	See (a) above.

QUESTION 8.1 (continued)

2. If: Imprest funds are under the custody of persons who have access to non-imprest funds,

Cash and income may be overstated. The risk of misappropriation or loss is increased because access to non-imprest funds can aid in the concealment of fraud.	The auditor should perform the procedures in 1 above at the year-end.

3. If: Imprest funds are not periodically verified and reconciled to the general ledger by someone other than the custodian,

Cash and income may be overstated because the company has not established that the funds still exist intact. Misappropriations would remain undetected.	The auditor should perform the procedures in 1 above at the year-end.

QUESTION 8.2

Are all disbursements from imprest and similar funds: (a) supported by adequate documentation; (b) approved where appropriate?

Purpose

1. To determine whether disbursements from imprest (or similar) funds are made only on the basis of adequately approved documentation.

2. If the procedure described above is not carried out, opportunities exist for fraud and invalid payments to be made.

What Constitutes Adequate Control Procedures?

If	Impact on Adequacy of Control	Example
1. All disbursements are supported by adequate documentation,	Control is adequate because the validity of the disbursements can be established.	All petty cash vouchers are supported by vendors' invoices, and the like.

2. Only disbursements over a specified monetary amount are required to be supported by adequate documentation,

The auditor should assess the reasonableness of the specified amount and whether controls are in effect to ensure that all disbursements over the amount are supported. If the amount involved is not reasonable, the control is not adequate because numerous invalid disbursements totalling a material sum could be processed.

Only disbursements in excess of $50.00 require supporting documentation. Such disbursements account for more than 90% of the monetary value of petty cash disbursements.

3. The documentation is cancelled after payment has been made,

Control is adequate because the same documentation cannot be used to support additional disbursements.

The petty cashier stamps the documents "paid" when he disburses the funds.

4. Part (b) of this question deals with controls for supervisory review and approval. Refer to the discussion under that heading on page 374.

Possible Errors in Financial Statements	Example	Effect on Audit Procedures
1. **If:** Disbursements are not supported by adequate documentation or are not cancelled upon payment,		
(a) Assets and income may be overstated because a fraudulent payment may be made and erroneously charged to an asset account.	An invalid payment is charged to fixed assets.	The auditor should vouch significant asset additions arising from imprest funds and physically inspect the related assets.
(b) A misclassification of expenses may have occurred. The loss from a fraudulent payment may not be properly classified.	A fictitious advertising invoice is charged to advertising expense rather than being disclosed as a loss from fraud.	If the auditor wishes to determine whether, and to what extent, fraudulent payments have been made (e.g., because disclosure is required in the financial statements or

QUESTION 8.2 (*continued*)

Possible Errors in Financial Statements	Example	Effect on Audit Procedures
		as a client service), he should consider vouching payments made during the year. The auditor should recognize that these procedures may not be conclusive.
2. If: Disbursements are not approved,		
Refer to 1 above. The possible errors are similar to those that may occur if disbursements are not documented.	Company employees, knowing that the petty cashier does not check for approvals, submit invalid requests for payment and thereby defraud the company.	The auditor should perform the more efficient and effective of the following procedures: (a) Those set forth in 1 above; (b) Extended functional tests of disbursements.

QUESTION 8.3

In the case of cash funds, are there reasonable limits on: (a) the size of individual disbursements; (C) (b) the extent to which personal checks of employees are cashed; (C) (c) loans and advances (e.g. for wages) made from such funds? (C)

Purpose

To determine whether reasonable limits have been placed on the above types of transactions in order to ensure that: (a) routine transactions do not bypass the normal payables procedures; and (b) the funds are not subjected to undue risks of loss.

What Constitutes Adequate Control Procedures?

If	Impact on Adequacy of Control	Example
Reasonable limits are established and approved in writing for each type of transaction,	Control is adequate if these limits are enforced by the custodian, and care is taken that payments are not "split" to avoid the limitations.	The petty cash custodian is prohibited from: (a) Making disbursements in excess of $100; (b) Cashing personal checks or making advances in excess of one-half of an employee's normal weekly pay.

Possible Errors in Financial Statements	Example	Effect on Audit Procedures
1. If: Reasonable limits are not placed on the size of individual disbursements,		
The likelihood of invalid payments is increased, and assets and expenses may be misstated. This is because large payments that should pass through the normal purchasing system may bypass the checks within that system.	A purchase of an inventory item may not be matched with the purchase order and the receiving report because the imprest custodian may accept an invoice as suitable supporting documentation.	The auditor should review the levels of imprest fund expenditures and vouch any large or unusual payments or any regularly recurring expenses that should have been processed through the purchasing system.
2. If: Reasonable limits are not placed on the extent to which personal checks of employees are cashed,		
The company's funds may be at risk because an employee check in excess of a reasonable amount may be cashed with a high risk of the check not being honored.	An employee who earns $150 per week cashes a check for $1,000.	The auditor should ensure that all checks in the fund at year-end are deposited promptly and should determine whether any are returned by the bank.

509

QUESTION 8.3 (*continued*)

Possible Errors in Financial Statements	Example	Effect on Audit Procedures
3. If: Reasonable limits are not placed on the extent to which loans and advances are made,		
Invalid and non-recoverable loans or advances may be made, thereby overstating income and receivables.	A loan of $5,000 is made to an office clerk by the petty cashier.	The auditor should review the collectibility of any advances or loans outstanding at the year-end.

QUESTION 8.4

Are all reimbursements made on an imprest basis?

Purpose

To determine whether the reimbursement procedures ensure that the funds remain at the level established by the company and the imprest procedures are employed. If reimbursements vary from the amounts expended, control is diminished.

What Constitutes Adequate Control Procedures?

If	Impact on Adequacy of Control	Example
Reimbursements differ from amounts actually expended,	Control is not adequate because: (a) The fund may expand in size beyond that authorized, thereby increasing the amount of risk;	The petty cashier decides that the funds should be larger and requests reimbursements in excess of the amounts spent.

510

Possible Errors in Financial Statements	Example	Effect on Audit Procedures
	(b) The documentation for expenditures will not support the reimbursement amount.	The petty cash custodian requests reimbursements each week that are $50 higher than amounts expended and steals the excess funds.
If: The imprest system is not in use,		
1. Cash and income may be overstated because disbursements from the fund are not recorded on a timely basis.	The petty cashier obtains cash advances on a "need" basis. As a result, he does not submit his disbursements on a regular basis and they are not accounted for promptly.	Either the company or the auditor should count the fund at year-end and ensure that the disbursements are properly recorded.
2. Cash is more likely to be misappropriated because "reimbursements" can be obtained that are in excess of disbursements, thus increasing cash on hand.	See 1 above. The cash advances exceed the disbursements and the petty cashier steals some of the "excess" cash.	See 1 above.
3. The unrecorded disbursements are more likely to be fraudulent because they are not reviewed on a regular basis.	The petty cashier has unwittingly been making disbursements in violation of company policy. His errors are not detected because the disbursements are not reviewed on a regular basis.	See 1 above. In addition, with respect to transactions during the year, see Question 8.2, item 1(b).

QUESTION 8.5

Are requests for reimbursement accompanied by details of expenditures and supporting vouchers?

Purpose

To determine whether the company's procedures ensure that reimbursements of imprest funds are made only on the basis of adequate supporting documentation.

511

QUESTION 8.5 (*continued*)

What Constitutes Adequate Control Procedures?

If	Impact on Adequacy of Control	Example
1. All requests for reimbursements are accompanied by details of the expenditures and the supporting vouchers,	Control is adequate because the petty cash disbursements can be reviewed for authenticity.	A check requisition together with the vouchers for reimbursement are presented to the official approving the payment.
2. The requests and the supporting documents are cancelled when the reimbursement is made,	Control is adequate because the custodian will not be able to resubmit the same documents for a further, fraudulent reimbursement.	See 1 above. The official stamps "paid" on the request and supporting documents.

Possible Errors in Financial Statements	Example	Effect on Audit Procedures
If: Requests for reimbursement are not accompanied by supporting vouchers,		
The company's funds may be misappropriated and consequently expenses and assets misstated. This can occur in either of the following ways: (a) The reimbursement requested exceeds the total of the expenditures; (b) The reimbursement requested equals the total expenditures but some of the latter are not valid.	A check requisition requesting reimbursement is not accompanied by the supporting documentation.	Refer to Question 8.2.

QUESTION 8.6

Are the reimbursements approved by an official who is not the custodian of the funds? (S)

Purpose

To determine whether reimbursements are approved by someone other than the custodian.

What Constitutes Adequate Control Procedures?

If	Impact on Adequacy of Control	Example
1. This question deals in part with controls for supervisory review and approval. Refer to the discussion under that heading on page 374.		
2. Someone other than the fund custodian approves the reimbursements,	Control is adequate because that person is more likely to detect and report any errors (deliberate or inadvertent) that may be present.	All requests for reimbursements of petty cash are approved by the assistant treasurer.

Possible Errors in Financial Statements

If: The supervisory control is absent,	Example	Effect on Audit Procedures
Refer to Question 8.5. The possible errors that could arise are similar to those that may occur when reimbursement requests are not supported by relevant vouchers.	The petty cash custodian realizes that the supervisor does not review the reimbursement and he therefore begins including invalid items.	To determine whether the related basic controls have continued to operate properly, the auditor should perform the supervisory review at year-end and for selected periods during the year. Refer to the common control procedure for supervisory review and approval (page 374) for guidance as to the procedures to follow.

QUESTION 9.2

Are supplies of unissued checks properly safeguarded? (C)

Purpose

To determine whether unissued checks are physically secured and whether access to them is limited, in order to ensure that they are not used for unauthorized or fraudulent disbursements.

What Constitutes Adequate Control Procedures?

If	Impact on Adequacy of Control	Example
1. Adequate physical safeguards for unissued checks are provided (e.g., keeping them in a fireproof safe) and physical access to the storage area is limited to the authorized custodian,	The basis for maintaining proper physical security has been established since only limited and authorized access to checks can occur.	Unissued checks are kept in a closed vault with a combination lock. Only the custodian has the combination and the vault is locked in his absence.
2. Adequate physical safeguards are not present but all checks are pre-numbered by the printer,	There may be an adequate compensating control if the company adopts appropriate alternative procedures (see "Example" column).	The following procedures constitute an adequate compensating control: (a) Unissued checks are physically inventoried weekly and compared to records of usage (e.g., cash disbursements books); (b) Stop-orders are issued immediately on all checks that cannot be accounted for; (c) The reconciliation and comparison (see (a) above) is either performed or checked by persons other than the check custodian and persons involved in the cash disbursements functions;

514

3. The custodian releases checks only with written authorization and records their release,	Proper physical security is maintained because checks are released only to authorized preparers (see Question 9.5) and this can be checked by others (see Question 9.3).	(d) The above procedures are reviewed by a responsible official. Authorized check preparers present an approved requisition for checks to be used and the custodian records the numbers of such checks. The recipient initials the register as evidence of having received the checks.
4. All new checks are sent directly to the custodian and he records their receipt,	Proper physical security is maintained because new, unissued checks are controlled without permitting unauthorized access. This procedure is especially important if checks are not pre-numbered.	All new checks are mailed or delivered directly to the custodian and the mail is opened by him; he maintains a record of the quantity of checks received.
5. The custodian is not an authorized signatory and does not have access to the mechanical check signer (see Question 9.12),	The basis for proper custodial control is established since (in the absence of forgery) the custodian cannot prepare and issue an unauthorized check unless someone else is involved.	The custodian is not a check signatory and does not have access to the mechanical check signer.
6. The company uses presigned checks,	Additional safeguards are necessary to prevent or limit unauthorized usage. A safeguard that may be considered is printing monetary limits on such checks.	All presigned checks bear the legend, "For amounts not to exceed ten dollars."

Possible Errors in Financial Statements	Example	Effect on Audit Procedures
1. **If:** Adequate safeguards over and limited access to unissued checks are not in effect,		If controls for safeguarding unissued checks are not in effect, the auditor should:
Material misappropriations of cash and related overstatements of income are possible because there is no assurance that checks are not being removed for unauthorized uses.	Unissued checks are kept in an unlocked cabinet. An employee takes some checks, forges the authorized signatures and cashes the checks.	(a) Perform extended validation procedures on bank accounts at year-end, including the following:
		(i) Review or prepare year-end bank reconciliations, ensuring that all items appearing on or returned with the bank statements have been properly accounted for;
2. **If:** The custodian receives or releases checks without recording them,		(ii) Obtain bank statements directly from the bank for a reasonable period of time in the new year (e.g., one month) and ensure that all significant or unissued items appearing on or returned with the bank statements have been properly accounted for.
Material misappropriations of cash and related overstatements of income are possible because the use of checks cannot be accounted for.	The custodian maintains checks under adequate physical security but keeps no record of new checks received or released.	
3. **If:** The custodian is an authorized signatory or has access to a mechanical check signer,		(b) Consider whether significant amounts of unauthorized checks may have been issued during the year. The auditor should consider reviewing the results of bank reconciliations performed during the year and related journal entries to determine whether significant amounts of unauthorized checks were
Material misappropriations of cash and related overstatement of income are possible because the custodian can issue unauthorized checks without involving anyone else in the company.	The custodian removes a checks without authorization, makes it payable to himself and signs it, all without (immediate) detection.	
4. **If:** The company does not maintain adequate control over presigned checks,		
Material misappropriations of cash and related overstatements of income could arise.	The custodian removes a presigned check without authorization and makes it pay-	

The likelihood that such checks will be stolen is greater because it is easier for unauthorized persons to use them, i.e., they are already signed.

able to himself. The check is not subject to normal check-signing approvals. (See Questions 9.9 and 9.10.)

issued during the year. The auditor should recognize that these procedures may not be conclusive.

QUESTION 9.3

Is the system such that: (a) the usage of checks is accounted for by persons other than those who have custody of unissued checks (9.2); (C) (b) spoiled checks are under adequate control? (C)

Purpose

1. To determine whether all checks that have been used are recorded appropriately in the cash disbursements records. To accomplish this, all checks, both used and unused, should be accounted for.

2. To determine whether all spoiled checks are controlled to ensure that:
   (a) They are actually spoiled and not used to justify omissions from cash disbursements entries;
   (b) They are not issued in error or converted to unauthorized use.

What Constitutes Adequate Control Procedures?

If	Impact on Adequacy of Control	Example
1. Checks are not pre-numbered or those numbers are not used in the cash disbursements records,	Control cannot be established over check usage because the company can never be sure that it has accounted for all checks on a timely basis.	Checks are not pre-numbered; the check preparer numbers them as used. Missing checks will not be detected until they appear on the bank statement.
2. A person other than the check custodian compares issued checks as recorded in the cash disbursements book with the in-	Control is adequate because the company can determine whether all checks that have been used are recorded. The company	The person determines that checks numbered 800 and 802 are neither on hand nor recorded as used. Stop-payment orders are

517

QUESTION 9.3 (*continued*)

If	Impact on Adequacy of Control	Example
ventory of unissued checks and investigates missing checks,	should follow up on missing checks (e.g., inquire of the persons to whom they were issued and place stop-orders with banks). The custodian should not perform the comparison because he can conceal unauthorized usage of checks.	placed with the bank on those checks.
3. Spoiled checks are retained at least until the comparison in 2 above (and the related supervisory review—see Question 9.4) has been completed,	Control is adequate because the person performing the comparison in 2 above can determine that the checks are in fact spoiled. Otherwise, the issuance of unauthorized checks could be concealed by the claim that the checks were spoiled.	All spoiled checks are returned to the check custodian and are examined by the person performing the comparison in 2 above.
4. Spoiled checks are mutilated,	Control is adequate because such checks cannot be used in error or for unauthorized disbursements.	The signature block is cut from spoiled checks.

Possible Errors in Financial Statements	Example	Effect on Audit Procedures

1. **If:** The usage of checks, including spoiled checks, is not adequately accounted for,

(a) Material misappropriations of cash and related overstatements of income are possible because the issuance of unauthorized checks may not be detected.	The custodian takes a check, makes it payable to himself, forges the signature and cashes the check.	Refer to Question 9.2. If the usage of checks is not accounted for, the effect on audit procedures is the same as when unissued checks are not adequately safeguarded.

518

(b) Cash and accounts payable may be overstated and asset and expense accounts may be understated because valid cash disbursements are not recorded.

As a result of clerical error, cash disbursements for the last three days of December are not recorded. The error is not detected because the usage of checks is not accounted for at year-end.

Refer to Question 9.2, item (a) for the effect on audit procedures. In addition, the auditor should review the December cash disbursements book to ensure that the posting of disbursements to the control account(s) is complete.

---

2. **If:** The usage of checks is not, but could be, accounted for (e.g., pre-numbered checks are used and are issued in sequence),

See 1 above.

See 1 above.

The auditor may be able to perform extended validation procedures (see Question 9.2) at an interim date, rather than at year-end, if either of the following conditions is present:

(a) The company agrees to install the desired controls during the intervening period (subject to review and test by the auditor); or

(b) The auditor exercises the control himself for the intervening period.

See 1 above.

QUESTION 9.4

Are the results of the procedures in 9.3 reviewed and approved by a responsible official? (S)

Purpose

To determine whether the control procedures in Question 9.3 are being performed regularly and effectively.

519

QUESTION 9.4 (*continued*)

What Constitutes Adequate Control Procedures?

This question deals with the controls for supervisory review and approval. Refer to the discussion under that heading on page 374.

Possible Errors in Financial Statements	Example	Effect on Audit Procedures
If: An adequate supervisory review is not performed,		
Refer to Question 9.3. In the absence of supervisory controls, the control procedures may not be performed. Accordingly, possible errors are the same as when no review is made.	The persons performing the controls in Questions 9.2 and 9.3 observe that their work is not reviewed by the supervisor and they stop exercising the controls.	The auditor should adopt the more efficient and effective of the following approaches: (a) Performing the procedures referred to in Question 9.3; (b) Performing the necessary supervisory reviews for all or selected periods of the year.

QUESTION 9.5

Are checks and bank transfers prepared by persons other than those who initiate or approve any documents which give rise to disbursements for: (a) payments of accounts payable (control objective 5); (D) (b) payrolls and payroll deductions (control objectives 6 and 7); (D) (c) reimbursements of imprest and similar funds (control objective 8)? (D)

Purpose

There is a greater likelihood that checks and bank transfers will be prepared only for valid disbursements if the persons preparing them are not involved in processing the documents giving rise to disbursements. The purpose of this question is to determine whether that division of duties is present.

520

What Constitutes Adequate Control Procedures?

If	Impact on Adequacy of Control	Example
The check preparer is not responsible for initiating documents authorizing disbursements,	Control is more effective because there is an additional person involved in the disbursements process. The check preparer may notice that certain documents do not appear to be authentic and question them, thereby reducing the opportunity for unauthorized disbursements.	The invoice supervisor forwards fictitious invoices from a dummy company. The check preparer observes that the payee's name is not familiar and that there are no supporting documents. He brings the invoice to the attention of the chief accountant and the attempted fraud is discovered.

Possible Errors in Financial Statements	Example	Effect on Audit Procedures
If: Persons who initiate or approve documents giving rise to disbursements also prepare checks and bank transfers,		
It is more likely that erroneous or fraudulent payments may be made, resulting in:		1. Initially, the auditor should determine if the control procedures discussed in Questions 9.9 and 9.10 are being performed effectively. If so, he may be able to conclude that the check signers' review of supporting documents (9.10) together with the separation of duties contemplated in 9.9 provides reasonable assurance that only valid cash disbursements are being made.
(a) Overstatement of assets;	A fictitious invoice is debited to fixed assets.	
(b) Understatement of liabilities;	A fraudulent payment is debited to accounts payable but the related liability was never recorded.	2. If the control procedures in Questions 9.9 and 9.10 are not effective for this
(c) Misclassification of expenses;	Payment of a fictitious freight bill is charged to freight expense rather than being identified as a fraud loss.	
(d) Failure to discover a contingent asset.	See (a), (b) and (c) above. The company has a claim against the persons who stole the money.	

521

QUESTION 9.5 (*continued*)

Possible Errors in Financial Statements	Example	Effect on Audit Procedures
		purpose, the auditor should perform extended validation procedures at year-end on the affected accounts:
		(a) Assets. Vouch and physically inspect significant additions or ending balances, as appropriate;
		(b) Accounts payable. Confirm with suppliers and/or reconcile suppliers' statements with recorded liabilities;
		(c) Transactions during the year. If the auditor wishes to determine the extent to which fraudulent payments may have been made (e.g., because disclosure is required in the financial statements or as a client service), he should consider vouching recorded disbursements with supporting documents for all or part of the year. The auditor should recognize that these procedures may not be conclusive.

QUESTION 9.6

Are checks and bank transfers prepared only on the basis of evidence that the validity of the transactions has been confirmed in accordance with the company's procedures, in respect of: (a) payments of accounts payable (control objective 5); (b) payrolls and payroll deductions (control objectives 6 and 7); (c) reimbursements of imprest and similar funds (control objective 8)?

Purpose

To determine whether checks and bank transfers are prepared only on the basis of appropriately approved supporting documentation.

What Constitutes Adequate Control Procedures?

If	Impact on Adequacy of Control	Example
1. The checks and bank transfers are prepared based on the original approved supporting documents,	Control is adequate because such documentation serves as the best evidence that a valid transaction requiring a cash disbursement has occurred.	(a) All requests for accounts payable disbursements are accompanied by approved suppliers' invoices. (b) All requests for payroll disbursements are accompanied by an approved payroll.
2. Checks and bank transfers are prepared based on substitute documents,	Control may not be adequate because errors, either deliberate or inadvertent, may be made in preparing the substitute documents.	Accounts payable disbursements are based on a list of vendors and amounts received from the invoice clerk. This procedure by itself is not adequate because there is no evidence of supervisory approval of the list.
3. Persons who prepare checks and bank transfers are knowledgeable about the company's controls and operations,	Control will be more effective because the preparers are more likely to detect invalid disbursements requests.	The preparers are familiar with the signatures of persons authorized to approve disbursements requests.
4. There is a supervisory review to determine that checks or bank transfers are	Control is adequate because there is greater assurance that checks or bank transfers are	A supervisor test checks the work of check preparers to determine if they are in fact

523

If	Impact on Adequacy of Control	Example
prepared on the basis of valid documentation,	prepared only on the basis of valid documentation. This procedure is more important in situations where: (a) Check signatories are not familiar with or do not closely supervise the company's transactions; (b) Substitute documents are used since there is a greater need to assure that evidence used as a basis for making disbursements is valid.	preparing checks only on the basis of valid documentation.

Possible Errors in Financial Statements	Example	Effect on Audit Procedures
If: The company's procedures do not ensure that checks and bank transfers are prepared only for valid transactions,		
Refer to Question 9.5. It is more likely that fraudulent or erroneous payments can be made.	Refer to Question 9.5 for various examples of possible errors.	Refer to Question 9.5 for the effect on audit procedures.

QUESTION 9.7

Are checks and bank transfers for transactions which, because of their nature, do not pass through the normal approval procedures as referred to in 9.6 (e.g. purchase of investments, payment of dividends, repayment of debt) initiated only on the basis of proper documentation of the validity of the transactions?

Purpose

To determine whether checks and bank transfers related to transactions outside the normal control procedures are prepared only on the basis of proper documentation supporting the validity of those transactions.

What Constitutes Adequate Control Procedures?

If	Impact on Adequacy of Control	Example
1. Disbursement requests are supported by original documents and are authorized by a responsible official (see Question 9.8),	Control is adequate because such documentation serves as the best evidence that a valid transaction requiring a cash disbursement has occurred.	A request for disbursement relating to the purchase of securities is supported by a broker's invoice and approved by the treasurer.
2. Standard check requisition forms are used for such disbursement requests,	Control is adequate because using a standard requisition form ensures that information and approvals required by company procedures are included in the documentation.	The check requisition form includes space for a description of the transaction, the amount, account to be charged and appropriate approvals.
3. The standard check requisition forms are kept in the custody of a responsible official,	Control is enhanced because disbursements will not be made without the standard form being released by the responsible official.	The treasurer acts as custodian of check requisition forms for payment of purchased securities.
4. Persons who prepare checks and bank transfers are knowledgeable about the company's controls and operations,	Control will be more effective because the preparers are more likely to detect invalid disbursements requests.	The preparers are familiar with the signatures of persons authorized to approve disbursements requests.
5. There are many transactions not subject to normal control procedures,	The company should install more formal basic and disciplinary control procedures similar to those found in Control Objectives 4 and 5.	The company engages in several securities transactions every day.

If	Impact on Adequacy of Control	Example
6. There is a supervisory review to determine that checks or bank transfers are prepared on the basis of valid documentation,	Control is adequate because there is greater assurance that checks or bank transfers are prepared only on the basis of valid documentation. This procedure is more important in situations where check signatories are not familiar with or do not closely supervise the company's transactions.	A supervisor test checks the work of check preparers to determine if they are in fact preparing checks only on the basis of valid documentation.

Possible Errors in Financial Statements	Effect on Audit Procedures	Example
If: The company's procedures do not ensure that checks and bank transfers are prepared only for valid transactions,		
Refer to Question 9.5. It is more likely that fraudulent payments may be made.	A check is prepared for the alleged purchase of securities based on a telephone request. However, the securities were not in fact purchased and the person making the request intends to defraud the company.	Refer to Question 9.5 for the effect on audit procedures.

QUESTION 9.8

Is the documentation in 9.7 reviewed and approved in writing by a responsible official before checks and bank transfers are initiated? (S)

Purpose

1. To determine whether checks and bank transfers related to transactions outside the normal control procedures are prepared only on the basis of proper documentation supporting the validity of those transactions and that they are approved by a responsible official.

2. Note that a "no" answer to this question should also result in a "no" answer to Question 9.7.

What Constitutes Adequate Control Procedures?

This question deals with the controls for supervisory review and approval. Refer to the discussion under that heading on page 374.

Possible Errors in Financial Statements	Example	Effect on Audit Procedures
If: The supervisory control is absent,		
Refer to Question 9.5. It is more likely that fraudulent or erroneous payments have been made.	See the example in Question 9.7. The absence of valid supporting documentation is not detected because no supervisory review is performed.	Refer to Question 9.5 for the effect on audit procedures.

QUESTION 9.9

Are checks signed by officials other than those who approve transactions for payment in respect of: (a) payment of accounts payable (control objective 5); (C) (b) payrolls and payroll deductions (control objectives 6 and 7); (C) (c) reimbursement of imprest and similar funds (control objective 8); (C) (d) other payments (9.7)? (C)

Purpose

To determine whether the indicated division of duties is present. There is a greater likelihood that checks will be issued only for valid transactions if the persons who sign checks are not also the persons who approve the underlying transactions for payment.

What Constitutes Adequate Control Procedures?

If	Impact on Adequacy of Control	Example
1. Persons who approve transactions for payment are not signatories,	Control is adequate because the signatory is a further check on the validity of the disbursement.	Disbursements are approved by the chief accountant or the controller, neither of whom is authorized to sign checks.

527

If	Impact on Adequacy of Control	Example
2. Neither the signatories nor the persons who approve transactions for payment are subordinate to one another,	Control is adequate because one function cannot instruct the other to circumvent control procedures.	Checks are approved by the controller and signed by the treasurer. They each report directly to the president.
3. All checks are signed by more than one responsible official,	Control is enhanced because more than one person reviews supporting documents (see Question 9.10) and each acts as a check on the other.	Two authorized signatures are required on each check. Each signatory reviews supporting documentation for validity.
4. Some or all checks are signed by only one responsible official,	The reviewer should carefully consider all the related controls to determine if this represents a control weakness. If there are no other weaknesses in the disbursement procedures, the reviewer may conclude that control is adequate.	The reviewer concludes that control is adequate because the controls in Questions 9.2 through 9.8 and 9.10 are effective and all checks are subject to supervisory review (see Question 9.6, item 4) before being forwarded to the signatory.
5. Signatories do not have access to un-issued checks,	Control is adequate because the signatory cannot issue an unauthorized check without someone else being involved.	Checks are signed by the treasurer, who does not have access to unissued checks.

Possible Errors in Financial Statements	Example	Effect on Audit Procedures
If: Check signers approve transactions for payment or do not exercise adequate control,		
Refer to Question 9.5. It is more likely that fraudulent or erroneous payments have been made.	Refer to Question 9.5 for various examples of possible errors.	Refer to Question 9.5, item 2, for the effect on audit procedures.

QUESTION 9.10

At the time of signing checks and bank transfers, does each signatory examine: (a) original supporting documents (e.g. invoices, payrolls, or imprest cash records) which have been checked and approved in accordance with the company's procedures (control objectives 4, 6, 7 and 8 and Question 9.7); (S) or (b) substitute documents (such as remittance advices or check requisitions) which provide adequate evidence of the validity of the related transactions? (S)

Purpose

To determine whether the signatories provide a final check on the validity of disbursements before signing checks or bank transfers. Their review would also indicate whether the controls in Questions 9.6, 9.7 and 9.8 appear to have been performed properly.

What Constitutes Adequate Control Procedures?

If	Impact on Adequacy of Control	Example
1. Each signatory examines original supporting documents,	Control is adequate because checks are signed only after the signatories have satisfied themselves as to the validity of the disbursement.	Company procedures require that supporting documentation accompany all checks to be signed. The signatories examine the documentation before signing the checks.
2. Substitute documents rather than original documents are forwarded to the check signatories,	Control is ordinarily not adequate. However, control may be adequate if *all* of the following conditions are present: (a) The controls in Questions 9.2 through 9.8 are operating effectively; (b) The check preparer has initialled or signed the substitute document as evidence that he has checked the payee and amount to the original supporting documentation;	Each check is accompanied by an approved check request. Approval procedures include the steps outlined in the adjacent column.

529

If	Impact on Adequacy of Control	Example
	(c) All substitute documents are approved by a responsible official who does not approve transactions for payment (see Question 9.9), as evidence that he has reviewed original documents and confirms the validity of the related checks; (d) All original documents are cancelled at the time of preparation of substitute documents and this is checked by the responsible official mentioned in the preceding step (see Question 9.11); (e) Substitute documents are cancelled by the signatories (see Question 9.11).	
3. The signatories are familiar with the company's control procedures,	Control is adequate because there is a greater likelihood that checks will be signed only on the basis of appropriate evidence.	The signatories know that all supporting documents must be initialled, recognize the initials of personnel authorized to approve transactions, and check each document for those initials.

Possible Errors in Financial Statements	Example	Effect on Audit Procedures
If: The signatories do not examine original supporting documents or adequate substitute documents before signing checks.		
Refer to Question 9.5. It is more likely that fraudulent or erroneous payments can be made.	Because check signers do not examine supporting documents, the check preparer prepares checks for more than the invoice amounts in order to pay for goods obtained from the same vendors for his own use.	Refer to Question 9.5, item 2.

QUESTION 9.11

Are the supporting documents effectively cancelled by, or under the control of, the signatories to prevent subsequent re-use? (C)

Purpose

To determine whether company procedures provide a safeguard against the subsequent reuse of supporting documents, either in error or intentionally, to support invalid payments.

What Constitutes Adequate Control Procedures?

If	Impact on Adequacy of Control	Example
1. Supporting documents are cancelled by the signatory at the time of signing,	Control is adequate because the documents provide evidence that they have been used.	The signatory initials each document upon signing the check.
2. Supporting documents are cancelled by someone under the signatory's control immediately after the checks are signed,	Control is adequate because the documents provide evidence that they have been used.	The signatory's secretary stamps each document with a "paid" stamp immediately after the checks are signed.
3. Supporting documents are returned for cancellation to the check preparers or persons who process disbursements for payment,	Control is not adequate because additional erroneous checks can be prepared, either inadvertently or deliberately, based on those documents.	(a) The check preparer does not realize that the documents have already served as the basis for a check and prepares another check. (b) The person who approves invoices for payment resubmits invoices from selected suppliers as part of a plan to defraud the company.
4. Supporting documents are not cancelled immediately,	Control is not adequate because the documents may be removed for reuse before they are cancelled.	The signatory's secretary holds documents awaiting cancellation. Some documents are removed from her desk before they are cancelled.

QUESTION 9.11 (*continued*)

Possible Errors in Financial Statements	Example	Effect on Audit Procedures
If: The cancellation of supporting documents is not adequately controlled,		
Refer to Question 9.5. It is more likely that fraudulent or invalid payments can be made.	Refer to Question 9.5 for various examples of possible errors.	Refer to Question 9.5, item 2, for the effect on audit procedures.

QUESTION 9.12

If a mechanical check signer is in use, is there adequate control over the custody and use of the signer and the signature plates? (C)

Purpose

1. To determine whether adequate physical safeguards are maintained when the mechanical check signer and signature plates are not in use.

2. To determine whether there is adequate control over the use of the mechanical check signer and signature plates.

3. Note that this question deals only with controls over a method for signing checks, i.e., mechanically rather than manually. All other questions dealing with controls over check signing, particularly Questions 9.9 through 9.11, apply to checks that are signed using a mechanical check signer as well as to checks that are signed manually. In other words, the "responsible official" (see item 1 below) should be considered the equivalent of a check signatory for purposes of completing this control objective.

What Constitutes Adequate Control Procedures?

If	Impact on Adequacy of Control	Example
1. The keys to the mechanical check signer and signature plates are under the control of a responsible official with no incompatible duties at all times,	Control is adequate because access to the machine and signature plates is restricted.	The keys to the mechanical check signer and signature plates are kept under lock and key by the treasurer.
2. The persons who operate the check signer do not have access to unissued checks,	Control is adequate because the operator cannot obtain blank checks and substitute them for the approved checks that are to be signed.	All unissued checks are in the custody of either the check custodian or the person who prepares checks, and are under adequate physical security. Neither of these persons operates the check signer.
3. The responsible official reconciles the number of checks signed with the number of checks approved for payment (normally the signer has a register of the cumulative number of checks signed),	Control is adequate because there is a comparison of the number of checks authorized with the number of checks signed, which should reveal any discrepancies.	The treasurer reviews payroll checks to be signed and notes that there are 102 in total. He checks the counter on the signer before and after the checks are run to determine that only 102 checks are signed.

Possible Errors in Financial Statements	Example	Effect on Audit Procedures
If: The controls over the use of the mechanical check signer are not adequate,		
Refer to Question 9.5. It is more likely that fraudulent payments can be made.	Refer to Question 9.5 for various examples of possible errors.	Refer to Question 9.5, item 2, for the effect on audit procedures.

After signing, are checks and bank transfers forwarded directly to the payees (or to the bank with the bank transfer lists) without being returned to the originators or others who are in a position to introduce documents into the cash disbursements system? (C)

Purpose

To determine whether control over signed checks is adequate. If signed checks are returned for mailing to persons who prepared them or who process transactions for payment, they can obtain checks issued for invalid transactions or alter checks issued for valid transactions.

What Constitutes Adequate Control Procedures?

If	Impact on Adequacy of Control	Example
1. Signed checks and bank transfers are mailed or delivered to the payee by the signatory or someone under his control soon after signing,	Control is adequate because signed checks or bank transfers do not remain in the company and the opportunity for misappropriation is minimized.	Signed checks are mailed by the signatory's secretary the same day they are signed. The secretary has no incompatible duties.
2. Signed checks are returned for mailing to the check preparers or persons involved in processing transactions for payment,	Control is not adequate because those persons can: (a) Extract invalid checks that they have prepared so that there is less chance of detection;	The signed checks are sent to the check preparer for mailing. Checks payable to fictitious suppliers are removed before mailing.
	(b) Alter valid checks by changing the payee or the amount.	The preparer changes the payee to himself.
3. The procedures in 2 above are followed,	Some control against unauthorized alterations of checks or bank transfers may be obtained if protective paper is used for all checks and the banks are instructed not to honor altered checks or bank transfers.	The payee's name cannot be altered without rendering the check invalid.

534

Possible Errors in Financial Statements	Example	Effect on Audit Procedures
If: Signed checks and bank transfers are returned to the check preparers or those involved in processing transactions for payment,		
Refer to Question 9.5. It is more likely that fraudulent payments have been made.	A check made payable to a supplier is altered so that the invoice clerk becomes the payee. Accounts payable is understated because the liability to the supplier is still open.	1. In the event of a "yes" answer to Questions 9.14 and 9.15, the auditor can extend his tests of the bank reconciliation procedures to gain assurance that misappropriations have not occurred because of the failure of this control procedure.
		2. In the event of a "no" answer to Question 9.14 or 9.15, or in the event that the tests indicate that these procedures are not operating effectively, the effect on audit procedures will be the same as that described for a "no" answer to Question 9.5.

QUESTION 9.14

Are all checks and individual bank transfers as listed in the disbursement records compared as to names, dates and amounts with transactions processed through the company's bank accounts, e.g. as part of the bank reconciliation procedures (control objective 56)?

Purpose

1. To determine whether there is a check for erroneous or invalid entries in the cash disbursements records. Intentional alterations of such records may be used to cover up alterations of checks or bank transfers.

2. To determine that a basis for valid entries in the detailed accounts payable records is provided.

QUESTION 9.14 (*continued*)

What Constitutes Adequate Control Procedures?

If	Impact on Adequacy of Control	Example
1. The payee, date, amount, signature and endorsements on all checks and bank transfers processed through the company's bank accounts are compared to disbursements records,	Control is adequate because there is a comparison between transactions processed through bank accounts and the company's records to identify any inaccurate entries in cash disbursements records or any unauthorized alterations.	Paid checks are returned by the bank monthly and are compared to the cash disbursements book.
2. Paid checks are sent directly to the person responsible for making the comparison,	Control is adequate because there is no opportunity to alter the paid checks to prevent detection of erroneous or fraudulent disbursements.	The bank mails the bank statement and related paid checks directly to the person making the comparison.
3. The person making the comparison reports all exceptions found,	Control is adequate because appropriate action can be taken to prevent recurrence of such exceptions and adjusting entries can be made to correct accounting records.	All exceptions found are reported to the corporate controller who corrects errors and establishes procedures to prevent similar occurrences.
4. There is a procedure to ensure that the comparisons are made for all bank accounts,	Control is adequate because any errors or fraudulent conversions should be detected.	The controller receives a monthly report showing the month-end cash balance, the bank accounts included in that balance, and an indication of whether the comparison has been made for each account.

Possible Errors in Financial Statements	Example	Effect on Audit Procedures
If: Cash disbursements processed through the company's bank accounts are not compared with the cash disbursements book,		
The possible errors are the same as when check preparers have incompatible duties. (See Question 9.5.) In addition, cash and income might be overstated because the cash books would not be adjusted to reflect checks that had fraudulently been increased in amount.	Signed checks are returned to the invoice clerk for mailing. He alters a check payable to a travel agent to increase the amount from $100 to $1,100. Cash and income will be overstated by $1,000 if this comparison is not made (assuming that the $1,000 cannot be recovered from the employee or the travel agent).	Refer to Questions 9.2 and 9.5 for the effect on audit procedures.

QUESTION 9.15

Is the comparison (9.14) carried out by persons other than those who prepare checks and bank transfers or who can introduce documents into the disbursements system? (D)

Purpose

To determine whether the indicated divisions of duties are present. There is a greater likelihood that the person performing the comparison will report exceptions if he does not prepare checks and bank transfers or introduce documents into the disbursements system.

What Constitutes Adequate Control Procedures?

If	Impact on Adequacy of Control	Example
The person performing the comparison does not introduce supporting documents or prepare checks or bank transfers,	Control is adequate because the person will be more likely to call attention to errors or differences.	While making the comparison, several errors in check preparation were discovered and reported. Since the person mak-

QUESTION 9.15 (continued)

If	Impact on Adequacy of Control	Example
		ing the comparison did not prepare the checks, he had no reason not to report the errors.

Possible Errors in Financial Statements	Example	Effect on Audit Procedures
If: The person making the comparison has incompatible duties,		
Refer to Question 9.14. If the comparison is done by a person with incompatible duties, the errors that can arise are the same as when the comparison is not made.	While making the comparison, several errors in check preparation are discovered. Since the person making the comparison prepared the checks, he does not report the errors and the necessary adjusting entries are not made.	1. If the answer to Question 9.14 is "yes," the auditor should consider extended testing of Question 9.14 to gain assurance that those procedures are being performed properly. 2. If the answer to Question 9.14 is "no," the results of the extended testing are not satisfactory, or the auditor thinks this would be more efficient, he should apply the procedures in Questions 9.2 and 9.5.

QUESTION 10.1

Are all movements of inventories that result in postings to the detailed records required to be: (a) supported by prescribed accounting documentation; (b) properly approved?

538

Purpose

To determine whether the company's procedures require that all entries to inventory records be made only on the basis of appropriate documentation, thereby enhancing the accuracy of the records.

What Constitutes Adequate Control Procedures?

If	Impact on Adequacy of Control	Example
1. The prescribed documentation contains sufficient detail regarding the inventory,	Control is adequate because the documentation enables accurate postings to be completed.	The receiving report contains description, part number and quantity.
2. The documentation contains the movement date,	Control is adequate because the appropriate date for posting is recorded. The use of the date of entry or preparation would produce erroneous balances.	A receipt on March 6 is not posted to the detailed records until March 15; however, March 6 is recorded as the receipt date in the detailed records.
3. The documentation is approved,	Control is adequate. The degree of approval of the documentation will depend on the entry itself; however, in order to ensure that only valid entries are processed, each entry should be approved.	All receiving reports are approved by the foreman of the receiving department, who supervises the receiving function and is familiar with the goods received by the company.

Possible Errors in Financial Statements

	Example	Effect on Audit Procedures
1. **If:** Movements are not supported by prescribed accounting documentation or the documentation is not complete,		
The inventory records may be misstated and are of no value for audit purposes because no audit trail exists. In addition, there is no means of determining if only valid entries are processed.	Receiving reports are not prepared when the receiving department is busy or when the items are needed urgently by the production department.	The company should take, and the auditor should observe, a complete physical inventory at year-end.

539

QUESTION 10.1 (*continued*)

Possible Errors in Financial Statements	Example	Effect on Audit Procedures
2. If: Movement documents are not properly approved,		
The inventory records may be misstated because unauthorized or invalid entries may be processed.	Receiving reports are not approved by the receiving department foreman. This could result in invalid entries, such as a wrong part number, being recorded.	Refer to 1 above. However, if the following conditions are present, the auditor may conclude that a complete year-end physical inventory is not required: (a) The detailed inventory records are otherwise well controlled; (b) The results of the company's physical inventories during the year, including investigation of differences, are satisfactory.
3. If: Movement documents do not contain date of movement or date in records is not the movement date,		
The inventory records will be misstated because the recorded entries will not reflect the quantities on hand on a particular date and erroneous adjustments may be made.	A receipt of goods on March 6 is not recorded in the detailed records until March 12 and that date is entered therin. A cycle count conducted on March 10 reveals an apparent overage that is erroneously adjusted for.	Refer to 1 above.

QUESTION 10.2

Is the system such that it can subsequently be established that all documentation has been (a) accounted for and (b) posted to the control accounts (e.g. by sequential pre-numbering of documents and/or batches or by reconciliation of records)? (N.B. The letters (a) and (b) have been inserted for convenience and do not appear in the question in the ICQ.)

Purpose

1. To determine whether the company's procedures are such that it can determine whether all inventory movements have been posted.

2. Note that the question is not whether the documents *are* in fact accounted for. Thus, if the documentation for controlling them exists (e.g., receiving reports are pre-numbered), the auditor may be able to use it to reduce the amount of audit work otherwise required in situations where the client can, but does not, account for the documents.

What Constitutes Adequate Control Procedures?

Part (a) of this question deals with two of the controls over completeness of processing. Refer to the discussion under that heading on page 363, items 1 and 2.

Part (b) of this question deals with one of the controls over maintenance of subsidiary records supporting a control account. Refer to the discussion under that heading on page 368, item 1.

Possible Errors in Financial Statements	Example	Effect on Audit Procedures
1. **If:** There are no completeness controls over the inventory movement documentation,		
Inventory may be misstated, because there is no means of determining that all transactions have been processed or posted.	Receiving reports are not accounted for by the persons posting the inventory records.	Refer to Question 10.1, item 1.
2. **If:** There are completeness controls over the inventory movement documentation for the control account but not for the detailed records,		

Possible Errors in Financial Statements	Example	Effect on Audit Procedures
The subsidiary records may be erroneous and, if so, will not reconcile with the control account.	The inventory control account is posted from the accounting department copy of all inventory documentation, the numerical sequence of which is accounted for.	Refer to Question 10.8.

QUESTION 10.3

Is a review made on a regular basis, e.g. monthly, to determine the reasons for any documents which have not been accounted for and posted within a reasonable period of time?

Purpose

1. To determine whether the company adequately investigates unmatched items, thereby ensuring that any necessary corrective action is taken.

2. Please note that this question deals with the follow-up of documents not accounted for. The ICQ does not specifically ask if the documents *are* accounted for. However, in order to answer this question "yes," the auditor should ensure that documents are accounted for (e.g., a numerical sequence check).

What Constitutes Adequate Control Procedures?

This question deals with two of the controls over completeness of processing. Refer to the discussion under that heading on page 365, items 2 and 3.

Possible Errors in Financial Statements	Example	Effect on Audit Procedures
If: A regular review is not made,		

The effectiveness of the controls in Question 10.2 is reduced and, therefore, similar errors could arise.

A sequence check on receiving reports is performed. Numerous missing numbers are found; however, no investigative action is undertaken.

The auditor should perform the more efficient of the following procedures:
(a) Review and evaluate the amount of unmatched items at the year-end; or
(b) Perform the extended validation procedures described in Question 10.1, item 1.

QUESTION 10.4

Is evidence that all documentation has been accounted for and posted to the control account (10.3) reviewed and approved by a responsible official? (S)

Purpose

To determine whether the operation of the completeness controls is adequately reviewed and approved by a responsible official. The existence of this supervisory control helps to ensure that the basic control is exercised regularly.

What Constitutes Adequate Control Procedures?

This question deals with the controls for supervisory review and approval. Refer to the discussion under that heading on page 374.

Possible Errors in Financial Statements	Example	Effect on Audit Procedures
If: The supervisory review is not performed,		
In the absence of a supervisory control, the review procedures may not be performed.	The clerk making the review and investigation notes that the supervisor does not	To determine whether the related basic and disciplinary controls have continued

543

QUESTION 10.4 (*continued*)

Possible Errors in Financial Statements	Example	Effect on Audit Procedures
Accordingly, the possible errors are the same as when no review is made. Refer to Question 10.2.	review his work and he stops making the review and investigation.	to operate properly, the auditor should perform the supervisory review at year-end. Refer to the common control procedure for supervisory review and approval (page 374) for guidance as to the procedures to follow.

QUESTION 10.5

Are the detailed records maintained by persons other than the storekeepers? (C)

Purpose

1. To determine whether the detailed records are maintained by persons with no incompatible duties, thereby helping to ensure that the detailed records are accurate.

2. If the segregation of duties described in 1 above is not present, unauthorized entries in the detailed records could be made to conceal misappropriations.

What Constitutes Adequate Control Procedures?

This question deals with one of the controls over maintenance of subsidiary records supporting a control account. Refer to the discussion under that heading on page 370, item 2.

Possible Errors in Financial Statements	Example	Effect on Audit Procedures
If: The detailed records are maintained by the stockkeepers,		
The inventory records may be misstated because invalid or unauthorized entries may be made, without being detected, to conceal theft or misappropriation.	The stockkeeper amends the detailed records to conceal a theft.	The company should take, and the auditor should observe, a complete physical inventory at year-end.

QUESTION 10.6

Are totals for posting to the control accounts established over all documentation before it is passed to the persons who post the detailed records?

Purpose

1. To determine whether control totals are established before the details are passed to the person who posts the detailed records. If they are not, the control account will not serve its intended purpose, i.e., to act as a control over the processing of transactions in the subsidiary records. Items could be added to or removed from the detail of transactions to be posted without such alterations being detected.

2. This question is relevant only when inventory records are maintained in monetary terms.

What Constitutes Adequate Control Procedures?

This question deals with one of the controls over maintenance of subsidiary records supporting a control account. Refer to the discussion under that heading on page 368, item 1.

QUESTION 10.6 (*continued*)

Possible Errors in Financial Statements	Example	Effect on Audit Procedures
If: Control totals are not established before the documentation is passed to persons who post the detailed records,		
The inventory records may be misstated because the inventory ledger clerk can add unauthorized items or delete valid items without (immediate) detection.	In order to reduce his workload, the inventory ledger clerk discards 25% of the documentation sent to him for posting.	The company should take, and the auditor should observe, a complete physical inventory at year-end.

QUESTION 10.7

Are the control accounts maintained by persons other than those who maintain the detailed records? (D)

Purpose

1. To determine whether the control accounts are maintained by persons with no incompatible duties, thereby helping to ensure that the control accounts are accurate.

2. This question is relevant only when inventory records are maintained in monetary terms.

What Constitutes Adequate Control Procedures?

This question deals with one of the controls over maintenance of subsidiary records supporting a control account. Refer to the discussion under that heading on page 370, item 2.

Possible Errors in Financial Statements	Example	Effect on Audit Procedures

If: The same persons maintain both the control account and the detailed records,

Possible Errors in Financial Statements	Example	Effect on Audit Procedures
Inventories may be misstated because the persons can conceal differences by altering one record to agree with the other.	The inventory clerk knows the detailed records do not agree with the control account and makes fictitious entries on the detailed records (affecting items that have already been cycle counted) to conceal the differences.	Refer to Question 10.6.

QUESTION 10.8

Are the balances in the detailed records periodically reconciled with the control account balances?

Purpose

1. To determine whether the accuracy of the control account and the detailed records is verified by reconciliation on a regular basis.

2. This question is relevant only when inventory records are maintained in monetary terms.

What Constitutes Adequate Control Procedures?

This question deals with one of the controls over maintenance of subsidiary records supporting a control account. Refer to the discussion under that heading on page 370, item 3.

Possible Errors in Financial Statements	Example	Effect on Audit Procedures

If: The control account and the detailed records are not reconciled periodically,

Possible Errors in Financial Statements	Example	Effect on Audit Procedures
Inventories may be misstated. This is obvious if a reconciliation and investigation	Entries recording the receipt of certain goods are made to the control account but	The auditor should reconcile the control account and the detailed records at year-

QUESTION 10.8 (*continued*)

Possible Errors in Financial Statements	Example	Effect on Audit Procedures
of differences reveals that the control account is wrong. However, inventories can be misstated even if an investigation of differences reveals that the control account is correct.	not to the detailed records. However, those goods require a provision for obsolescence of 50% of their cost. The provision is understated because it is based on detailed records that do not reflect the complete book inventory of those items.	end and investigate any differences.

QUESTION 10.9

Are there adequate procedures for investigating differences disclosed by the reconciliations (10.8) before any adjustments are made?

Purpose

1. To determine whether the investigation of differences is adequate. If it is not, the reconciliation procedures are incomplete.

2. This question is relevant only when inventory records are maintained in monetary terms.

What Constitutes Adequate Control Procedures?

This question deals with one of the controls over maintenance of subsidiary records supporting a control account. Refer to the discussion under that heading on page 371, item 4.

Possible Errors in Financial Statements	Example	Effect on Audit Procedures
If: The differences disclosed by the reconciliation are not investigated,		

The reconciliation procedure is incomplete and the possible errors are the same as if the reconciliation was not performed. Refer to Question 10.8.

The company performs the reconciliation monthly but investigates only significant differences. However, unbeknown to the company, a small difference is actually the net effect of a significant error that should be corrected and a significant valid reconciling item that need not be adjusted.

The auditor should investigate all differences disclosed by the year-end reconciliation.

QUESTION 10.10

Are the reconciliations and investigation of differences (10.8 and 10.9) either performed or checked by individuals other than those who: (a) post the detailed records; (D) (b) are responsible for the physical custody of the stock; (C) (c) maintain the control account? (D)

Purpose

1. To determine whether the persons performing the reconciliations and investigations have no incompatible duties, thereby helping to enhance their reliability.

2. This question is relevant only when inventory records are maintained in monetary terms.

What Constitutes Adequate Control Procedures?

This question deals with one of the controls over maintenance of subsidiary records supporting a control account. Refer to the discussion under that heading on page 372, item 5.

Possible Errors in Financial Statements	Example	Effect on Audit Procedures
If: Persons with incompatible duties either perform or check the reconciliations and investigations,		
The possible errors are similar to those that may arise if the reconciliations and investi-	The person who maintains the detailed records performs the reconciliation and	Ordinarily, the auditor should perform the procedures set forth in Question 10.8. How-

Possible Errors in Financial Statements	Example	Effect on Audit Procedures
gations are not completed. Refer to Question 10.8.	conceals the differences in order to avoid criticism of his job performance.	ever, if it would be more efficient, the auditor may, instead, increase his tests of the controls covered by Questions 10.8 and 10.9, both at year-end and for selected periods during the year.

QUESTION 10.11

Are the reconciliations in 10.10 reviewed and approved by a responsible official? (S)

Purpose

1. To determine whether the reconciliations and investigations are suitably reviewed and approved.

2. The existence of the supervisory control described in 1 above helps to ensure that the basic control is exercised regularly.

3. This question is relevant only when inventory records are maintained in monetary terms.

What Constitutes Adequate Control Procedures?

This question deals with the controls for supervisory review and approval. Refer to the discussion under that heading on page 374.

Possible Errors in Financial Statements	Example	Effect on Audit Procedures
If: The supervisory control is absent,		

550

In the absence of a supervisory control, the reconciliations and investigations may not be performed adequately or at all. Accordingly, the possible errors are the same as when no review is made. Refer to Question 10.8.

The person performing the reconciliation and investigation notes that the supervisor does not review his work. Accordingly, he decides to do these jobs only when time permits.

The auditor should perform the supervisory review at the year-end and extend his level of functional tests on the reconciliations and investigations.

QUESTION 10.12

In cases where adjustments to the detailed records are required and amounts are not easily quantified (e.g. losses due to evaporation) do the methods used to determine such adjustments appear reasonable?

Purpose

To determine whether all special adjustments are made only on the basis of approved and reasonable methods.

What Constitutes Adequate Control Procedures?

If	Impact on Adequacy of Control	Example
1. The results obtained by the estimation procedures are compared to the actual results when the physical inventory is taken,	Control is adequate because the company's estimation techniques can be modified based on actual results.	A mining company estimates "weather" losses to stockpiles based on past experience. The actual losses, as determined when the stockpile is completely used up, are considered when revising the estimated loss factor.
2. The estimation technique is changed to reflect changes in the company's operations,	Control is adequate because the recorded inventory should approximate the physical quantity on hand.	See 1. The mining company provides physical protection for its stockpiles and reduces the estimated loss factor.

551

Possible Errors in Financial Statements	Example	Effect on Audit Procedures
If: The estimation methods used by the company are not reasonable,		
Inventories may be misstated because the recorded amount will not approximate physical quantities on hand.	A mining company estimates its "weather" losses on outdoor stockpiles at 2% per annum. However, physical inventory results suggest that such losses approximate 10% per annum.	1. If the auditor believes that the losses can be reliably estimated by varying the company's method, he should prepare or review the necessary computations. Using the example in the adjacent column, the company adjusts its estimated losses to 10% per annum and the auditor is satisfied. 2. If the auditor believes that the losses cannot be reliably estimated, the company should take, and the auditor should observe, a physical inventory at year-end.

QUESTION 10.13

Are separate general or subsidiary ledger accounts maintained for all adjustments to inventory valuations (e.g. for provisions, variances, adjustments arising on physical verification)?

Purpose

To determine whether inventory adjustments are appropriately segregated in the accounts. If separate accounts are maintained, the company can identify readily the amounts of those adjustments; that information should assist the company in evaluating the effectiveness of its inventory control procedures.

What Constitutes Adequate Control Procedures?

If	Impact on Adequacy of Control	Example
Separate accounts are maintained,	Control is adequate because the amounts of the adjustments can be obtained readily.	Separate subsidiary accounts are maintained for all inventory adjustments.

Possible Errors in Financial Statements	Example	Effect on Audit Procedures

If: Separate accounts for inventory adjustments are not maintained,

Inventory may be overstated because the failure to identify such adjustments may conceal the existence of large losses that would, in turn, suggest the need for year-end physical inventory counts and/or increased estimated loss provisions.	The company records all inventory adjustments as part of its cost of sales entry without separate identification. The existence of large losses is thereby obscured.	The auditor should obtain or prepare an analysis of all physical inventory adjustments for the year and adjust his audit procedures accordingly. See Question 10.12.

QUESTION 10.14

Are areas where materials and supplies are held protected against access by unauthorized personnel? (C)

Purpose

1. To determine whether the company's control procedures prevent unauthorized access to inventories and the consequent risk of theft or misappropriation.

2. If the control described in 1 above is not carried out, the company has no means to ensure that the physical inventory is safeguarded and that the records reflect actual physical inventory on hand.

553

What Constitutes Adequate Control Procedures?

If	Impact on Adequacy of Control	Example
1. Access to the inventory storage areas is restricted by policy to authorized personnel,	Control is adequate because the likelihood of theft is reduced.	Materials and supplies inventory is kept in a locked storeroom to which only authorized personnel have a key.
2. There is adequate physical security over inventory storage areas,	Control is adequate because the likelihood of theft, unauthorized destruction or damage (e.g., by fire) is reduced.	Materials and supplies inventory stored outside is kept in a fenced, well-lit area and entrances and exits are either observed by a guard or controlled by lock and key.
3. All shipments are required to be supported by appropriate documentation and are checked upon leaving the company's premises,	Control is adequate because all goods are controlled and can be accounted for. (See Control Objectives 3, 31 and 32.)	A gatekeeper inspects all goods leaving the premises. He counts the goods and compares the quantity to the appropriate copy of a properly approved shipping advice.

Possible Errors in Financial Statements	Example	Effect on Audit Procedures
If: Materials and supplies inventories are not adequately protected against unauthorized access,		
Inventories may be overstated because of theft, damage or failure to record valid shipments.	Company employees are able to steal inventory because it is unprotected.	The company should take, and the auditor should observe, a complete physical inventory at year-end.

QUESTION 10.15

Are all materials and supplies inventories physically verified at least annually, either by cycle or periodic counts (control objective 51)?

Purpose

1. To determine whether the company verifies the accuracy of its inventory records by physical count at least annually.

2. This question does not deal with the adequacy of the physical inventory procedures (see Control Objective 51).

What Constitutes Adequate Control Procedures?

If	Impact on Adequacy of Control	Example
All classes of materials and supplies inventory are physically counted at least once a year, either by cycle, periodic, or year-end counts,	Control is adequate if: (a) The results of the physical inventories do not indicate that significant adjustments to book inventory are required; (b) The counts are made at year-end or at date(s) reasonably close to year-end (depending upon the adequacy of other controls).	The company counts all materials and supplies inventory on a cycle basis twice a year, once during the first half and again during the second half. The company knows of no weaknesses in the relevant internal controls. Differences disclosed by the counts, which are not material, are investigated and, where necessary, adjusted promptly.

Possible Errors in Financial Statements

	Example	Effect on Audit Procedures
If: Materials and supplies inventories are not subject to adequate physical verification during the year,		
Inventory may be misstated because the records may not reflect the goods actually on hand.	The company's control over posting issue slips to the detailed records has broken down and, consequently, materials and supplies inventory is overstated.	The company should take, and the auditor should observe, a year-end physical inventory of those classes of materials and supplies inventory that have not been adequately physically verified during the year.

555

QUESTION 11.1

Are formal written requests and authorizations required for the following (if appropriate, over a certain limit): (a) individual property, plant and equipment additions; (b) individual property, plant and equipment disposals; (c) major maintenance or repair of property, plant and equipment; (d) expenditures on property, plant and equipment over the amount initially authorized?

Purpose

To determine whether all significant non-routine expenditures and dispositions of assets are properly authorized.

What Constitutes Adequate Control Procedures?

If	Impact on Adequacy of Control	Example
1. Written authorizations are obtained for all the matters discussed in the question,	Control is adequate because non-routine expenditures cannot be made without appropriate approval.	The board of directors approves "capital expenditure authorizations" for all additions and disposals and for maintenance projects costing $5,000 or more. The board also approves all overruns exceeding $10,000 or 10% of the estimated cost, whichever is less.
2. Written authorizations are obtained only for expenditures over a specified monetary amount,	The reviewer should evaluate the reasonableness of the specified amount and determine whether there are sufficient controls to ensure that all expenditure over that amount is authorized in writing. If the specified amount is too high, then material unauthorized expenditure may occur.	Board approval of "capital expenditure authorizations" is required only for expenditures over $10,000. Proposed expenditures of less than $10,000 are authorized by the president.

Possible Errors in Financial Statements	Example	Effect on Audit Procedures
If: Written authorizations are not obtained,		
1. Property, plant and equipment (and income) may be overstated because:		
(a) Assets were acquired that were not needed;	The distribution manager acquired 5 new, special-purpose trucks. However, the board of directors had decided to ship the company's goods by rail and the trucks must be sold at a loss.	The auditor should review with appropriate senior company officials the usefulness to the company of assets acquired during the year.
(b) Capitalized overruns include wasted expenditures that should be expensed.	A company decides to build a machine for an estimated cost of $50,000, rather than to purchase a similar machine for $60,000. However, because of inexperience, the machine actually costs $75,000. Some portion of the overrun probably should be expensed.	The auditor should review the reasons for overruns on capital projects and evaluate the appropriateness of the related accounting.
2. Property, plant and equipment may be understated because capital items may be included in repairs and maintenance expense.	A company requires board approval for acquisitions of property, plant and equipment but not for major maintenance and repair projects. Local managers who wish to avoid the approval process charge asset purchases to maintenance expense.	The auditor should: (a) Vouch major repair and maintenance expenditures and consider whether they have been properly classified; (b) During plant tours, inventory observation, and the like, consider whether there are any significant property, plant and equipment items that have not been recorded as additions.

557

QUESTION 11.2

Do the above requests include: (a) the reasons for the expenditures or disposals; (b) the estimated amount of expenditures?

Purpose

To determine whether capital expenditure authorizations contain sufficient detail to provide adequate information for the persons who approve them.

What Constitutes Adequate Control Procedures?

If	Impact on Adequacy of Control	Example
The authorizations state the reasons for the project and the estimated amount of expenditures,	Control is adequate because there is sufficient information to make the approvals meaningful.	The capital expenditure authorization includes a description of the assets to be acquired, their estimated cost, the reason for the expenditure (e.g., to reduce labor costs), any related dispositions of assets, and the proposed accounting (see Question 11.6).

Possible Errors in Financial Statements	Example	Effect on Audit Procedures
1. **If:** The reason for the expenditure or disposal is not given,		
Acquisitions or disposals may be duplicated or made unnecessarily because the official approving them does not have sufficient details to judge their validity.	An authority for the purchase of a new typewriter does not state why the typewriter is needed (e.g., as replacement of old machine).	See Question 11.1, item 1(a).

2. If: The estimated amount of expenditure is not given,

Invalid or excess payments may be made because the estimated amount acts as a measure of reasonableness of expenditure.	The official authorizing an acquisition of a new office machine considers $10,000 a reasonable price. However, because the estimated cost was not entered on the authorization, the company paid $15,000 for the machine.	The auditor should consider whether the accounting for any invalid or excessive payments is appropriate.

QUESTION 11.3

Where the expenditure is for the replacement of an existing asset, is the system such that the related retirement or disposal is accurately recorded in the accounts?

Purpose

To determine whether the company's control procedures are such that all assets no longer in use or disposed of are properly recorded as retirements.

What Constitutes Adequate Control Procedures?

If	Impact on Adequacy of Control	Example
The written approval for a capital expenditure indicates that an existing asset will be replaced,	Control is adequate if the company's procedures ensure that the asset will be retired in the accounts when it is removed from service.	(a) The company's procedures require that all the accounting entries related to each capital project be summarized and approved each quarter. The approval process includes comparing the summarization to the written approval for capital expenditures, at which time any failure to record a retirement would be noticed and corrected.

559

If	Impact on Adequacy of Control	Example
		(b) When the capital expenditure is approved by the board, the company immediately makes the entry to record the assets to be removed from service (less any depreciation related to the period between date of authorization and estimated date of removal from service). The chief accountant ensures that an entry is made for each approved capital expenditure.

Possible Errors in Financial Statements	Example	Effect on Audit Procedures
If: The company's procedures do not ensure that all replaced assets are retired from the accounts,		
Property, plant and equipment and income may be overstated because an asset no longer in the company's use or possession is still recorded in the accounts.	An office machine was traded in on a new machine and, although the new machine was capitalized, the old machine remained on the books.	1. The auditor should review additions for the year to determine if they are replacements. If so, the auditor should ensure that the replaced assets have been correctly accounted for. 2. If the company has performed a physical verification of its property, plant and equipment (Control Objective 54), the above procedure should be performed only for the period since the last verification.

3. The auditor should review miscellaneous income accounts for evidence of sale or disposal of assets. Where applicable, the auditor should determine that those assets have been retired.

QUESTION 11.4

Are the above requests authorized by the Board of Directors or, if amounts are under a specified limit, by designated officials?

Purpose

To determine whether all capital expenditures are authorized by the board of directors or designated officials before the work begins.

What Constitutes Adequate Control Procedures?

If	Impact on Adequacy of Control	Example
1. The board of directors authorizes all capital expenditures,	Control is adequate because all capital expenditures are appropriately approved.	All capital expenditures are approved by the board of directors.
2. The board of directors authorizes all capital expenditures over a specified monetary amount,	The reviewer should evaluate the reasonableness of the specified amount. If it is too high, the board may not approve major capital expenditure projects that it should review.	The board authorizes capital expenditures over $10,000. Amounts below $10,000 are approved by the chief executive officer.

QUESTION 11.4 (*continued*)

Possible Errors in Financial Statements	Example	Effect on Audit Procedures
If: Requests are not authorized by the board or designated officials (as appropriate),		
Refer to Question 11.1. The errors that can arise are similar to those that may occur if written authorizations are not used.	The production manager buys two new machines to make a particular product. However, the board has decided to discontinue that product and the machines must be sold at a loss.	Refer to Question 11.1.

QUESTION 11.5

Are the actual expenditures compared with the authorized requests and approvals obtained for excess expenditures?

Purpose

To determine whether appropriate approvals are obtained for overruns.

What Constitutes Adequate Control Procedures?

If	Impact on Adequacy of Control	Example
Actual expenditures and estimates to complete are compared to authorized amounts, and overruns are submitted to the board or designated officials for approval,	Control is adequate because the excess expenditures are approved by the persons who approved the estimated expenditures. In this regard, control is enhanced if:	Company prepares a summary of capital projects monthly. Supplemental requests are forwarded to the board for all projects that have or are expected to overrun.

(a) The approvals are obtained before the overruns are incurred;
(b) The accounting treatment of the overruns is also approved.

Possible Errors in Financial Statements	Example	Effect on Audit Procedures
If: Overruns are not approved,		
Refer to Question 11.1, item 1(b).	Refer to Question 11.1, item 1(b).	Refer to Question 11.1, item 1(b).

QUESTION 11.6

Is the allocation of expenditure between capital expenditures and charges to current operations approved as part of the authorization for the expenditure?

Purpose

To determine whether the accounting classification of the expenditure is approved by the board or the designated officials, thus helping to ensure that the classifications are appropriate.

What Constitutes Adequate Control Procedures?

If	Impact on Adequacy of Control	Example
Allocation is approved as part of the authorization procedure,	Control is adequate because this should provide assurance that the accounting classification is correct. Ordinarily, the account coding of the actual disbursements will be based on the accounting classification approved as part of the written approval for a capital expenditure.	Written approvals for capital expenditures include the ledger account allocation, which is completed before board (or designated official) approval.

563

QUESTION 11.6 (*continued*)

Possible Errors in Financial Statements	Example	Effect on Audit Procedures
If: The allocation of expenditures is not approved,		The auditor should:
Property, plant and equipment and repairs and maintenance expense may be misstated because invalid or incorrect allocation of expenditures may pass undetected.	A major repair on a machine is capitalized instead of being expensed.	(a) Review the levels of capitalization, disposals, and repairs and maintenance expense for reasonableness in relation to budgets and to the previous year. Obtain explanation for any large or unusual fluctuations;
		(b) Review the propriety of the account distribution for all major additions and disposals during the year;
		(c) Vouch significant charges to the repairs and maintenance expense account and review the propriety of the account allocation.

QUESTION 12.1

Are property, plant and equipment subsidiary ledgers maintained for the following classifications: (a) land and buildings; (b) leasehold improvements; (c) plant and machinery; (d) furniture, fixtures and fittings; (e) office equipment; (f) motor vehicles; (g) property, plant and equipment leased or loaned to third parties; (h) other property, plant and equipment (specify below)?

Purpose

To determine whether adequate subsidiary records are maintained for each category of property, plant and equipment.

What Constitutes Adequate Control Procedures?

If	Impact on Adequacy of Control	Example
Subsidiary ledgers are maintained for each category of property, plant and equipment.	The company has records that should enable it to maintain control over property, plant and equipment.	The subsidiary ledger consists of a card for each asset. The card includes description, location, date of acquisition, identifying number, cost, depreciation method and rate, salvage value, depreciation for the period and cumulative depreciation.

If	Possible Errors in Financial Statements	Example	Effect on Audit Procedures
If: Subsidiary ledgers are not maintained,	Property, plant and equipment may be misstated because the company cannot determine the individual items that comprise the control account balance and whether they are still used in the company's business.	The company maintains only general ledger control accounts.	Depending on the circumstances, the auditor should: (a) Arrange for the company to take and price a complete or partial inventory of property, plant and equipment at or near year-end; or (b) Perform extended validation procedures on additions and retirements during the year, paying particular attention to the possibility of unrecorded disposals.

QUESTION 12.2

Do the subsidiary ledgers provide the following details for each item: (a) adequate identification; (b) cost; (c) accumulated depreciation?

Purpose

To determine whether there is sufficient information in the subsidiary ledgers to identify each asset and permit reconciliation of cost and accumulated depreciation with the control accounts.

What Constitutes Adequate Control Procedures?

If	Impact on Adequacy of Control	Example
1. Individual assets can be identified in the subsidiary ledgers,	Control is adequate because the subsidiary ledger contains sufficient detail to enable physical verification of the assets at a later date (see Control Objective 54).	The subsidiary ledger includes description, date of acquisition, supplier, location and, where possible, an identification number that is also marked on the asset.
2. The subsidiary ledgers contain original cost, depreciation rate and accumulated depreciation,	Control is adequate because the subsidiary ledgers provide a control on the accuracy of the general ledger.	Errors in posting to either record are revealed when the two records are reconciled.

Possible Errors in Financial Statements	Example	Effect on Audit Procedures
1. **If:** Individual assets cannot be identified,		
Property, plant and equipment may be misstated because physical verification of individual assets is not possible.	The subsidiary records contain information only as to cost and year of acquisition.	See Question 12.1.

2. **If:** The subsidiary records do not include cost,

Property, plant and equipment may be misstated because the company cannot determine whether the cost of assets on hand agrees with the control account.	The subsidiary ledgers identify the individual assets but contain no information as to cost.	Depending on the circumstances, the auditor should: (a) Arrange for the company to price the subsidiary ledgers at year-end; or (b) See Question 12.1, item (b). The auditor should determine whether the additions and disposals recorded in the general ledger agree with the activity recorded in the subsidiary records.

3. **If:** The subsidiary records do not include accumulated depreciation,

Property, plant and equipment (net) may be misstated because the company cannot determine whether the accumulated depreciation on the individual assets agrees with the control account.	The subsidiary ledgers have cost and identification details only.	If the auditor is not satisfied as to accumulated depreciation based on other tests, he should arrange for the company to calculate accumulated depreciation on the individual assets and compare the total with the control account at year-end. If the company will not make the calculations, the auditor should make them himself.

QUESTION 12.3

Are the subsidiary ledgers posted regularly, e.g. quarterly, for: (a) cost of additions and disposals; (b) depreciation for the period?

Purpose

To determine whether subsidiary ledgers are updated on a regular basis. The update helps to ensure their completeness and accuracy.

What Constitutes Adequate Control Procedures?

If	Impact on Adequacy of Control	Example
1. The subsidiary ledgers are updated on a regular basis,	Control is adequate because the likelihood of error is reduced.	The subsidiary ledgers are updated and balanced with the general ledger monthly.
2. The subsidiary ledgers are not updated regularly but are updated annually,	Control is adequate as long as the procedures in Questions 12.4 to 12.6 are performed.	The subsidiary ledgers are posted annually as part of the year-end closing procedures.

Possible Errors in Financial Statements	Example	Effect on Audit Procedures
1. If: The subsidiary ledgers are not updated regularly,		
Property, plant and equipment and income may be misstated because the subsidiary ledgers may not agree with the control accounts.	The subsidiary ledger is updated only when time permits. Upon updating, the company discovers that a number of invoices have been processed and paid twice in error, so that the control account is overstated.	The auditor should determine that the posting is up-to-date before he performs his year-end validation procedures. He should also extend his tests of the reconciliation of the subsidiary ledgers with the control account.
2. If: The subsidiary ledgers are updated regularly for cost only,		
Accumulated depreciation may be misstated because of errors or invalid entries in the depreciation control account.	Depreciation is entered in the subsidiary ledger annually.	See Question 12.2, item 3.

QUESTION 12.4

Are the subsidiary ledgers balanced at least annually with the general ledger for: (a) cost; (b) accumulated depreciation?

Purpose

To determine whether the subsidiary ledgers are regularly agreed to the general ledger control accounts, thereby helping to ensure their accuracy.

What Constitutes Adequate Control Procedures?

This question deals with one of the controls over maintenance of subsidiary records supporting a control account. Refer to the discussion under that heading on page 370, item 3.

Possible Errors in Financial Statements	Example	Effect on Audit Procedures
1. If: The reconciliation is not completed,		
Property, plant and equipment may be misstated because the company has no means of determining the accuracy of the control accounts.	The person maintaining the subsidiary ledgers records disposals based on information received from the plant manager. However, through oversight, the entries are not recorded in the general ledger. The error is not detected because the reconciliation is not performed.	The auditor should add the balances in the subsidiary ledgers, compare the totals with the control account and investigate any differences at year-end.
2. If: The reconciliation is prepared for cost only,		
Accumulated depreciation may be misstated because the company cannot determine the accuracy of the control account.	Accumulated depreciation calculation or posting errors are not detected.	The auditor should perform the procedures in 1 above for accumulated depreciation at year-end.

QUESTION 12.5

Are there adequate procedures for investigating differences disclosed by the reconciliations (12.4) before any adjustments are made?

Purpose

To determine whether all differences disclosed by reconciliations are adequately investigated before adjustments are made.

What Constitutes Adequate Control Procedures?

This question deals with two of the controls over maintenance of subsidiary records supporting a control account. Refer to the discussion under that heading on page 371, items 4 and 5.

Possible Errors in Financial Statements	Example	Effect on Audit Procedures
If: Differences are not investigated before adjustments are made,		
Refer to Question 12.4. The possible errors are the same as those that may occur if the reconciliation is not performed.	The company adjusts the control account to agree with the total of the subsidiary ledgers. However, this entry is erroneous because the control account was correct. The difference was caused by a posting error in the subsidiary ledger.	The auditor should: (a) Examine the year-end reconciliations and investigate reconciling items; (b) Vouch adjustments made during the year to determine their validity.

QUESTION 12.6

Are the results of the procedures in 12.5 reviewed and approved by a responsible official before any adjustments to the accounts are made? (S)

Purpose

To determine whether such a review is performed. The review helps to ensure that the basic control is exercised regularly and effectively.

What Constitutes Adequate Control Procedures?

This question deals with the controls for supervisory review and approval. Refer to the discussion under that heading on page 374.

Possible Errors in Financial Statements	Example	Effect on Audit Procedures
If: The supervisory control is absent,		
Refer to Question 12.4. The possible errors are the same as those that may occur when no adequate reconciliation procedures exist.	The persons performing the reconciliations and investigations observe that the supervisor does not review their work and they stop making the reconciliations and investigations.	To determine whether the basic controls have continued to operate properly, the auditor should perform the supervisory review at year-end and at dates during the year when adjustments were made. Refer to the common control procedure for supervisory review and approval (page 374) for guidance as to the procedures to follow.

QUESTION 12.7

Are suitable records maintained of assets leased or on loan from third parties?

Purpose

1. To determine whether adequate records are maintained for leased or borrowed assets.

2. This question is not applicable to leased assets that have been capitalized by the company/lessee. Those assets should be considered when answering Question 12.1.

QUESTION 12.7 (*continued*)

What Constitutes Adequate Control Procedures?

If	Impact on Adequacy of Control	Example
The records of borrowed or leased assets indicate description, location, identifying number (where applicable) and owner,	Control is adequate because the company has a complete record of leased or borrowed assets and can distinguish them from its own assets.	The company maintains a register of leased vehicles indicating, for each vehicle, the lessor; make and model and serial number.

Possible Errors in Financial Statements	Example	Effect on Audit Procedures

If: Adequate records of leased or borrowed assets are not maintained,

| Income may be overstated and liabilities understated. Leased or borrowed assets may be stolen, destroyed or sold in error without the company's resulting liability to the owner being recorded. | Leased equipment that is obsolete is sold for scrap value but the company does not record as a liability the present value of the remaining lease payments. | The company should perform, and the auditor should test, the following procedures:
 (a) Establish a complete list of leased or borrowed assets by correspondence with lessors, review of company records such as details of rentals paid, and the like;
 (b) Determine by physical count whether all of the leased or borrowed assets are on hand;
 (c) Record a liability for any leased or borrowed assets not on hand or in use. |

QUESTION 13.1

Is the coding of the following transactions for posting to general ledger accounts checked to an appropriate extent: (a) invoices and other supporting documentation related to the payment of accounts payable; (b) payrolls; (c) reimbursements of imprest and similar funds; (d) disbursements from bank accounts not covered in (a) to (c) above; (e) depreciation of property, plant and equipment?

Purpose

To determine whether the transactions arising from the payments cycle are checked to ensure that the general ledger account coding is appropriate.

What Constitutes Adequate Control Procedures?

If	Impact on Adequacy of Control	Example
1. The person performing the check has a working knowledge of the company's business and the transactions,	Control is adequate because the checker should be able to detect errors made by the person who entered the account code.	The chief bookkeeper checks the coding of all payments cycle transactions.
2. The person performing the check has a current chart of accounts,	Control is adequate because the checker can ensure that the current codes have been used.	Both the person entering the account codes and the checker receive copies of revisions to the chart of accounts on a timely basis.

Possible Errors in Financial Statements

If	Example	Effect on Audit Procedures
Account codings are not adequately checked,		
Assets, liabilities, income and expense accounts may be misstated.	Because the entries were coded improperly, credits related to goods returned to suppliers were credited to other income rather than to inventory. As a result, income and inventory are overstated.	1. The auditor should consider whether the supervisory review (Question 13.2) provides sufficient assurance that the transactions are coded properly. 2. If not, he should adopt the more effi-

573

QUESTION 13.1 *(continued)*

Possible Errors in Financial Statements	Example	Effect on Audit Procedures
		cient of the following procedures: (a) Extend his tests of coding, including transactions during the intervening period when early validation procedures have been applied; or (b) Perform extended validation procedures at year-end on affected accounts.

QUESTION 13.2

Is the coding (13.1) of the following transactions approved by responsible officials: (a) invoices and other supporting documentation related to the payment of accounts payable; (S) (b) payrolls; (S) (c) reimbursements of imprest and similar funds; (S) (d) disbursements from bank accounts not covered in (a) to (c) above; (S) (e) depreciation of property, plant and equipment? (S)

Purpose

To determine whether the account coding and checking thereof is approved by a responsible official, thereby helping to ensure its accuracy.

What Constitutes Adequate Control Procedures?

This question deals with the controls for supervisory review and approval. Refer to the discussion under that heading on page 374.

Possible Errors in Financial Statements | Example | Effect on Audit Procedures

Possible Errors in Financial Statements	Example	Effect on Audit Procedures
If: A responsible official does not approve the account coding,		
Refer to Question 13.1. The possible errors are similar to those that may arise when the coding is not checked.	The person checking the coding notes that the supervisor does not review his work. Accordingly, he decides to make these checks only when time permits.	Refer to Question 13.1, item 2.

QUESTION 13.3

Are there adequate controls (e.g. reconciliation of totals) to verify that the summaries which are used as a basis for making the general ledger entries are arithmetically accurate in respect of: (a) invoices and other supporting documentation related to the payments of accounts payable; (b) payrolls; (c) reimbursements of imprest and similar funds; (d) disbursements from bank accounts not covered in (a) to (c) above; (e) depreciation of property, plant and equipment?

Purpose

To determine whether the company's control procedures ensure that all summaries of payments cycle transactions are checked for arithmetic accuracy before processing.

What Constitutes Adequate Control Procedures?

If	Impact on Adequacy of Control	Example
1. Summaries are checked arithmetically,	Control is adequate because any errors in addition should be detected.	The addition of the voucher register is checked by a comptometrist.
2. Summaries are agreed to independent control totals,	Control is adequate because any errors in addition should be detected.	The entries in the cash disbursements book are checked against the items marked as paid in the voucher register and the totals are compared.

QUESTION 13.3 (*continued*)

Possible Errors in Financial Statements	Example	Effect on Audit Procedures
If: The arithmetic accuracy of the posting summaries is not checked,		
Assets, liabilities, income and expense accounts may be misstated.	A voucher register is totalled at $10,000 that actually totals $11,000. The general ledger will still balance; however, purchases and accounts payable are understated.	1. The auditor should adopt the more efficient of the following approaches: (a) Extend his tests of the arithmetic accuracy of the posting summaries, including those for the intervening period when early validation procedures have been applied; or (b) Perform extended validation procedures at year-end on the accounts affected. 2. He should also bear in mind that arithmetic errors that are not self-compensating should be detected either at the time of preparing the trial balance (Questions 50.7 to 50.10) or when reconciling subsidiary ledgers with related control accounts (50.20).

QUESTION 13.4

Are the summaries referred to in 13.3 approved by a responsible official before posting to the general ledger accounts? (S)

Purpose

To determine whether the summaries are approved as being arithmetically accurate and valid before posting to the general ledger.

What Constitutes Adequate Control Procedures?

This question deals with the controls for supervisory review and approval. Refer to the discussion under that heading on page 374.

Possible Errors in Financial Statements	Example	Effect on Audit Procedures
If: A responsible official does not review the posting summaries,		
Refer to Question 13.3. The possible errors are similar to those that may arise if the posting summaries are not checked for arithmetic accuracy.	The clerk responsible for checking the addition of the voucher register observes that the responsible official never inquires about or reviews his work. Accordingly, the clerk stops making the check of additions.	Refer to Question 13.3.

E

Functional Tests and
Operational Reviews

1.   This Appendix contains instructions for documenting functional tests and operational reviews, and schedules of specimen tests.

2.   The documentation for functional tests and operational reviews consists of:

a. Program and Record of Functional Tests and Operational Reviews (PRT)—page 581;
b. Summary Sheet to (a) above—page 584;
c. Record of Control-Operation Exceptions (RCE)—page 586.

In addition, specimen tests have been prepared for many common internal accounting control techniques (page 590).

PROGRAM AND RECORD OF FUNCTIONAL TESTS AND
OPERATIONAL REVIEWS

3.   The PRT, like the ICQ, is designed to be used for more than one period. In the period of introduction, the program should be prepared in the manner described in paragraph 5 below. After management has reviewed and agreed to the program of proposed tests and reviews, photocopies may be taken for use in subsequent periods. In each of the subsequent periods, the system evaluator should consider the continued appropriateness of the program in the light of:

a.   Experience in carrying out the tests or reviews in previous periods; and

b.   Any changes in control procedures, as identified during the preparation or updating of the ICQ for the current period.

When a proposed functional test or operational review is no longer appropriate, or if different or additional tests are necessary, the program should be amended accordingly. The program should indicate proposed functional tests or operational reviews intended to be performed on a cycle basis, i.e., not every year. If substantial changes are required, for example, as a result of a fundamental change in the system, it is normally preferable to prepare a new PRT.

4.   To facilitate review, the functional tests and operational reviews should be grouped on the PRT sheet(s) in the order in which they may be carried out most efficiently. Since this is usually the order of the control objectives in the ICQ, the form is arranged in that order. However, other arrangements may also be useful; for example, tests and reviews of controls relating to the payroll activity might be listed on one sheet and those relating to fixed assets on another sheet. Tests and reviews might also be grouped by transaction type or by activity as shown on the flowcharts. The activity or other grouping to which the tests and reviews included on a PRT sheet relate should be entered individually on the PRT summary sheet under the heading "Control Objective No."

5.   Generally the PRT should be used as follows:

Preparation of Program (Period of Introduction)

a.   A separate sheet should be used for each control objective for which functional testing or an operational review is proposed.

b.   The ICQ reference for each question should be entered in column

Program and Record of Functional Tests and Operational Reviews

Control Objective No. _____

Site _____

Period _____

(1)	(2)	(3)	(4)	(5)	(6)	(7)	(8)	(9)
ICQ Ref.	Details of Test or Reason for Omitting Test	Level of Test	Prog Uart Prog Udate ram (✓)	Evidence Seen Period(s) Selected	Exceptions Yes/ No	Exceptions RCE Ref.	W.P. Ref.	Signing and Date

581

1. At the same time, the PRT page reference number should be entered on the ICQ.

c.   Complete details of tests or reviews to be performed should be entered in column 2. The specimen tests contained in this Appendix should be used as a guide in designing functional tests. A mere cross-reference to the specimen tests without further discussion of the work performed ordinarily does not constitute a satisfactory description of the functional test performed.

d.   The reasons for omitting functional tests of internal accounting controls should be recorded in column 2. Management may also give reasons for omitting reviews of operational controls.

Tests or reviews are normally omitted because:

i. there is a "No" answer to a question; or
ii. the control cannot be relied on because of other "No" answers related to the same control objective; or
iii. management has decided that testing or review is inefficient or otherwise inappropriate.

e.   The proposed levels of tests or reviews should be entered in column 3.

f.   The program should be reviewed and approved by responsible supervisory management before the tests or reviews are performed.

g.   The work in (b) to (e) above should be carried out at the same time as, or immediately following, the completion of the ICQ, preferably by the same system evaluator who prepared the flowcharts, performed the transaction reviews, and completed the ICQ for the related controls.

Updating of Program (Subsequent Periods)

h.   A mark should be placed in column 4 to indicate the continued appropriateness of the proposed functional tests or operational reviews (paragraph 3 above). If column 2 was completed for operational controls in the period of preparation of the program and such controls are not to be reviewed in the current period, the letter "o" (for operational control) should be entered in column 4 to indicate that the review will not be performed in the current period. If the operational controls were not reviewed in the period the program was prepared but are to be reviewed in the current period, columns 1, 2, and 3 should be completed as described above.

Completion of Program

i. After the functional tests or operational reviews have been carried out, the evidence seen and period(s) selected should be entered in column 5 or, if space is insufficient, on a separate working paper which should be cross-referenced in column 8. Preparation of working papers is dealt with in paragraph 8 below.

j. The existence or absence of exceptions resulting from the functional tests or operational reviews should be indicated, respectively, by a "Yes" or "No" answer in column 6. All "No" answers should be appropriately recorded on the RCE (see detailed instructions regarding the use of this form on pages 587 to 589). The RCE highlights exceptions, thus facilitating subsequent review and reporting. Details of exceptions and action taken should be recorded on a working paper which should be cross-referenced to the RCE.

k. The PRT should be signed and dated in column 9 by the person carrying out the tests or reviews.

PRT Summary Sheet

6. A PRT summary sheet should be completed each period for each cycle of the ICQ. This provides a means of evidencing:

a. Approval by responsible supervisory management of the preparation or up-dating of the program of functional tests and operational reviews;
b. Completion by the system evaluator of the functional tests and operational reviews; and
c. Review by the responsible supervisor of the work performed.

The PRT summary sheet also serves as an index to the individual PRTs. Detailed instructions for the completion of this document are contained in the notes following it.

Summary Sheet
Program and Record of Functional Tests and Operational Reviews
Record of Control-Operation Exceptions

_____ Cycle

Site_____Period_____

1. Completion of PRT and RCE

Index		Completion of Program		Completion of RCE	
Control Objective No.	File Reference	(Signature)	(Date)	(Signature)	(Date)

2. Review and Approval

   Preparation/updating of program

   Completion of program and RCE

Notes to Summary Sheet

1. *Index.* The index to the summary sheet (first two columns) should be completed each period for each control objective. If some other activity or grouping is used [see paragraph 4 above of this Appendix], the index entries should agree with the identification used in the individual PRTs.

2. *Completion of Program.* On completion of the functional tests and operational reviews relevant to each PRT, the system evaluator should sign and date the column under the heading "Completion of Program" as evidence that:

   a. The functional tests and operational reviews were carried out satisfactorily; and

   b. Any amendments or additions to the program were clearly recorded on the PRT or on a working paper cross-referenced thereto.

Similarly, the evaluator should sign and date the column under the heading "Completion of RCE" as evidence that any exceptions noted during the functional tests and operational reviews were recorded on the RCE.

3. *Review and Approval.* The supervisor should review the completed PRT, RCE, and supporting working papers. The appropriate box should be signed and dated as evidence that:

   a. The program of tests and reviews appears to have been properly completed;

   b. All exceptions noted were correctly disposed of; and

   c. Consideration was given to advising senior management immediately of any significant exceptions in internal control.

Record of Control-Operation Exceptions

Site_____   Page_____of_____
ICQ Section _____

ICQ Ref.	Nature of Control-Operation Exception and Possible Effects on Internal Accounting Control or Efficiency of Operations	Could a Material Error Arise?		Notification of Exception to Responsible Management		
		Yes/No	Justification	Informal Discussion With Site Management (Date)	Report to Senior Management (Date)	Response/ Comments (If Applicable)
(1)	(2)	(3)	(4)	(5)	(6)	(7)

Record of Control-Operation Exceptions

7.   The purpose of the RCE is to ensure that the system evaluator summarizes and considers the effect of all exceptions identified (columns 2, 3, and 4). The system evaluator is required to make a judgment as to whether a recorded exception could result in material error. The RCE also provides a record that control exceptions that may lead to a potentially material error have been discussed informally with site personnel (column 5) and considered for formal reporting to senior management (column 6). Column 7 is also provided to record any corrective action taken. For convenience, column 1 shows a cross-reference to the ICQ.

Evidence of Work Performed

8.   Sufficient detail should be recorded, either on the PRT, RCE, or a separate working paper, to enable the record, document, or other evidence examined to be identified. If complete reperformance of an internal accounting control is not appropriate, it is normally necessary to prepare a working paper to record the extent of reperformance carried out. For example, if the reconciliation of a control account is reperformed, it is ordinarily desirable to summarize the reconciliation on a working paper and indicate thereon the specific balances checked to the ledgers, the extent to which additions were reperformed, and any other tests performed. For disciplines over basic controls and operational controls, supporting working papers should be prepared to record the specific evidence examined, the procedures reperformed, or the nature and circumstances of observations.

INSTRUCTIONS FOR COMPLETING RECORD OF CONTROL-OPERATION EXCEPTIONS

1.   All control exceptions identified during functional tests or operational reviews should be recorded on the Record of Control-Operation Exceptions. Separate RCE sheets or series of sheets should usually be prepared for each relevant section of the PRT.

Internal Accounting Control Exceptions

2.   Columns 1 and 2 of the RCE are provided, respectively, to identify the numbers of the related ICQ questions (including those applicable to supplementary control objectives) and to explain the nature of the exceptions and their possible effect on the financial statements and on internal

accounting control objectives. Each exception should be described in the context of the control objective to which it relates. Guidance as to possible effects of exceptions is contained in the Internal Control Reference Manual, which indicates for each question:

    a. The items in the financial statements that are directly related thereto; and/or
    b. The possibility of major error in the financial statements, e.g., a loss may not be disclosed in the income statement or may be carried forward in the balance sheet as a fictitious asset or an understated liability.

    3.   The system evaluator should next consider whether the exceptions identified could give rise to material error. This decision must be made in the light of all the circumstances, including such factors as the number and size of the transactions affected and the existence of other control procedures that would detect a material error. The system evaluator should also consider whether an exception could have a cumulative effect on a judgment relating to any other exception, e.g., a breakdown in the capital expenditure authorization procedure combined with inadequate control over the coding of purchase invoices.

    4.   If the evaluator decides, taking all the circumstances into account, that the exception could not give rise to a material error, this decision should be recorded in column 3 and the justification for it in column 4. Such exceptions should be considered for reporting to senior management, as mentioned in paragraph 13 below.

    5.   If the evaluator believes that a material error could arise, this possibility together with the justification for the decision should be recorded in columns 3 and 4.

    6.   The information and conclusions recorded in columns 2, 3, and 4 should be discussed with site personnel to:

    a. Identify any other relevant factors that should be considered to place the exception in proper perspective; and
    b. Enable corrective action to be taken at the earliest opportunity.

The date of the discussion, the name and title of the personnel involved, and details of the discussion should be recorded in columns 5 and 7.

Operational Control Exceptions*

    7.   If operational control questions are answered, the RCE is prepared

---

*The following paragraphs may be applicable to internal accounting control exceptions as well as operational control exceptions.

in the manner described in paragraph 2 above and the following paragraphs of this section.

8. The system evaluator should consider whether the operational control exceptions identified could have implications for meeting the objectives of the internal accounting control system (see paragraphs 2 and 3 above). If it is decided that an exception could give rise to a material error, this possibility, together with the justification for the decision, should be recorded in columns 3 and 4, and the procedures described in paragraph 6 above should be followed.

9. To make the report to senior management as meaningful as possible, the system evaluator should quantify, where practicable, the effect of an exception in terms of revenue losses or cost increases. If that is not practicable, an effort should be made to determine the order of magnitude of the transactions or operations to which the control exception relates. For example, if it is not possible to determine the revenue lost or additional costs incurred due to failure to calculate economic order quantities, the system evaluator may comment on the total volume of purchases, purchased goods inventory, etc.

10. Exceptions can be evaluated in terms of monetary significance by analyzing the operational effects of failure to perform the control procedures. Considerations would include:

 a. The potential profitability significance of a control exception; and
 b. Dollarization of the effect of a control exception.

11. Operational control exceptions should be evaluated with respect to materiality. If an exception has only an insignificant effect on operations, it may be included in a miscellaneous section of, or an appendix to, the evaluator's report to senior management or excluded from the report altogether. However, all exceptions should be discussed with site personnel for possible correction.

Reporting Exceptions

13. All uncleared internal accounting control and operational control exceptions recorded on the RCE should be considered for reporting to senior management. Column 6 of the RCE should be completed to provide a record of the dates on which exceptions were reported or a note that it was not considered necessary to report them.

14. When an exception to control operations is subsequently rectified, this should be evidenced on the RCE by recording the date in column 7.

INDEX TO SPECIMEN FUNCTIONAL TESTS

Note: The purpose of this index is to provide a direct link between the ICQ for the Payments Cycle and the specimen functional tests. It lists in column (1) all the internal accounting control questions in the ICQ and provides in column (2), where applicable, a cross-reference to the typical related specimen tests.

(1) ICQ Reference	(2) Specimen Test No.	(1) ICQ Reference	(2) Specimen Test No.	(1) ICQ Reference	(2) Specimen Test No.
1.1		5.6	7	9.8	
1.17		5.7	8	9.9	
1.18		5.8	8	9.10	5
1.20	2/3	5.9	9	9.11	5
1.21	4	5.10	9	9.12	12
1.22	2	5.11	9	9.13	12
1.23	4	5.12	9	9.14	5/9
1.24	4	5.13	10	9.15	5/9
1.25	4	5.14	10		
		5.15	10		
2.1	1			10.1	
2.5	2/3	6.1		10.2	2/9
2.6	4	6.2		10.3	2/9
2.7	2	6.3		10.4	2/9
2.8	4	6.4		10.5	
2.9	4	6.5		10.6	8
2.10	4	6.6		10.7	8
2.11		6.7		10.8	9
2.12		6.8	6/9	10.9	9
2.13		6.9	6/9	10.10	9
		6.10	6	10.11	9
3.1	1	6.11	6/9	10.12	
3.3	2/3	6.12	6/9	10.13	
3.4	4	6.13	7	10.14	12
3.5	2	6.14	5	10.15	11
3.6	4	6.15(b)	12		
3.7	4			11.1	
3.8	4	7.1		11.2	
3.9		7.2	9	11.3	
		7.3	9	11.4	
4.1	5			11.5	
4.2	5	8.1(a,b)		11.6	
4.5	5	8.1(c)	11		
4.6	5	8.2		12.1	
4.7	6	8.3		12.2	
4.8	6	8.4		12.3	
4.9	7	8.5		12.4	9
4.10	7	8.6	7	12.5	9
4.11	7			12.6	9
		9.2	12	12.7	
5.1	2/3	9.3	2/3		
5.2	2/3	9.4	2/3	13.1	
5.3	2/3	9.5		13.2	7
5.4	2/3	9.6		13.3	6/8
5.5	8	9.7		13.4	7

SPECIMEN FUNCTIONAL TESTS

Nature of Control	Specimen Test
1. Control over physical movements (goods and services received, goods shipped, goods returned, services performed, goods held in store or production areas).	Visit relevant department and verify, by examination or appropriate source documents, by examination of exception reports and memoranda, and by observation of procedures, that goods are: a. moved only on the basis of valid authorizations; b. appropriately verified as to both description and quantity (e.g. weight, count); c. accurately recorded.

2A. Completeness control—sequential prenumbering.	a. Examine records, lists, or other documentary evidence indicating that the numerical sequence of prenumbered documents is periodically checked and missing numbers investigated by persons with no incompatible duties (see ICQ).
	b. Where appropriate, examine evidence indicating that the results of the procedures in (a) above have been reviewed and approved by a responsible official.
	c. Reperform control by selecting batches of documents, or entries in register and:
	  i. check numerical sequence;
	  ii. obtain satisfactory explanations for any missing numbers;
	  iii. confirm that procedures for dealing with cancelled or spoiled documents have been followed.

2B. Completeness control—batching.	a. Examine batch control registers, sheets, or other documentary evidence indicating that batch control totals have been periodically agreed with related totals derived from appropriate source documents, and that any differences have been investigated by persons with no incompatible duties (see ICQ).
	b. Where appropriate, examine evidence indicating that the results of the procedures in (a) above have been reviewed and approved by a responsible official.
	c. Reperform the control by selecting batches of documents, and:
	  i. check batch totals with batch control registers;
	  ii. inspect batch control registers and ensure that all batches have been processed;
	  iii. obtain satisfactory explanation for any discrepancies.

Nature of Control	Specimen Test
3. Completeness control—entry in register.	a. Examine register for evidence that entries therein appear to be up to date and are being systematically cleared. b. Where appropriate, examine evidence indicating that the results of the procedures in (a) above have been reviewed and approved by a responsible official. c. Reperform control by testing entries with relevant documentation to establish that the transaction has either been cleared or is a valid outstanding item. d. Confirm that procedures for dealing with cancelled or spoiled documents have been followed.
4. Control over unmatched/outstanding items.	a. Examine records or files of unmatched items and reports, listings, memoranda, or other evidence indicating that the records are periodically reviewed, long-outstanding items investigated by persons with no incompatible duties (see ICQ), and the results thereof approved by a responsible official. b. Reperform control by reviewing files or records and obtaining satisfactory explanations for long-outstanding items.
5. Matching/comparison control (purchase/sales invoices, credit memoranda, journal vouchers, checks).	a. Examine items for evidence of matching/comparison with related documentation (e.g., authorized orders, records of goods received/shipped, price lists, etc.) by persons with no incompatible duties (see ICQ). b. Reperform control by matching a number of items selected in (a) above with related documentation verifying, as appropriate, description, quantities, prices, terms, amounts, and authorization. c. Where appropriate, e.g., in the case of payments and credit memoranda, see that supporting documentation has been effectively cancelled to prevent subsequent reuse.
6. Checks of calculations, extensions, and additions (purchase/sales invoices, credit memoranda, payroll summaries).	a. Examine evidence of checks or tests of the calculations, extensions, and additions by persons with the degree of independence stated in the ICQ. b. Reperform control by checking a sample of calculations and extensions and testing additions.
7. Final approval of documentation (purchase/sales invoices, credit memoranda, journal vouchers, payrolls, reimbursements of imprest funds) and allocation to the general ledger.	a. Examine documentation for evidence of final approval by a responsible official with no incompatible duties (see ICQ) before entry into the relevant records. b. Examine available evidence of rejections or queries raised by the official and of checks performed before giving final approval. c. Reperform control by selecting a sample of documents examined in (a) above and:

592

Nature of Control	Specimen Test
	i. seeing that necessary supporting documentation is attached, that such supporting documentation bears adequate evidence that prior required clerical checks have been performed, and that the transaction does not appear to be unreasonable; ii. reperforming any other steps that the responsible official is supposed to follow; iii. seeing that the allocation to the general ledger is accurate.
8. Summarization of transactions and posting to control accounts (purchase/sales invoices, credit memoranda, journal vouchers).	a. Examine postings in the control account(s) in the general ledger and confirm that these have been made by persons with no incompatible duties (see ICQ) from totals in batch register/control log/day book/cash book established prior to posting of entries into the detailed records. b. Reperform control by testing: i. postings to control accounts in the general ledger; ii. additions of batches, journals, payroll summaries; iii. batch registers and control logs with batch totals and subsequent reconciliations or agreement with totals of documents processed.
9. Reconciliation controls (control accounts with detailed records; specific items of income or expenditure with predetermined totals or with totals of previous periods).	a. Examine periodic reconciliations and confirm that such reconciliations have been prepared and, where appropriate, subsequently reviewed and approved: i. regularly throughout the year; ii by persons with no incompatible duties (see ICQ). b. In respect of differences arising from the reconciliations, confirm by examination that such differences have been fully investigated and examine authority for write-offs signed by a responsible official. c. Reperform control by testing: i. reconciliations with detailed records and appropriate supporting documentation; ii. the additions and agreeing the total with the control account; iii. contras or unusual items in the reconciliations with supporting evidence; iv. the subsequent clearance of reconciling items.
10. Agreement with third parties (bank statements, suppliers' statements, customers' records).	a. Examine periodic reconciliations/agreements of balances with statements received from third parties and confirm that such reconciliations have been prepared and, where appropriate, subsequently reviewed and approved: i. regularly throughout the year; ii. by persons with no incompatible duties (see ICQ); iii. by persons who receive the statements directly from the third parties and retain them until agreement is completed.

Nature of Control	Specimen Test

	b. In respect of differences arising from the reconciliations, confirm by examination that such differences have been fully investigated and see authority for write-offs signed by a responsible official.
	c. Reperform control by testing balances in the records with third parties' statements, seeing that:
	   i. unmatched items are investigated and cleared;
	   ii. contras or unusual items in the reconciliations are substantiated with supporting evidence;
	  and in respect of bank reconciliations, testing the additions of the cash books and testing the balances forward at the end of selected periods.

11. Verification of physical existence of assets (fixed assets, investments, inventories).	a. Examine evidence (including, where appropriate, reports of planned and actual coverage) that physical verification has been carried out at appropriate intervals in accordance with procedures by persons with no incompatible duties (see ICQ).
	b. In respect of differences arising from the above checks confirm by examination that such differences have been:
	   i. properly recorded;
	   ii. adequately investigated by persons with no incompatible duties (see ICQ);
	   iii. reviewed and approved by a responsible official;
	   iv. correctly disposed of (e.g., by adjustment to the detailed records and/or posting to a separate ledger account maintained for such adjustments).
	c. Reperform control by testing balance on the detailed records with the existence of corresponding assets.
	d. In the case of investments, see that they are registered either in the name of the company or in the name of a wholly owned nominee company.
	e. In the case of inventory, as the actual procedures for physical inventory verification tend to vary from client to client, such procedures should be evaluated each year by obeservation.

12. Other controls of a physical nature.	Such controls can usually be tested only by observation. The exact nature of the observation required will be evident from the ICQ and should be specified in the PRT. Reference should be made to the Internal Control Reference Manual.

F

SEC Releases

ACCOUNTING SERIES RELEASE NO. 242/FEBRUARY 16, 1978

NOTIFICATION OF ENACTMENT OF FOREIGN CORRUPT PRACTICES ACT OF 1977

AGENCY: Securities and Exchange Commission

ACTION: Notification of enactment of Foreign Corrupt Practices Act of 1977.

SUMMARY: The Commission wishes to call to the attention of issuers, accountants, attorneys and other interested persons the enactment of the Foreign Corrupt Practices Act of 1977. The Act, which is described in detail below, requires issuers subject to the registration and reporting provisions of the Securities Exchange Act of 1934, as amended, among other things to comply with certain accounting standards. It also makes unlawful the use of any means or instrumentality of interstate commerce by any such issuer, or by any domestic concern not subject to the Securities Exchange Act, in furtherance of any offer, payment, promise to pay or authorization of the payment of any money, or offer, gift, promise to give or authorization of the giving of anything of value, to foreign officials and certain other persons for certain corrupt purposes.

FOR FURTHER INFORMATION CONTACT: Frederick B. Wade, Office of the General Counsel (202/755-1229), Barbara L. Leventhal, Division of Corporation Finance (202/755-1750), or Edward R. Cheramy, Office of Chief Accountant (202/376-8020), Securities and Exchange Commission, 500 North Capitol Street, Washington, D.C. 20549.

SUPPLEMENTARY INFORMATION: The Securities and Exchange Commission wishes to call to the attention of issuers, attorneys, accountants and other interested persons, the recent enactment of the Foreign Corrupt Practices Act of 1977 [the "Act"].[1] The Act, which was signed by the President on December 19, 1977, and became effective on that date, amends Section 13(b) of the Securities Exchange Act of 1934 [15 U.S.C. 78m(b)] to require every issuer which has a class of securities registered pursuant to Section 12 of the Securities Exchange Act, and every issuer which is required to file reports pursuant to Section 15(d) of the Securities Exchange Act, to comply with certain accounting standards. The Act also makes it unlawful for such issuers, or any domestic concern not subject to the Securities Exchange Act, to engage in certain corrupt practices with respect to foreign officials. Because the Act became effective upon signing, it is important that issuers subject to the new requirements review their accounting procedures, systems of internal accounting controls and business practices in order that they may take any actions necessary to comply with the requirements contained in the Act.

The Act, which is set forth in its entirety in Appendix A, is described below.

A.   Accounting Standards

Section 13(b) of the Securities Exchange Act is amended by renumbering existing subsection (b) as paragraph (b)(1) of Section 13, and by adding two new paragraphs to that subsection. New paragraph 13(b)(2) applies to issuers which have a class of securities registered pursuant to Section 12 of the Securities Exchange Act, and issuers required to file reports pursuant to Section 15(d) of the Securities Exchange Act (hereinafter referred to collectively as "reporting companies"). It required reporting companies to make and keep books, records and accounts which, in reasonable detail, accurately and fairly reflect the transactions and dispositions of the assets of the issuer. The maintenance of accurate books and records by publicly-held companies is a necessary concomitant of the existing requirement for full, fair and accurate periodic reports. Inaccurate books, off-the-book accounts, and related practices are proscribed by the Act.

Reporting companies are also required to devise and maintain a system of internal accounting controls sufficient to provide reasonable assurances that:

    i.   Transactions are executed in accordance with management's specific authorization;
    ii. Transactions are recorded as necessary: (a) to permit preparation of financial statements in conformity with generally accepted accounting principles or other applicable criteria; and (b) to maintain accountability for its assets;
   iii. Access to assets is permitted only in accordance with management authorization; and
   iv. The recorded accountability for assets is compared with existing assets at reasonable intervals and appropriate action is taken with respect to any differences.

New paragraph 13(b)(3) of the Securities Exchange Act provides that, with respect to "matters concerning the national security of the United States, no duty or liability under paragraph (2)*** shall be imposed upon any person acting in cooperation with the head of any Federal department or agency responsible for such matters if such act in cooperation

---

[1]The Act is contained in Title I of Public Law No. 95-213 (Dec. 19, 1977). Title II of the legislation, the Domestic and Foreign Investment Improved Disclosure Act of 1977, amends Section 13 of the Securities Exchange Act of 1934 (15 U.S.C. 78m) to require expanded disclosure by persons who acquire or possess beneficial ownership of more than 5 percent of a class of securities which is registered pursuant to Section 12 of the Exchange Act, or any equity security of an insurance company, which would have been required to be so registered except for the exemption contained in Section 12(g)(2)(G) or any equity security issued by a closed end investment company registered under the Investment Company Act of 1940. Rulemaking to implement Section 13(g) as part of a uniform integrated approach to disclosure under Sections 13(d), (f) and (g) is under consideration and will be the subject of a separate release.

with such head of a department or agency was done upon the specific, written directive of the head of such department or agency pursuant to Presidential authority to issue such directives.'' Each such directive shall expire one year after it is issued unless it is renewed in writing.

B.   Foreign Corrupt Practices by Issuers

Pursuant to the Act, a new Section 30A has been added to the Securities Exchange Act, which makes it unlawful for any reporting company, or any officer, director, employee, or agent of the company, or any shareholder acting on behalf of such a company, to make use of the mails or any means or instrumentalities of interstate commerce, corruptly, in furtherance of an offer, payment, promise to pay, or authorization of the payment of any money, or offer, gift, promise to give or authorization of the giving of anything of value, to three classes of persons:

1.   An official of a foreign government or instrumentality of a foreign government;
2.   A foreign political party or official thereof, or any candidate for a foreign political office; or
3.   Any other person where the reporting company knows, or has reason to know, that all or a portion of such money or thing of value will be offered, given or promised, directly or indirectly to any foreign official, foreign political party or official thereof, or any candidate for a foreign political office.

New Section 30A applied to payments made for the purpose of influencing an act or decision of a foreign official, foreign political party or candidate for foreign political office (including a decision not to act), or inducing such a person or party to use his or its influence to affect any government act or decision, in order to assist an issuer in obtaining, retaining or directing business to any person. A ''foreign official'' is defined to mean any officer or employee of a foreign government or any department, agency or instrumentality thereof, or any person acting in an official capacity for or on behalf of such government. The term does not include employees whose duties are essentially ministerial or clerical.

C.   The Commission's Enforcement Responsibilities

The legislative history of the Act reflects that the Commission's enforcement responsibilities extend to conducting investigations, bringing civil injunctive actions, commencing administrative proceedings if appropriate, including public or private disciplinary proceedings pursuant to Rule 2(e) of the Commission's Rules of Practice,[2] and referring cases to the Justice Department for criminal prosecution where warranted, just as the Commission currently does with respect to its existing responsibilities under the federal securities laws.[3] In addition, as is true with respect to violations of other provisions of the Securities Exchange Act, controlling persons of an issuer may be liable for violations of the new requirements,[4] and a negligence standard will govern civil injunctive actions brought to enforce the Act.[5] The legislative history of the Act also contemplates that private rights of action properly could be implied under the Act on behalf of persons who suffer injury as a result of prohibited corporate bribery.[6]

---

[2] 17 CFR 201.2(e).

[3] S. Rep. No. 95-114, 95th Cong., 1st Sess. (1977) at 12; H.R. Rep. No. 95-640, 95th Cong., 1st Sess. (1977) at 10.

[4] *See* Section 20 of the Securities Exchange Act, 15 U.S.C. 78t.

[5] H.R. Rep. No. 95-640, 95th Cong., 1st Sess. (1977) at 10.

[6] *Id.*

In the case of an individual, the penalties for each criminal violation of the corrupt practices provisions of new Section 30A are a fine of up to $10,000 or imprisonment for up to 5 years, or both; in the case of a corporation, the penalties for violation of the Section include a fine of up to $1,000,000. In this regard, the Act provides that any fines imposed upon individuals may not be paid directly or indirectly by an issuer.

D.   Foreign Corrupt Practices by Domestic Concerns

The Act also subjects any domestic business concern, other than one subject to the reporting requirements of the Securities Exchange Act, and any officer, director or agent of such a domestic business concern or any natural person in control of such a domestic concern to the same prohibitions and penalties that are applicable to reporting companies. The provisions applicable to domestic concerns will be administered and enforced by the Justice Department rather than the Commission.

E.   Impact on Disclosure Policies

While the Act imposes new requirements on reporting companies with respect to the maintenance of internal accounting controls, and outlaws certain foreign corrupt practices, it does not alter the existing obligation of such companies adequately to disclose material questionable and illegal corporate payments and practices. In addition to providing all information called for by the specific disclosure requirements of the various registration and reporting forms promulgated pursuant to the Securities Act of 1933 and the Securities Exchange Act of 1934, registrants have a continuing obligation to disclose all material information and all information necessary to prevent other disclosures made from being misleading with respect to such transactions.[7] Although the legality or illegality of a particular transaction is one of the factors that must be assessed in determining its materiality, other factors must also be considered. A transaction which is not unlawful under the Act may still be material to investors and therefore required to be disclosed under the federal securities laws. For guidance in determining whether or not a specific fact is material, attention is directed to the discussion of materiality contained in Securities and Exchange Commission, **Report on Questionable and Illegal Corporate Payments and Practices,** which was submitted to the Senate Committee on Banking, Housing and Urban Development on May 12, 1976, at 16-32 (''Report'').

F.   Effect on Outstanding Rule Proposals

On January 19, 1977 the Commission published for comment a series of rulemaking proposals designed to promote the reliability and completeness of financial information, prevent concealment of questionable or illegal corporate payments and practices, and provide information to investors concerning management involvement in such transactions.[8] The proposals were substantially similar to a legislative proposal submitted by the Commission to the Senate Committee on Banking, Housing and Urban Affairs on May 12, 1976, parts of which were ultimately incorporated in the Act.[9] The Commission is considering the numerous comments it has received on these proposals and will determine whether to

---

[7]*See e.g.*, 17 CFR 230.405(1); 17 CFR 230.408; 17 CFR 240.12b-20; 17 CFR 240.10b-2; 17 CFR 240.14a-9.

[8]Securities Exchange Act Release No. 13185 (Jan. 19, 1977), *11 SEC Docket 1514* (1977).

[9]The proposals were contained in the Commission's Report, *supra,* at 63, which is, accordingly, a part of the legislative history of the Act. The Commission's proposals were originally introduced by Senator Proxmire, Chairman of the Senate Committee on Banking, Housing and Urban Affairs, as S.3418. Following hearings, the committee referred the bill to the Senate floor—S.3664—which embodied the Commission's recommendations as well as certain other proposals. S.3664 was passed by

adopt, modify or withdraw those rulemaking proposals.[10] In view of the extensive comments which already have been received no further comments on these proposals are being solicited. An appropriate announcement respecting the Commission's determination with respect to these rule proposals will be published in the near future.

G. Inquiries to the Staff

A number of inquiries have been received by the staff which relate to the scope of the Act and the applicability of its criminal provisions to specific factual situations. The staff has declined to address these issues on an **ad hoc** basis. As a matter of policy and in light of the legislative and administrative history of the Act, the Commission does not intend to render interpretive advice on the applicability of the Act's proscriptions to particular factual situations.

By the Commission.

George A. Fitzsimmons
Secretary

SECURITIES EXCHANGE ACT OF 1934 AMENDMENT

An Act

To amend the Securities Exchange Act of 1934 to make it unlawful for an issuer of securities registered pursuant to section 12 of such Act or an issuer required to file reports pursuant to Section 15(d) of such Act to make certain payments to foreign officials and other foreign persons, to require such issuers to maintain accurate records, and for other purposes.

---

the Senate unanimously on September 15, 1976. The House of Representatives, however, was unable to complete work on the legislation before adjournment *sine die* on October 2, 1976.

The substance of the Commission's proposals was again included in S.305, which was passed by the Senate on May 2, 1977, but two of the proposals were deleted in the joint conference committee appointed to reconcile the differences in the Senate and House versions of the bill, prior to final enactment of the legislation.

[10]The accounting provisions in the new law, which are described above, are similar to proposed Rules 13b-1, and 13b-2. The rulemaking proposals not incorporated in the legislation include proposed Rule 13b-3, which would prohibit the falsification of corporate books or records; proposed Rule 13b-4, which would prohibit the making of false or misleading statements to an accountant; and proposed Item 6(d) of Schedule 14A relating to disclosure of management involvement in questionable or illegal payments or practices.

Be it enacted by the Senate and House of Representatives of the United States of America in Congress assembled,

TITLE I—FOREIGN CORRUPT PRACTICES

SHORT TITLE

Sec. 101.　This title may be cited as the "Foreign Corrupt Practices Act of 1977."

ACCOUNTING STANDARDS

Sec. 102.　Section 13(b) of the Securities Exchange Act of 1934 (15 U.S.C. 78q(b)) is amended by inserting "(1)" after "(b)" and by adding at the end thereof the following:
"(2)　Every issuer which has a class of securities registered pursuant to section 12 of this title and every issuer which is required to file reports pursuant to section 15(d) of this title shall—
"(A) make and keep books, records, and accounts, which, in reasonable detail, accurately and fairly reflect the transactions and dispositions of the assets of the issuer; and
"(B) devise and maintain a system of internal accounting controls sufficient to provide reasonable assurances that—

"(i) transactions are executed in accordance with management's general or specific authorization;
"(ii) transactions are recorded as necessary (I) to permit preparation of financial statements in conformity with generally accepted accounting principles or any other criteria applicable to such statements, and (II) to maintain accountability for assets:
"(iii) access to assets is permitted only in accordance with management's general or specific authorization; and
"(iv) the recorded accountability for assets is compared with the existing assets at reasonable intervals and appropriate action is taken with respect to any differences.

"(3)(A) With respect to matters concerning the national security of the United States, no duty or liability under paragraph (2) of this subsection shall be imposed upon any person acting in cooperation with the head of any Federal department or agency responsible for such matters if such act in cooperation with such head of a department or agency was done upon the specific, written directive of the head of such department or agency pursuant to Presidential authority to issue such directives. Each directive issued under this paragraph shall set forth the specific facts and circumstances with respect to which the provisions of this paragraph are to be invoked. Each such directive shall, unless renewed in writing, expire one year after the date of issuance.
"(B) Each head of a Federal department or agency of the United States who issues a directive pursuant to this paragraph shall maintain a complete file of all such directives and shall, on October 1 of each year, transmit a summary of matters covered by such directives in force at any time during the previous year to the Permanent Select Committee on Intelligence of the House of Representatives and the Select Committee on Intelligence of the Senate."

FOREIGN CORRUPT PRACTICES BY ISSUERS

Sec. 103. (a) The Securities Exchange Act of 1934 is amended by inserting after section 30 the following new section:

"Foreign Corrupt Practices by Issuers

"Sec. 30A. (a) It shall be unlawful for any issuer which has a class of securities registered pursuant to section 12 of this title or which is required to file reports under section 15(d) of this title, or for any officer, director, employee, or agent of such issuer or any stockholder thereof acting on behalf of such issuer, to make use of the mails or any means or instrumentality of interstate commerce corruptly in furtherance of an offer, payment, promise to pay, or authorization of the payment of any money, or offer, gift, promise to give, or authorization of the giving of anything of value to—

"(1) any foreign official for purposes of—

"(A) influencing any act or decision of such foreign official in his official capacity, including a decision to fail to perform his official functions: or

"(B) inducing such foreign official to use his influence with a foreign government or instrumentality thereof to affect or influence any act or decision of such government or instrumentality,

in order to assist such issuer in obtaining or retaining business for or with, or directing business to, any person;

"(2) any foreign political party or official thereof or any candidate for foreign political office for purposes of—

"(A) influencing any act or decision of such party, official, or candidate in its or his official capacity, including a decision to fail to perform its or his official functions; or

"(B) inducing such party, official, or candidate to use its or his influence with a foreign government or instrumentality thereof to affect or influence any act or decision of such government or instrumentality,

in order to assist such issuer in obtaining or retaining business for or with, or directing business to, any person; or

"(3) any person, while knowing or having reason to know that all or a portion of such money or thing of value will be offered, given, or promised, directly or indirectly, to any foreign official, to any foreign political party or official thereof, or to any candidate for foreign political office, for purposes of—

"(A) influencing any act or decision of such foreign official, political party, party official, or candidate in his or its official capacity, including a decision to fail to perform his or its official functions; or

"(B) inducing such foreign official, political party, party official, or candidate to use his or its influence with a foreign government or instrumentality thereof to affect or influence any act or decision of such government or instrumentality, in order to assist such issuer in obtaining or retaining business for or with, or directing business to, any person.

"(b) As used in this section, the term 'foreign official' means any officer or employee of a foreign government or any department, agency, or instrumentality thereof, or any person acting in an official capacity for or on behalf of such government or department, agency, or instrumentality. Such term does not include any employee of a foreign government or any department, agency, or instrumentality thereof whose duties are essentially ministerial or clerical."

(b)(1) Section 32(a) of the Securities Exchange Act of 1934 (15 U.S.C. 78ff(a)) is amended by inserting "(other than section 30A)" immediately after "title" the first place it appears.

(2) Section 32 of the Securities Exchange Act of 1934 (15 U.S.C. 78ff) is amended by adding at the end thereof the following new subsection:

"(c)(1) Any issuer which violates section 30A(a) of this title shall, upon conviction, be fined not more than $1,000,000.

"(2) Any officer or director of an issuer, or any stockholder acting on behalf of such issuer, who willfully violates section 30A(a) of this title shall, upon conviction, be fined not more than $10,000, or imprisoned not more than five years, or both.

"(3) Whenever an issuer is found to have violated section 30A(a) of this title, any employee or agent of such issuer who is a United States citizen, national, or resident or is otherwise subject to the jurisdiction of the United States (other than an officer, director, or stockholder of such issuer), and who willfully carried out the act or practice constituting such violation shall, upon conviction, be fined not more than $10,000, or imprisoned not more than five years, or both.

"(4) Whenever a fine is imposed under paragraph (2) or (3) of this subsection upon any officer, director, stockholder, employee, or agent of an issuer, such fine shall not be paid, directly or indirectly, by such issuer."

Foreign Corrupt Practices by Domestic Concerns

Sec. 104.   (a) It shall be unlawful for any domestic concern, other than an issuer which is subject to section 30A of the Securities Exchange Act of 1934, or any officer, director, employee, or agent of such domestic concern or any stockholder thereof acting on behalf of such domestic concern, to make use of the mails or any means or instrumentality of interstate commerce corruptly in furtherance of an offer, payment, promise to pay, or authorization of the payment of any money, or offer, gift, promise to give, or authorization of the giving of anything of value to—

(1) any foreign official for purposes of—

(A) influencing any act or decision of such foreign official in his official capacity, including a decision to fail to perform his official functions; or

(B) inducing such foreign official to use his influence with a foreign government or instrumentality thereof to affect or influence any act or decision of such government or instrumentality,

in order to assist such domestic concern in obtaining or retaining business for or with, or directing business to, any person;

(2) any foreign political party or official thereof or any candidate for foreign political office for purposes of—

(A) influencing any act or decision of such party, official, or candidate in its or his official capacity, including a decision to fail to perform its or his official functions; or

(B) inducing such party, official, or candidate to use its or his influence with a foreign government or instrumentality thereof to affect or influence any act or decision of such government or instrumentality,

in order to assist such domestic concern in obtaining or retaining business for or with, or directing business to, any person; or

(3) any person, while knowing or having reason to know that all or a portion of such money or thing of value will be offered, given, or promised, directly or indirectly, to any foreign official, to any foreign political party or official thereof, or to any candidate for foreign political office, for purposes of—

(A) influencing any act or decision of such foreign official, political party, party official, or candidate in his or its official capacity, including a decision to fail to perform his or its official functions; or

(B) inducing such foreign official, political party, party official, or candidate to use his or its influence with a foreign government or instrumentality thereof to affect or influence any act or decision of such government or instrumentality, in order to assist such domestic concern in obtaining or retaining business for or with, or directing business to, any person.

(b)(1)(A) Except as provided in subparagraph (B), any domestic concern which violates subsection (a) shall, upon conviction, be fined not more than $1,000,000.

(B) Any individual who is a domestic concern and who willfully violates subsection (a) shall, upon conviction, be fined not more than $10,000, or imprisoned not more than five years, or both.

(2) Any officer or director of a domestic concern, or stockholder acting on behalf of such domestic concern, who willfully violates subsection (a) shall, upon conviction, be fined not more than $10,000, or imprisoned not more than five years, or both.

(3) Whenever a domestic concern is found to have violated subsection (a) of this section, any employee or agent of such domestic concern who is a United States citizen, national, or resident or is otherwise subject to the jurisdiction of the United States (other than an officer, director, or stockholder acting on behalf of such domestic concern), and who willfully carried out the act or practice constituting such violation shall, upon conviction, be fined not more than $10,000, or imprisoned not more than five years, or both.

(4) Whenever a fine is imposed under paragraph (2) or (3) of this subsection upon any officer, director, stockholder, employee, or agent of a domestic concern, such fine shall not be paid, directly or indirectly, by such domestic concern.

(c) Whenever it appears to the Attorney General that any domestic concern, or officer, director, employee, agent, or stockholder thereof, is engaged, or is about to engage, in any act or practice constituting a violation of subsection (a) of this section, the Attorney General may, in his discretion, bring a civil action in an appropriate district court of the United States to enjoin such act or practice, and upon a proper showing a permanent or temporary injunction or a temporary restraining order shall be granted without bond.

(d) As used in this section:

(1)   The term "domestic concern" means (A) any individual who is a citizen, national, or resident of the United States; or (B) any corporation, partnership, association, joint-stock company, business trust, unincorporated organization, or sole proprietorship which has its principal place of business in the United States, or which is organized under the laws of a State of the United States, or a territory, possession or commonwealth of the United States.

(2)   The term "foreign official" means any officer or employee of a foreign government or any department, agency, or instrumentality thereof, or any person acting in an official capacity for or on behalf of any such government or department, agency, or instrumentality. Such term does not include any employee of a foreign government or any department, agency or instrumentality thereof whose duties are essentially ministerial or clerical.

(3)   The term "interstate commerce" means trade, commerce, transportation, or communication among the several States, or between any foreign country and any State or between any State and any place or ship outside thereof. Such term includes the intrastate use of (A) a telephone or other interstate means of communication, or (B) any other interstate instrumentality.

TITLE II—DISCLOSURE

SEC. 201.   This title may be cited as the "Domestic and Foreign Investment Improved Disclosure Act of 1977."

SEC. 202.   Section 13(d)(1) of the Securities Exchange Act of 1934 (15 U.S.C. 78m) is amended to read as follows:

"(d)(1) Any person who, after acquiring directly or indirectly the beneficial ownership of any equity security of a class which is registered pursuant to section 12 of this title, or any equity security of an insurance company which would have been required to be so registered except for the exemption contained in section 12(g)(2)(G) of this title, or any equity security issued by a closed-end investment company registered under the Investment Company Act of 1940, is directly or indirectly the beneficial owner of more than 5 per centum of such class shall, within ten days after such acquisition, send to the issuer of the security at its principal executive office, by registered or certified mail, send to each exchange where the security is traded, and file with the Commission, a statement containing such of the following information, and such additional information, as the Commission may by rules and regulations, prescribe as necessary or appropriate in the public interest or for the protection of investors—

"(A)　the background, and identity, residence, and citizenship of, and the nature of such beneficial ownership by, such person and all other persons by whom or on whose behalf the purchases have been or are to be effected:

"(B)　the source and amount of the funds or other consideration used or to be used in making the purchases, and if any part of the purchase price is represented or is to be represented by funds or other consideration borrowed or otherwise obtained for the purpose of acquiring, holding, or trading such security, a description of the transaction and the names of the parties thereto, except that where a source of funds is a loan made in the ordinary course of business by a bank, as defined in section 3(a)(6) of this title, if the person filing such statement so requests, the name of the bank shall not be made available to the public;

"(C)　if the purpose of the purchases or prospective purchases is to acquire control of the business of the issuer of the securities, any plans or proposals which such persons may have to liquidate such issuer, to sell as assets to or merge it with any other persons, or to make any other major change in its business or corporate structure;

"(D)　the number of shares of such security which are beneficially owned, and the number of shares concerning which there is a right to acquire, directly or indirectly, by (i) such person, and (ii) by each associate of such person, giving the background, identity, residence, and citizenship of each such associate; and

"(E)　information as to any contracts, arrangements, or understanding with any person with respect to any securities of the issuer, including but not limited to transfer of any of the securities, joint ventures, loan or option arrangements, puts or calls, guaranties of loans, guaranties against loss or guaranties of profits, division of losses or profits, or the giving or withholding of proxies, naming the persons with whom such contracts, arrangements, or understandings have been entered into, and giving the details thereof."

SEC. 203.　Section 13 of the Securities Exchange Act of 1934, as amended (15 U.S.C. 78m), is amended by adding at the end thereof the following new subsection:

"(g)(1)　Any person who is directly or indirectly the beneficial owner of more than 5 per centum of any security of a class described in subsection (d)(1) of this section shall send to the issuer of the security and shall file with the Commission a statement setting forth, in such form and at such time as the Commission may, by rule, prescribe—

"(A)　such person's identity, residence, and citizenship; and

"(B)　the number and description of the shares in which such person has an interest and the nature of such interest.

"(2)　If any material change occurs in the facts set forth in the statement sent to the issuer and filed with the Commission, an amendment shall be transmitted to the issuer and shall be filed with the Commission, in accordance with such rules and regulations as the Commission may prescribe as necessary or appropriate in the public interest or for the protection of investors.

"(3)　When two or more persons act as a partnership, limited partnership, syndicate, or other group for the purpose of acquiring, holding, or disposing of securities of an issuer, such syndicate or group shall be deemed a 'person' for the purposes of this subsection.

"(4)　In determining, for purposes of this subsection, any percentage of a class of any security, such class shall be deemed to consist of the amount of the outstanding securities of such class, exclusive of any securities of such class held by or for the account of the issuer or a subsidiary of the issuer.

"(5)   In exercising its authority under this subsection, the Commission shall take such steps as it deems necessary or appropriate in the public interest or for the protection of investors (A) to achieve centralized reporting of information regarding ownership, (B) to avoid unnecessarily duplicative reporting by and minimize the compliance burden on persons required to report, and (C) to tabulate and promptly make available the information contained in any report filed pursuant to this subsection in a manner which will, in the view of the Commission, maximize the usefulness of the information to other Federal and State agencies and the public.

"(6)   The Commission may, by rule or order, exempt, in whole or in part, any person or class of persons from any or all of the reporting requirements of this subsection as it deems necessary or appropriate in the public interest or for the protection of investors.

"(h)   The Commission shall report to the Congress within thirty months of the date of enactment of this subsection with respect to (1) the effectiveness of the ownership reporting requirements contained in this title, and (2) the desirability and the feasibility of reducing or otherwise modifying the 5 per centum threshold used in subsections (d)(1) and (g)(1) of this section, giving appropriate consideration to—

"(A)   the incidence of avoidance of reporting by beneficial owners using multiple holders of record;

"(B)   the cost of compliance to persons required to report;

"(C)   the codisseminating the reported information;

"(D)   the effect of such action on the securities markets, including the system for the clearance and settlement of securities transactions;

"(E)   the benefits to investors and to the public;

"(F)   any bona fide interests of individuals in the privacy of their financial affairs;

"(G)   the extent to which such reported information gives or would give any person an undue advantage in connection with activities subject to sections 13(d) and 14(d) of this title;

"(H)   the need for such information in connection with the administration and enforcement of this title; and

"(I)   such other matters as the Commission may deem relevant, including the information obtained pursuant to section 13(f) of this title."

SEC. 204.   Section 15(d) of the Securities Exchange Act of 1934 is amended by inserting immediately before the last sentence the following new sentence: "The Commission may, for the purpose of this subsection, define by rules and regulations the term 'held of record' as it deems necessary or appropriate in the public interest or for the protection of investors in order to prevent circumvention of the provisions of this subsection."

Approved December 19, 1977.

Title 17—Commodity and Securities Exchanges

CHAPTER II—SECURITIES AND EXCHANGE COMMISSION
[Release No. 34-15570]
PART 240—GENERAL RULES AND REGULATIONS, SECURITIES EXCHANGE ACT OF 1934

Promotion of the Reliability of Financial Information and Prevention of the Concealment of Questionable or Illegal Corporate Payments and Practices

AGENCY: Securities and Exchange Commission.

ACTION: Final rules.

SUMMARY: The Commission is adopting rules intended to assure that an issuer's books and records accurately and fairly reflect its transactions and dispositions of assets; to protect the integrity of the independent audit of issuer financial statements that is required under the Securities Exchange Act of 1934 (''Securities Exchange Act'') and existing Commission rules; to promote the reliability and completeness of financial information that issuers are required to file with the Commission, or disseminate to investors, pursuant to the Securities Exchange Act; to promote compliance with new Sections 13(b)(2)(A) and (B) of the Securities Exchange Act; and to prevent the concealment of questionable or illegal corporate payments and practices. The rules expressly prohibit the falsification of corporate books, records, or accounts and prohibit the officers and directors of an issuer from making false, misleading or incomplete statements to any accountant in connection with any audit or examination of the issuer's financial statements or the preparation of required reports. Although the Commission's authority to promulgate rules of this nature does not rest solely on Section 13 of the Securities Exchange Act, these rules have been codified in a new Regulation 13B-2, entitled "Maintenance of Records and Preparation of Required Reports."

The Commission believes that these rules, while intended to deal with a much broader range of practices than the problem of questionable or illegal corporate payments and practices, will serve to discourage repetition of the serious abuses which the Commission has uncovered in this area. The Commission's experience indicates that improper corporate payments and practices are rarely reflected in corporate books, records and accounts in an accurate manner and that the desire to conceal information concerning such activities frequently entails the falsification of books, records and accounts and the making of false, misleading or incomplete statements to accountants.

EFFECTIVE DATE: March 23, 1979.

FOR FURTHER INFORMATION CONTACT:

Barbara Leventhal, Division of Corporation Finance (202-755-1750); Frederick B. Wade, Office of the General Counsel (202-755-1229); Ernest Ten Eyck, Office of the Chief Accountant (202-755-7471); Securities and Exchange Commission, 500 North Capitol Street, Washington, D.C. 20549.

SUPPLEMENTARY INFORMATION: The SEC today announced the adoption of two rules under the Securities Exchange Act, 15 U.S.C. 78a *et seq.*, as amended by the Foreign Corrupt Practices Act ("FCPA"), Pub. L. No. 95-213 (Dec. 19, 1977). The rules are codified in a new Regulation 13B-2, entitled "Maintenance of Records and Preparation of Required Reports." New Rule 13b2-1 (17 CFR 240.13b2-1) provides that "no person shall, directly or indirectly, falsify or cause to be falsified, any book, record or account subject to Section 13(b)(2)(A) of the Securities Exchange Act."[1] In addition, new Rule 13b2-2 (17 CFR 240.13b2-2) prohibits officers and directors of an issuer from making materially

---

[1]Section 13(b)(2)(A) of the Securities Exchange Act was added to the Act by the FCPA. It requires issuers subject to the Act to "make and keep books, records and accounts, which, in reasonable detail, accurately and fairly reflect the transactions and dispositions of the assets of the issuer."

Section 3(a)(37) of the Securities Exchange Act defines the term "records" to mean "accounts, correspondence, memorandums, tapes, discs, papers, books and other documents or transcribed information of any type, whether expressed in ordinary or machine language."

false, misleading or incomplete statements to an accountant in connection with any audit or examination of the financial statements of the issuer or the filing of required reports.[2]

The rules were initially published for comment in Securities Exchange Act Release No. 13185 (Jan. 19, 1977), together with a proposed amendment to Item 6 of Schedule 14A (17 CFR 240.14a-101).[3] The rules are designed to promote the reliability and completeness of the financial information that issuers are required to file with the Commission, or disseminate to investors, pursuant to the Securities Exchange Act; to protect the integrity of the independent audit of issuers' financial statements required under that Act and existing Commission rules; to promote compliance with new Sections 13(b)(2)(A) and (B) of the Securities Exchange Act; and to prevent the concealment of questionable or illegal payments and practices. In this regard, although the rules are intended, in part, to eliminate certain serious abuses the Commission has uncovered in connection with questionable and illegal payments and practices, the rules are addressed to a much broader range of practices than the problem of questionable or illegal corporate payments and practices.

I. Background

Beginning in 1973, as a result of the work of the Office of the Watergate Special Prosecutor, the Commission became aware of a pattern of conduct involving the use of corporate funds for illegal domestic political contributions. Because these activities often involved matters of significance to public investors, the nondisclosure of which entailed violations of the federal securities laws, the Commission published a statement, on March 8, 1974, expressing the views of its Division of Corporation Finance concerning disclosure of these matters in documents filed with the Commission, Securities Act Release No. 5466 (Mar. 8, 1974).

Subsequent Commission investigations and enforcement actions revealed that instances of undisclosed questionable or illegal corporate payments—both domestic and foreign—were widespread, that they represented a serious breach in the system of corporate disclosure administered by the Commission and that such payments threatened public confidence in the integrity of the system of capital formation, which rests on a foundation of full and fair disclosure of corporate business and financial transactions. On May 12, 1976, the Commission submitted a detailed "Report on Questionable and Illegal Corporate Payments and Practices" ("May 12 Report") to the Senate Committee on Banking, Housing and Urban Affairs. That report describes and analyzes the Commission's activities concerning such payments and practices and outlines the legislative and other responses that the Commission, based on its experience, recommended to remedy these problems. One of the key conclusions drawn in the May 12 Report was that:

---

[2]As proposed, Rules 13b2-1 and 13b2-2 were designated 13b-3 and 13b-4, respectively. *See* Securities Exchange Act Release No. 13185 (Jan. 19, 1977), 42 FR 4854 (Jan. 26, 1977). The rules promulgated today have been renumbered to reflect the intervening enactment of the FCPA, which incorporated the substance of proposed rules 13b-1 and 13b-2 in new Section 13(b)(2) of the Securities Exchange Act, and the Commission's determination that enactment of the FCPA makes it unnecessary to adopt proposed Rules 13b-1 and 13b-2.

[3]As proposed, a new subsection (d) would be added to Item 6 of Schedule 14A, requiring disclosure of management involvement in specified types of questionable or illegal payments and practices and of corporate policies relating to such matters. The Commission expects to consider this proposal in the near future.

"The almost universal characteristic of the cases reviewed to date by the Commission has been the apparent frustration of our system of corporate accountability which has been designed to assure that there is proper accounting of the use of corporate funds and that documents filed with the Commission and circulated to shareholders do not omit or misrepresent material facts. Millions of dollars of funds have been inaccurately recorded in corporate books and records to facilitate the making of questionable payments. Such falsification of records has been known to corporate employees and often to top management, but often has been concealed from outside auditors and counsel and outside directors."[4]

On the basis of the conclusions in the May 12 Report, the Commission, in addition to active pursuit of its enforcement and disclosure programs, proposed a multi-faceted approach to prevent further abuses. First, the Commission recommended that Congress enact legislation aimed expressly at enhancing the accuracy of corporate books and records and the reliability of the audit process, which together constitute foundations of the system of corporate disclosure. Specifically, the Commission proposed legislation to:

(1) require issuers subject to the periodic reporting requirements of the Securities Exchange Act (i.e., "reporting companies") to make and keep accurate books and records;

(2) require such issuers to devise and maintain a system of internal accounting controls meeting the objectives articulated by the American Institute of Certified Public Accountants in Statement on Auditing Standards No. 1, Section 320.28 (1973);

(3) prohibit the falsification of corporate accounting records; and

(4) prohibit the making of false, misleading or incomplete statements to an accountant in connection with any examination or audit.

In addition, because of the magnitude of the problem, and the need to supplement the Commission's own enforcement capabilities, a voluntary disclosure program was developed. Companies participating in this program were encouraged to conduct careful investigations of their operations under the auspices of persons not involved in the questionable activities and to discuss the question of appropriate disclosure of these matters with the Commission's staff before filing any document with the Commission.[5]

The Commission also proposed means of strengthening the effectiveness and vitality of corporate boards of directors by suggesting that issuers maintain audit committees composed of non-management directors unrelated to the company and its management and by encouraging the separation of the functions of independent corporate counsel and director. In the May 12 Report, the Commission proposed that, at least initially, these principles could best be implemented by an amendment to the listing requirements of the New York Stock Exchange and the rules of the other self-regulatory organizations, rather than by direct Commission action.[6]

---

[4]May 12 Report at p.a.

[5]The voluntary program was announced in several public statements, including the testimony of Commissioner Philip A. Loomis on July 17, 1975, before the Subcommittee on International Economic Policy of the House Committee on International Relations and the testimony of former Commission Chairman Roderick M. Hills before the Subcommittee on Priorities and Economy in Government on January 14, 1976. *See* May 12 Report, supra, at pp. 7-8. Since the program was announced, more than 450 companies have disclosed information relating to questionable or illegal activities in filings with the Commission.

[6]*See* letter from former Chairman Roderick M. Hills to William Batten, Chairman, New York Stock Exchange (NYSE), dated May 11, 1976 (May 12 Report, Exhibit D). The NYSE subsequently adopted a requirement that listed companies have an audit committee which meets certain specified criteria by June 30, 1978. Similar rules have been considered by other national exchanges and the NASD.

II. ENACTMENT OF THE FOREIGN CORRUPT PRACTICES ACT OF 1977

The Commission's legislative proposals were considered by the 94th Congress, but Congress adjourned before taking final action on the legislation. Following adjournment of the 94th Congress, the Commission, on January 19, 1977, published proposed rules for public comment in language substantially identical to the legislative proposals it had submitted to the Congress in the May 12 Report.[7]

The Commission's legislative proposals were given additional consideration by the 95th Congress. Two of the four proposals, the legislative analogs to proposed rules 13b-1 and 13b-2, were eventually incorporated in the FCPA in language virtually identical to that proposed by the Commission. The FCPA was signed by the President on December 19, 1977, and became effective on that date.[8]

The primary impetus for enactment of the FCPA arose from disclosures of widespread corporate bribery. As the House Report concerning the legislation declared:

> "More than 400 corporations have admitted making questionable or illegal payments. The companies, most of them voluntarily, have reported paying out well in excess of of $300 million in corporate funds to foreign government officials, politicians, and political parties. These corporations have included some of the largest and most widely held public companies in the United States; over 117 of them rank in the top Fortune 500 industries. The abuses disclosed run the gamut from bribery of high foreign officials in order to secure some type of favorable action by a foreign government to so-called facilitating payments that allegedly were made to ensure that government functionaries discharged certain ministerial or clerical duties."[9]

The legislative history makes clear that Congress viewed such questionable or illegal payments as: (a) unethical and reprehensible; (b) inconsistent with the principles of a free market economy; (c) unnecessary to the successful conduct of business; and (d) a source of serious difficulties with respect to conduct of the nation's foreign policy.[10] In this regard, the FCPA creates a new Section 30A of the Securities Exchange Act, which makes it unlawful for any reporting company, or any officer, director, employee, or agent of such company, or any shareholder acting on behalf of such company, to make use of the mails or any means or instrumentality of interstate commerce, corruptly, in furtherance of an offer, payment, or gift, of any money or thing of value, to certain classes of persons.[11] The new provision applies to payments made for the purpose of influencing any act or decision of a foreign official, foreign political party or candidate for foreign political office (including a decision not to act), or inducing such a person or party to use his or its influence to affect any govern-

---

[7]*See* Securities Exchange Act Release No. 13185, *supra* (Jan. 19, 1977).
[8]As noted, *supra*, p. 3, the FCPA is contained in Title I of Pub. L. No. 95-213.
[9]H. Rept. No. 95-640, 95th Cong., 1st Sess. 4 (1977).
[10]*Id.* at 4-5; S. Rep. No. 114, 95th Cong., 1st Sess. 3-4 (1977).
[11]These classes include an official of a foreign government; a foreign political party or an official thereof; a candidate for foreign political office; or any other person where the reporting company knows, or has reason to know, that all or a portion of such money or thing of value will be offered, given or promised, directly or indirectly, to one of the foregoing persons.

A "foreign official" is defined by Section 30A to mean "any officer or employee of a foreign government or any department, agency or instrumentality thereof, or any person acting in an official capacity for or on behalf of such government or department, agency, or instrumentality." The term does not include employees "whose duties are essentially ministerial or clerical."

ment act or decision in order to assist an issuer in obtaining, retaining or directing business to any person.[12]

New Section 13(b)(2) of the Securities Exchange Act incorporates two of the four legislative proposals that the Commission made in the May 12 Report. In this regard, the new provision requires every issuer that has a class of securities registered pursuant to Section 12 of the Securities Exchange Act, and every issuer that is required to file reports pursuant to Section 15(d) of the Securities Exchange Act (*i.e.,* "reporting companies"):

(1) to make and keep books, and records and accounts which, in reasonable detail, accurately and fairly reflect the transactions and dispositions of the assets of the issuer; and

(2) to devise and maintain a system of internal accounting controls sufficient to provide reasonable assurances that:

(i) transactions are executed in accordance with management's general or specific authorization;

(ii) transactions are recorded as necessary: (a) to permit preparation of financial statements in conformity with generally accepted accounting principles or other applicable criteria; and (b) to maintain accountability for assets;

(iii) access to assets is permitted only in accordance with management's general or specific authorization; and

(iv) the recorded accountability for assets is compared with existing assets at reasonable intervals and appropriate action is taken with respect to any differences.

The Senate Report concerning the legislation indicates that the "accounting standards * * * [provisions] are intended to operate in tandem with the criminalization provisions of the bill to deter corporate bribery."[13] In this regard, the Report states that the accounting provisions are intended "to strengthen the accuracy of the corporate books and records and the reliability of the audit process which constitute the foundations of our system of corporate disclosure."[14] It also declares that "the affirmative duties" contained in the accounting provisions "will go a long way to prevent the use of corporate assets for corrupt purposes * * * [and that] public confidence in securities markets will be enhanced by assurance that corporate recordkeeping is honest."[15]

As noted above, the May 12 Report also proposed that Congress prohibit the falsification of corporate books, records and accounts and the making of false, misleading or incomplete statements to an accountant in connection with any examination or audit. The Senate bill contained such provisions, but limited the applicability of the provisions to violative conduct that was performed "knowingly."[16] The House bill "contained no comparable provi-

---

[12]Violations of new Section 30A may result in the imposition of a fine of "not more than $1,000,000" upon any issuer convicted of a violation and, with respect to individuals, in the imposition of a fine of not more than $10,000, or imprisonment for not more than 5 years, or both.

The FCPA also subjects any domestic business concern, other than one subject to the reporting requirements of the Securities Exchange Act, and any officer, director or agent of such a domestic business concern, or any natural person in control of such a domestic concern, to the same prohibitions and penalties that are applicable to reporting companies. That portion of the FCPA is administered and enforced, however, by the Department of Justice rather than the Commission.

[13]S. Rept. No. 114, *supra,* at 7.

[14]*Id.*

[15]*Id.* The Report of the Conference Committee concerning the FCPA makes clear that the requirement that corporate books and records be "accurate" is intended "to prevent off-the-books slush funds and payments of bribes" without regard to whether such funds or payments are material in amount. H. Rept. No. 95-831, 95th Cong., 1st Sess. 10 (1977).

[16]S. Rept. No. 114, *supra,* at 9. In this regard, the Senate Report declared that the latter proposal "is designed to encourage careful communications between auditors and persons from whom the auditors seek information in the audit process. The Committee is of the view that a proscription on knowing false statements to auditors will enhance the integrity of the audit process" (*Id.*).

sions because the SEC had already published for comment [the instant] rules designed to accomplish similar objectives under its existing authority."[17]

In the Conference Committee, the Senate receded to the House.[18] Although the conferees agreed that the two proposals "were supportive of the basic accounting section" enacted into law as part of the FCPA,[19] they determined to delete the provisions from the proposed legislation because use of the word "knowingly" in the Senate bill had become "involved in an issue never intended to be raised or resolved by the Senate bill—namely whether or not the inclusion or deletion of the word 'knowingly' would or would not affirm, expand, or overrule the decision of the Supreme Court in *Ernst & Ernst* v. *Hochfelder* (425 U.S. 185)."[20] In deleting the provisions, the conferees stated that they had decided not to "debate * * * the important issues raised by the *Hochfelder* decision" and that "no inference should be drawn [on the basis of the deletions] with respect to any rulemaking authority the SEC may or may not have under the securities laws."[21]

IV.　BASIS FOR ADOPTION OF REGULATION 13B-2

Section 23(a) of the Securities Exchange Act provides, in pertinent part, that the Commission shall "have power to make such rules and regulations as may be necessary or appropriate to implement the provisions of * * *" the Act. In this regard, the enactment of new Section 13(b)(2) provides a basis for promulgation of the new rules in addition to the various provisions cited in the release requesting comments concerning the rule proposals.[22]

It bears emphasis that the accounting provisions of the FCPA are *not* exclusively concerned with the preparation of financial statements. An equally important objective of the new law, as well as pre-existing provisions of the federal securities laws cited in Securities Exchange Act Release No. 13185, *supra,* is the goal of corporate accountability.

In this context, new section 13(b)(2)(A) embodies certain requirements of integrity in corporate record-keeping. Thus, it requires issuers "to make and keep books, records, accounts, which, in reasonable detail, accurately and fairly reflect the transactions and dispositions of the assets of the issuer." This provision is designed, not only to provide a more reliable basis for the preparation of financial statements, but also, among other things, for the purpose of confirming the Commission's authority "effectively to prevent off-the-books slush funds"[23] and to assure that "there is proper accounting of the *use* of corporate funds * * *."[24]

In addition, new Section 13(b)(2)(B) requires issuers to "devise and maintain a system of internal accounting controls sufficient to provide reasonable assurances that * * *" certain statutory objectives are met. These objectives include not only the recording of transactions "as necessary * * * to permit preparation of financial statements in accordance with

---

[17]*See* H. Rept. No. 95-831, *supra,* at 10.

[18]*Id.*

[19]*Id.*

[20]*Id.* at 10-11. In *Hochfelder,* the Supreme Court held that a plaintiff in an implied private action for damages under Section 10(b) of the Securities Exchange Act, 15 U.S.C. 78j(b), and Rule 10b-5 promulgated thereunder, 17 CFR 240.10b-5, must allege and prove that the defendant acted with *scienter,* i.e., "a mental state embracing intent to deceive, manipulate or defraud" (*see* 425 U.S. at 193-194, n. 12). The Court specifically left open "the question whether *scienter* is a necessary element in an action for injunctive relief under Section 10(b) and Rule 10b-5" (*Id.*).

[21]H. Rept. No. 95-831, *supra,* at 11.

[22]*See* Securities Exchange Act Release No. 34-13185, *supra.*

[23]*See* H.R. Rep. No. 95-831, *supra,* at 10.

[24](Emphasis added.) *See* May 12 Report at a.

generally accepted accounting principles * * *'' or other applicable criteria, but also the recording of such transactions "as necessary * * * to maintain accountability for assets." In addition, these objectives expressly include the goals of providing reasonable assurances that access to corporate assets is permitted, and that corporate assets transactions are executed, "in accordance with management's general or specific authorization."

Accordingly, new Section 13(b)(2) establishes requirements concerning the internal activities of reporting companies that are supportive of the disclosure system mandated by the Securities Exchange Act, but should not be analyzed solely from that point of view. The new requirements may provide an independent basis for enforcement action by the Commission, whether or not violation of the provisions may lead, in a particular case, to the dissemination of materially false or misleading information to investors.[25]

As is set forth in more detail below, the rules promulgated today are intended to discourage the kind of abuses that led to enactment of the FCPA, and to promote compliance with new Section 13(b)(2) of the Securities Exchange Act. Accordingly, the Commission has determined that the rules are "necessary or appropriate," within the meaning of the Commission's general rulemaking authority, to implement new Section 13(b)(2).

Although the rules adopted today will be codified with rules promulgated under Section 13 of the Securities Exchange Act, the Commission is not relying exclusively on Section 13 as a foundation for the rules. As the Commission noted, in publishing the instant rule proposals for public comment:

". . . the close relationship between the [disclosure] objectives which Congress, in 1934, sought to accomplish by enactment of the Securities Exchange Act and the substance of its legislative proposals places those proposals within the reach of the Commission's general rulemaking authority under Section 23(a) of the Securities Exchange Act."[26]

In this context, the rules adopted today are also based, in part, upon a number of disclosure-related provisions, including: (a) Sections 13(a), 13(b)(1) and 15(d) of the Act, which set forth certain periodic reporting requirements; (b) Section 10(b), which prohibits fraud; (c) Section 14(a), which governs proxy solicitations; (d) Section 20(b), which prohibits unlawful conduct performed by any person "through or by means of any other person"; and (e) Section 20(c), which prohibits any director or officer of, or any owner of securities issued by, any issuer required to file any document, report or information under * * * "the Securities Exchange Act without just cause to hinder, delay or obstruct the making or filing of any such document, report or information * * *," these provisions are sometimes referred to collectively in the remainder of this release as "the disclosure provisions" in order to distinguish them from new Section 13(b)(2) of the Securities Exchange Act.[27]

The Commission has determined, on the basis of the findings set forth in the May 12

---

[25] For example, although new Section 13(b)(2) imposes requirements upon issuers that are designed, in part, to promote the reliability and completeness of financial information and to protect the integrity of the independent audit of an issuer's financial statements, these new statutory requirements are qualified by the terms "in reasonable detail" and "reasonable assurances," as distinguished from the concept of materiality.

[26] *See* Securities Exchange Act Release No. 34-13185, *supra.*

[27] In this context, of course, Sections 20(b) and 20(c) are "disclosure provisions" only insofar as they may be applicable in tandem with one or more of the other provisions noted above.

Report and its experience in various enforcement actions involving questionable or illegal payments,[28] the legislative history of the FCPA[29] and careful consideration of the comments received concerning the rule proposals, that false corporate books and records and the making of false, misleading and incomplete statements to auditors often lead to a variety of activities that the Commission is authorized to curtail through exercise of its rulemaking authority to implement the "disclosure provisions." These activities include, but are not limited to:

(1) the utilization of deceptive devices, such as materially false statements or material omissions, in connection with the purchase or sale of securities in interstate commerce;

(2) the filing of inaccurate and incomplete periodic reports with the Commission and the dissemination of such reports to investors;

(3) the solicitation of proxies in contravention of the proxy rules, including Rule 14a-9, 17 CFR 240.14a-9; and

(4) the hindrance, delay, and obstruction of the making and filing of required documents, reports and information.

Accordingly, the Commission has determined that the rules adopted today are "necessary or appropriate," within the meaning of Section 23(a) of the Securities Exchange Act, to implement the foregoing "disclosure provisions" and that such rules are "necessary or appropriate" in the public interest, for the protection of investors and to insure fair dealing in securities.

A.   Adoption of Rule 13b2-1 (Proposed Rule 13b-3)

Proposed Rule 13b-3 would have prohibited any person from falsifying corporate books and records maintained pursuant to proposed Rule 13b-1. As adopted, Rule 13b2-1 has been modified to reflect the enactment of new Section 13(b)(2)(A) of the Securities Exchange Act, the Commission's concomitant decision not to adopt proposed rule 13b-1 and certain technical or clarifying changes in the language of the rule. Thus, the new rule provides that "no person shall, directly or indirectly, falsify or cause to be falsified, any book, record or account subject to Section 13(b)(2)(A) of the Securities Exchange Act."

The Commission has determined that Rule 13b2-1, while not directed solely to the problem of questionable or illegal corporate payments and practices, should serve to discourage a repetition of the serious abuses the Commission has uncovered. The Commission's experience, as set forth in the May 12 Report and subsequent enforcement actions,[30] demonstrates that questionable or illegal payments are rarely reflected correctly in corporate books and records and that the need to suppress information concerning such payments has frequently entailed the falsification of corporate books, records or accounts.

New Section 13(b)(2)(A) of the Securities Exchange Act requires that corporate books and records "accurately and fairly reflect the transactions and dispositions of the assets of the issuer." This provision is intended, among other things, to preclude the maintenance of

---

[28]*See e.g.,* the May 12 Report, Exhibit B; *Securities and Exchange Commission* v. *Aminex Resources Corp., et al.* (D.D.C., Civil Action No. 78-0410) *Securities and Exchange Commission* v. *Page Airways, Inc.* (D.D.C., Civil Action No. 78-0656) *Securities and Exchange Commission* v. *Katy Industries* (N.D. Ill., No. C 78-3476).

[29]*See* S. Rept. No. 114, *supra;* H.R. Rep. No. 95-640, *supra;* and H. Rept. No. 95-831, *supra.*

[30]*See, e.g.,* n. 28, *supra.*

off-the-books slush funds and to insure that corporate transactions and dispositions are properly recorded. It bears emphasis, in this context, that the new requirement is qualified by the phrase "in reasonable detail" rather than by the concept of "materiality."

In the Commission's judgment, new Rule 13b2-1 should promote compliance with the statutory requirement that issuers have accurate books and records by discouraging person from falsifying any corporate book, record, or account subject to new Section 13(b)(2)(A) and by making individuals directly liable for such conduct. Accordingly, the Rule is "necessary or appropriate," within the meaning of the Commission's general rulemaking authority, to implement new Section 13(b)(2) of the Securities Act.

In addition, the maintenance of accurate books and records by reporting companies is one of the foundations of the system of corporate disclosure embodied in the Securities Exchange Act. In this regard, the disclosure requirements of the Securities Exchange Act are based on the premise that "No investor * * * can safely buy or sell securities * * * without having an intelligent basis for forming his judgment as to the value of the securities he buys or sells."[31]

As the Commission has previously indicated, "The maintenance of accurate books and records by publicly-held companies is a necessary concomitant of the existing requirement for full, fair and accurate periodic reports."[32] In addition, as the May 12 Report reflects, the Commission's experience is that the falsification of corporate books and records has often been associated with the making of questionable and illegal payments.[33] In certain cases, concealed corporate payments and off-the-books slush funds were the result of actions by particular individuals, who acted with or without the knowledge of corporate management, to cause such transactions to be improperly recorded.[34] Given the importance of adequate information to "the maintenance of fair and honest [securities] markets,"[35] the sensitivity of securities prices to the availability of material information, and the close nexus between the maintenance of accurate books and records and the ability of reporting companies to disclose such information, the Commission has determined that the new rule is "necessary or appropriate" to implement "the disclosure provisions," and that, in this context, the rule is also "necessary or appropriate" in the public interest, for the protection of investors and to insure fair dealing in securities.

The Commission received comments from approximately 70 persons with respect to proposed Rule 13b-3, most of which expressed opposition to aspects of the rule. Many comments advocated changes that would: (a) limit application of the rule to "material" falsifications of corporate books, records and accounts; (b) require a showing of *"scienter"* before a person could be held liable for violations of the rule; and (c) limit application of the rule to persons having certain affiliations with an issuer, rather than "any person."

The advocates of a "materiality" standard expressed concern that false entries of insignificant or nominal amounts would give rise to a violation of the rule. In addition, some comments asserted that, in view of the large number of books, records and accounts kept by some corporations, particularly large corporations, application of the rule to any falsification of such books, records and accounts would make compliance impossible.

The Commission has considered these concerns and determined that it would not be desirable to modify the rule as suggested. New Rule 13b2-1 is, as noted above, applicable to

---

[31]H. Rept. No. 1383 73rd Cong., 2nd Sess. 11 (1934); *see* S. Rept. No. 1455, 73rd Cong., 2nd Sess. 68 (1934).

[32]*See* Securities Exchange Act Release No. 14478 (Feb. 16, 1978.)

[33]May 12 Report at a.

[34]*Id.*

[35]*See* Section 2 of the Securities Exchange Act, 15 U.S.C. 78b.

"any book, record or account subject to section 13(b)(2)(A) of the Securities Exchange Act." That provision was qualified by the Conference Committee, prior to enactment of the FCPA, to make clear that issuers are required to "make and keep books, records and accounts, which, *in reasonable detail,* accurately and fairly reflect the transactions and dispositions of the assets of the issuer * * *."[36] The Report of the Conference Committee indicates the change was made because the provision, "if unqualified, might connote a degree of exactitude and precision which is unrealistic."[37] It adds, "The amendment makes clear that the issuer's records should reflect transactions in conformity with accepted methods of recording economic events and effectively prevent off-the-books slush funds and payments of bribes."[38]

The Commission believes the presence of the words "in reasonable detail" in Section 13(b)(2)(A) should alleviate much of the concern expressed in comments concerning proposed rule 13b-3. In addition, it bears emphasis that compliance with new Section 13(b)(2)(B) of the Securities Exchange Act, concerning systems of internal accounting control, and increased use of audit committees composed of persons unaffiliated with the corporation or its management should facilitate compliance with new Rule 13b2-1. A further consideration is the Commission's concern that a limitation concerning "material" falsity would unduly narrow the scope of the rule and result in an unwarranted diminution of investor protection. Under these circumstances, the Commission has determined that it would be inappropriate to limit application of the Rule in the manner suggested.

Many comments expressed the view that a showing of *"scienter"* ought to be required in order to establish violations of the Rule. These comments were premised on the views that some false entries in corporate books, records and accounts result from inadvertent errors or oversights, and that a number of such entries are inevitable, particularly in view of the volume of transactions that must be recorded on a daily basis by large public companies. Some comments added that it would be unfair to impose liability upon persons who acted in good faith and made inadvertent or unintentional mistakes.

After careful consideration of the comments, the Commission has determined that a *"scienter"* requirement should not be included in the Rule. The inclusion of such a requirement would be inconsistent with the language of new section 13(b)(2)(A), which contains no words indicating that the Congress intended to impose a *"scienter"* requirement. It would be anomalous, under these circumstances, to include a *"scienter"* requirement in the new Rule.

Moreover, the Commission believes that the concern expressed with respect to inadvertent and inconsequential errors is unwarranted. The statute does not require perfection but only that books, records and accounts *"in reasonable detail,* accurately and fairly reflect the transactions and dispositions of the assets of the issuer" (emphasis added). In addition, the legislative history reflects that "standards of reasonableness" are to be used in applying this provision.[39]

Although Section 13 of the Securities Exchange Act authorizes the Commission to impose certain requirements upon issuers, Rule 13b2-1 provides that "no person" shall violate the terms of the Rule. The Rule, as proposed, contained substantially similar language applicable to "any person." In this regard, a number of commentators suggested that the rule should be applicable only to certain persons affiliated with an issuer rather than to "any person."

[36]H. Rept. No. 93-831, *supra,* at 10 (emphasis added).
[37]*Id.*
[38]*Id.*
[39]S. Rept. 95-114, *supra,* at 8.

The Commission has considered these comments, but has determined to promulgate the rule in a form substantially the same as that proposed. The effect of falsifications of books, records or accounts, in making reports required under Section 13 misleading or incomplete, is not necessarily contingent on the identity of the wrongdoer or on whether he acts with the knowledge or acquiescence of management. Moreover, while normally only officers and employees of the issuer are in a position to falsify corporate records, it is not feasible to identify in the Rule all categories of persons who might violate it. Consequently, the Commission believes that the rule should apply to any person who, in fact, does cause corporate books and records to be falsified.

Accordingly, because the falsification of accounting records, especially if falsified in order to conceal questionable corporate practices, may lead, among other things, to the concealment of material information that should be disclosed in periodic reports or to purchasers and sellers of the issuer's securities and to the omission of such information from proxy solicitations, and may also hinder the preparation of required reports, the Commission believes that the extension of Rule 13b2-1 to any person who violates the prohibition is "necessary or appropriate" to implement the "disclosure provisions" set forth as a basis for promulgation of the rule.[40]

B.   Adoption of Rule 13b2-2 (Proposed Rule 13b-4)

Rule 13b2-2 prohibits any officer[41] or director of an issuer, directly or indirectly, from making any materially false or misleading statement, or omitting to state any material fact necessary to make statements made not misleading, to an accountant in connection with an audit of the financial statements of the issuer or the filing of required reports. The Rule is similar to proposed rule 13b-4, although certain technical or clarifying changes have been made and the Rule has been narrowed by the deletion of "security holders" from the class of persons subject to the Rule.[42]

Based on its review of cases involving questionable or illegal corporate payments, the Commission's May 12 Report concluded:

> "The almost universal characteristic of the cases * * * has been the apparent frustration of our system of corporate accountability which has been designed to

---

[40]In this regard, Section 10(b) of the Act authorizes the Commission to prohibit manipulative or deceptive devices—regardless of by whom employed—in connection with the purchase or sale of securities. Section 14(a) of the Act, as implemented by Rule 14a-9, 17 CFR 240.14a-9, prohibits "any person" from soliciting proxies by means of proxy materials that contain false or misleading statements. In addition, Section 20(c) of the Act prohibits "any director or officer of, or any owner of any securities issued by, any issuer required to file any document, report or other information" from hindering, delaying or obstructing the making or filing of such document, report or information.

[41]Securities Exchange Act Rule 3b-3, 17 CFR 240.3b-3, defines the term "officer" to mean "a president, vice-president, treasurer, comptroller, and any other person who performs for an issuer, whether incorporated or unincorporated, functions corresponding to those performed by the foregoing officers."

[42]It bears emphasis, however, that controlling persons of an issuer may be liable for violations of the new Rule by virtue of Section 20(a) of the Securities Exchange Act. In addition, insofar as any director or officer of, or any owner of securities issued by, any issuer, engages in conduct prohibited by the new Rule in order to hinder, delay or obstruct the making or filing of any required report, document or information, such persons may be liable by virtue of Section 20(c) of the Act.

assure that there is proper accounting for the use of corporate funds and that documents filed with the Commission and circulated to shareholders do not omit or misrepresent material facts.''[43]

In this context the new Rule is primarily intended to help restore the efficacy of the system of corporate accountability and to encourage boards of directors to exercise their authority to deal with the problem.[44]

The Commission intends that the new rule encompass the audit of financial statements by independent accountants, the preparation of any required reports, whether by independent or internal accountants, the preparation of special reports to be filed with the Commission, as, for example, those filed pursuant to judicial orders incident to Commission enforcement proceedings, and any other work performed by an accountant that culminates in the filing of a document with the Commission.

As noted above, new Rule 13b2-2 is being promulgated, in part, pursuant to Section 13(b)(2) of the Securities Exchange Act. In this regard, the Commission has determined that the adoption of the Rule will promote compliance with the requirement of new Section 13(b)(2)(B) that issuers devise and maintain a system of internal accounting controls sufficient to achieve certain statutory objectives by assisting auditors in evaluating an issuer's system of internal accounting controls in connection with an examination or audit of the issuer's financial statements or the preparation or filing of any document or report with the Commission. Although the auditor's evaluation of the system of internal accounting control is traditionally conducted principally for the purpose of assisting the auditor in determining the scope and nature of his examination, such evaluations also frequently result in weaknesses in internal accounting controls being brought to the attention of the issuer by the auditor. The authoritative auditing literature (Statement on Auditing Standards No. 20) requires that defined ''material weaknesses'' which came to the attention of the auditor be communicated to the issuer.

Similarly, new Section 13(b)(2)(A) requires reporting companies to ''make and keep books, records, and accounts which in reasonable detail, accurately and fairly reflect the transactions and disposition of the assets of the issuer.'' The Commission believes that the adoption of new Rule 13b2-2 will act as a deterrent to the falsification of corporate books, records and accounts and to the making of false, misleading or incomplete statements to an accountant or auditor that might conceal the falsification of such books and records. Accordingly, the Commission has determined that adoption of Rule 13b2-2 is ''necessary or appropriate,'' within the meaning of Section 23(a), to implement the provisions of new Section 13(b)(2).

The prohibition against making false, misleading or incomplete statements to accountants, in connection with an audit, or the filing of required reports, is also being promulgated as ''necessary or appropriate'' to implement the various ''disclosure provisions,'' discussed above in connection with Rule 13b2-1, and as ''necessary or appropriate'' in the public interest, for the protection of investors and to insure fair dealing in securities. In this regard, the accountant's examination or audit of the financial statements of the issuer is a crucial element in safeguarding the reliability of the information that is disclosed to the public pursuant to the disclosure requirements of the Securities Exchange Act. The integrity of the financial disclosure system is diminished when issuers impede accountants or auditors in

[43]May 12 Report at a.
[44]*See* May 12 Report at b.

the discharge of their responsibilities by providing them with false, misleading or incomplete information.

In this context, the Commission believes that new Rule 13b2-2 will encourage careful and accurate communications between auditors and issuers from whom they request information during the audit process, deter the making of false, misleading or incomplete statements to accountants, and thereby enhance the integrity of financial disclosure system.

The Commission received comments from approximately 80 persons with respect to proposed Rule 13b-4, most of which questioned certain aspects of the proposal. The majority of these comments expressed concern that the proposed rule would: (a) require no showing of *scienter* in order to establish a violation based upon the making of false, misleading or incomplete statements to an accountant in the course of an examination or audit; (b) impose liability for oral, as well as written, statements made to an accountant; and (c) make minority shareholders of an issuer liable for violations of the rule. In addition, many of the comments asserted that imposition of liability for misstatements or omissions, in the absence of a *scienter* requirement, would be counterproductive and impede communications between auditors and those from whom they seek information in the course of an audit. In fact, a number of comments suggested that some persons would refuse to communicate with an auditor rather than expose themselves to potential liability.

The Commission disagrees with the assertion that a *scienter* requirement should be added to the Rule for the reasons set forth above at pp. 24-25 with respect to Rule 13b2-1.[45] In addition, the Commission believes its experience concerning questionable and illegal payments is more persuasive as to the need for such a rule than the opinions expressed by some commentators to the effect that the rule will impede communications between auditors and those from whom they seek information. Under these circumstances, the Commission has decided that the advantages of the new Rule outweigh the potential disadvantages suggested by certain commentators.

Some of the comments suggested that the proposed rule should be applicable only to written statements that are submitted to an auditor in the course of an examination or audit and that oral statements should not be covered by the rule. In this regard, it was suggested that auditors will usually obtain written representations concerning matters of material significance and that such a limitation would permit persons to review written communications and thereby minimize the possibility that false, misleading or incomplete statements would be made in the absence of *scienter* or an intent to deceive.

The Commission believes that a distinction between written and oral statements is inappropriate, primarily because oral statements may be no less harmful to investors than a misleading written statement. Moreover, section 12(2) of the Securities Act,[46] and the anti-fraud provisions of the Securities Exchange Act, have long been applied in Commission enforcement actions and private actions to oral misstatements without unusual or unintended consequences. While the Commission is sensitive to concerns expressed by some commentators that oral statements which are inaccurately recorded in accountants' work papers may become the basis for liability under the Rule, on balance, the Commission believes a distinction between written and oral statements would unduly narrow the scope of the Rule. Moreover, this concern can be alleviated to some degree by the exercise of care in the preparation of accountants' work papers and by accountants' requesting written confirmations of material representations.

New Rule 13b2-2, as adopted, is applicable only to any director or officer of an issuer. In

---

[45]*See* pp. 24-25, *supra.*
[46]15 U.S.C. 77l(2).

this regard, most of the comments concerning the proposed rule questioned the applicability of the rule to any owner of securities issued by a reporting company. Several suggested that the rule should be applicable only to controlling shareholders, or the beneficial owners of a certain percentage of a class of securities, while others expressed the view that the rule, as drafted, would discriminate between employees of an issuer who own the issuer's securities and those employees who do not. In addition, some comments opined that shareholders might be deterred from providing confirmations to accountants if they were made subject to the rule. After careful consideration of these comments, the Commission decided to delete shareholders from the coverage of the new Rule.

It must be stressed, however, that the exclusion from the express language of the new Rule of shareholders, low-level corporate employees of an issuer, and persons unaffiliated with the issuer does not indicate that those individuals may mislead the issuer's accountants with impunity. As noted above, controlling persons of an issuer may be held liable for such conduct by virtue of Section 20 of the Securities Exchange Act.[47] In addition, the existing antifraud provisions of the federal securities laws, and the concept of aiding and abetting, can be invoked, in appropriate circumstances, against those who deceive the auditors of a publicly held corporation. In this area, as in other areas where duties and liabilities are created under the federal securities laws, case-by-case balancing is essential with respect to the needs of the investing public and the interests of those who have engaged in conduct injurious to investors.

V.   OTHER MATTERS

The Commission specifically requested comments concerning "the likely impact, if any, which * * * [the proposed rules] would have on conpetition."[48] Approximately ten comments addressed this issue, but the comments were primarily directed toward proposed rules 13b-1 and 13b-2, which would have imposed requirements upon reporting companies. The Commission has determined that the instant rules will not impose a "burden on competition" within the meaning of Section 23(a)(2) of the Securities Exchange Act.

The Commission has also considered whether it might be appropriate to republish these rules for further public comment. In this regard, the Commission decided that it is not necessary to obtain additional comments before promulgating the new rules ånd that the delay inherent in republication would not be in the public interest. The Commission intends, however, to monitor the impact of the new rules and invites comments from interested persons concerning that subject.

VI.   TEXT OF RULES

Accordingly, 17 CFR 240 is amended by adding §§ 240.13b2-1 and 240.13b2-2 as set forth below:

REGULATION 13b-2: MAINTENANCE OF RECORDS AND PREPARATION OF REQUIRED REPORTS

§ 240.13b2-1   Falsification of accounting records.

No person shall directly or indirectly, falsify or cause to be falsified, any book, record or account subject to Section 13(b)(2)(A) of the Securities Exchange Act.

---

[47]*See* n. 42, *supra.*

[48]*See* Securities Exchange Act Release No. 34-13185, *supra.*

§ 240.13b2-2   Issuer's representations in connection with the preparation of required reports and documents.

No director or officer of an issuer shall, directly or indirectly,

(a) Make or cause to be made a materially false or misleading statement, or

(b) Omit to state, or cause another person to omit to state, any material fact necessary in order to make statements made, in the light of the circumstances under which such statements were made, not misleading to an accountant in connection with (1) any audit or examination of the financial statements of the issuer required to be made pursuant to this subpart of (2) the preparation or filing of any document or report required to be filed with the Commission pursuant to this subpart or otherwise.

By the Commission (Chairman Williams and Commissioners Loomis, Evans, and Pollack concurring; Commissioner Karmel dissenting).

GEORGE A. FITZSIMMONS,
Secretary

FEBRUARY 15, 1979.

SEPARATE STATEMENT OF VIEWS BY COMMISSIONER KARMEL

The Foreign Corrupt Practices Act of 1977 was enacted after the comment period had closed with respect to the proposals for these rules. Therefore, I believe it would have been desirable as a matter of policy to republish the proposals and seek additional comments concerning the relationship between the proposed rules and the accounting provisions of the new statute.

With respect to the substance of the new rules, I would have preferred a more restrained implementation of the Commission's statutory authority. In my view, the Commission should have limited the applicability of Rule 13b2-1, as a matter of policy, to cases of intentional falsification of accounting records, or deliberate circumvention of internal accounting control systems. Although, in my view, "falsify" implies an element of deceit, it does not go far enough in articulating a standard of wrongful intent for culpable conduct. In addition, I do not believe it is necessary or appropriate to regulate communications between accountants and their clients by way of the prohibitions contained in Rule 13b2-2.

For the foregoing reasons, I disagree with the Commission's determination to promulgate new Regulation 13B-2 as drafted at this time.

SECURITIES AND EXCHANGE COMMISSION
[17 CFR Parts 211, 229, 240, 249]
[Release No. 34-15772, File No. S7-779]
STATEMENT OF MANAGEMENT ON INTERNAL ACCOUNTING CONTROL

AGENCY: Securities and Exchange Commission.

ACTION: Proposed rules.

SUMMARY: Since the enactment of the Foreign Corrupt Practices Act of 1977, interest in the effectiveness of internal accounting controls has been enhanced. To provide information about the effectiveness of systems of internal accounting control, the Commission is proposing for comment rules which would require inclusion of a statement of management on internal accounting control in annual reports on Form 10-K filed with the Commission under the Securities Exchange Act of 1934, and in annual reports to security holders furnished pursuant to the proxy rules. The Commission also is proposing that such statement be examined and reported on by an independent public accountant.

DATES: Comments should be received by the Commission on or before July 31, 1979.

ADDRESS: Comments should be submitted in triplicate to George A. Fitzsimmons, Secretary, Securities and Exchange Commission, 500 North Capitol Street, Washington, D.C. 20549. Comment letters should refer to File No. S7-779. All comments received will be available for public inspection and copying in the Commission's Public Reference Room, 1100 L Street, N.W., Washington, D.C. 20549.

FOR FURTHER INFORMATION CONTACT: James J. Doyle (202-472-3782), Office of the Chief Accountant, Securities and Exchange Commission, 500 North Capitol Street, Washington, D.C. 20549.

SUPPLEMENTARY INFORMATION: The Securities and Exchange Commission is proposing for public comment amendments to Form 10-K (17 CFR 249.310); Regulation 14A (17 CFR 240.14a-1 *et seq.*); and Regulation S-K (17 CFR 229.20). The proposed amendments, if adopted, would require inclusion of a statement of management on internal accounting control in Forms 10-K and in annual reports to security holders furnished pursuant to Rule 14a-3 [17 CFR 240.14a-3]. To standardize the disclosure requirements, the information to be included in the statement of management on internal accounting control would be specified in proposed new Item 7 of Regulation S-K.

The amendments are proposed to be adopted in two stages. As of dates after December 15, 1979 and prior to December 16, 1980 for which audited balance sheets are required, the statement of management on internal accounting control would be required to include the following:

1. Management's opinion as to whether, as of the date of such audited balance sheet, the systems of internal accounting control of the registrant and its subsidiaries provided reasonable assurances that specified objectives of internal accounting control were achieved; and

2. A description of any material weaknesses in internal accounting control communicated by the independent accountants of the registrant or its subsidiaries which have not been corrected, and a statement of the reasons why they have not been corrected.

For periods ending after December 15, 1980 for which audited statements of income are required, the statement of management on internal accounting control would be required to include management's opinion as to whether, for such periods, the systems of internal accounting control of the registrant and its subsidiaries provided reasonable assurances that the specified objectives of internal accounting control were achieved. In addition, the statement of management on internal accounting control would be required to be examined and reported on by an independent public accountant for such periods.

Thus, initially the management opinion which would be required would extend only to conditions existing as of the balance sheet date, and the statement of management would not be required to be examined and reported on by an independent accountant. There would be a specific disclosure requirement relating to any material weaknesses in internal accounting control communicated by the independent accountants which have not been corrected.

After the initial stage, the management opinion which would be required would extend to conditions which existed during the periods for which audited statements of income are required, and the statement of management would be required to be examined and reported on by an independent public accountant.

I. Background and Basis for Proposed Rules

In December, 1977, Congress enacted the Foreign Corrupt Practices Act of 1977 ("FCPA").[1] Among other things, the FCPA requires that issuers subject to the registration and reporting provisions of the Securities Exchange Act of 1934, as amended, devise and maintain a system of internal accounting control sufficient to provide reasonable assurances that

"(i) transactions are executed in accordance with management's general or specific authorization;

"(ii) transactions are recorded as necessary (a) to permit preparation of financial statements in conformity with generally accepted accounting principles or any other criteria applicable to such statements, and (b) to maintain accountability for assets;

"(iii) access to assets is permitted only in accordance with management's general or specific authorization; and

"(iv) the recorded accountability for assets is compared with the existing assets at reasonable intervals and appropriate action is taken with respect to any differences."[2]

While the FCPA, which was effective upon enactment,[3] contains a specific statutory requirement that certain issuers devise and maintain an effective system of internal accounting control, the establishment and maintenance of such a system have always been important responsibilities of management. An effective system of internal accounting control has always been necessary to produce reliable financial statements and other financial information generated from the accounting system, as well as to assure that assets and transactions of the business are adequately controlled.

The Commission believes that information regarding the effectiveness of an issuer's system of internal accounting control may be necessary to enable investors to better evaluate management's performance of its stewardship responsibilities and the reliability of interim financial statements and other unaudited financial information generated from the accounting system, and that, therefore, the proposed rules may be necessary to the interests of investors and other users of financial information.[4]

---

[1]Title I of Public Law No. 95-213 (December 19, 1977).

[2]These internal accounting control provisions of the FCPA are codified in Section 13(b)(2)(B) of the Securities Exchange Act of 1934, 15 U.S.C. 78m(b)(2)(B).

[3]The Commission discussed the enactment of the FCPA in Accounting Series Release No. 242 (Securities Exchange Act Release No. 14478, February 16, 1978, 43 FR 7752), in which it stated:

"Because the Act became effective upon signing, it is important that issuers subject to the new requirements review their accounting procedures, systems of internal accounting controls and business practices in order that they may take any actions necessary to comply with the requirements contained in the Act."

The Commission also discussed the provisions of the FCPA in Securities Exchange Act Release No. 34-15570 (44 FR 10964), February 15, 1979.

[4]The Commission on Auditor's Responsibilities ("Cohen Commission") concluded that users of financial information are interested in whether controls are adequate to reduce the risk of loss of assets through unauthorized use or misappropriation and to produce reliable financial information, and that users may need to be informed, as part of adequate disclosure, about the condition of controls. See the Commission on Auditor's Responsibilities: "Report, Conclusions, and Recommendations" (1978) (hereinafter cited as "Cohen Commission Report"), p. 55. See also M. V. Brown, "Auditors and Internal Controls: An Analyst's View," *CPA Journal* 47 (September, 1977), pp. 27-31.

In proposing to require a statement of management on internal accounting control, the Commission is not setting forth detailed, prescriptive rules for control procedures and techniques which will ensure compliance with the internal accounting control provisions of the FCPA. The Commission believes that the control procedures and techniques which will provide for compliance with those provisions must be determined in the context of the circumstances of each issuer, and it is the responsibility of management to make those determinations.

As noted above, the Commission is proposing that, for periods ending after December 15, 1980 for which audited statements of income are required, the statement of management on internal accounting control be examined and reported on by an independent public accountant. Because of the independent public accountant's expertise with respect to internal accounting control and the fact that internal accounting control is integral to preparation of financial statements, the Commission believes that an examination by an independent public accountant of a statement of management on internal accounting control would result in increased reliability of such a statement. It should be emphasized, however, that the independent accountant's responsibility will be more limited than that of management. The responsibility for complying with the substantive internal accounting control provisions of the FCPA, as well as with the disclosure requirements of these proposed rules, rests with the issuer and its management.

The Commission notes that increasing attention recently has been focused on the need for a "management report" directed to management responsibilities for financial reporting. The principal initiative in this regard was taken by the Cohen Commission, which recommended, among other things, that companies include with the financial statements a report that acknowledges management's responsibilities with respect to the financial information reported.[5] The Financial Executives Institute ("FEI") responded to the Cohen Commission's recommendation by endorsing the furnishing of a management report and, in June 1978, issued suggested guidelines for preparation of a management report. Those guidelines generally follow the recommendations of the Cohen Commission. In addition, the American Institute of Certified Public Accountants ("AICPA") formed the Reports by Management Special Advisory Committee, consisting of financial executives, attorneys, a financial analyst, and other users of financial information, to consider the Cohen Commission's recommendations pertaining to management reports and to develop guidance on matters that should be included in a management report. In December 1978, the Reports by Management Special Advisory Committee issued, for public comment, a report of its tentative conclusions and recommendations.[6]

The Cohen Commission's report, the FEI guidelines, and the AICPA Special Advisory Committee's tentative report each contain the suggestion that a management report include an assessment of the company's system of internal accounting control.[7] This aspect of a

---

[5]Cohen Commission Report. See generally pp. 76-80.

[6]Tentative Conclusions and Recommendations of the Reports by Management Special Advisory Committee, AICPA, December 8, 1978.

[7]The example of a management representation regarding assessment of the company's system of internal accounting control contained in the tentative report of the Reports by Management Special Advisory Committee is limited to "errors or irregularities that could be material to the financial statements"(*id.* at p. 5). As discussed herein, neither the internal accounting control provisions of the FCPA nor the representations which would be required in the proposed statement of management on internal accounting control are so limited. *See also* Securities Exchange Act Release No. 15570, *supra*, n. 3.

management report has received significantly more attention than any other, in large part as a result of the enactment of the FCPA.

It should be noted that the management statement which the Commission is proposing today does not involve matters other than internal accounting control that might be included in a management report. The Commission intends to follow closely the further initiatives of the private sector and will consider the need to propose additional rules relating to such other matters. In the meantime, the Commission encourages issuers to provide meaningful disclosure regarding management responsibilities. At this time, however, the Commission is proposing to require only the more limited management statement discussed and set forth below.

II. DISCUSSION OF PROPOSED RULES
A. Management Opinion

Proposed Item 7(a) of Regulation S-K would require a statement of management's opinion as to whether, as of any date after December 15, 1979 and prior to December 16, 1980 for which an audited balance sheet is required, and for periods ending after December 15, 1980 for which audited statements of income are required, the systems of internal accounting control of the registrant and its subsidiaries provided reasonable assurances that:

1. Transactions were executed in accordance with management's general or specific authorization;
2. Transactions were recorded as necessary (a) to permit preparation of financial statements in conformity with generally accepted accounting principles (or other applicable criteria), and (b) to maintain accountability for assets;
3. Access to assets was permitted only in accordance with management's general or specific authorization; and
4. The recorded accountability for assets was compared with the existing assets at reasonable intervals and appropriate action was taken with respect to any differences.

1. *Objectives of Internal Accounting Control*

Proposed Item 7(a) is based upon the broad objectives of internal accounting control stated in the FCPA. In this regard, the Commission recognizes that systems of internal accounting control must be designed to fit individual circumstances. Numerous factors, such as the types of products or services provided, types of customers, degree of centralization, and methods of data processing, will affect the choice of control procedures that may be necessary or appropriate to achieve the broad control objectives. Consequently, it is not practicable to prepare a comprehensive list of internal accounting control procedures, nor is it possible to prepare a list of certain internal accounting control procedures which would be appropriate for all organizations.

2. *Internal Accounting Controls*

The Commission believes that it is important to emphasize that the scope of internal accounting control cannot be defined in terms of types of control procedures or in terms of organizational or functional departments. Any factors within an organization which affect the achievement of the objectives of internal accounting control must be considered in evaluating the effectiveness of a system of internal accounting control, and may often include factors which also are concerned with what the authoritative auditing literature defines as "administrative control." [8]

In this connection, the AICPA's Special Advisory Committee on Internal Accounting Control emphasized the importance to the effectiveness of systems of internal accounting control of factors in addition to specific internal accounting control procedures:

"The internal accounting control environment established by management has a significant impact on the selection and effectiveness of a company's accounting control procedures and techniques.

"The control environment is shaped by several factors. Some are clearly visible, like a formal corporate conduct policy statement or an internal audit function. Some are intangible, like the competence and integrity of personnel. Some, like organizational structure and the way in which management communicates, enforces, and reinforces policy, vary so widely among companies that they can be contrasted more easily than they can be compared.

"Although it is difficult to measure the significance of each factor, it is generally possible to make an overall evaluation. The committee believes that an overall evaluation of a company's internal accounting control environment is a necessary prelude to the evaluation of control procedures and techniques.

"A poor control environment would make some accounting controls inoperative for all intents and purposes because, for example, individuals would hesitate to challenge a management override of a specific control procedure. On the other hand, a strong control environment, for example, one with tight budgetary controls and an effective internal audit function, can have an important bearing on the selection and effectiveness of specific accounting control procedures and techniques." [9]

The Commission concurs with the foregoing statements of the Special Advisory Committee regarding the importance of the control environment to the effectiveness of a system of internal accounting control. The Commission also agrees that, in addition to the overall importance of an environment which provides a high level of control consciousness, individual environmental factors, such as strong budgetary controls and an effective, objective internal audit function, can contribute directly to achievement of internal accounting control objectives and must be considered in evaluating whether reasonable assurance of achievement of such objectives is provided.

3. *Reasonable Assurance*

Like the specified objectives of internal accounting control, the phrase "reasonable assurance" is contained in the FCPA. The concept of reasonable, as opposed to absolute, assurance is incorporated in the proposed rules in recognition that it is not in the interest of shareholders for the cost of internal accounting control to exceed the benefits thereof. Such benefits, and in many cases such costs, are not likely to be precisely quantifiable. Therefore,

---

[8]See Statement on Auditing Standards No. 1, AICPA, Section 320.27, for the definition of administrative control. That statement also recognizes, at Section 320.29, that administrative controls and accounting controls are not mutually exclusive.

[9]Tentative Report of the Special Advisory Committee on Internal Accounting Control, AICPA, September 15, 1978 (hereinafter cited as "Tentative Report"), p. 9. See generally pp. 9-12 for a discussion of the control environment. The Special Advisory Committee was formed to develop criteria for evaluating internal accounting controls. The Tentative Report was issued to solicit comments from interested parties and, thus, is not the final work product of the Special Advisory Committee. The Special Advisory Committee plans to issue a final report in the near future.

many decisions on reasonable assurance will necessarily depend in part on estimates and judgments by management which are reasonable under the circumstances.

Consideration of the benefits of internal accounting controls generally will involve some degree of estimation of the possible effects and the likelihood of occurrence of various future conditions and events. In addition, the benefits to be considered often may include not only quantitative benefits, such as reduction in exposure to theft of assets, but also qualitative benefits, such as the reputation of the company and its management. For example, the benefits to be considered in connection with evaluating controls intended to prevent bribes and other illegal payments cannot be measured solely by the amounts of such payments which might be prevented. Rather, as the Commission repeatedly has emphasized,[10] the relationship between such illegal payments, and other questionable activities—whether or not the amounts are significant—and the reputation of the company and integrity of its management is a significant benefit to be considered. The Commission recognizes that placing a value on such qualitative factors will almost invariably involve judgments by management.

Many managements may decide that it is desirable to discuss in the statement on internal accounting control the concept of reasonable assurance and the extent to which decisions on reasonable assurance depend on management estimates and judgments. Some may believe that such a discussion is essential for informed use of the statement.[11] Comments are requested on whether such a discussion should be required in all statements of management on internal accounting control.

The Commission recognizes that there are limitations upon the effectiveness of any system of internal accounting control.[12] However, limitations upon the effectiveness of a system of internal accounting control do not limit the responsibility of registrants to maintain a system of internal accounting control which provides reasonable assurances that the objectives of internal accounting control are achieved. Indeed, the fact that errors may arise as a result of human frailties, that systems of internal accounting control may be circumvented as a result of collusion or overridden by management,[13] and that changes in conditions may require changes in control procedures, mandates ongoing review and monitoring of any internal accounting control system if such reasonable assurance is to be provided.

4. *Evaluation of Internal Accounting Controls*
   a. *Conceptual Elements*

The Commission believes that specific methods of approaching and implementing evaluations of systems of internal accounting control will vary from company to company. Accordingly, the proposed rules do not specify the method of or procedures to be performed in an evaluation of internal accounting control.

[10]See generally Report of the Securities and Exchange Commission on Questionable and Illegal Payments and Practices Submitted to the Committee on Banking, Housing and Urban Affairs, United States Senate (May 12, 1976). Also see, e.g., *S.E.C. v. Sharon Steel Corporation,* Civil No. 77-1631 (D.C.D.C., September 20, 1977) and *S.E.C. v. Ormand Industries, Inc.,* Civil No. 77-0790 (D.C.D.C., May 9, 1977).

[11]The Cohen Commission's example of a management report includes such a discussion. See Cohen Commission Report, p. 79.

[12]Limitations of internal accounting control are discussed in Statement on Auditing Standards No. 1, AICPA, Section 320.4.

[13]In this regard, in February 1979 the Commission adopted Regulation 13B-2, which expressly prohibits the falsification of corporate books, records, or accounts and prohibits the officers and directors of an issuer from making false, misleading or incomplete statements to any accountant in connection with any audit or examination of the issuer's financial statements or the preparation of required reports. See Securities Exchange Act Release No. 15570, *supra,* n. 3.

However, the Commission believes that evaluations by managements of systems of internal accounting control should encompass certain conceptual elements.[14] Determination of whether a system of internal accounting control provides reasonable assurances that the broad objectives of internal accounting control are achieved generally will involve the following:

- First, evaluation of the overall control environment;
- Second, translation of the broad objectives of internal accounting control into specific control objectives applicable to the particular business, organizational and other characteristics of the individual company;
- Third, consideration of the specific control procedures and individual environmental factors which should contribute to achievement of the specific control objectives;
- Fourth, monitoring of control procedures and consideration of whether they are functioning as intended; and
- Finally, consideration of the benefits (consisting of reductions in the risk of failing to achieve the objectives) and costs of additional or alternative controls.

The first element of such a determination is evaluation of the overall control environment. The Commission recognizes that such evaluations will require a careful exercise of management's judgment, generally involving consideration of matters such as the organizational structure, including the role of the board of directors; communication of corporate procedures, policies and related codes of conduct; communication of authority and responsibility; competence and integrity of personnel; accountability for performance and for compliance with policies and procedures; and the objectivity and effectiveness of the internal audit function. The role of the board of directors in overseeing the establishment and maintenance of a strong control environment, and in overseeing the procedures for evaluating a system of internal accounting control, is particularly important. The Commission has often stressed the importance of audit committees to enable boards of directors to better fulfill their oversight responsibilities with respect to an issuer's accounting, financial reporting and control obligations.[15]

A strong control environment will not, in itself, provide a basis for reasonable assurance

---

[14]The Commission believes that the conceptual elements discussed herein also are reflected in the Tentative Report of the AICPA's Special Advisory Committee on Internal Accounting Control (see Note 11, *supra*). The Commission believes that the work of the Special Advisory Committee should be very useful to managements by providing a framework which will be helpful to all companies in establishing an approach, or appraising the effectiveness of an existing approach, to evaluate whether the broad objectives of internal accounting control are achieved. However, the Special Advisory Committee's Tentative Report does not represent a manual that can be followed by companies in evaluating their accounting control systems. This was recognized by the Special Advisory Committee (at p. 8 of the Tentative Report):

"[T]he approach to an evaluation suggested in this report is not the only way an evaluation can be performed, and the criteria included . . . are not and cannot be detailed rules. However, the committee believes that the recommendations in this report should help management in its continuing evaluation and monitoring of internal accounting control."

[15]See Securities Exchange Act Release No. 14970 (43 FR 31945), July 18, 1978, in which the Commission proposed rules requiring issuers to state whether they have an audit committee and whether it performs "customary functions" of such committees, and which includes a discussion of previous Commission actions regarding audit committees. The Commission adopted the proposal in Securities Exchange Act Release No. 15384 (43 FR 58522), December 6, 1978, after amending it to require disclosure of the functions which the audit committee actually performs.

that the broad objectives of internal accounting control are achieved. However, the Commission agrees with the AICPA's Special Advisory Committee on Internal Accounting Control that

". . . [i]t is unlikely that management can have reasonable assurance that the broad objectives of internal accounting control are being met unless the company has an environment that establishes an appropriate level of control consciousness."[16]

For that reason, an evaluation of the overall control environment is a necessary first step in evaluating a system of internal accounting control.

The second and third conceptual elements of an evaluation of a system of internal accounting control might be characterized as review of the system. The effectiveness of the design of control procedures in place cannot be evaluated without first relating the broad objectives of internal accounting control to the particular circumstances of a company. The AICPA's Special Advisory Committee on Internal Accounting Control found a transaction cycle approach a convenient way to develop illustrative specific control objectives and examples of specific control procedures and techniques.[17] Some companies might use a transaction cycle approach in reviewing the system; others might organize a review of the system by functional area within the organization or use some other approach or combination of approaches. Regardless of the way in which the review of the system is organized, what is important is that the specific control objectives appropriate for the company, and the specific control procedures and individual environmental factors which should contribute to achievement of those specific objectives, are identified and considered.

The fourth conceptual element of an evaluation of a system of internal accounting control might be characterized as monitoring compliance with control procedures. Management must have reasonable assurance not only that the system of internal accounting control is appropriately designed, but also that it is functioning as designed. In addition, knowledge that adherence to company policies and procedures will be monitored is an important element of an overall control environment. Monitoring compliance with control procedures may take place through observation and supervision and through testing of controls in effect. An objective, effective internal audit function can play an important role in monitoring compliance.

The final conceptual element of an evaluation of a system of internal accounting control might be characterized as determination of reasonable assurance. As discussed previously, determining whether reasonable assurance of achievement of control objectives is provided often will depend in part on estimates and judgments by managements.

b. *Documentation*

Appropriate documentation is important to each aspect of an evaluation of internal accounting control. The overall control environment often will be enhanced by written policies and procedures, formalized reporting responsibilities within the organization, and written descriptions of authority and responsibility. Very few, if any, registrants could perform an effective review of their systems of internal accounting control without documenting their specific control objectives and the control procedures in place which should contribute to achieving those objectives. Documentation of tests of controls in effect is necessary to determine that the tests were appropriately planned and performed and that the results of the tests were appropriately considered. Because of the judgmental aspects of cost-benefit analyses, a record of the bases for management's conclusions with respect to reasonable assurance considerations may be particularly important.

[16]Tentative Report, p. 8.
[17]See Tentative Report, p. 12.

c. *Performance of Evaluation Procedures*

Because of the interaction of numerous factors both within and outside the organization which affects the choice of control procedures necessary to obtain reasonable assurances that the broad objectives of internal accounting control have been achieved, control systems are necessarily dynamic. As a result of this dynamic nature and the possibilities that controls may be circumvented or overridden and that compliance with control procedures may deteriorate, evaluation of any system of internal accounting control requires ongoing review of the system and monitoring compliance with control procedures.

It should be emphasized that the management opinion which would be required by proposed Item 7(a) for periods ending after December 15, 1980 would encompass reasonable assurances of achievement of the broad objectives of internal accounting control during the periods for which audited statements of income are required. The Commission believes that effective, ongoing evaluations of systems of internal accounting control often may result in identification of the need for and implementation of improvements in a system. To the extent that such improvements are necessitated by changing circumstances (including both circumstances which affect the benefits of controls by changing the risks of failing to achieve the broad objectives of internal accounting control and circumstances which change the costs of controls) and are made on a timely basis, the Commission believes that they do not indicate that the system did not provide reasonable assurances of achievement of the objectives of internal accounting control. In this connection, the Commission encourages the process of interaction between registrants and their independent accountants whereby independent accountants suggest ways in which management might improve its internal accounting controls.

On the other hand, weaknesses which have existed but have not been identified on a timely basis as a result of inadequate procedures for review and monitoring of the system of internal accounting control would indicate that the system did not provide reasonable assurances of achievement of the objectives of internal accounting control throughout the period and, therefore, would preclude an unqualified management opinion under proposed Item 7(a) for periods ending after December 15, 1980. Of course, any weaknesses which have been identified but not appropriately corrected also would preclude such an unqualified opinion.

The Commission recognizes that some registrants may conclude that maintenance of review and monitoring procedures which will be sufficient to obtain reasonable assurances that the objectives of internal accounting control are achieved does not require performance of all such procedures at all locations in each reporting period. Because of the dynamic nature of internal accounting control and the resultant continuing nature of the evaluation process, the extent and timing of the review and monitoring of a system of internal accounting control are among the cost-benefit judgments involved in the concept of reasonable assurance. In its determinations regarding the need to take enforcement action with respect to the internal accounting control provisions of the FCPA, among other things the Commission will consider the nature of weaknesses in a system of internal accounting control and efforts to identify and correct such weaknesses.

B.   "Material Weaknesses" in Internal Accounting Control

Proposed Item 7(b) of Regulation S-K would require that statements of management on internal accounting control as of dates after December 15, 1979 and prior to December 16, 1980 include a description of any "material weaknesses" in internal accounting control which have been communicated by the independent accountants of the registrant or its subsidiaries which have not been corrected and a statement of the reasons why they have not been corrected.

Present auditing standards with respect to internal accounting control are directed to, and were developed in the context of, examinations of financial statements. Under generally accepted auditing standards, the auditor's purpose in reviewing and evaluating internal accounting control is not to determine whether the broad objectives of internal accounting control have been achieved, but rather to form a basis for determining the scope of the examination of the financial statements. Under present auditing standards,[18] the responsibility of an independent public accountant for reporting on the results of the review and evaluation of internal accounting control performed in connection with an examination of financial statements is limited to reporting to management and the board of directors or audit committee "material weaknesses" which came to the accountant's attention.[19]

The examination by an independent public accountant of the statement of management on internal accounting control which would be required by proposed Item 7(c) of Regulation S-K would be required initially for periods ending after December 15, 1980. The Commission believes it is appropriate in the first, more limited, stage of the proposed rules, wherein an examination by an independent public accountant would not be required by the proposed rules, to require disclosure by management relating to any uncorrected "material weaknesses" communicated by independent accountants as a result of their present responsibilities with respect to examinations of financial statements, including disclosure of the reasons why such "material weaknesses" were not corrected.

It should be noted that the independent accountant will have certain responsibilities, including revision of his report on the financial statements to include an explanatory paragraph, in the event management does not appropriately disclose uncorrected "material weaknesses" under proposed Item 7(b).[20]

C. Examination by Independent Public Accountant

Proposed Item 7(c) of Regulation S-K would require that, for periods ending after December 15, 1980, the statement of management on internal accounting control be examined and reported on by an independent public accountant.

Independent public accountants have long been involved with internal accounting control. The auditing profession's second standard of field work states:

> "There is to be a proper study and evaluation of the existing internal control as a basis for reliance thereon and for the determination of the resultant extent of the tests to which auditing procedures are to be restricted."[21]

In addition, the objectives of internal accounting control set forth in the FCPA, which are the same as those in proposed Item 7(a) of Regulation S-K, were taken directly from Section 320.28 of Statement on Auditing Standards No. 1. Because of the independent public

---

[18]See Statement on Auditing Standards No. 20, AICPA.

[19]A "material weakness" is defined in Statement on Auditing Standards No. 1, AICPA, Section 320.68, as

". . . [a] condition in which the auditor believes the prescribed procedures or the degree of compliance with them does not provide reasonable assurance that errors or irregularities in amounts that would be material in the financial statements being audited would be prevented or detected within a timely period by employees in the normal course of performing their assigned functions."

[20]Statement on Auditing Standards No. 8, AICPA, sets forth the independent accountant's responsibilities when the accountant is aware of any material inconsistencies or material misstatements of fact in documents containing audited financial statements.

[21]Statement on Auditing Standards No. 1, AICPA, Section 150.02.

accountant's expertise with respect to internal accounting control and the fact that internal accounting control is integral to preparation of financial statements, the Commission believes that an examination by an independent public accountant of a statement of management on internal accounting control would result in increased reliability of such a management statement.

1. *Objectives of Examination*

Proposed Item 7(c) specifies that the examination be sufficient to enable the independent public accountant to express an opinion as to (1) whether the representations of management in response to proposed Item 7(a) are consistent with the results of management's evaluation of the systems of internal accounting control, and (2) whether such management representations are, in addition, reasonable with respect to transactions and assets in amounts which would be material when measured in relation to the registrant's financial statements. The proposed examination by an independent public accountant of the statement of management on internal accounting control would, therefore, require expansion of the independent public accountant's present responsibilities with respect to internal accounting control.

To reach an opinion, as would be required by proposed Item 7(c)(1), as to whether the management representations were consistent with the results of management's evaluation of the systems of internal accounting control, the independent public accountant would have to review management's procedures for reviewing, monitoring and evaluating the systems of internal accounting control and the results thereof. The purposes of this review would be to determine whether the management representations recognized any conditions which indicated that reasonable assurances of achievement of the objectives of internal accounting control were not provided, and to determine that management's procedures for reviewing, monitoring and evaluating the systems of internal accounting control were not insufficient as a basis for its representations. Although the independent accountant would not necessarily be required to perform independent tests to reach the opinion which would be required under proposed Item 7(c)(1), that opinion would, of course, also have to reflect any other knowledge which the accountant may have as a result of an examination of the financial statements, as a result of the more extensive examination procedures which would be required under proposed Item 7(c)(2), or through other means.

The independent public accountant's responsibilities under proposed Item 7(c)(2) would be more extensive. To reach the reasonableness opinion which would be required under proposed Item 7(c)(2) the independent accountant would, in effect, have to reach independent conclusions as to whether the systems of internal accounting control provided reasonable assurances that transactions were recorded as necessary to permit preparation of annual and interim financial statements in conformity with generally accepted accounting principles; that transactions in amounts which would be material when measured in relation to the registrant's financial statements were appropriately authorized; and that assets in amounts which would be material when measured in relation to the registrant's financial statements were appropriately safeguarded, and there was appropriate accountability for such assets.

The independent public accountant would, therefore, have to independently evaluate and test the underlying bases for management's conclusions as to the effectiveness of the design and functioning of the systems of internal accounting control and as to cost-benefit considerations, to the extent that those conclusions relate to reasonable assurances of achievement of the objectives of internal accounting control with respect to transactions and assets in amounts which would be material when measured in relation to the registrant's financial statements.

It should be emphasized that the materiality limitation contained in proposed Item 7(c)(2) would apply only to the objectives and scope of the independent public accountant's examination. The proposed materiality limitation reflects a cost-benefit judgment by the Commission with respect to the appropriate extent of the independent accountant's examination for purposes of the proposed rule. In contrast, the management representations which would be required by proposed Item 7(a) would not be, and the internal accounting control provisions of the FCPA are not, so limited. Rather each extends to reasonable assurances that the broad objectives of internal accounting control were achieved, without regard to materiality of amounts.

2. *Examination and Reporting Standards*

The Commission recognizes that examinations by independent public accountants of statements of management on internal accounting control will require development of appropriate professional standards with respect to such matters as examination procedures; procedures for consideration of other knowledge, gained from the accountant's examination of the financial statements or other means, which may be inconsistent with management's representations; and procedures when the accountant believes that management does not have a sufficient basis for its representations. The Commission notes that a task force of the AICPA's Auditing Standards Board is currently considering the general issue of reporting to the public on internal accounting control. The Commission believes that it is appropriate to continue its past policy of permitting the accounting profession to determine the standards and procedures underlying accountants' reports as long as this policy is consistent with the interests of investors, the federal securities laws, and the Commission's rules and regulations thereunder.

Since the standards applicable to reporting should be integrated with those applicable to the conduct of the examination, the Commission also believes that it is appropriate to allow the accounting profession to take the lead in determining the standards applicable to the specific form and content of an accountant's report on an examination of a statement of management on internal accounting control.

Accordingly, the Commission urges the AICPA's Auditing Standards Board to continue its study of reporting on internal accounting control in the light of the Commission's proposed requirement for an examination by an independent public accountant of a statement of management on internal accounting control, and to be prepared to adopt, on a timely basis, an authoritative pronouncement which sets forth the standards and procedures to be followed in connection with such an examination, and the form and content of a report thereon. The Commission intends to follow this work closely. If it appears that sufficient progress is not being made toward development of appropriate standards and procedures, the Commission will undertake to develop such standards and procedures.

III. OTHER ISSUES
A. Costs of Proposed Rules

The Commission is aware that in most cases an expansion of the independent accountant's work with respect to internal accounting control would be necessitated by this proposal. While such an expansion of work would probably result in additional costs to registrants,[22] the Commission believes that such costs likely would be in large part of an

---

[22]As to the basic proposal for a statement of management on internal accounting control, the Commission believes that this proposal will not establish requirements for maintenance of systems of internal accounting control which exceed those already required by the FCPA. Consequently, the costs of providing the proposed statement of management on internal accounting control should not be substantial.

initial rather than a continuing nature. In addition, the Commission believes that in many instances the additional work of the independent accountant with respect to internal accounting control would result in reductions in costs of the examination of the financial statements, as independent accountants would be able to place more reliance on internal accounting control.[23] The Commission believes that the additional costs of the proposed requirement that the statement of management on internal accounting control be examined by an independent public accountant would be outweighed by the increased reliability of the statement of management which would result from such examination.

The Commission believes that the benefits of new requirements to present and prospective investors should outweigh any additional costs involved. Since the benefits of the proposed examination by an independent public accountant of the statement of management on internal accounting control are not subject to quantification, and the measurement of costs includes many variables which are highly uncertain, the weighing of costs and benefits of such an examination will inevitably require the Commission's judgment. The Commission specifically requests comments on the costs and benefits of the proposed requirement for examination by an independent public accountant, including possible alternatives to the proposed scope of such examination.

In particular, comments are requested on the costs and benefits of the following alternatives to the proposed examination by an independent public accountant:

1. A requirement for an examination which would be sufficient to enable the independent public accountant to express an opinion as to whether the representations of management in response to proposed Item 7(a) are reasonable. In effect, this would require the independent public accountant to reach independent conclusions as to whether the systems of internal accounting control provided reasonable assurances (cost-benefit judgments not limited to material amounts) of achievement of the broad objectives of internal accounting control.

2. No requirement for an examination by an independent public accountant. Rather, require registrants to state whether or not the statement of management on internal accounting control had been examined by an independent public accountant, and require the filing of the related accountant's report if an affirmative statement is made. This would, of course, also require development of professional standards for examinations by independent public accountants of statements of management on internal accounting control. It might also necessitate specific professional standards for responsibilities of an independent accountant as a result of association with such a statement of management which accompanies audited financial statements.

To the extent possible, commentators are requested to supply empirical data in support of their comments.

In addressing this issue, commentators also are requested to consider whether certain registrants should be exempted from the requirement that the proposed statement of management be examined and reported on by an independent public accountant. The costs of such an examination may fall with the greatest severity on smaller registrants; however, systems of internal accounting control of smaller registrants may be generally less sophisticated and less well documented so that examination by an independent public accountant may be particularly needed.

---

[23]However, registrants' selections of independent accountants for examinations of statements of management on internal accounting control would not be restricted to the same independent accountants who are engaged to examine the financial statements.

As part of its response to issues relating to the impact on small businesses of the disclosure requirements of the federal securities laws, the Commission recently announced the adoption of a simplified form, Form S-18, under the Securities Act.[24] Form S-18 is available to issuers not subject to the Commission's continuous reporting requirements when they register securities to be sold for cash not exceeding an aggregate offering amount of $5 million. Comments are also specifically requested on whether a registrant filing on Form S-18, and thereby becoming subject to the reporting provisions of section 15(d) of the Securities Exchange Act, should be exempt from the requirement for an examination by an independent public accountant with respect to the statement of management on internal accounting control contained in its initial annual report on Form 10-K.[25]

B.   Disclosure of Basis for Management Opinion

In addition to the opinion which would be required by proposed Item 7(a) of Regulation S-K (and, in the initial stage, the disclosures relating to uncorrected "material weaknesses" which would be required by proposed Item 7(b)), registrants are encouraged to include in the statement of management on internal accounting control whatever information they believe would make the statement most useful. Some may believe that disclosure of the basis for the management opinion, including a description of the general approach applied in evaluating internal accounting controls and the extent to which the procedures comprised by such approach were performed in the periods encompassed by such opinion, should be required. Comments on this issue are specifically requested.

C.   Signing of Management Statement

Some may believe that the statement of management should be required to be signed by a a certain representative or representatives of management, such as the chief executive officer or the chief financial officer. Comments on this issue are specifically requested.

IV.   PROPOSED EFFECTIVE DATES

The Commission recognizes that the enactment of the FCPA has prompted many registrants to reevaluate their procedures for reviewing, monitoring and evaluating their systems of internal accounting control and that issuance of these rule proposals may provide additional focus for such reevaluation. The Commission also recognizes that, as a result of recently establishing sound procedures for reviewing, monitoring and evaluating their systems of internal accounting control, some registrants may have identified and corrected conditions which had not provided reasonable assurance of achievement of the objectives of internal accounting control.

Accordingly, these amendments are proposed to be effective with respect to reports for fiscal periods ending after December 15, 1979. Statements of management on internal accounting control would not be required for reports for periods ending prior to December 15, 1979. In addition, by proposing to adopt these amendments in two stages as discussed herein, representations regarding the effectiveness of systems of internal accounting control would be required to encompass only conditions existing as of and after the end of the first fiscal period for which the amendments would be effective.

[24]*See* Securities Act Release No. 6049, April 3, 1979 (44 FR 21562).

[25]Similarly, the Commission has amended its requirements to permit Form S-18 registrants to include in their initial filing on Form 10-K, in lieu of similar information called for by Form 10-K, information concerning the registrant's business, the remuneration of its officers and directors, and the interest of management and others in certain transactions which had been provided in the registration statement on Form S-18.

Nevertheless, it again should be emphasized that the FCPA was effective upon enactment in December 1977. Registrants would be well advised to ensure that any weaknesses in internal accounting control are identified and corrected on the most timely basis.

V.   AUTHORITY FOR, AND REQUEST FOR COMMENT ON SCOPE OF, PROPOSED AMENDMENTS

The Commission is not at this time proposing to require the disclosures outlined in this release in registration statements filed pursuant to the Securities Act of 1933. The Commission recognizes, however, that much of the rationale which supports the furnishing of this information to investors in Securities Exchange Act filings may apply with equal force to Securities Act registration statements. The Commission therefore invites comments concerning whether these proposals should be extended to filings under that Act. In that connection, the Commission invites commentators to consider whether the applicability of these proposals to Securities Act registration statements would have any impact—whether favorable or unfavorable—on the capital formation process and whether the Commission should consider exempting any category of issuers from those requirements, should it determine to extend them to Securities Act registration statements.

The Commission also invites comment concerning whether it would be appropriate to extend these requirements to Forms N-1 and N-2 for use by open-end and closed-end management investment companies; Form N-1R for annual reports of registered management investment companies; Form N-5R for annual reports of small business investment companies; and to Forms U5A, U5B, U5S, and U-6B-Z promulgated under the Public Utility Holding Company Act of 1935. Similarly, commentators are requested to consider whether these disclosure items should be incorporated in Forms 20 and 20-K for use by certain foreign private issuers.

The Commission is proposing these amendments pursuant to its general rulemaking authority contained in Section 23(a) of the Securities Exchange Act of 1934, 15 U.S.C. 78w(a). That provision empowers the Commission to promulgate "such rules and regulations as may be necessary or appropriate to implement the provisions" of the Act.

The internal accounting control requirements of the Foreign Corrupt Practices Act—which these amendments would, in part, implement—appear in Section 13(b)(2)[B] of the Securities Exchange Act, 15 U.S.C. 78m(b)(2). The various disclosure forms and schedules which these proposals would amend have been promulgated pursuant to Sections 12, 13, 14 and 15(d) of the 1934 Act, 15 U.S.C. 78*l*, 78m, 78n, 78*o*.

Section 23(a) of the Securities Exchange Act requires the Commission to consider the impact which any proposed rule would have on competition. While the Commission is not aware of any competitive impact likely to result from the proposals described in this release, commentators are invited to address that issue.

VI.   REQUEST FOR COMMENTS

All interested persons are invited to submit their views and comments on the foregoing in triplicate to George A. Fitzsimmons, Secretary, Securities and Exchange Commission, Washington, D.C. 20549 on or before July 31, 1979. Such communications should refer to File S7-779 and will be available for public inspection.

VII.   TEXT OF PROPOSED RULES

In consideration of the foregoing, it is proposed to amend 17 CFR Chapter II as follows:

PART 229—STANDARD INSTRUCTIONS FOR FILING FORMS UNDER SECURITIES ACT OF 1933 AND SECURITIES EXCHANGE ACT OF 1934—REGULATION S-K

1.   By amending §229.20 by adding Item 7 to read as follows:
§229.20 Information required in document.

*   *   *   *   *

Item 7.   Statement of management on internal accounting control.

(a) State management's opinion as to whether, as of any date after December 15, 1979 and prior to December 16, 1980 for which an audited balance sheet is required, and for periods ending after December 15, 1980 for which audited statements of income are required, the systems of internal accounting control of the registrant and its subsidiaries provided reasonable assurances that:

(1)   Transactions were executed in accordance with management's general or specific authorization;

(2)   Transactions were recorded as necessary (i) to permit preparation of financial statements in conformity with generally accepted accounting principles (or other applicable criteria), and (ii) to maintain accountability for assets;

(3)   Access to assets was permitted only in accordance with management's general or specific authorization; and

(4)   The recorded accountability for assets was compared with the existing assets at reasonable intervals and appropriate action was taken with respect to any differences.

(b) For statements of management on internal accounting control as of dates after December 15, 1979 and prior to December 16, 1980, describe any material weaknesses in internal accounting control which have been communicated by the independent accountants of the registrant or its subsidiaries which have not been corrected, and state the reasons why they have not been corrected.

(c) For periods ending after December 15, 1980, the statement of management on internal accounting control shall be examined and reported on by an independent public accountant. The examination shall be sufficient to enable the independent public accountant to express an opinion as to (1) whether the representations of management in response to paragraph (a) are consistent with the results of management's evaluation of the systems of internal accounting control; and (2) whether such representations of management are, in addition, reasonable with respect to transactions and assets in amounts which would be material when measured in relation to the registrant's financial statements.

Instructions.

1.   The statement of management on internal accounting control should accompany the financial statements.

2.   The independent public accountant's report of examination shall accompany or be included within the accountant's report on the financial statements.

*   *   *   *   *

PART 240—GENERAL RULES AND REGULATIONS, SECURITIES EXCHANGE ACT OF 1934

2.   By amending §240.14a-3 by adding a new paragraph (b)(4), renumbering present

paragraphs (b)(4) to (12) as (b)(5) to (13), and amending the references to the renumbered paragraphs as follows (changes italicized):

§240.14a-3 Information to be furnished to security holders.

*   *   *   *   *

(b) * * *

(4)   The report shall contain a statement of management on internal accounting control prepared in accordance with the provisions of Item 7 of Regulation S-K.

(5)   Note 1: Subparagraph (b) (*11*) permits. . . .

(6)   (No change.)

(7)   Note: Subparagraph (b) (*11*) permits. . . .

(8)   (No change.)

(9)   (No change.)

(10)   Note: Pursuant to the undertaking required by the above paragraph, (b) (*10*). . . .

(11)   Subject to the foregoing requirements, the report may be in any form deemed suitable by management and the information required by subparagraphs (b)(*5*) to (b) (*10*). . . .

(12)   Subparagraphs (b)(*5*) through (b) (*11*) shall not apply. . . .

(13)   (No change.)

*   *   *   *   *

PART 249—FORMS, SECURITIES EXCHANGE ACT OF 1934

3.   By amending §249.310 by renumbering Items 13-15 of Part II as Items 14-16 and by adding a new Item 13 to Part I to read as follows:

§249.310 Form 10-K, annual report pursuant to section 13 or 15d of the Securities Exchange Act of 1934.

*   *   *   *   *

Item 13.   Statement of Management on Internal Accounting Control. A statement of management on internal accounting control shall be furnished in accordance with the provisions of Item 7 of Regulation S-K.

*   *   *   *   *

By the Commission.

GEORGE A. FITZSIMMONS
Secretary

April 30, 1979

Index